"Today virtually all scholars agree that there are readings in the transmission history of the Greek New Testament that more likely reflect the theology, not of the New Testament authors, but of scribes who changed the text. As Wallace points out in his introduction, this is not the issue at stake. The problem that this volume of essays seeks to address is when 'orthodox corruption' is made the default explanation whenever there is a grain of suspicion that a passage may have been tampered with for doctrinal reasons, or when it is used as a heuristic device to harvest the entire textual tradition in search for suitable variants to label as 'anti-adoptionistic', 'anti-separationist', 'anti-docetic' or 'anti-patripassianist'. As A. E. Housman remarked, 'every problem which presents itself to the textual critic must be regarded as possibly unique'. Such a sound view of textual criticism excludes every mechanical application of any principle to account for textual variation."

—Tommy Wasserman,
Academic Dean and Lecturer in New Testament,
Örebro School of Theology, Örebro, Sweden

"This collection of stimulating essays, edited by Dan Wallace, renowned scholar of New Testament manuscripts, interacts with Bart Ehrman's own groundbreaking book *The Orthodox Corruption of Scripture*. These essays deal mainly with issues of New Testament textual criticism, and each responds to a specific aspect of Ehrman's work. The studies attempt to 'push back' against some of Ehrman's stimulating theories. Their value lies in clarifying arguments, re-examining primary evidence, and advancing debates concerning fundamental issues surrounding the text of the New Testament. With the recent reissue of Ehrman's book, this collection forms a stimulating dialogue partner to be read alongside that work. It is essential reading for anybody interested in the text of the New Testament and in the way that text was brought together."

—Paul Foster,
Senior Lecturer in New Testament Language, Literature, and Theology,
School of Divinity, University of Edinburgh, Edinburgh, Scotland

"If I could choose only five scholars in the world from whom to learn and whom to emulate, Dan Wallace would unquestionably be one of them. His commitment to rigorous, authentic inquiry is unsurpassed. And that is just one of the reasons this volume is welcomed. Wallace has also enlisted new work in the field of textual criticism from five emerging scholars. That these essays also address issues raised by Bart Ehrman provides additional value for those wanting to learn a more sober-minded view."

—Michael R. Licona,
External Research Collaborator,
North-West University, Potchefstroom, South Africa

D0992961

These essays do not hesitate to get into the details of key discussions and to show that the differences in the manuscript tradition really do not impact core Christian teaching. Balanced, worth reading, and well done."

—Darrell Bock,
Research Professor of New Testament Studies,
Professor of Spiritual Development and Culture,
Dallas Theological Seminary

"Dan Wallace is definitely among the elite, foremost scholars in establishing the nature of the New Testament text. He has done us a favor here by editing a volume of critical essays regarding the ongoing dialogue on the transmission of the New Testament, taking careful aim at those who would question the accuracy of the text. These detailed distinctions, time and again, provide crucial insights that add much to the current debate. I am pleased to recommend this volume."

—Gary R. Habermas,
Distinguished Professor,
Liberty University

"A favorite habit of biblical critics is to take something well-known to scholars of the Bible, put a sensational spin on it that induces wrong conclusions, and then offer it as something new to threaten the reliability of Scripture for the general public. They are aided in this mischief by publishers who will title their works in a misleading and even false manner. Bart Ehrman is a prime example of this unfortunate development in the publishing industry, with works of increasing shock value, such as *Misquoting Jesus* or *Forged*. Now, in the name of ethics and honesty, it is time for a sober response to such excesses, and this book is an excellent start. Daniel Wallace nicely dismantles the wrong-headed and pretentious conclusions of Ehrman and others who love to frighten the faithful, adding a welcome dose of sanity in the process."

—Paul L. Maier,
Professor Emeritus of Ancient History and Early Christianity,
Western Michigan University

"Professor Daniel Wallace, a well-known and respected New Testament textual critic, has assembled an important collection of scholarly, yet very accessible essays, that shed much needed light on the question of how old and how good the New Testament manuscripts really are. In recent years this important topic has become a hot button at every level of public discourse, from scholarly books to late-night television talk shows. Wallace and his colleagues set the record straight and show convincingly that the New Testament manuscript record is strong and the text is reliable."

Craig A. Evans,
Payzant Distinguished Professor of New Testament,
Acadia Divinity College

TEXT AND CANON OF THE NEW TESTAMENT

REVISITING THE CORRUPTION OF THE NEW TESTAMENT

Manuscript, Patristic, and Apocryphal Evidence

DANIEL B. WALLACE

EDITOR

Kregel
Academic & Professional

Revisiting the Corruption of the New Testament: Manuscript, Patristic, and Apocryphal Evidence

© 2011 Daniel B. Wallace

Published by Kregel Publications, a division of Kregel, Inc., P.O. Box 2607, Grand Rapids, MI 49501.

Library of Congress Cataloging-in-Publication Data

Revisiting the corruption of the New Testament : manuscript, patristic, and apocryphal evidence / [edited by] Daniel B. Wallace.
      p. cm.—(The text and canon of the New Testament)
  1. Bible. N.T.—Evidences, authority, etc. 2. Bible. N.T.—Canon. I. Wallace, Daniel B.
    BS2332.R48 2010
    225.1—dc22

                           2010029717

ISBN 978–0–8254–3338–2

Printed in the United States of America
12 13 14 15 16 / 7 6 5 4 3

Contents

Preface

This inaugural volume of the Text and Canon of the New Testament series includes essays by six authors. All of the chapters focus on issues in textual criticism—in particular, how badly the scribes, who copied their exemplars by hand, corrupted the text. All but one of the chapters deals specifically with NT textual criticism; one addresses textual issues related to an early apocryphal text, the Gospel of Thomas.

The writing of each essay tells its own story. Chapter 1 is an expansion of a paper I delivered at the fourth annual Greer-Heard Point-Counterpoint Forum, held at New Orleans Baptist Seminary in April 2008. Dr. Bart Ehrman and I dialogued there over the issue of corruption of the NT manuscripts. Four other scholars joined the debate: David Parker (Birmingham University), Dale Martin (Yale University), Michael Holmes (Bethel University and Seminary), and William Warren (New Orleans Baptist Seminary). The text of all the presentations, along with a few others, was published by Fortress Press in 2010 as *The Reliability of the New Testament: Bart D. Ehrman and Daniel B. Wallace in Dialogue*, edited by Robert Stewart. I express my gratitude to Fortress Press for allowing me to publish an expansion of my paper in this book. This first chapter, because it was delivered to a nonspecialist and, to a large degree, lay audience, is in some ways out of sync with the rest of the chapters in this book. But because it frames the discussion that the rest of the book addresses, it is appropriate as the entrée to the topic of this volume.

The other five chapters were written by former interns of mine in the ThM program at Dallas Theological Seminary. I am immensely grateful to DTS for having an academic intern program, which allows faculty to help develop scholars in the making. Since the early 1990s, I have had multiple interns every year. To date, I have enjoyed the privilege of mentoring more than fifty students through this δοῦλος program—an apt nickname because each student is required to put in 400 hours of work without pay. Each professor shapes the internship how he or she wants. My own approach has been to spend between sixty and one hundred hours with the interns during the school year: we usually meet in my home for several hours each week. Each intern is required to write a paper that he or she will present at a regional scholarly conference. That paper is read to the intern group in rough draft and, later, final draft before it is read at the conference. The greatest joy of my academic career has been to work closely with these future professors, pastors, priests, missionaries, and leaders of the church and to see them mature through the rigors of our year together. Most have gone on for doctoral work, and they collectively have published dozens of articles in theological journals, as well as an increasing number of scholarly monographs. Many, if not most, of these publications were expansions on these students' intern papers.

The chapters in this volume went through multiple layers of peer review. These five men all read their papers first at the Southwestern Regional Evangelical Theological Society conference. I was impressed with each of these papers sufficiently that I requested that these ThM students be allowed to read them at the national Evangelical Theological Society conference in November 2008, held in Providence, Rhode Island. Normally, master's students are not permitted to read papers at the annual ETS conference, but these essays were so good that permission was granted. Several textual critics interacted with the papers—both before the conference and at it. Valuable feedback thus came from the intern group initially, then from the regional conference and individual scholars, and finally from the national conference of the ETS.

When I proposed to Dr. Bruce Ware, the program chair of the 2008 ETS conference, that these papers be considered for the conference, I soon realized that they should get even wider exposure. Jim Weaver, director of Academic & Ministry Resources at Kregel Publications, was enthusiastic about the possibility of these essays comprising the bulk of the inaugural volume of the Text and Canon of the New Testament series.

All five chapters address, directly or indirectly, issues raised in Bart Ehrman's *The Orthodox Corruption of Scripture*, a monumental work that has raised numerous questions about intentional corruption of the NT by proto-orthodox scribes in the early centuries. Two of the essays address a single verse (Matt 24.36 and John 1.1), one a methodological issue (whether the least orthodox reading is to be preferred), one an analogous matter (the textual transmission of the Gospel of Thomas), and one a foundational theological issue (whether the autographic text ever spoke of Jesus as θεός). Thus three of the essays deal with global issues (i.e., not focused on a single verse or textual problem), while two deal with an individual textual problem; one of these latter two focuses on patristic interactions over Matthew 24.36, while another examines the texts of two manuscripts in John 1.1. The chapter on the text of Thomas may seem out of place in this volume, but it is both groundbreaking in its treatment and highly relevant for the transmission of the NT text: the text of Thomas has undergone significant changes that made it more compatible with the rest of the Nag Hammadi codices.

As this manuscript was going to the publisher, I received an email from Dr. Ehrman requesting critical input on his *Orthodox Corruption of Scripture*. Oxford University Press had requested that he update that eighteen-year-old work. In response, I sent Dr. Ehrman the drafts of most of the chapters of this manuscript. This volume might, then, have some impact on the second edition of *Orthodox Corruption of Scripture*. Regrettably, because of where our respective manuscripts were in the publishing pipeline, the reverse could not be the case.

My fellow contributors and I offer up these essays in the spirit of collegial dialogue and bring them as offerings of the mind to our Lord Jesus Christ. May he be pleased and magnified by our efforts.

—Daniel B. Wallace, editor

Series Preface
Text and Canon of the New Testament

Few would question that Jesus Christ is the most important figure in human history, let alone in Western civilization. Our primary sources for him are the twenty-seven books that we call the New Testament. There are numerous challenges that face historians, Christians, theologians, and skeptics alike: Do the Gospels tell the truth about Jesus? Are they historically reliable? Were they later documents, written by noneyewitnesses in every case? Was Paul's view of Jesus contrary to the view of the early apostles? Do the books of the New Testament contradict each other theologically or historically? Were the letters purported to be by Paul, Peter, James, and Jude really written by these men? Can we recover the autographic text of the New Testament with any reasonable assurance? What about the other NT documents—is the authorship traditionally assigned to them accurate? How should we interpret these books? Are they normative for Christians today—that is, do they speak to believers authoritatively with reference to faith and practice?

All these and many more questions are exceedingly important. But two areas are foundational: First, can we recover the autographic text; that is, can we determine, through rigorous analysis of surviving manuscripts and scribal methods, what that text, in all its essentials, looked like? Do we dare go further, even hoping to recover the autographic wording in all its particulars? If so, what methods and materials would be of critical importance in this endeavor? Second, should these twenty-seven books be treated with more authority than the myriad of books that were written by Christians in the early centuries after the death and resurrection of Jesus? If so, why? Did the early church get it right concerning these books and their authors, or do we need to modify their conclusions or even revamp them? This series explores these questions of textual and canonical criticism. Its focus is whether these books bear an authority above all others and, if so, what these books actually say. The hope for the series is that fresh dialogue, collegial interaction, and new evidence and arguments will enable us to better grasp the text of the New Testament and its place in the life of the church today.

—Daniel B. Wallace, editor

Abbreviations

APOCRYPHA AND PSEUDEPIGRAPHA

Gos Heb	Gospel of the Hebrews
Sir	Sirach
Wisd Sol	Wisdom of Solomon

APOSTOLIC FATHERS

1 Clem.	*1 Clement*
Herm. Sim.	*Shepherd of Hermas, Similitudes*
Ign., *Eph.*	Ignatius, *To the Ephesians*
Ign., *Trall.*	Ignatius, *To the Trallians*
Ign., *Phld.*	Ignatius, *To the Philadelphians*
Ign., *Pol.*	Ignatius, *To Polycarp*
Ign., *Rom.*	Ignatius, *To the Romans*
Ign., *Smyrn.*	Ignatius, *To the Smyrnaeans*
Mart. Pol.	*Martyrdom of Polycarp*
Pol., *Phil.*	Polycarp, *To the Philippians*

BIBLE
Old Testament

Exod	Exodus
Deut	Deuteronomy
1 Chr	1 Chronicles
Job	Job
Ps/Pss	Psalm(s)
Prov	Proverbs
Isa	Isaiah
Mic	Mic

New Testament

Matt	Matthew
Mark	Mark
Luke	Luke
John	John
Rom	Romans
1 Cor	1 Corinthians
2 Cor	2 Corinthians
Gal	Galatians
Eph	Ephesians

Phil	Philippians
Col	Colossians
1 Thess	1 Thessalonians
2 Thess	2 Thessalonians
1 Tim	1 Timothy
2 Tim	2 Timothy
Titus	Titus
Phlm	Philemon
Heb	Hebrews
Jas	James
1 Pet	1 Peter
2 Pet	2 Pet
1 John	1 John
2 John	2 John
3 John	3 John
Jude	Jude
Rev	Revelation

Greek Texts

NA^{27}	*Novum Testamentum Graece*, 27th ed.
Tischendorf^8	*Novum Testamentum Graece*, 8th ed.
UBS^4	*Greek New Testament*, 4th revised ed.

Modern English Versions

CSB	The Christian Standard Bible
ESV	The Holy Bible: English Standard Version
KJV	King James Version
NASB	New American Standard Bible
NET	The New English Translation
NIV	New International Version
NJB	The New Jerusalem Bible
NLT	New Living Translation
NRSV	New Revised Standard Version
RSV	Revised Standard Version

CLASSICAL AND ANCIENT CHRISTIAN SOURCES

Eusebius, *Eccl. theol.*	Eusebius, *De ecclesiastica theologia* (*Ecclesiastical Theology*)
Eusebius, *Hist. eccl.*	Eusebius, *Historia ecclesiastica* (*Ecclesiastical History*)
Hippolytus, *Philos.*	Hippolytus, *Refutatio omnium haeresium* (*Philosophoumena*) (*Refutation of All Heresies*)
Josephus, *Ap.*	Josephus, *Contra Apionem* (*Against Apion*)

Origen, *Comm. Jo.*	Origen, *Commentarii in evangelium Joannis* (*Commentary on John*)
Origen, *Matt. Comm.*	Origen, *Commentarium in evangelium Matthaei* (*Commentary on Matthew*)
Philo, *Somn.*	Philo, *De somniis* (*On Dreams*)
Tertullian, *Ad uxor.*	Tertullian, *Ad uxorem* (*To His Wife*)

GENERAL

ca.	circa
CE	Common Era
LXX	Septuagint
MS, MSS	manuscript(s)
MT	Majority Text, Masoretic Text
NT	New Testament
OT	Old Testament
TR	Textus Receptus
TSKS	Article-substantive-καί-substantive

MAJOR REFERENCE WORKS AND SERIES

ANF	*Ante-Nicene Fathers*
BDAG	*A Greek-English Lexicon of the New Testament and Other Early Christian Literature*
BP	*Biblia Patristica: Index des Citations et Allusions Bibliques dans la Littérature Patristique*
IGNT/IGNTP	International Greek New Testament Project
L&N	*The Greek/English Lexicon of the NT Based on Semantic Domains*
MPG/PG	*Patrologia Graecae*
NPF/NPFS	*The Nicene and Post-Nicene Fathers: First Series*
PL	*Patrologia Latina*
TCE	*The Catholic Encyclopedia*
TLG	*Thesaurus Linguae Graecae*

PAPYRI

NHC	Nag Hammadi Codices
P. Oxy.	Oxyrhynchus Papyri

PERIODICALS

AJT	*American Journal of Theology*
Bib	*Biblica*
BSac	*Bibliotheca Sacra*

CBQ	*Catholic Biblical Quarterly*
CRBR	*Critical Review of Books in Religion*
CT	*Cuneiform Texts from Babylonian Tablets in the British Museum*
EFN	*Estudios de filologia neotestamentaria*
EvT	*Evangelische Theologie*
ExpTim	*Expository Times*
HibJ	*Hibbert Journal*
HTR	*Harvard Theological Review*
HTS	*Harvard Theological Studies*
JBL	*Journal of Biblical Literature*
JETS	*Journal of the Evangelical Theological Society*
JSNT	*Journal for the Study of the New Testament*
JTS	*Journal of Theological Studies*
Mus	*Muséon: Revue d'études orientales*
NovT	*Novum Testamentum*
NTS	*New Testament Studies*
PSB	*Princeton Seminary Bulletin*
RelSRev	*Religious Studies Review*
ResQ	*Restoration Quarterly*
SJT	*Scottish Journal of Theology*
ThTo	*Theology Today*
TJ	*Trinity Journal*
TRu	*Theologische Rundschau*
TS	*Theological Studies*
TSK	*Theologische Studien und Kritiken*
TynBul	*Tyndale Bulletin*
VC	*Vigilae Christianae*
ZNW	*Zeitschrift für die neutestamentliche Wissenschaft und die Kunde der älteren Kirche*

1

LOST IN TRANSMISSION

How Badly Did the Scribes Corrupt
the New Testament Text?

Daniel B. Wallace[1]

For well over a century, the principal attacks on the earliest MSS of the NT have come from the far right, theologically speaking. Most of the attackers are fanatics, but there are some scholars among them. Occasionally, vitriolic language comes from even those who work with the Greek text and thus, in some measure, stand apart from the Bible-thumping preachers in America's backwaters. They speak of the early manuscripts as "bastard Bibles" and as coming from a "sewer pipe."

Such verbal abuse might be expected from the ultraconservative wing, because their method is apparently dictated, from beginning to end, by their theological presuppositions. But in recent years, the attack on the earliest witnesses has also come from the left side of the theological aisle. Liberals, too, have their fanatics, some of whom may be bona fide scholars but with expertise far removed from textual matters. They nevertheless freely opine that the state of the text is in such bad repair that we must abandon all hope of recovering anything remotely close to the original wording.

Things have changed in the last few years, however: some respectable textual critics have joined the ranks of the scornful. Bart Ehrman—a scholar with impeccable credentials in textual criticism—has arguably led the charge. He has been the most prolific among these scholars and the most intentional in bypassing peer review, appealing directly to the

---

1. This chapter is an expanded version of a lecture delivered at the fourth annual Greer-Heard Point-Counterpoint Forum, held at New Orleans Baptist Seminary on April 4–5, 2008. A more succinct version appeared in Robert Stewart's *The Reliability of the New Testament: Bart Ehrman and Daniel Wallace in Dialogue* (Minneapolis: Fortress, 2010). Thanks are due to Fortress Press for permission to publish this expanded essay here.

general reader. His wildly popular book *Misquoting Jesus*, published in 2005 and based on his 1993 scholarly tome *Orthodox Corruption of Scripture*, has had a huge impact among nonscholars.

Normally, Ehrman writes in a clear, forceful style and punctuates his writing with provocative one-liners and a good measure of wit. I must confess, however, that his *Misquoting Jesus* left me more perplexed than ever. I was not sure exactly what he was saying. Read one way, the book contradicted what he had written elsewhere; read another way, it was hardly controversial—and certainly not the sort of book that would warrant being a blockbuster on the *New York Times* Bestseller List. So I acknowledge that I am not sure what all the points of disagreement between us are. But I do know some.

Whatever our disagreements, there are issues on which we agree. There is often a gulf between those "inside" a particular scholarly discipline and those on the outside. When outsiders hear what insiders are talking about, sometimes they can get quite alarmed. Ehrman says in the appendix to *Misquoting Jesus*, "The facts that I explain about the New Testament in *Misquoting Jesus* are not at all 'news' to biblical scholars. They are what scholars have known, and said, for many, many years."[2] He is right. We do walk on common ground.

There are basically five things that we agree on:

1.   The handwritten copies of the NT contain a lot of differences. We are not sure exactly what the number is, but the best estimate is somewhere between 300,000 and 400,000 variants. This means, as Ehrman is fond of saying, that there are more variants in the MSS than there are words in the NT.

2.   The vast bulk of these differences affect virtually nothing.

3.   We concur on the wording of the original text almost all the time.[3]

---

2. Bart D. Ehrman, *Misquoting Jesus: The Story behind Who Changed the Bible and Why*, 1st paperback ed. (New York: HarperOne, 2007), 253. All quotations are from the paperback edition.

3. In the appendix to *Misquoting Jesus*, Ehrman says about his disagreements with Bruce Metzger, whom Ehrman described as his doctor-father and to whom he had dedicated *Misquoting Jesus*: "[E]ven though we may disagree on important religious questions—he is a firmly committed Christian and I am not—we are in complete agreement on a number of very important historical and textual questions. If he and I were put in a room and asked to hammer out a consensus statement on what we think the original text of the New Testament probably looked like, there would be very few points of disagreement—maybe one or two dozen places out of many thousands" (252). My views of the original text of the NT would tend to be closer to Metzger's but would certainly not line up there all the time (e.g., I agree with Ehrman that Jesus was angry in Mark 1.41). My point is that those who

Daniel B. Wallace

4.   We are even in harmony over several well-known or controversial passages:

Mark 16.9–20—Here Jesus tells his disciples that they can drink poison and handle snakes and not get hurt. I agree with Ehrman that this passage is not part of the original text of Mark.

John 7.53–8.11—We both agree that the story of the woman caught in adultery was not part of the original text of John. It is my favorite passage that is *not* in the Bible.

1 John 5.7—The King James Bible says, "For there are three that bear record in heaven, the Father, the Word, and the Holy Ghost: and these three are one." This would be the most explicit statement about the Trinity in the Bible, but it is definitely not part of the original text. This fact has been known by scholars for more than half a millennium.

Mark 1.41—Although most MSS here say that Jesus was moved with compassion when he healed a leper, we both agree that the original text probably said that he was angry when he did so. One of Ehrman's finest pieces is his provocatively titled article "A Leper in the Hands of an Angry Jesus."[4] He there gave very strong evidence that Mark 1.41 spoke of Jesus' anger rather than his compassion. I agree.

5.   We both are of the same mind that the orthodox scribes occasionally changed the NT text to bring it more into conformity with their views.

All these agreements raise a fundamental point: even though we are looking at the same textual problems and arriving at the same answers most of the time, conservatives are still conservative, and liberals are still liberal.

What is the issue then? The text is not the basic area of our disagreement; the *interpretation* of the text is. Even here, it is not so much the interpretation of the text[5] as the interpretation of *how* the textual variants arose and how *significant* those variants are—that is where

---

are "reasoned eclectics" (the dominant school of thought in NT textual criticism) would agree with each other on the vast majority of textual problems.

4. Bart D. Ehrman, "A Leper in the Hands of an Angry Jesus," in *New Testament Greek and Exegesis: Essays in Honor of Gerald F. Hawthorne* (Grand Rapids: Eerdmans, 2003), 77–98.

5. To be sure, Ehrman would regard the NT books to be in contradiction with each other over many issues, while I would regard the basic beliefs of the authors to be in general agreement. The larger issue is whether what the NT essentially teaches is true. Here, the bedrock of all three branches of Christendom is that Jesus Christ,

our differences lie. Ehrman puts a certain spin on the data.[6] If you have read *Misquoting Jesus*, you may have come away with an impression of the book that is far more cynical than what Ehrman is explicitly saying. Whether that impression accurately reflects Ehrman's views is more difficult to assess, but one thing is clear: Ehrman sees in the textual variants something more pernicious, more sinister, more conspiratorial, and therefore more controlled than I do. This chapter—indeed, this book—offers a different narrative.

TWO ATTITUDES, THREE QUESTIONS

To begin with, there are two attitudes that we should try to avoid: absolute certainty and total despair. On the one side are King James Only advocates; they are absolutely certain that the KJV, in every place, exactly represents the original text. To be frank, the quest for certainty often overshadows the quest for truth in conservative theological circles and is a temptation that we need to resist. It is fundamentally the temptation of *modernism*. To our shame, evangelicals have too often been more concerned to protect our presuppositions than to pursue truth at all costs.

On the other side are a few radical scholars who are so skeptical that no piece of data, no hard fact, is safe in their hands. It all turns to putty because *all views are created equal.* If everything is equally possible, then no view is more probable than any other view. In Starbucks and on the street, in college classrooms and on the airwaves, you can hear the line "We really don't know what the NT originally said since we no longer possess the originals *and* since there could have been tremendous tampering with the text before our existing copies were produced."

But are any biblical scholars *this* skeptical? Robert Funk, the head of the Jesus Seminar, seemed to be. In *The Five Gospels* he said,

> Even careful copyists make mistakes, as every proofreader knows. So we will never be able to claim certain knowledge of exactly what the original text of *any* biblical writing was.[7]

---

the theanthropic person, died for humanity's sin on a Roman cross outside of Jerusalem and later rose from the dead.

6. Although Ehrman speaks frequently about the hopelessness of the task of trying to recover the wording of the original text or about the irrelevance of such a task (two views that seem mutually exclusive), he also speaks about what he and Bruce Metzger "think the *original* text of the New Testament probably looked like" (*Misquoting Jesus*, 252; italics added), as though the task were neither hopeless nor irrelevant.

7. Robert W. Funk, Roy W. Hoover, and the Jesus Seminar, *The Five Gospels: The Search for the Authentic Words of Jesus* (New York: Macmillan, 1993), 6 (italics added).

Daniel B. Wallace

The temporal gap that separates Jesus from the first surviving copies of the gospels—about one hundred and seventy-five years—corresponds to the lapse in time from 1776—the writing of the Declaration of Independence—to 1950. What if the oldest copies of the founding document dated only from 1950?[8]

Funk's attitude is easy to see: rampant skepticism over recovering the original wording of any part of the NT. This is the temptation of *postmodernism*.[9] The only certainty is uncertainty itself. It is the one absolute that denies all the others. Concomitant with this is an intellectual pride—pride that one "knows" enough to be skeptical about all positions.

Where does Ehrman stand on this spectrum? I do not know. On the one hand, he has said such things as the following:

> If the primary purpose of this discipline is to get back to the original text, we may as well admit either defeat or victory, depending on how one chooses to look at it, because we're not going to *get* much closer to the original text than we already are.
>
> . . . [A]t this stage, our work on the *original* amounts to little more than tinkering. There's something about historical scholarship that refuses to concede that a major task has been accomplished, but there it is.[10]

---

8. Ibid.
9. Those whose writings are very influential in the marketplace of ideas but who are not biblical scholars make even more unguarded statements. For example, Earl Doherty declared in *Challenging the Verdict* (Ottawa: Age of Reason, 2001), "Even if we had more extensive copies of the Gospels from within a couple of generations of their writing, this would not establish the state of the originals, nor how much evolution they had undergone within those first two or three generations. It is precisely at the earliest phase of a sect's development that the greatest mutation of ideas takes place, and with it the state of the writings which reflect the mutation" (39).
10. Bart D. Ehrman, "*Novum Testamentum Graecum Editio Critica Maior*: An Evaluation," *TC: A Journal of Biblical Textual Criticism* (1998), revision of a paper presented at the Textual Criticism Section of the 1997 Society of Biblical Literature conference in San Francisco. He goes on to argue (in point 20 of his review), "We can still make small adjustments in the text in places—change the position of an adverb here, add an article there—we can still dispute the well known textual problems on which we're never going to be agreed, piling up the evidence as we will. But the reality is that we are unlikely to discover radically new problems or devise radically new solutions; at this stage, our work on the *original* amounts to little more than tinkering. There's something about historical scholarship that refuses to concede that a major task has been accomplished, but there it is." This sounds, for the most part, as though he thinks the primary task of textual criticism—that of recovering the wording of the autographic text—has been accomplished.

In spite of these remarkable [textual] differences, scholars are convinced that we can reconstruct the original words of the New Testament with reasonable (although probably not 100 percent) accuracy.[11]

The first statements were made at the Society of Biblical Literature in an address to text-critical scholars. The last is in a college textbook. All of this sounds as if Ehrman would align himself more with those who are fairly sure about what the wording of the autographic text is.

But here is what Ehrman wrote in his immensely popular book *Misquoting Jesus*:

Not only do we not have the originals, we don't have the first copies of the originals. We don't even have copies of the copies of the originals, or copies of the copies of the copies of the originals. What we have are copies made later—much later. . . . And these copies all differ from one another, in many thousands of places. . . . [T]hese copies differ from one another in so many places that we don't even known how many differences there are.[12]

We could go on nearly forever talking about specific places in which the texts of the New Testament came to be changed, either accidentally or intentionally. . . . [T]he examples are not just in the hundreds but in the thousands.[13]

And here is what he wrote in another popular book, *Lost Christianities:*

The fact that we have thousands of New Testament manuscripts does not in itself mean that we can rest assured that we know what the original text said. If we have very few early copies—in fact, scarcely

---

11. Bart Ehrman, *The New Testament: A Historical Introduction to the Early Christian Writings*, 3rd ed. (New York: Oxford University Press, 2003), 481. All quotations are from this edition.
12. *Misquoting Jesus*, 10.
13. Ibid., 98. Elsewhere Ehrman says, "Given the problems, how can we hope to get back to anything like the original text, the text that an author actually wrote? It is an enormous problem. In fact, it is such an enormous problem that a number of textual critics have started to claim that we may as well suspend any discussion of the 'original' text, because it is inaccessible to us. That may be going too far" (58); "In short, it is a very complicated business talking about the 'original' text of Galatians. We don't have it. The best we can do is get back to an early stage of its transmission, and *simply hope* that what we reconstruct about the copies made at that stage—based on the copies that happen to survive (in increasing numbers as we move into the Middle Ages)—reasonably reflects what Paul himself actually wrote, or at least what he intended to write when he dictated the letter" (58; italics added).

any—how can we know that the text was not changed significantly *before* the New Testament began to be reproduced in such large quantities?[14]

The cumulative effect of these latter statements seems to be not only that we have no certainty about the wording of the original but that, even where we are sure of the wording, the core theology is not nearly as "orthodox" as we had thought. According to this line of thinking, the message of whole books has been corrupted in the hands of the scribes; and the church, in later centuries, adopted the doctrine of the winners—those who corrupted the text and conformed it to their own notion of orthodoxy.

So you can see my dilemma. I am not sure what Ehrman believes. Is the task done? Have we essentially recovered the wording of the original text? Or should we be hyperskeptical about the whole enterprise? It seems that Ehrman puts a far more skeptical spin on things when speaking in the public square than he does when speaking to professional colleagues.[15]

---

14. Bart Ehrman, *Lost Christianities: The Battles for Scripture and the Faiths We Never Knew* (New York: Oxford University Press, 2005), 219.
15. Part of the evidence for this is what he says in interviews. In one posted on September 25, 2006, on the Evangelical Textual Criticism website (http://evangelical-textualcriticism.blogspot.com/), he was asked by host P. J. Williams, "Do you think that anyone might ever come away from reading *Misquoting Jesus* with the impression that the state of the New Testament text is worse than it really is?" Ehrman responded, "Yes I think this is a real danger, and it is the aspect of the book that has apparently upset our modern day apologists who are concerned to make sure that no one thinks anything negative about the holy Bible. On the other hand, if people misread my book—I can't really control that very well." The cynicism and implicit condemnation of apologists, coupled with a denial of his own radical skepticism about the original text, clearly suggests that Ehrman feels that he has not contributed to this false impression. Further, in his final chapter of *Misquoting Jesus*, Ehrman declares, "The reality, I came to see, is that meaning is not inherent and texts do not speak for themselves" (216). But if he really believed this, would he have the right to complain about how people are reading *his* books?

    The reality seems to be that Ehrman has had the opportunity to alter such a false impression in his many radio, TV, and newspaper interviews. But instead of tempering the misimpression, he usually feeds it. For example, in an interview in the *Charlotte Observer* (Dec. 17, 2005)—nine months before his interview by P. J. Williams—he said, "When I talk about the hundreds and thousands of differences, it's true that a lot are insignificant. But it's also true that a lot are highly significant for interpreting the Bible. Depending on which manuscript you read, the meaning is changed significantly." No quantitative distinction is made between insignificant variants and significant variants; both are said to be "a lot." But a qualitative distinction is made: "a lot are insignificant," while "a lot are highly significant." Further, in many of his interviews, he leads off with what appears to have a calculated shock value, viz., denial of the authenticity of the *pericope adulterae*.

    One other comparison can be made: Both Ehrman and KJVers have a major point in agreement. They both view the early scribes as having almost a conspiratorial motive behind them. (*Webster's* defines the word *conspire* in three ways: "*1 a:* to

These two attitudes—total despair and absolute certainty—are the Scylla and Charybdis that we must steer between. There are also three questions that we need to answer:

1. What is the *number* of variants—how many scribal changes are there?

2. What is the *nature* of variants—what kinds of textual variations are there?

3. What *theological* issues are at stake?

THE NUMBER OF VARIANTS

A textual variant is *any place among the MSS in which there is variation in wording, including word order, omission or addition of words, even spelling differences.* The most trivial changes count, and even when all the manuscripts except one say one thing, that lone MS's reading counts as a textual variant.[16] The best estimate is that there are between 300,000 and 400,000 textual variants among the manuscripts. Yet there are only about 140,000 words in the NT. That means that there is an average of between two and three variants for every word in the Greek NT. If this were the only piece of data, it would discourage anyone from attempting to recover the wording of the original. But there is more to this story.

---

join in a secret agreement to do an unlawful or wrongful act or an act which becomes unlawful as a result of the secret agreement <accused of *conspiring* to overthrow the government>[;] *1 b:* scheme[;] *2* to act in harmony toward a common end." Ehrman does not necessarily see what the proto-orthodox scribes did as a "secret agreement," but he certainly sees them as doing more than acting in harmony toward a common end. And if what became the orthodox view started out in a minority camp struggling for survival, then the fact of the changes the scribes made could certainly not be made public.) The basic difference is that KJVers think that *heretics* corrupted the text, while Ehrman thinks that *orthodox* scribes did. (Of course, Ehrman is not adamantly against the early Alexandrian manuscripts. But it does seem that his overriding criterion for determining the wording of the original [as seen in *Orthodox Corruption*] is that if a reading even gives off a faint scent of perhaps being an orthodox corruption, that trumps all other considerations, both external and internal. In addition to my discussion later in this chapter, see Philip Miller's "The Least Orthodox Reading Is to be Preferred: A New Canon for New Testament Textual Criticism," also in this book.)

16. On a popular level among evangelicals, a textual variant is erroneously defined in terms of the number of MSS that support a reading rather than the number of textual differences regardless of MS support. For a discussion of this erroneous definition, see D. B. Wallace, "The Number of Textual Variants: An Evangelical Miscalculation," at http://bible.org/article/number-textual-variants-evangelical-miscalculation, accessed September 3, 2011..

There are two points to ponder: First, *the reason we have a lot of variants is that we have a lot of manuscripts.* It is simple, really. No classical Greek or Latin text has nearly as many variants, because they do not have nearly as many manuscripts. With virtually every new manuscript discovery, new variants are found.[17] If there were only one copy of the NT in existence, it would have zero variants.[18] Several ancient authors have only one copy of their writings in existence, and sometimes that lone copy is not produced for a millennium. A lone, late manuscript would hardly give us confidence that that single manuscript duplicated the wording of the original in every respect.[19] To speak about the number of variants without also speaking about the number of manuscripts is simply an appeal to sensationalism.[20]

Second, as Samuel Clemens said, "There are lies, damn lies, and statistics." A little probing into these 400,000 variants puts these statistics in a context.

In Greek alone, there are more than 5,600 manuscripts today.[21] Many of these are fragmentary, especially the older ones, but the av-

---

17. For example, the recently cataloged Codex 2882, a MS of Luke from the tenth or eleventh century, has 29 singular readings not found in any other manuscripts. Yet the manuscript is, for the most part, an ordinary Byzantine manuscript, and none of the singular readings is even remotely compelling.

18. Of course, if a lone MS also had corrections, those readings would count as variants.

19. This was recognized three hundred years ago by the brilliant Richard Bentley in his work *Remarks upon a Discourse of Free Thinking* (London: J. Morphew and E. Curll, 1713; 8th ed., London: Knaptons, Manby, and Beecroft, 1743), 349 (the eighth edition, quoted here, was published a year after Bentley's death, with additions from his manuscript):

> If there had been but one manuscript of the Greek Testament at the restoration of learning about two centuries ago, then we had had no *various readings* at all. . . . And would the text be in a better condition then, than now [that] we have 30,000 [variant readings]?
>
> It is good, therefore . . . to have more anchors than one; and another MS. to join the first would give more authority, as well as security.

Bentley's discussion that the number of variants among NT MSS gives us more assurance, not less, concerning the wording of the original occupies a major section in this book (347–64).

20. Although Ehrman does both in *Misquoting Jesus*, he seems to emphasize the former far more than the latter. As NT professor Craig Blomberg observes, "What most distinguishes the work are the spins Ehrman puts on some of the data at numerous junctures and his propensity for focusing on the most drastic of all the changes in the history of the text, leaving the uninitiated likely to think there are numerous additional examples of various phenomena he discusses when there are not" (*Denver Journal* 9 [2006]; accessed online).

21. Eldon Jay Epp, "Are Early New Testament Manuscripts Truly Abundant?," in *Israel's God and Rebecca's Children: Christology and Community in Early Judaism and Christianity; Essays in Honor of Larry W. Hurtado and Alan F. Segal*, ed. David B.

erage Greek NT MS is over 450 pages long. Altogether, there are more than 2.6 million pages of texts, leaving hundreds of witnesses for every book of the NT.

It is not just the Greek MSS that count, either. Early on, the NT was translated into a variety of languages—Latin, Coptic, Syriac, Georgian, Gothic, Ethiopic, Armenian. There are more than 10,000 Latin MSS alone. No one really knows the total number of all these ancient versions, but the best estimates are close to 5,000—plus the 10,000 in Latin.[22] It would be safe to say that we have altogether about 20,000 handwritten manuscripts of the NT in various languages, including Greek.

If someone were to destroy all those manuscripts, we would not be left without a witness, because the church fathers wrote commentaries on the NT. To date, more than one million quotations of the NT by the fathers have been recorded. "[I]f all other sources for our knowledge of the text of the New Testament were destroyed, [the patristic quotations] would be sufficient alone for the reconstruction of practically the entire New Testament," wrote Bruce Metzger and Bart Ehrman.[23]

These numbers are *breathtaking*! But if left by themselves, they also resemble Samuel Clemens's quip about statistics. Far more important than the numbers is the *date* of the MSS. How many manuscripts do we have in the first century after the completion of the NT, in the second, and in the third? Although the numbers are significantly lower for the early centuries, they are still rather impressive. Today we have as many as 12 MSS from the second century, 64 from the third, and 48 from the fourth—a total of 124 MSS within 300 years of the composition of the

---

Capes, April D. DeConick, Helen K. Bond, and Troy A. Miller (Waco, TX: Baylor University Press, 2007), 77–107, notes on 395–99. Epp notes that the official tally is 5,752 manuscripts but that this "count of manuscripts . . . cannot simply be looked up, because duplications and items misplaced in the lists must be eliminated" (78). This brings his numbers to 5,494. However, in the summer of 2007, the Center for the Study of New Testament Manuscripts (see www.csntm.org) sent a team to Albania to photograph Greek NT manuscripts housed in the National Archive in Tirana. In the process, at least 24 manuscripts and as many as 30 were photographed for the first time—MSS that had not been cataloged by the Institut für neutestamentliche Textforschung in Münster, Germany (the differences being that some of these MSS may have been among the 17 that had been presumed lost for decades. In the summer of 2008, before these MSS had been tabulated by the Münster institute, Ulrich Schmid of the INTF informed me that the number of extant MSS now stood at 5,555. As of May 2011, CSNTM had discovered more than 70 Greek NT MSS. Thus the number of extant MSS will soon officially stand at over 5,600.

22. Curiously, Epp claimed as recently as 2007 that there were about "10,000 versional manuscripts" (Epp, "Are Early New Testament Manuscripts Truly Abundant?," 77) although the number of *Latin* MSS alone reaches that number.

23. Bruce M. Metzger and Bart D. Ehrman, *The Text of the New Testament: Its Transmission, Corruption, and Restoration*, 4th ed. (New York: Oxford University Press, 2005), 126.

NT. Most of these are fragmentary, but the whole NT text is found in this collection multiple times.[24]

How does the average Greek or Latin author stack up? If we are comparing the same time period—300 years after composition—the average classical author has *no literary remains*. But if we compare all the MSS of a particular classical author, regardless of when they were written, the total would still average at least less than 20 and probably less than a dozen—and they would all be coming much more than three centuries later. In terms of extant MSS, the NT textual critic is confronted with an embarrassment of riches. If we have doubts about what the autographic NT said, those doubts would have to be multiplied a *hundredfold*[25] for the average classical author.[26] When we compare the

---

24. Epp's numbers are slightly different: 11 MSS from the second and third centuries, 52 from the third and fourth, and 48 from the fourth and fifth, for a total of 111 MSS within 300 years of the completion of the NT ("Are Early New Testament Manuscripts Truly Abundant?," table 6.2, p. 80). The different counts are due to (1) new discoveries since 2006 (when he tabulated his data) and (2) some MSS that he did not consider or perhaps overlooked. (Bagnall has recently offered a different view on the date of our earliest NT MSS, considering them much later than almost all other textual critics and paleographers have [Roger S. Bagnall, *Early Christian Books in Egypt* [Princeton, NJ: Princeton University Press, 2009].) What is most telling in his essay is that he hardly speaks of the value of these numbers in relation to other ancient literature. It is remarkable that in an article intended to show how sparse the early data for the NT are (e.g., "If the early manuscripts are most valuable, what value and how much abundance do we have in the mere eleven manuscripts that have survived from the period up to and around 200 C.E.? At that point, Christianity had been in existence for two hundred years!" [88]), the author makes no comparison with other ancient Greco-Roman literature. Without such a comparison, there is no way to tell how *relatively* abundant the early NT MSS are. Further, nowhere does he discuss how much text of the NT was found in these early MSS.

25. Technically, our doubts should be a thousandfold if there are 20,000 NT MSS (in Greek and the ancient versions) and less than 20 MSS of an average classical author. However, if one were only to look at the more ancient copies of such documents, the ratios could be closer. A hundredfold is an amount that is hard to dispute.

26. Note that I did not say that we have no doubts about the autographs of these other ancient writers. But far greater skepticism toward the NT is shown than its MS testimony would warrant. Further, it is curious that Ehrman can sound so skeptical of the wording of the original NT in *Misquoting Jesus* when a part of his basis for such skepticism is *certainty* about what some ancient writers said. Part of his argument against the reliability of NT MSS is his assumption of accuracy of what certain ancient writers' texts read, even though we have to do textual criticism on *their* extant MSS to try to reconstruct what they wrote. He enlists Seneca (46), Martial (47), Hermas (48), Irenaeus (53), Dionysius (53), and Rufinus (54). Most significantly, he discusses Origen's *quotations* of Celsus, an antagonist to the Christian faith who wrote about seventy years before Origen did, with the tacit assumption that the *copies* of Origen that we have accurately reflect what Origen wrote *and* that Origen accurately recorded what Celsus wrote, even though seventy years separated the two men. If we had the original text of Origen, we would still be dealing with a seventy-year gap after Celsus. But when a similar gap occurs for the

NT MSS to the very best that the classical world has to offer,[27] the NT MSS still stand high above the rest. The NT is by far the best-attested work of Greek or Latin literature from the ancient world.

There is another way to look at this. If all of the NT MSS that are definitely or possibly dated to the second century are fragmentary—and they are—*how* fragmentary are they? We can measure this in different ways. First, three out of the four Gospels are attested in the MSS, as well as nine of Paul's letters, Acts, Hebrews, and Revelation—in other words, most of the NT books. Another way to look at this is that over 40 percent of all the verses in the NT are already found in MSS within 150 years of the completion of the NT.[28]

Ehrman seems to say in a couple places that we do not have *any* second-century MSS.[29] He declared in an interview in the *Charlotte Observer*,[30] "If we don't have the original texts of the New Testament—or even copies of the copies of the copies of the originals—what do we have?" His response is illuminating: "We have copies that were made *hundreds* of years later—in most cases, many hundreds of years later. And these copies are all different from one another."[31] He is saying that we do not have *any* manuscripts of the NT until hundreds of years after the NT was completed. He repeated this statement at the 2008 Greer-Heard Forum debate and, more recently, on the TC-List, an

---

NT MSS, Ehrman says, "We don't even have copies of the copies of the originals, or copies of the copies of the copies of the originals. What we have are copies made later—much later" (*Misquoting Jesus*, 10); "If we have very few early copies—in fact, scarcely any—how can we know that the text was not changed significantly *before* the New Testament began to be reproduced in such large quantities?" (*Lost Christianities*, 219).

27. Homer's *Iliad* has just over 2,200 extant MSS, while his *Odyssey* has 141 (Martin L. West, *Homeri Ilias*, vol. 1, *Rhapsodias I–XII Continens*, Bibliotheca Scriptorum Graecorum et Romanorum Teubneriana [Stuttgart: In Aedibus B. G. Teubneri, 1998], xxxviii–liv; Victor Berard, *L'Odyssee: Poesie Homerique*, vol. 1, *Chants 1–VII*, Collection des Universités de France [Paris: Societe D'Edition Les Belles Lettres, 1924], xxxvi–xxxix. The data on the *Odyssey*, however, need to be updated). Nothing in the ancient Greco-Roman world comes close to this—except, of course, for the NT and some patristic writers such as Chrysostom. Not counting patristic citations of the NT, there are still almost ten times as many copies of the NT as there are Homeric MSS extant today.

28. The specific number is 43 percent. But this does not necessarily mean that every portion of each of these verses is in these MSS. Thanks are due to Brett Williams for doing the painstaking work of tabulating the number of verses that are found in the definite and possible second-century manuscripts.

29. He does not say this in any of his books, as far as I am aware, but he does discount the number of early MSS by noting their fragmentary character. Cf. *Lost Christianities*, 219.

30. Dec. 17, 2005.

31. Italics added.

Daniel B. Wallace

international Internet discussion group of biblical textual critics.[32] But this is demonstrably not true. The impression Ehrman sometimes gives throughout *Misquoting Jesus*—but especially repeats in interviews—is that of wholesale uncertainty about the original wording, a view that is probably far more radical than the one he actually embraces.

In light of comments such as these, the impression that many readers get from *Misquoting Jesus* is that the transmission of the NT resembles the "telephone game."[33] This is a game every child knows. It involves a line of people, with the first one whispering some story into the ear of the second person. That person then whispers the story to the next person in line, and that person whispers it to the next, and so on down the line. As the tale goes from person to person, it gets terribly garbled. The whole point of the telephone game, in fact, is to see how garbled it can get. *There is no motivation to "get it right."* By the time it gets to the last person, who repeats it aloud for the whole group, everyone has a good laugh.

But the copying of NT manuscripts is hardly like this parlor game, for many reasons:

1. The message is passed on in writing, not orally. Passing a message in writing would make for a pretty boring telephone game!

2. Rather than having one line, there are *multiple* lines or streams of transmission.[34]

---

32. "[W]e don't know how much the texts got changed in all those decades/*centuries before* our *earliest* manuscripts, and we have no way of knowing" (TC-List, Nov. 1, 2008; italics added to "centuries" and "earliest").

33. The impression that the transmission of NT manuscripts is like the telephone game is reinforced by Ehrman's almost complete lack of discussion of early versions, patristic comments, or the relation between manuscripts that surely brings us back much earlier than our extant witnesses can do. He knows better than this, as is revealed by a perusal of Metzger and Ehrman's *Text of the New Testament*.

34. Elsewhere Ehrman seems to argue that Christians simply destroyed the original documents "for some unknown reason." In his discussion of manuscript production in *Lost Christianities*, he says, "In this process of recopying the document by hand, what happened to the original of 1 Thessalonians? For some unknown reason, it was eventually thrown away or burned or otherwise destroyed. Possibly it was read so much that it simply wore out. The early Christians saw no need to preserve it as the 'original' text. They had copies of the letter. Why keep the original?" (217). He is here presupposing two unlikely attitudes: first, that early Christians just did not care about original documents at all; second, that early Christians made only one copy of the original text of a NT book.
Kirsopp Lake, Robert P. Blake, and Silva New ("The Caesarean Text of the Gospel of Mark," *HTR* 21 [1928]: 348–49) argued that the scribes in the monasteries at Sinai, Patmos, and Jerusalem probably destroyed their exemplars. This opinion was just one way to make sense of the fact that most of the manuscripts in these monasteries were "orphan children without brothers or sisters." There is, however, no evidence that early Christians destroyed their own revered manuscripts. The only evidence we have of MS destruction by Christians, as far as I am

3.   Textual critics do not rely on just the last person in each line but can interrogate several folks who are closer to the original source.

---

aware, is of destruction of documents that were viewed as heretical. We have two statements, both from the fifth century, to this effect. Theodoret of Cyrrhus seems to imply that he destroyed two hundred copies of Tatian's *Diatessaron* (*Compendium haereticarum fabularum* 1.20 [MPG 83, cols. 369, 372]), though this is not exactly stated. Rabbula of Edessa, writing in the early fifth century, explicitly says that the writings of the heretics *needed* to be destroyed ("Commands and Admonitions . . . to the Priests and the Benai Qeiama," in *Syriac and Arabic Documents regarding Legislation Relative to Syrian Asceticism* , ed. Arthur Vööbus [Stockholm: Etse, 1960], 48). Though there is no reason to think that his orders were not carried out, there is again no statement of fact about such destruction. But the fact that both of these references are from the fifth century (well after heresy and orthodoxy had been clearly defined) and that copies of the *NT* per se were not among the documents destroyed leaves us guessing as to whether earlier groups of Christians actually did this sort of thing.

Further, there is some evidence that the NT autographa were revered in the second century. Tertullian, a church father living up through the first quarter of the third century, chastised his theological opponents about their doubts over what the original text said. The exact meaning of his statement is somewhat controversial: "Come now, you who would indulge a better curiosity, if you would apply it to the business of your salvation, run over to the apostolic churches, in which the very thrones of the apostles are still pre-eminent in their places, in which their own *authentic writings* are read, uttering the voice and representing the face of each of them severally" (Tertullian, *The Prescription against Heretics*, chap. 36; italics added). What is at issue here is the meaning of "authentic" writings. If this refers to the *original* documents, as the word in Latin (*authenticae*) normally does, Tertullian is saying that several of the original NT books still existed in his day, well over a century after the time of their writing. He specifically refers to Paul's letters sent to Corinth, Philippi, Thessalonica, Ephesus, and Rome, urging his reader to visit these sites to check out these authentic writings. But if *authenticae* does not mean original documents, it would at least mean, in this context, carefully produced copies. Most likely, the term is here referring to the originals, but Tertullian's testimony may not be credible. However, by Tertullian's day, carefully done copies of the originals both were considered important for verifying what the NT authors wrote and may have still been available for consultation. Even taking the worst-case scenario, Tertullian's statement is an early documented concern about having the original text or at least accurate copies *in circulation*, rather than quietly put on the shelf never to be consulted again. (See George Houston, "Papyrological Evidence for Book Collections and Libraries in the Roman Empire," in *Ancient Literacies: The Culture of Reading in Greece and Rome*, ed. William A. Johnson and Holt N. Parker [Oxford: Oxford University Press, 2009], 233–67, for evidence of the longevity of well-used papyrus MSS in the ancient world. Houston points out that literary documents were in use an average of two hundred or more years [248–51]).

Regarding the second assumption—that the original text was copied only once (Ehrman says that it may have worn out from being read, but not from being copied)—surely it was copied often if it was read often. To suppose that the early Christians just somehow forgot about the originals or, worse, destroyed them is contrary to human nature, to at least one early patristic writer's testimony, and to all the evidence we have from the first several centuries of the Christian era.

4. Patristic writers are commenting on the text as it is going through its transmissional history. And when there are chronological gaps among the manuscripts, these writers often fill in those gaps by telling us what the text said in that place in their day.

5. In the telephone game, once the story is told by one person, that individual has nothing else to do with the story. It is out of his or her hands. But the original NT books were most likely copied more than once and may have been consulted even after a few generations of copies had already been produced.[35]

6. There was at least one very carefully produced stream of transmission for the NT MSS, and there is sufficient evidence to show that even a particular fourth-century MS in this line is usually more accurate than *any* second-century MS.

We can illustrate this with two manuscripts that Ehrman and I would both agree are two of the most accurate MSS of the NT, if not *the* two most accurate: $\mathfrak{P}^{75}$ and Codex Vaticanus (or B). These two MSS have an incredibly strong agreement. Their agreement is higher than the agreement of any other two early MSS. $\mathfrak{P}^{75}$ is 100 to 150 years older than B, yet *it is not an ancestor of B*. Instead, B copied from an *earlier* common ancestor that both B and $\mathfrak{P}^{75}$ were related to.[36] The combination of both of these manuscripts in a particular reading goes back to early in the second century.[37]

---

35. Ehrman has suggested that as the copying was done, discrepancies would be noted. At the Greer-Heard Forum, in fact, he painted a scenario in which early copies of Mark would have been compared to earlier copies to clear up these discrepancies. If these discrepancies were large enough from the earliest period of copying, would it not seem likely that the autographs would have been consulted?

36. See C. L. Porter, "Papyrus Bodmer XV ($\mathfrak{P}^{75}$) and the Text of Codex Vaticanus," *JBL* 81 (1962): 363–76; Porter, "An Evaluation of the Textual Variation between Pap75 and Codex Vaticanus in the Text of John," in *Studies in the History and Text of the New Testament in Honor of Kenneth Willis Clark*, ed. Boyd L. Daniels and M. Jack Suggs, Studies and Documents 29 (Salt Lake City: University of Utah Press, 1967), 71–80; Gordon D. Fee, "$\mathfrak{P}^{75}$, $\mathfrak{P}^{66}$, and Origen: The Myth of Early Textual Recension in Alexandria," in Eldon J. Epp and Gordon D. Fee, *Studies in the Theory and Method of New Testament Textual Criticism*, ed. Irving Alan Sparks, Studies and Documents 45 (Grand Rapids: Eerdmans, 1993), 247–73.

37. Fee argues that their agreement goes back to the second century, but he adds that since $\mathfrak{P}^{75}$ was not a recension but a relatively pure copy in a relatively pure stream of transmission, Hort had good instincts when he thought of Codex B as representing "a 'relatively pure' line of descent from the original text" (Fee, "Myth of Early Textual Recension in Alexandria," 272). Ehrman acknowledges the significance of Codex Vaticanus and $\mathfrak{P}^{75}$ in the appendix to *Misquoting Jesus*. Regarding $\mathfrak{P}^{75}$, he says, "This is arguably the most valuable ancient papyrus manuscript of

---

Ehrman has asserted, "If we have very few early copies—in fact, scarcely any—how can we know that the text was not changed significantly *before* the New Testament began to be reproduced in such large quantities?"[38] I am not sure what large quantities he is speaking about, since there are more MSS from the *third* century than there are from the fourth *or* fifth century.[39]

But how can we know? It is a legitimate question. There is a way to be relatively confident that the text of the fourth century looked remarkably like the earliest form of the text. 𝔓⁷⁵ has large portions of Luke and John in it—and nothing else. Codex B has most of the NT in it. If B and 𝔓⁷⁵ are very close to each other yet B often has the more primitive reading, we can extrapolate that the text of B is pretty decent for the rest of the NT. When it agrees with a MS such as Codex Sinaiticus, which it usually does, that combined reading almost surely goes back to a common archetype from deep in the second century.[40]

Nevertheless, Ehrman has carefully and ably described the transmission of the text. He has detailed how the winners succeeded in conquering all with their views and emerged as the group we might call "orthodox." What he has said is fairly accurate overall. The only problem is that his is the right *analysis* but for the wrong *religion.* Ehrman's basic argument about theological motives describes Islam far more than Christianity. Recent work on the transmissional history of both the NT and the Qur'an shows this clearly. Consider the following points:

---

the Gospels" (263). Concerning Vaticanus, he says, "This is probably the highest quality manuscript of the New Testament" (ibid.).

38. *Lost Christianities*, 219.

39. The next line, however, suggests that he is speaking about *medieval* MSS: "Most surviving copies were made during the Middle Ages, many of them a thousand years after Paul and his companions had died" (ibid.). The juxtaposition of this sentence with the one questioning whether we can know how significant the changes were prior to this time is, at best, misleading. Ehrman would acknowledge, as would most textual critics, that the MSS produced in the Middle Ages are hardly our most reliable witnesses to the NT text *and* that we have several sufficient witnesses prior to that time on which to reconstruct the wording of the earliest form of the text.

40. Cf., e.g., Metzger and Ehrman, *Text of the New Testament*, 277–78, 312. Hort believed that when ℵ and B agreed, their reading went back to a very ancient common ancestor. That it was not a near ancestor was demonstrated by the thousands of disagreements between these two manuscripts, suggesting that there were several intermediaries between the common ancestor and these two majuscule documents (B. F. Westcott and F. J. A. Hort, *The New Testament in the Original Greek*, vol. 2, Introduction [and] Appendix [Cambridge: Macmillan, 1882], 212–50). Cf. also Metzger and Ehrman, *The Text of the New Testament*, 312: "With the discovery . . . of 𝔓66 and 𝔓75, both dating from about the end of the second or the beginning of the third century, proof became now available that Hort's Neutral text goes back to an archetype that must be put early in the second century."

1.   Within just a few decades of the writing of the Qur'an, it underwent a strongly controlled, heavy-handed editing, geared toward "orthodoxy," that weeded out variants that did not conform.

But the NT, as even Ehrman argues, did not suffer this sort of control early on. Instead, Ehrman has often suggested that the earliest decades were marked by free, even *wild* copying.[41]

2.   Calif Uthman was in charge of the earliest segment of this heavy-handed editing of the Qur'an. He systematically gathered up any nonconforming MSS and destroyed them. The originals were destroyed as well.[42] Uthman then claimed that his "canonical" text was the exact equivalent of the autographs.

There is no real evidence that inexact copies of the NT were destroyed by ecclesiastical authorities.[43] Indeed, there is evidence that just the opposite took place: defective or deteriorating copies might be placed in a jar or storage room but not destroyed.[44]

---

41. Cf., e.g., Ehrman, *Misquoting Jesus*, 124. I will discuss the nature of the early copying soon enough, but for now I simply point out that according to Ehrman, there was extensive uncontrolled copying of the NT in the earliest period.
42. Ehrman opines that perhaps the NT autographs were destroyed. Not only is there no evidence that this was the case, there is second-century evidence that the autographs would have been revered.
43. See nn. 34 and 44 for discussion.
44. Colin H. Roberts (*Manuscript, Society, and Belief in Early Christian Egypt* [London: Oxford University Press, 1979], 6–8) gives ample evidence that early Christians took over the practice of Jews to "dispose of defective, worn-out, or heretical scriptures by burying them near a cemetery, not to preserve them but because anything that might contain the name of God might not be destroyed" (ibid., 7). He was dealing with the earliest period of Christian copying but noted that the Nag Hammadi MSS ("outside our period") seem to fit this pattern as well. In addition, he cited the Dead Sea Scrolls, the Chester Beatty papyri, as well as several other examples. In more modern times, it is noteworthy to mention the New Finds manuscripts at St. Catherine's Monastery of Mt. Sinai. Discovered in 1975, quite by accident, was a geniza that housed about 1,200 manuscripts and 50,000 fragments of manuscripts. The latest date of any of the MSS was from the eighteenth century; the earliest was the fourth century (about two dozen leaves or fragments from Codex Sinaiticus). Among the less orthodox MSS were the Protevangelium of James and the Assumption of the Virgin. When I visited the monastery in September 2002, Archbishop Damianos expressed surprise to me that the Protevangelium was among the New Finds manuscripts. I discovered the Assumption of the Virgin inside the Protevangelium, occupying a new quire.

What the New Finds illustrate is that the practice of burying MSS at Mt. Sinai was taking place after the eighteenth century and sufficiently prior to modern times to have been forgotten by the monks. After Tischendorf's last visit in 1859, the monastery became increasingly flooded with visitors. This suggests that the geniza was filled prior to this time. And the fact that leaves from Sinaiticus were buried there—both from the Pentateuch and from the Apostolic Fathers (i.e., the outer leaves of the codex, which would be most prone to be loosed from the book)—may imply that Tischendorf was mistaken when he said that the monks were burning

3. The closest we come to heavy-handed control for NT MSS did not occur until at least the *ninth* century, long after the major Christological disputes had ended.[45] Even then, we do not see defective MSS getting destroyed.

4. One cannot have it both ways; there cannot be wild copying by untrained scribes *and* a proto-orthodox conspiracy simultaneously producing the same variants. Conspiracy implies control, and wild copying is anything but controlled.

On the one hand, there *was* uncontrolled copying of MSS in the earliest period, but this was largely restricted to the Western text form.[46] On the other hand, there was a strand of early copying that may *appear* to be controlled. This is the Alexandrian family of MSS. Yet the reason that MSS of this text form look so much like each other is largely because they were in a relatively pure line of transmission.[47] There was no conspiracy, just good practices.

5. The reason why Islam has Qur'an MSS that so closely resemble each other is precisely because this was official dogma, there was over-zealous control in the copying of the MSS, and there were severe repercussions to any who erred significantly in their scribal duties. All MSS ultimately derived from a single copy—a copy that was *not* identical to the original text.[48]

---

leaves of this codex. For our purposes, it is enough to note that the normative practice of ancient Christians, even perhaps to modern times, was to bury or hide sacred texts rather than destroy them.

45. T. J. Ralston ("The Majority Text and Byzantine Texttype Development: The Significance of a Non-Parametric Method of Data Analysis for the Exploration of Manuscript Traditions" [PhD diss., Dallas Seminary, 1994]) notes (in agreement with von Soden's assessment) that there was a large editorial push by at least one scriptorium in the ninth and eleventh centuries, resulting in carefully produced copies that were very close to each other.

46. It is not entirely insignificant that Ehrman's preferred reading in several places that seem to impact Christology is found in the Western text (e.g., Luke 3.22; John 20.28). The burden of proof certainly rests with the one who would argue that such a textual tradition has the original wording when the carefully copied tradition of Alexandria does not. He admits that the Western text is less likely to preserve the best reading when it lacks support of the Alexandrian witnesses (*Misquoting Jesus*, 131). I do agree with Ehrman in at least one Western reading, however. But ὀργισθείσ in Mark 1.41 has compelling internal evidence in its favor.

47. Ehrman, *Misquoting Jesus*, 131.

48. This is not at all what the NT transmission was like. See the following discussion of the work of Uthman in canonizing the Qur'an by starting with his own MS as the progenitor of all that would follow. Ehrman speculates, without a shred of evidence, that this same phenomenon occurred for NT books: "[W]hat if only *one* of the copies served as the copy from which all subsequent copies were made . . . ?" (*Misquoting Jesus*, 59).

Contrast this with the NT: from the earliest times, the NT was translated into a multitude of languages.[49] The transmission of the text was a growing, living thing, not constrained by ecclesiastical controls until *long* after Christianity became legalized. Even then, we know of nothing like what we see in Islam: scribes not only made plenty of mistakes, but they even complained in the margins of their manuscripts about the weather, the length of the MS they were copying, the clogging of the ink, and so on.[50] This sort of living, hands-on, messy relationship of the scribes to their holy scriptures is unheard of in Islam. In short, the Qur'an copying practices were more related to *apologetics*, while the NT practices were more related to *life*.

6.   Further, ever since *canon* was a term meaningfully applied to the NT, there was never a sense that only the Greek MSS were Scripture. To be sure, the Reformation sparked a return to the original languages of the Bible, but the reason was not only purity of the text but clarity in the proclamation of the message. It is no accident that the Reformers were the catalyst for the great European translations of the Bible—translations into the language of the people that could be considered the very Word of God by the average layman. By way of contrast, the only true Qur'an is the Arabic Qur'an. All translations are officially suspect. Thus what Ehrman is describing is right on target but for the wrong religion. He is describing what has occurred in Islam, not in Christianity.

7.   What Westcott said over a century ago is relevant to this discussion:

> When the Caliph Othman fixed a text of the Koran and destroyed all the old copies which differed from his standard, he provided for the uniformity of subsequent manuscripts at the cost of their historical

---

49.   Keith Small, a scholar in the United Kingdom who has recently completed his doctoral thesis on a comparison of the NT textual transmission and the Qur'an textual transmission ("Mapping a New Country: Textual Criticism and Qur'an Manuscripts" [London School of Theology, 2008]), noted in an email on March 25, 2008, "There was not a program of translation to spread Islam through having people read the Qur'an, like there was with the Christian Scriptures. Though one early jurist, Abu Hanifah (d. AD 767), did rule that a person could recite a vernacular translation in their prayers, he also is said to have retracted that ruling. The earliest extant translation I know of is one done into Persian about AD 956 (Ekmeleddin Ihsanoglu, *World Bibliography of Translations of the Meanings of the Holy Qur'an, Printed Translations 1515-1980* [Istanbul: Research Centre for Islamic History, Art and Culture], xxiii)."

50.   See Metzger and Ehrman, *Text of the New Testament*, 29, for illustrations. Having this sort of marginal note in the Qur'an is unheard of. But some of the marginal notes in the NT MSS are rather impious, showing that the copying was meant more for the masses than for apologetic reasons.

foundation. *A classical text which rests finally on a single archetype is that which is open to the most serious suspicions.*[51]

What we see in the NT copies is absolutely nothing like this. Ehrman tries to make a case for *significant* theological alterations to the text of the NT *by a group that did not have control over the text from the beginning*, but the historical ingredients for his hypothesis are missing. It is like trying to bake a cake with romaine lettuce and ranch dressing.

As Small points out,

> The original NT text (the autographic text-form in Epp's categories) has been kept remarkably well, and *one form* of the Qur'an text, a strongly edited one (a canonical text-form in Epp's words), has been preserved remarkably well. This Qur'anic text form (the one attributed to Uthman though probably a little later—ca. 700 AD) preserves authentic material, but not in the forms in which it was originally used or in the complete collection assembled in writing or orally during Muhammad's lifetime. Instead, it is a very selective, heavily edited text. In contrast, the NT is not really the product of an official process of intentional editing and so preserves more of the original text within the extant manuscripts. This can be said just on the basis of Islamic tradition concerning the collections attributed to have been made by the companions of Muhammad. In the twenty years after Muhammad's death until Uthman's project to standardize the text, these versions were used extensively in other parts of the growing Islamic empire, apparently as authoritative scripture. Some of these are reported to have been in use into the 900's AD until they were finally suppressed around 934. My research in the manuscripts also demonstrates that the majority of the earliest manuscripts contain this edited text, with the handful of palimpsests pointing to other textual traditions that were successfully suppressed. These palimpsests contain the same variety of textual variants that one can see between the Western and Alexandrian text-types in the NT tradition—showing that there was a period when the Qur'an text was more fluid than the majority of manuscripts and Islamic dogma would lead one to believe. Muslims assume and state that this Uthmanic text was the original text, though even their traditions go against the view. It contains original material, but the original form of that material cannot be reconstructed because Uthman destroyed the autographs and had his authoritative version written in a defective script which allowed the growth of competing written

---

51. Brooke Foss Westcott, *Some Lessons of the Revised Version of the New Testament*, 2nd ed. (London: Hodder and Stoughton, 1897), 8–9 (italics added). Credit is due to Keith Small for pointing this reference out to me.

Daniel B. Wallace

versions and oral recitation systems. Their theological view of mechanical inspiration keeps them from adequately engaging with their own historical sources. What they have done instead is selectively choose reports that they can use to construct a straight line of "perfect" transmission while ignoring the facts which disagree with the theological construct they want to hold of an eternal book perfectly transmitted. I think Uthman's version does probably represent the main lines of Muhammad's teaching, though for political reasons certain parts may have been left out. But we can't tell for sure because the autographs were destroyed, not that they wore out in use. And the main point to get to in all of this is still that the NT and the Qur'an teach very different things. Also, for whatever integrity one wants to grant to the transmission of the Qur'an, the NT needs to be regarded as having more integrity in its transmission process since there was not such an official editing process after the books were written. In light of all of this, I think Bart Ehrman's arguments are much more appropriate for the Qur'an because for it there can be demonstrated an official program of textual standardization which was maintained over three centuries, and in some respects to this day.[52]

Concerning conforming the text to the Medieval standard, though there is a general parallel to this situation to the Qur'an's, I see it having a fundamental difference, that while the changes to the NT were gradual, relatively late in the history of transmission, and primarily for liturgical reasons and to improve the style, the Qur'an's form of the consonantal text was determined and maintained from very early on (within 30–70 years after Muhammad's death) for reasons which had a large ideological/dogmatic component at the outset, and then that form was further shaped and developed with diacritics and vowels to maintain and serve various agendas during the next 200 years until the Sunnis came out on top politically in the 900's and were able to canonize their version of the text.[53]

In another respect, when Ehrman discusses whether God has preserved the text of the NT, he places on the NT transmissional process some rather unrealistic demands—demands that Islam traditionally claims for itself with respect to the Qur'an but that no bona fide Christian scholar would ever claim was true of the NT MSS. As is well known, most Muslims claim that the Qur'an has been transmitted

---

52. Email from Keith Small, Mar. 11 2008,
53. Email from Keith Small, Dec. 30, 2007. For an excellent survey on the transmission of the Qur'an, see now Keith E. Small, *Textual Criticism and Qur'an Manuscripts* (Idaho Falls, Idaho: Lexingon, 2011).

perfectly, that all copies are exactly alike. This is what Ehrman demands of the NT text *if* God has inspired it. Methodologically, he did not abandon the evangelical faith; he abandoned a faith that in its bibliological constructs is what most Muslims claim for their sacred text. Or as C. S. Lewis put it,

> The moment [the miracle] enters [nature's] realm, it obeys all her laws. Miraculous wine will intoxicate, miraculous conception will lead to pregnancy, *inspired books will suffer all the ordinary processes of textual corruption*, miraculous bread will be digested.[54]

To sum up the evidence on the *number* of variants, there are a lot of variants because there are a lot of manuscripts. Even in the early centuries, the text of the NT is found in a sufficient number of MSS, versions, and writings of the church fathers to give us the *essentials* of the original text.

THE NATURE OF THE VARIANTS

How many differences affect the meaning of the text? How many of them are "plausible" or "viable"—that is, found in manuscripts with a sufficient pedigree that they have some likelihood of reflecting the original wording? The variants can be broken down into the following four categories:

- spelling differences and nonsense errors

- minor differences that do not affect translation or that involve synonyms

- differences that affect the meaning of the text but are not viable

- differences that both affect the meaning of the text and are viable

Of the hundreds of thousands of textual variants in NT MSS, the great majority are spelling differences that have no bearing on the meaning of the text.[55] The most common textual variant involves what

---

54. C. S. Lewis, *Miracles: A Preliminary Study*, 1st Touchstone ed. (New York: Touchstone, 1996) 95 (italics added).

55. Even in the earliest form of the text, we see spelling variations by the same author. Perhaps the most notable example is to be found in John 9.14–21: in the space of eight verses, the evangelist manages to spell the third-person singular aorist active indicative of ἀνοίγω *three* different ways (ἀνέῳξεν in v 14, ἠνέῳξεν in v 17, ἤνοιξεν in v 21).

Daniel B. Wallace

is called a movable *nu*. But whether the *nu* appears in these words or not, there is absolutely no difference in meaning.

Several of the spelling differences are nonsense readings. These occur when a scribe is fatigued, inattentive, or perhaps does not know Greek very well. For example, in 1 Thessalonians 2.7, the manuscripts are divided over a very difficult textual problem. Paul is describing how he and Silas acted among the new converts in their visit to Thessalonica. Some manuscripts have "we were gentle among you," while others have "we were little children among you." The difference between the two variants is a single letter in Greek (νήπιοι vs. ἤπιοι). A lone medieval scribe changed the text to "we were *horses* among you"! The Greek word for *horses* (ἵπποι) is similar to the other two words. Or consider a reading that Matthew Morgan noted in his chapter for this book: in John 1.30, the scribe of Codex L writes "after me comes air" instead of "after me comes a man" (ὀπίσω μου ἔρχεται ἀήρ for ὀπίσω μου ἔρχεται ἀνήρ).

After spelling differences, the next largest category of variants are those that involve synonyms or do not affect translation. They are wordings other than mere spelling changes, but they do not alter the way the text is translated or, at least, understood. A very common variant involves the use of the article with proper names. Greek can say "the Mary" or "the Joseph" (as in Luke 2.16), while English usage requires the dropping of the article. So, whether the Greek text has "the Mary" or simply "Mary," English will always translate this as "Mary."

Another common variant is when words in Greek are transposed. Unlike English, Greek word order is used more for emphasis than for basic meaning. That is because Greek is a highly inflected language, with a myriad of suffixes on nouns and verbs, as well as prefixes and even infixes on verbs. One can tell where the subject is by its ending, regardless of where it stands in the sentence.

Take, for example, the sentence, "Jesus loves John." In Greek, that statement can be expressed in a minimum of *sixteen* different ways, though the translation would be the same in English every time. Once we factor in different verbs for "love" in Greek, the presence or absence of little particles that often go untranslated, and spelling differences, the possibilities run into the *hundreds*. Yet all of them would be translated simply as "Jesus loves John." There may be a slight difference in emphasis, but the basic meaning is not disturbed.

If a three-word sentence like this could potentially be expressed by hundreds of Greek constructions, how should we view the number of *actual* textual variants in the NT manuscripts? That there are only three variants for every word in the NT, when the potential is almost infinitely greater, seems trivial—especially when we consider how many thousands of manuscripts there are.

The third largest category involves wording that is meaningful but not viable. These are variants found in a single MS or group of MSS that, by themselves, have little likelihood of reflecting the wording of the autographic text. In 1 Thessalonians 2.9, one late medieval MS speaks of "the gospel of Christ" instead of "the gospel of God," while almost all the other MSS have the latter. Here, "the gospel of Christ" is a meaningful variant, but it is not viable because there is little chance that one medieval scribe somehow retained the wording of the original text while all other scribes for centuries before him missed it.

The final, and by far the smallest, category of textual variants involves those that are both meaningful *and* viable. Less than 1 percent of all textual variants belong to this group, but even saying this may be misleading. By "meaningful," we mean that the variant changes the meaning of the text *to some degree*. It may not be terribly significant, but if the reading impacts our understanding of the passage, then it is meaningful.

For example, consider a textual problem in Revelation 13.18:

Let the one who has insight calculate the beast's number, for it is the number of a man, and his number is 666.

- A few years ago, a scrap of papyrus was found at Oxford University's Ashmolean Museum. It gave the Beast's number as 616. And it just happens to be the oldest manuscript of Revelation 13 now extant.

- This was just the second MS to do so. (The other MS, not quite so early, is a very important witness to the text of the Apocalypse, known as Codex Ephraimi Rescriptus.) Most scholars think that 666 is the number of the Beast and that 616 is the *neighbor* of the Beast. But it is possible that the Beast's number is really 616.

- But what is the significance of this, really?[56] I know of no church, no Bible college, no theological seminary that has a doctrinal statement that says, "We believe in the deity of Christ, we believe in the virgin birth of Christ, we believe in the bodily resurrection of Christ, and we believe that the number of the Beast is 666."

---

56. That this variant is not entirely trivial can be confirmed by Ehrman's view of things: in discussing Johann Albrecht Bengel's quirky views of eschatology, Ehrman declares, "If the number of the Antichrist were not 666 but, say, 616, that would have a profound effect" (*Misquoting Jesus*, 111).

Daniel B. Wallace

- This textual variant does not change any cardinal belief of Christians, but, if original, it would send about seven tons of *dispensational* literature to the flames!

Although the quantity of textual variants among the NT MSS numbers in the hundreds of thousands, those that change the meaning pale in comparison. Less than 1 percent of the differences are both meaningful and viable. There are still hundreds of texts that are in dispute. I do not want to give the impression that textual criticism is merely a mop-up job nowadays, that all but a handful of problems have been resolved. That is not the case. There are hundreds of passages whose interpretation depends, to some degree, on which reading is followed, but the nature of the remaining problems and their interpretive significance are probably far less monumental than many readers of *Misquoting Jesus* have come to believe.

THE THEOLOGICAL ISSUES INVOLVED

Finally, what theological issues are involved in these textual variants? Ehrman argues that the major changes that have been made to the text of the NT have been produced by "orthodox" scribes, that they have tampered with the text in hundreds of places, with the result that the basic teachings of the NT have been drastically altered. Ehrman's basic thesis that orthodox scribes have altered the NT text for their own purposes is certainly true, and this occurs in hundreds of places. Ehrman has done the academic community a great service by systematically highlighting so many of these alterations in his *Orthodox Corruption of Scripture*. However, the extent to which these scribes altered these various passages and whether such alterations have buried forever the original wording of the NT are a different matter. Indeed, the very fact that Ehrman and other textual critics can place these textual variants in history and can determine the original text that was corrupted presupposes that the authentic wording has hardly been lost.[57]

In the concluding chapter of *Misquoting Jesus*, Ehrman summarizes his findings as follows:

---

57. In response to Eldon Epp's adoption of a new direction for the goal of NT textual criticism, Moisés Silva noted, "[F]or us to retreat from the traditional task of textual criticism is equivalent to shooting ourselves in the foot. And my exhibit A is Bart Ehrman's brilliant monograph *The Orthodox Corruption of Scripture*. . . . Although this book is appealed to in support of blurring the notion of an original text, there is hardly a page in that book that does not in fact mention such a text or assume its accessibility. . . . Indeed, Ehrman's book is unimaginable unless he can identify an initial form of the text that can be differentiated from a later alteration" (M. Silva, "Response," in *Rethinking New Testament Textual Criticism*, ed. David Alan Black [Grand Rapids: Baker, 2002], 149).

It would be wrong . . . to say—as people sometimes do—that the changes in our text have no real bearing on what the texts mean or on the theological conclusions that one draws from them. . . . In some instances, the very meaning of the text is at stake, depending on how one resolves a textual problem: Was Jesus an angry man [Mark 1.41]? Was he completely distraught in the face of death [Heb 2.9]? Did he tell his disciples that they could drink poison without being harmed [Mark 16.9–20]? Did he let an adulteress off the hook with nothing but a mild warning [John 7.53–8.11]? Is the doctrine of the Trinity explicitly taught in the New Testament [1 John 5.7–8]? Is Jesus actually called the "unique God" there [John 1.18]? Does the New Testament indicate that even the Son of God himself does not know when the end will come [Matt 24.36]? The questions go on and on, and all of them are related to how one resolves difficulties in the manuscript tradition as it has come down to us.[58]

I have dealt with the referenced passages in detail in my essay "The Gospel according to Bart," published in the *Journal of the Evangelical Theological Society*.[59] What I present here is much briefer and more selective.

Ehrman's summary paragraph gives us seven passages to consider:

Mark 16.9–20
John 7.53–8.11
1 John 5.7 (in the KJV)
Mark 1.41
Hebrews 2.9
John 1.18
Matthew 24.36

The first three passages have been considered inauthentic by most NT scholars—including most *evangelical* NT scholars—for well over a century.[60] The presence or absence of these passages changes no fun-

---

58. Ehrman, *Misquoting Jesus*, 207–8.
59. "The Gospel according to Bart: A Review Article of *Misquoting Jesus* by Bart Ehrman," *JETS* 49 (2006): 327–49.
60. Ehrman writes as though the excision of such texts could shake up orthodox convictions. Such is hardly the case. I am aware of no confessional statements at seminaries, Christian colleges, or major denominations that were retooled in the slightest because of the excision of these verses. Yet it should be noted that these two passages are the largest textual problems in the NT by far. As one scholar complains, "[Ehrman's] first extended examples of textual problems in the New Testament are the woman caught in adultery and the longer ending of Mark. After demonstrating how neither of these is likely to be part of the originals of either Gospel, Ehrman concedes that 'most of the changes are not of this magnitude' (p. 69). But this sounds as if there are at least a few others that are of similar size, when in fact there are no other textual variants anywhere that are even one-fourth as

damental doctrine, no core belief—despite the fact that there is much emotional baggage and certainly historical significance attached to them.

In the next three passages, Ehrman adopts readings that most textual critics would consider spurious. I think his assessment is correct in one of them (Mark 1.41), possibly correct in one (Heb 2.9),[61] and almost surely incorrect in the last (John 1.18).[62] Nevertheless, even if his text-critical decisions are correct in all three passages, the theological reasons he gives for the changes are probably overdone, as, for example, in the case of Matthew 24.36.[63]

In Matthew's version of the Olivet Discourse, we read, "But about that day and hour no one knows, neither the angels of heaven, nor the Son, but only the Father" (NRSV). The words "nor the Son" are not found in all the MSS, which raises a significant issue: Did some scribes *omit* these words from the text of Matthew, or did other scribes *add* these words? Ehrman is firmly convinced that the words were expunged by proto-orthodox scribes who bristled at the idea of the Son of God's ignorance.

As Adam Messer notes, this passage "is Ehrman's example *par excellence.*"[64] Ehrman discusses it explicitly at least half a dozen times in *Misquoting Jesus.*[65] And in an academic publication, he calls it "the most famous instance" of doctrinal alteration.[66]

In *Misquoting Jesus*, he argues, "The reason [for the omission] is not hard to postulate; if Jesus does not know the future, the Christian claim that he is a divine being is more than a little compromised."[67] Ehrman does not qualify his words here; he does not say that *some* Christians would have a problem with Jesus' ignorance. No, he says that *the* Christian claim would have a problem with it.[68] If he does not mean this,

---

long as these thirteen- [*sic*] and twelve-verse additions" (Blomberg, *Denver Journal* 9 [2006]; accessed online).

61. But see Krista M. Miller, "Evaluating the Reading Χωρὶς Θεοῦ in Hebrews 2:9 in Light of Patristic Evidence" (Th.M. thesis, Dallas Theological Seminary, 2010).

62. See Brian Wright, "Jesus as Θεός: A Textual Examination," in this book, for a discussion of John 1.18.

63. See Adam G. Messer's extended treatment of this verse, especially in relation to patristic writings, in "Patristic Theology and Recension in Matthew 24.36: An Evaluation of Ehrman's Text-Critical Methodology," in this book.

64. Messer, "Patristic Theology and Recension in Matthew 24.36," 130.

65. *Misquoting Jesus*, 95, 110, 204, 209, 223 n. 19, 224 n. 16.

66. Bart D. Ehrman, *Studies in the Textual Criticism of the New Testament*, vol. 33 in NTTS, ed. Bruce M. Metzger and Bart D. Ehrman (Leiden: Brill, 2006), 333.

67. *Misquoting Jesus*, 204.

68. This sort of absolute statement seems to be either intentionally provocative or unintentionally ambiguous. Either way, it leaves a distinct impression on the reader that Jesus' deity is foreign to the original NT. This impression was reinforced by Ehrman himself in an interview with Diane Rehm on National Public Radio (Dec. 8, 2005). Ms. Rehm asked a vital question: "Has any central doctrine of Christian

---

he is writing more provocatively than is necessary and is misleading his readers. If he does mean it, he has overstated his case.

Ehrman suggests that the omission would have arisen in the late second century, as a proto-orthodox response to the Adoptionist heresy. This is possible, but there are three problems with this hypothesis.

1. It is somewhat startling that virtually no church father seems to have any problem with the words "nor the Son" until the fourth century,[69] though several comment on this very passage. Irenaeus (late second century), Tertullian (late second and early third century), and Origen (early third century) all embraced the deity of Christ, yet none of them felt that this passage caused any theological problems.[70] Irenaeus goes so far as to use Christ's ignorance as a model of humility for Christians.[71] If the scribes were simply following the leads of their theological mentors, the lack of any tension over this passage by second- and third-century fathers suggests that the omission of "nor the Son" either was not a reaction to Adoptionism or was not created in the late second century.

2. If the omission was created intentionally by proto-orthodox scribes in the late second century, it most likely would have been created by scribes who followed Irenaeus's view that the four Gospels were

---

faith been called into question by any of these variations?" Ehrman's response is illuminating:

> Well, yes. In the eighteenth century one of the first scholars to start studying these materials was a man in Germany named Wettstein, who ended up losing his teaching post because he pointed out that a number of the changes in the oldest manuscripts compromised the teaching of the deity of Christ, and they threatened the doctrine of the Trinity, that some of the oldest manuscripts didn't support the view of Jesus as divine.

Two things are notable about this response. First, rather than citing any textual problems in the NT, Ehrman enlists the name of Wettstein, a scholar who, more than two centuries ago, came to the conclusion that the deity of Christ and the Trinity had a dubious textual basis. Second, he seems to say that these fundamental doctrines are in jeopardy. Essentially, Ehrman appears to be agreeing with Wettstein's assessment. It is no wonder that toward the end of the interview, Ms. Rehm sighs, "Very, very confusing for everyone who hears you, reads the book, and thinks about their beliefs."

69. Athanasius is the first father to mention any problem with the Son's omniscience when discussing this passage (see Messer, "Patristic Theology and Recension in Matthew 24.36," 153).

70. Messer, "Patristic Theology and Recension in Matthew 24.36." Specifically, Messer challenged Ehrman's claim that Origen knew of the shorter reading (ibid., 151).

71. See Messer, "Patristic Theology and Recension in Matthew 24.36," 146.

Daniel B. Wallace

the only authoritative books on the life of Jesus.[72] But the parallel passage in Mark 13.32 definitely has the words "nor the Son." (We know of almost no MSS that omit the phrase there.) Even though Mark was not copied as frequently as Matthew in the early centuries of the Christian faith, the proto-orthodox would have regarded it as Scripture by the end of the second century. Why did they not strike the offensive words from Mark?

3. If the scribes had no qualms about deleting "nor the Son" in Matthew, why did they not delete the word "alone"? Without "nor the Son," the passage still implies that the Son of God does not know the date of his return: "But as for that day and hour no one knows it—not even the angels in heaven–except the Father *alone*." Since the Father is specified as the only person who intimately knows the eschatological calendar, it is difficult to argue that the Son is included in that knowledge.[73]

This point is not trivial. It cuts to the heart of Ehrman's entire method. In *Orthodox Corruption*, he argues that the reason the same MS can vacillate in the kinds of theological changes it makes is due to "the individuality of the scribes, who, under their own unique circumstances, may have felt inclined to emphasize one component of Christology over another."[74] But he immediately adds,

> It strikes me as equally likely, however . . . , that the same scribe may have seen different kinds of problems in different texts and made the requisite changes depending on his perceptions and moods at the moment of transcription.[75]

If this kind of logic is applied to Matthew 24.36, we would have to say that the scribe had a major mood swing, because *just four words* after he deleted "nor the Son," he could not bring himself to drop "alone."

---

72. Irenaeus speaks of them as though they were as certain as the four winds of the earth (Irenaeus, *Against Heresies* 3.11.8). Although his logic may leave something to be desired, it is not insignificant that he speaks as though this matter had been settled for some time—at least for the proto-orthodox. The Ebionites, however, utilized only Matthew's Gospel, but they would have nothing to gain from omitting "nor the Son" from their copies of Matthew.

73. It is not until Basil (mid- to late fourth century) that we see a patristic writer affirm the omission *and* argue that "alone" in Matt 24.36 does not exclude the Son. See Messer, "Patristic Theology and Recension in Matthew 24.36," 160. Basil could have easily changed the text or argued that "alone" was not found in all the MSS, if that were the case. But the fact that he attempts to adjust to the passage with the "alone" as a lone speed bump shows that, like other fathers, he "tended to clarify [his] theology rather than change texts" (ibid., 161).

74. Ehrman, *Orthodox Corruption*, 282 n. 16.

75. Ibid.

A recent critique of Ehrman's overarching method at this juncture did not mince words:

> If this view is accurate, then how can we have any possibility of determining the theological motivations involved in textual changes? With statements such as these, it becomes nearly impossible to falsify any hypothesis regarding theological tendencies. . . . Rather than verify his conclusions through the rigorous work of evaluating individual manuscripts, the major prerequisite in Ehrman's methodology is the alignment of a favorable theological heresy with particularly intriguing variants.[76]

Another reviewer complained about the wax nose on Ehrman's pronouncements over the theological *Tendenz* of the orthodox scribes with these words:

> [N]o matter what textual problem relating to the central theme and soul of the Bible (i.e., the Trinitarian God) may be found in the manuscript tradition . . . , one can always postulate a motivation for an orthodox corruption, whether or not it is probable. This disingenuous method can be applied because no matter whether an article is left off or added, a word slightly shifted or removed, due to orthographic errors or any other unintentional type, it often changes the meaning just enough that there is bound to be a heresy which would contemn the change. If an article is missing, it may seem that the unity of the Godhead is in danger. If the article is present, it may appear to threaten their distinct personalities. If a phrase exemplifying Jesus' humanity is removed, it was obviously to combat the heresy of Adoptionism. If it is added, it was obviously to combat the heresy of Sabellianism.[77]

My point on Matthew 24.36 is not that Ehrman's argument about the omission of "nor the Son" is entirely faulty, just that it is not the only option and does not tell the whole story. In fact, several aspects of the problem have apparently not been considered by him, yet this is his *prime* example of orthodox corruption. It strikes me that *Ehrman is often certain in the very places where he needs to be tentative, and he is tentative where he should have much greater certainty.* He is more certain about what the corruptions are than about what the original wording is, but his certitude about the corruptions

---

76. Matthew P. Morgan, "The Legacy of a Letter: Sabellianism or Scribal Blunder in John 1:1c?" (paper presented at the Southwestern Regional Meeting of the Evangelical Theological Society, Southwestern Baptist Theological Seminary extension campus, Houston, TX, Mar. 29, 2008), 31.

77. Messer, "Patristic Theology and Recension in Matthew 24.36," 181.

Daniel B. Wallace

presupposes, as Silva has eloquently pointed out, a good grasp of the original wording.

To sum up, although Ehrman's reconstructions of the reasons for certain textual corruptions are *possible*, they often reveal more about Ehrman's ingenuity than about the scribes' intentions. Or, as Gordon Fee said, "[u]nfortunately, Ehrman too often turns mere *possibility* into *probability*, and probability into *certainty*, where other equally viable reasons for corruption exist."[78] A very high proportion of Ehrman's examples could easily be classified as accidental errors rather than intentional changes. If they are accidental, then, by definition, one cannot claim theological motives.

THE ESSENTIAL RELIABILITY
OF THE NEW TESTAMENT MANUSCRIPTS

Finally, I offer three arguments for the essential reliability of the NT MSS:

1.   Ehrman argues repeatedly in *Misquoting Jesus* that we do not have the earliest copies of the NT and that the copies we do have are several generations removed from the autographs. From this, he suggests that we have to be agnostic about what these early copies looked like, that they could have changed the original text in some very significant ways. But he elsewhere contradicts this argument by *assuming* that the earliest copies were virtually flawless.

In *Misquoting Jesus*, he observes that although we do not have first-century MSS, we get a glimpse of what they would have looked like by an examination of the Synoptic Gospels. He argues that Mark was the first Gospel and that Matthew and Luke each independently copied it. Most students of the NT agree with this assessment.

Ehrman then suggests that Matthew and Luke give us the best clue about how scribes did their work. He claims that "the authors of the NT were very much like the scribes"[79] and that "they, like the scribes, were changing scripture."[80] A comparison of virtually any triple-tradi-

---

78.   Gordon D. Fee, review of *The Orthodox Corruption of Scripture*, in *Critical Review of Books* in *Religion* 8 (1995): 204.

79.   *Misquoting Jesus*, 211.

80.   Ibid., 213. See the whole discussion on pp. 211–15. On p. 135, in discussing the textual problem in Mark 1.41, Ehrman suggests, "There is even better evidence than this speculative question of which reading the scribes were more likely to invent. As it turns out, we don't have any Greek manuscripts of Mark that contain this passage until the end [sic] of the fourth century, nearly three hundred years after the book was produced. But we do have two authors who copied this story within *twenty years* of its first production." He goes on to tacitly assume that the copy of Mark that the other evangelists were using was virtually identical to the original, when he says, "It is possible . . . to examine Matthew and Luke to see how they

tion pericope in the Synoptic Gospels reveals that, indeed, Matthew and Luke exercised some freedom in their use of Mark. But in order for Ehrman to make his point that Matthew and Luke changed the text of Mark, he assumes that the copies of Mark that they each used had not *already* gone through drastic changes. Ehrman is not alone in this assumption. Virtually every Gospels scholar begins with the assumption that Matthew and Luke were reading nearly identical copies of Mark. All of redaction criticism is based on this assumption. But if their copies of Mark were not significantly changed by the time that they got to Matthew and Luke, then the evangelists are not at all like the scribes. One cannot have it both ways.

Indeed, the evangelists were not like the scribes. They each had something to contribute to the story from their own perspective and certainly did not envision themselves as mere copyists of Mark's Gospel. Matthew has a style of writing, as well as certain motifs, that are different from Luke's. Each evangelist displays a clear pattern in his presentation of the gospel. How can each Gospel be so distinctive if scribes had *already* drastically changed the text of Mark? Either Matthew came across a copy of Mark that was prefabricated in exactly the same direction that he would have taken *his* Gospel, or he was the creative source that changed it. The very fact that Gospels scholars assume that the Matthean motifs are really Matthew's—rather than some nameless scribe's—suggests that any scribal corruptions to Mark before Matthew came across it were trivial and insignificant. And the fact that Matthew's motifs are clearly distinguishable from Luke's indicates that the important changes to Mark's Gospel were made by the evangelists rather than by a *previous* scribe.

There are hints here and there that the copies of Mark that Matthew and Luke used were not identical to Mark's original. But they almost always involve minor alterations.[81] Since that is the case, what can we say about the scribes in the very first generation of copies? Although

---

changed Mark, wherever they tell the same story but in a (more or less) different way."

81. Perhaps the most significant alteration involves μόνος in Matt 24.36, assuming that οὐδὲ ὁ υἱός is authentic (though see my previous discussion of this text, as well as Messer's chapter): this does not seem to be in line with Matthew's elevated Christology, for it makes it doubly explicit that the Son does not know the day or the hour. What would possess Matthew to add insult to injury by adding the μόνος? Where else in Matthew is his Christology ever lower than Mark's? Also, there may be some instances in which Matthew has a historical present that parallels an aorist in Mark; since Mark has twice as many historical presents as Matthew (151 to 78), while Matthew has about 50 percent more material, the ratios are greater than two to one. The instances of εὐθύς are not significant, since this is always Mark's word choice (over εὐθέως), except in 7.35, which has no parallel in Matthew. Other instances are surely to be found, but to my knowledge, no one has done any serious work on this matter.

Daniel B. Wallace

they certainly were not professional scribes, they did not significantly alter the text.[82]

2.   Ehrman repeatedly speaks of the first two hundred years of copying as uncontrolled, giving the impression that all MSS of this era were riddled with mistakes, both unintentional and intentional. The scribes, it seems, were undisciplined and wild, freely adding or subtracting words whenever they wanted to.[83] But this is not the whole story. It certainly describes the *Western* text type, but the Western text does not comprise the only family of MSS in the early centuries.[84] (And even if it did, the very nature of an *uncontrolled* tradition is antithetical to changes that conformed to a singular system of beliefs, because one does not get order out of chaos.)[85]

The standard introduction to NT textual criticism puts things in perspective:

> It would be a mistake to think that the uncontrolled copying practices that led to the formation of the Western textual tradition were followed everywhere that texts were reproduced in the Roman Empire. In particular, there is solid evidence that in at least one major see of early Christendom, the city of Alexandria, there was conscious and

---

82. Ehrman holds that Matthew and Luke were written within twenty years of Mark (*Misquoting Jesus*, 135). His dates for Matthew and Luke would thus probably be ca. 85 CE. But he also holds that the Alexandrian stream of transmission finds its roots deep in the second century and that it was a very pure stream. Consequently, we are dealing with a gap of two or three *decades* in which we have nothing to go on for what the scribes were doing. Rather than having *hundreds of years* without a witness to the NT, then (as Ehrman said), we have a few decades. But these few years will hardly bear the weight of his thesis of radical changes to the text. Further, on a trajectory, the reconstructions scholars make of the Synoptic Gospels' texts really show how little these documents must have changed prior to the Alexandrian scribes doing their work. Finally, if we can pinpoint the greatest textual upheaval as between 85 CE and as late as 110 or 120 CE, Ehrman's main thesis of theological change by proto-orthodox is shipwrecked on the rocks of theological trajectories, since the great majority of orthodox convictions, according to Ehrman, arose *after* this time.

83. *Misquoting Jesus*, 45–69 and passim.

84. Even here, Ehrman is not playing fair with the data. He *assumes* early corruption by Western scribes, yet this is based on patristic testimony, not MS evidence. There are *no* second-century Western MSS, but there are second-century Alexandrian MSS. Ehrman's thesis thus implodes on the only basis that he considers valid.

85. If *all* of our early MSS were products of uncontrolled copying practices and sloppy scribes, we would still be in relatively good shape to recover the original wording; the many differences among the MSS, precisely because they were not controlled, would significantly help scholars to weed out the variants. If there is, in addition, one stream of transmission that was relatively pure, our lot is improved immeasurably.

conscientious control exercised in the copying of the books of the New Testament.

Alexandria ... had a long history of classical scholarship. .... It is no surprise, then, to find that textual witnesses connected to Alexandria attest a high quality of textual transmission from the *earliest* times. It was there that *a very ancient line* of text was copied and preserved.[86]

These words are found in the fourth edition of *The Text of the New Testament*, by Bruce Metzger and Bart Ehrman. As I have already pointed out, the kind of scenario Ehrman needs in order to demonstrate any kind of subversive *and* pervasive orthodox corruption involves *both* control *and* conspiracy. The Qur'an fits the bill, but the NT does not.

3. Although it is true that the orthodox occasionally corrupted the Scriptures (just as the nonorthodox occasionally corrupted the Scriptures),[87] the emerging Christology of the proto-orthodox was not the major force behind most of the intentional changes to the NT MSS. The larger impetus was *harmonization*, especially in the Gospels. As Ehrman recognizes,

[t]his scribal tendency to "harmonize" passages in the Gospels is ubiquitous. Whenever the same story is told in different Gospels, one scribe or another is likely to have made sure that the accounts are perfectly in harmony, eliminating differences by strokes of their pens.[88]

Although Ehrman overstates the point, it is true that narrative harmonization was a stronger impetus than a high Christology. To put it bluntly, to the early Christian scribes, the *historicity* of Christ was more important than their *doctrine* of Christ. Virtually all Gospels MSS harmonized passages between Matthew, Mark, and Luke.[89] They even did

---

86. Metzger and Ehrman, *Text of the New Testament*, 277–78 (italics added).
87. Ehrman insists that history was written by the winners; in Ehrman's construct, this mantra seems to assume that only the winners' *writings* will be found. But his entire edifice is based on the belief that he can locate earlier layers of the NT copies that were undefiled by the proto-orthodox. He does not deal with the possibility that some of the MSS may have been tampered with by the nonorthodox. In his reconstruction, there are thus only two types of readings: pure readings and those corrupted by the orthodox. But if some readings that have escaped the net of the proto-orthodox have survived, is it not equally possible that some readings that were created by the nonorthodox also have survived?
88. *Misquoting Jesus*, 97.
89. Fee puts it more strongly: "[C]ertain MSS and text-types have a much higher frequency of harmonization than others, although no MS is completely guiltless" ("Myth of Early Textual Recension in Alexandria," 269).

Daniel B. Wallace

so in such a way that would, at times, turn a high Christology into a highly suspect Christology.

As an example, consider the story of the rich young man who asks Jesus how to obtain eternal life:

> "Good teacher, what must I do to inherit eternal life?" Jesus said to him, "Why do you call me good? No one is good except God alone." (Mark 10.17–18)

Matthew changes this passage in a couple of key ways:

> "Teacher, what good thing must I do to gain eternal life?" He said to him, "Why do you ask me about what is good? There is only one who is good." (Matt 19.16–17)

In Mark's story, the reader is confronted with the question of Jesus' identity in a startling way: Is Jesus suggesting that he is *not* God? Vincent Taylor argued that "[Jesus'] use of the question along with [his] statement that God alone is good implies a contrast of some kind between Jesus and God."[90] But in Matthew's version, "good" is no longer attached to "teacher" in the young man's question. This allows Jesus' response to be less of a threat to an orthodox Christology.

As we would expect, many scribes—especially the later *orthodox* scribes—harmonized these two passages. But what they changed was not *Mark's* Gospel but *Matthew's*. In the hands of these scribes, the young man now says in *both* Gospels, "*Good* teacher," and Jesus says in *both* Gospels, "Why do you call *me* good?"[91]

Why would these scribes change Matthew's wording instead of Mark's? The most likely reason was because the story in Luke's Gospel already conformed to the wording in Mark's, and it was easier to change

---

90. Vincent Taylor, *The Gospel according to St. Mark* (London: Macmillan, 1952), 426. Taylor, Swete, Lagrange, and others mention several patristic writers who commented on this text. It seems that they struggled with this one yet did not, for the most part, change the text.

91. Mark 10.17 has the rich young man say, διδάσκαλε ἀγαθέ, τί ποιήσω ἵνα ζωὴν αἰώνιον κληρονομήσω; Jesus responds, τί με λέγεις ἀγαθόν; οὐδεὶς ἀγαθὸς εἰ μὴ εἷς ὁ θεός. NA[27] lists no variants here. Matt 19.16 has the young man say (in NA[27]) διδάσκαλε, τί ἀγαθὸν ποιήσω ἵνα σχῶ ζωὴν αἰώνιον; Jesus responds (v. 17), τί με ἐρωτᾷς περὶ τοῦ ἀγαθοῦ; εἷς ἐστιν ὁ ἀγαθός. But several witnesses in Matthew, particularly of the Byzantine strain, have the young man say, διδάσκαλε ἀγαθέ, τί ἀγαθὸν ποιήσω, ἵνα ἔχω ζωὴν αἰώνιον; Jesus responds, τί με λέγεις ἀγαθόν; οὐδεὶς ἀγαθὸς εἰ μὴ εἷς ὁ θεός. Orthodox Byzantine scribes, along with a host of others, changed the young man's address to Jesus in Matthew to "*good* teacher," and Jesus' response to "Why do you call me good? No one is good except one, God." At these points, the wording in both Gospels is now identical, but the scribes have made it so by harmonizing Matthew to Mark, rather than the other way around.

one story rather than two. But this clearly illustrates that the scribal tendency to harmonize the Gospels could trump their tendency toward a high Christology. What seems to drive much of Ehrman's text-critical method is the belief that the *least* orthodox reading is to be preferred.[92] But the story of the rich young man shows that there are other factors that need to be weighed and that this criterion clearly is not the most important.

CONCLUSION

It would have been an impossible task for me to try to address all the passages that Ehrman puts forth as examples of early orthodox corruption of the text, but I have tried to raise some questions about his method, his assumptions, and his conclusions. I do not believe that the orthodox corruptions are nearly as pervasive or as significant as Ehrman does. I have tried to show that there is no ground for wholesale skepticism about the wording of the autographic text and that Ehrman is far less skeptical than the impression he gives in the public square.[93]

Even Ehrman does not think that any essential belief of the Christian faith is jeopardized by the variants. In the appendix to *Misquoting Jesus*, added to the paperback version, there is a Q&A section. I do not know who the questioner is, but it is obviously someone affiliated with the editors of the book. Consider this question asked of Ehrman:

> Bruce Metzger, your mentor in textual criticism to whom this book is dedicated, has said that there is nothing in these variants of Scripture that challenges any essential Christian beliefs (e.g., the bodily

---

92. This has been carefully documented by Philip Miller's chapter in this book, "The Least Orthodox Reading Is to be Preferred: A New Canon for New Testament Textual Criticism?"

93. Ehrman hints here and there that he is not nearly as skeptical as reading his *Misquoting Jesus* might lead one to believe. For example, in his conclusion to the section "Examples of the Problem," which illustrates "complications in knowing the 'original text,'" he says (62),

> For my part, however, I continue to think that even if we cannot be 100 percent certain about what we can attain to, we can at least be certain that all the surviving manuscripts were copied from other manuscripts, which were themselves copied from other manuscripts, and that it is at least possible to get back to the *oldest* and *earliest* stage of the manuscript tradition for each of the books of the New Testament. All our manuscripts of Galatians, for example, evidently go back to *some* text that was copied; all our manuscripts of John evidently go back to a version of John that included the prologue and chapter 21. And so we must rest content knowing that getting back to the earliest attainable version is the best we can do, whether or not we have reached back to the "original" text. This oldest form of the text is no doubt closely (*very* closely) related to what the author originally wrote, and so it is the basis for our interpretation of his teaching.

Daniel B. Wallace

resurrection of Jesus or the Trinity). Why do you believe these core tenets of Christian orthodoxy to be in jeopardy based on the scribal errors you discovered in the biblical manuscripts?[94]

Note that the wording of the question is not *"Do* you believe . . ." but *"Why* do you believe these core tenets of Christian orthodoxy to be in jeopardy . . . ?" This is a question that presumably came from someone who read the book very carefully. How does Ehrman respond?

> The position I argue for in *Misquoting Jesus* does not actually stand at odds with Prof. Metzger's position that the essential Christian beliefs are not affected by textual variants in the manuscript tradition of the New Testament.[95]

Suffice it to say that viable textual variants that disturb cardinal doctrines found in the NT have not yet been produced.[96]

---

93. *Misquoting Jesus*, 252.
95. Ibid. He goes on to say, "What he means (I think) is that even if one or two passages that are used to argue for a belief have a different textual reading, there are still other passages that could be used to argue for the same belief. For the most part, I think that's true."
96. Yet, surprisingly, Ehrman at times seems to suggest that we must know exactly what an author wrote—down to the very words—before we can understand *any* of his message ("[T]he only way to understand what an author wants to say is to know what his words—*all* his words—actually were" [*Misquoting Jesus*, 56; italics added]). The fact that he can argue for the authenticity of certain variants because of how they fit in with the biblical author's argument presupposes that he has sufficient data from the rest of the Gospel or epistle to determine what that author's viewpoint is. And if this is the case, would this not undercut his entire skeptical position, since otherwise we could not understand any of the NT because we are not sure of all the particular words in any book?

2

THE LEAST ORTHODOX READING IS TO BE PREFERRED:

A New Canon for New Testament Textual Criticism?

Philip M. Miller[1]

Prior to the publication of *Novum Instrumentum Omne* by Desiderius Erasmus on March 1, 1516, the text of the Greek NT was hand copied for over fourteen centuries by ancient scribes who introduced variant readings as they transcribed the text. Textual critics usually group sources of these variant readings into two categories: unintentional alterations (e.g., dittography, haplography) and intentional alterations (e.g., harmonization, conflation).

Within the category of intentional alterations, those alterations made for theological and doctrinal considerations have garnered particular interest. While nearly all modern textual critics would acknowledge that scribes did alter the text for such reasons at times, Bart Ehrman has argued that theologically motivated alterations in the NT are both more significant and more pervasive than was previously understood.[2] Ehrman has concluded that the NT text was corrupted at

---

1. This chapter is dedicated to my grandparents, Jesse and Elizabeth Hensarling, who have shown me the priceless value of abandoning one's life for Christ, and to Eugene and LaVerne Miller, who have taught me the value of encouragement, leadership, and service to one's family, church, and country. They are my heroes. I want also to express my gratitude to my wife and dear friend, Krista, whose love and encouragement have been the fuel of this project from the very beginning. Thank you.
2. See especially Bart D. Ehrman, *The Orthodox Corruption of Scripture: The Effect of Early Christological Controversies on the Text of the New Testament* (Oxford: Oxford University Press, 1993); Bart D. Ehrman, *Misquoting Jesus: The Story behind Who Changed the Bible and Why* (San Francisco: HarperSanFrancisco, 2005).

the hands of orthodox scribes who "occasionally altered their texts to make them say what they were already believed to mean."[3] Ehrman's increasing commitment to this judgment appears to significantly shape his approach to textual criticism.

As this chapter will show, a new, implicit canon is emerging as an underlying influence in Ehrman's text-critical methodology: *the least orthodox reading is to be preferred.* While Ehrman denies the influence of such a canon, his methodology and resulting textual decisions indicate otherwise.[4] This chapter explores this undeclared canon of unorthodoxy—(1) surveying its historical backdrop; (2) examining its influence on Ehrman's methodology in *The Orthodox Corruption of Scripture* and, secondarily, in his popular work *Misquoting Jesus;*[5] and (3) critiquing its role within Ehrman's methodology and considering its value to the discipline of NT textual criticism.

To show that a new, implicit canon of unorthodoxy is emerging as an undeclared tenet in Ehrman's text-critical methodology, the second section of this chapter is devoted to examining his methodology both deeply and broadly. Detailed examination of three textual problems reveals the readings can be explained without resorting to orthodox corruption. Having examined these three problems in depth, attention shifts to a synthetic approach to surveying the major textual problems discussed by Ehrman in *The Orthodox Corruption of Scripture.* Such a survey reveals that Ehrman has consistently argued for the least orthodox readings, which are often at odds with the NA[27]/UBS[4] text, even in "A"- and "B"-rated decisions.

In addition to describing the line of argument, it seems prudent to mention the limitations of this chapter. First, it is not my intention to draw any textual conclusions or even to add to the discussion of the textual issues under consideration. Rather, my aim is to highlight

---

3. Ehrman, *Misquoting Jesus*, 175.
4. In an online posting on March 27, 2009, on the Yahoo! group *textualcriticism*, Ehrman wrote in response to Tommy Wasserman's question about using orthodox corruption as a canon,, "I have never argued, and never plan to argue, that the theological orthodoxy of a reading should be used as a **criterion** for deciding the text" ("RE: Greenlee's strawman (??) in The Text of the NT," http://groups.yahoo.com/group/textualcriticism/message/4608 [accessed Mar. 27, 2009]). In a subsequent reply to the same thread on the same day, he added, "I may have overstated the case when I said that I never **would** consider theological orthodoxy as a 'criterion.' Maybe I would eventually. . . . I thought then, and still think now, to use orthodoxy as a criterion would involve presupposing my conclusions. If it is widely accepted that there were such forces at work, however, I suppose I could see the possibility of using the question of orthodoxy as a criterion. But I would be very very careful in doing so, as there were often lots of other factors at work" (http://groups.yahoo.com/group/textualcriticism/message/4611 [accessed Mar. 27, 2009]).
5. Ehrman's Misquoting Jesus reflects his more recent thinking on these issues. However, due to its popular nature, our interaction with Misquoting Jesus will be limited here.

the evidence that reveals the influence of the canon of unorthodoxy in Ehrman's methodology. Second, my reliance on secondary literature is intentional, since my focus here is chiefly text-critical methodology. Third, for the sake of space, only a selection of the textual problems in *The Orthodox Corruption of Scripture* and *Misquoting Jesus* are explored; the texts selected are representative of how Ehrman employs his canon of unorthodoxy. Fourth, the critique of Ehrman's canon of unorthodoxy offered in this chapter is an initial one; this is not the final assessment. As more data become available, greater clarity will surely result.

THE CANON OF UNORTHODOXY AND ITS HISTORICAL BACKDROP

When I assert that a new, implicit canon of unorthodoxy has become an influence in Ehrman's text-critical methodology, I do not mean that textual critics have never argued along these lines before. In fact, the reality of theologically motivated alterations is rooted deep in the history of textual criticism.[6]

The Early Church

Perhaps the earliest reference to theologically motivated alterations may be in Revelation 22.18–19, possibly a condemnation of scribes who might be tempted to add to or subtract from the words of prophecy contained therein.[7] Clearer evidence is the almost unanimous opinion of the early church fathers that the NT texts were sometimes changed in light of Christological concerns.[8] This assessment was normally expressed in the context of accusing heretics of changing the text for their own interests.

---

6. For further support and detail for this chapter, see Peter M. Head's excellent article "Christology and Textual Transmission: Reverential Alterations in the Synoptic Gospels," *NovT* 35, no. 2 (1993): 105–29, to which this chapter is greatly indebted.

7. Jewish and early Christian literary works sometimes concluded with an admonition to later scribes to copy carefully (so *Letter of Aristeas* 310–11; Eusebius, *Hist. eccl.* 5.20.2, citing Irenaeus; cf. 1 Enoch 104.10–13; 2 Enoch 48.6–9; *b. Megilloth* 14a). Due to the use of these kinds of warnings in apocalyptic literature as well as possible allusions to the Deuteronomic warning passages (Deut 4.1–2; 12.32; 29.19–20; cf. Josephus, *Ap.* 1.42–43), the case can be made that careless scribal alterations are not the primary aim of this warning. Rather, it is most likely intended for more meddlesome parties bent on distorting the contents of the book for their own purposes (cf. Rev 2.14, 20–23). See G. K. Beale, *The Book of Revelation*, New International Greek Testament Commentary (Grand Rapids: Eerdmans, 1999), 1150–54.

8. Several of these opinions will be discussed here. For a fuller treatment, see Head, "Christology and Textual Transmission," 106; E. S. Buchanan, "Ancient Testimony to the Early Corruption of the Gospels," *BSac* 73 (1916): 177–91.

Origen (185–254 CE) at times indicated that the source of textual variations was in either the negligence of some scribes or the perverse audacity of others.[9] When refuting the accusation of Celsus—that Christians altered the text of the Gospels repeatedly in order to avoid criticism—Origen argued that it was the heretics, not the orthodox, that were responsible for variation in the textual tradition.[10]

The writings of Eusebius (263–339 CE) preserve portions of Dionysius's writings that mention some heretics who went so far as to falsify even the Scriptures.[11] Eusebius also recorded an anonymous account of some disciples of Theodotus the Cobbler who intentionally corrupted their copies of the Scriptures.[12] The reality of theologically motivated alterations to the text is therefore acknowledged early on by the church fathers.

Regarding specific textual problems, the fathers argued that certain readings arose precisely because of theological meddling. For example, Origen argued that heretics were responsible for adding "Jesus" to the name of Barabbas in Matthew 27.16–17, because an evildoer could not bear the name "Jesus."[13] Again, Origen claimed that in Luke 23.45 the enemies of the church refashioned the text as an attack on the Gospels, since an eclipse was impossible at the time of a full moon.[14] Ambrose (339–97 CE) suggested that the Arians inserted "nor the Son" in Matthew 24.36 to strengthen their cause.[15] Of particular interest is the argument by Epiphanius (315–403 CE) that the *orthodox* removed Luke 22.43–44 out of fear, because they did not understand the strength and perfection of Jesus' moment of vulnerability and need in Gethsemane.[16] Numerous other examples could be given.[17] Certainly many of the fathers' text-critical conclusions would be considered unpersuasive in light of current scholar-

---

9. Origen, *Matt. Comm. ser.* 15.14; see Bruce M. Metzger, "Explicit References in the Words of Origen to Variant Readings in New Testament Manuscripts," in *Historical and Literary Studies: Pagan, Jewish, and Christian*, New Testament Tools and Studies 8 (Leiden: Brill, 1968), 78–79.

10. Origen, *c. Celsus* 2.27.

11. Eusebius, *Hist. eccl.* 4.23.12.

12. Eusebius, *Hist. eccl.* 5.28.16.

13. Origen, *Matt. Comm. ser.* 121; see Metzger, "Explicit References in the Words of Origen," 94.

14. Origen, *Matt. Comm. ser.* 134; see Metzger, "Explicit References in the Words of Origen," 96.

15. Ambrose, *De fide* 5.16.

16. Epiphanius, *Ancoratus* 31. This perspective is echoed by Anastasius Sinaita (*Hodegos* 148) and Photius (*Epistle 138 to Theodore*). However, Ehrman and Plunkett have persuasively argued that these verses were added by the orthodox to combat against docetic theology. See Bart D. Ehrman and Mark A. Plunkett, "The Angel and the Agony: The Textual Problem of Luke 22:43–44," *CBQ* 45 (1983): 401–16; Ehrman, *Orthodox Corruption*, 187–94.

17. See Bruce M. Metzger, "The Practice of Textual Criticism among the Church Fathers," in *New Testament Studies: Philological, Versional, and Patristic*, New

ship, yet it is significant that they believed theologically motivated alterations to be a reality.

Modern Textual Criticism

As modernism was dawning, Richard Simon was at the front in
suggesting that such variants in the text were the result of scribal activity rather than intentional distortion by heretics, as the church fathers usually indicated.[18] Simon postulated that difficult texts prompted
marginal explanations that eventually were copied into the text by later
scribes.

Johann Wettstein was the first to discuss a principle for textual criticism in passages that have variants with theological impact. In 1730,
Wettstein argued that when there are two variant readings, the one that
seems more orthodox is not immediately to be preferred.[19] Wettstein understood "more orthodox" readings as those favoring the orthodox side
of a doctrinal dispute and "less orthodox" readings as those that were
neutral, favoring neither theological position. He asserted that the heterodox could not have corrupted the text, because the manuscripts were
in the possession of the orthodox. He also contended that since scribes
altered the writings of the church fathers in the direction of orthodoxy,
similar changes should be expected in the NT text. Thus, for Wettstein,
the more orthodox reading was not to be given immediate preference.

Johann J. Griesbach extended Wettstein's position, claiming that the
reading that favored orthodoxy was an object of suspicion.[20] Griesbach

---

Testament Tools and Studies 10 (Leiden: Brill, 1980), 189–98; Head, "Christology
and Textual Transmission," 105–29.

18. Richard Simon, *Histoire critique du texte du Nouveau Testament, Ou l'on etablit
la Verite des Actes sur lesquels la Religion Chretienne est fondee* (Rotterdam: Chez
Reinier Leers, 1689), 355; Simon, *A Critical History of the Text of the New Testament*, 3 vols. (London: R. Taylor, 1689), 2:123.

19. Johann J. Wettstein, *Novum Testamentum Graecum editionis receptae, cum Lec-
tionibus Variantibus Codicum MSS., Editionum aliarum, Versionum et Patrum,
necnon Commentario pleniore ex Scriptoribus veteribus, Hebraeis, Graecis, et
Latinis, historiam et vim verborum illustrante*, 2 vols. (Amsterdam: Ex officina
Dommeriana, 1751–52), 2:864. The masterful prologue to this work, *Animadversiones et cautiones* (2:851–74), is a republication of his earlier *Prolegomena ad
Testamenti Graeci editionem accuratissimam, e vetustissimis codicibus denuo pro-
curandam: in quibus agitur de codicibus manuscriptis Novi Testamenti, Scriptoribus qui Novo Testamento usi sunt, versionibus veteribus, editionibus prioribus,
et claris interpretibus; et proponuntur animadversiones et cautiones, ad examen
variarum lectionum Novi Testamenti*, 4 vols. (Amsterdam: Rengeriana, 1730),
1:165–201.

20. Johann J. Griesbach, *Novum Testamentum Graece, Textum ad fidem Codicum Ver-
sionem et Patrum recensuit et Lectionis Variatatem*, 2nd ed., 2 vols. (London: P.
Elmsly, 1796), 1:62.

viewed these readings with suspicion because a spurious reading that beautifully confirmed a dogma of the church or forcefully destroyed a heresy would most likely work its way into the text due to the scribes' general tendency toward inclusiveness.

In terms of dissent, Frederick Scrivener did not regard Griesbach's rule as generally acceptable, although he conceded its utility in navigating a few variants.[21] John Burgon more adamantly criticized the principle, calling it a "monstrous canon."[22] However, his critique must be tempered by his arguments elsewhere that both heretics and the orthodox were responsible for corrupting the NT text.[23] The most significant and decisive voice of dissent came from Hort[24] in 1882, when he wrote that "even among the numerous unquestionably spurious readings of the New Testament there are no signs of deliberate falsification of the text for dogmatic purposes."[25] According to Hort, dogmatic positions may have *influenced* the choice between rival readings, but they were not the *cause* for the readings in the first place.[26] Instead, Hort suggested that passages that appear to be doctrinally motivated are the result of carelessness or laxity, not malice. In concert with this assertion was Bludau's argument that the manuscripts of the NT were not easily susceptible to deliberate falsification, given the vigilance exercised over their production by all concerned, including, at times, opposing parties.[27]

Many scholars have subsequently challenged Hort's statement, insisting that theological considerations played a role in the rise of variant readings. Significant textual critics of the twentieth century viewed Hort's

---

21. Frederick H. A. Scrivener, *A Plain Introduction to the Criticism of the New Testament, for the Use of Biblical Students*, ed. Edward Miller, 4th ed., 2 vols. (London: George Bell and Sons, 1894), 2:251–52.

22. John W. Burgon, *The Traditional Text of the Holy Gospels Vindicated and Established*, ed. Edward Miller, 2 vols. (London: George Bell and Sons, 1896), 1:66.

23. John W. Burgon, *The Causes of the Corruption of the Traditional Text of the Holy Gospels* (London: George Bell and Sons, 1896), 191–231.

24. While both Brooke Foss Westcott and Fenton John Anthony Hort were responsible for their foundational text *Introduction [and] Conclusion* (New York: Harper and Brothers, 1882), Hort is the one usually credited with the major advancements in the text-critical methodology found therein.

25. Westcott and Hort, *Introduction [and] Conclusion*, 282; Hort notes that Marcion is the one exception to this rule.

26. Westcott and Hort, *Introduction [and] Conclusion*, 282–83; see also J. M. Bebb, "The Evidence of the Early Versions and Patristic Quotations on the Text of the Books of the New Testament," in *Studia Biblica et Ecclesiastica*, vol. 2 (Oxford: Clarendon, 1890), 224–26.

27. August Bludau, *Die Schriftfälschungen der Häretiker: Ein Beitrag zur Textkritik der Bibel* (Münster: Aschendorffschen Verlagsbuchhandlung, 1925); cf. also Bruce M. Metzger and Bart D. Ehrman, *The Text of the New Testament: Its Transmission, Corruption, and Restoration*, 4th ed. (Oxford: Oxford University Press, 2005), 282–83.

position to be untenable, including Harris,[28] Howard,[29] Conybeare,[30] and Lake.[31] Of note was Howard's suggestion that there was a "tendency on the part of the scribes to insert in the text of the Gospels what they knew to be established in the belief and practice of the Church."[32] According to Conybeare, the church ensured that only orthodox readings were preserved in the manuscript tradition.[33] For him, the most likely place to find the earliest reading was in the early church fathers, since he believed the manuscript tradition to be dominated by readings approved by the church.[34] Building on the foundation Conybeare laid, Lake added further that only the slightest manuscript evidence was needed to determine the earliest reading.[35] These four scholars stood in sharp contrast to Hort's position and argued that theological corruption significantly shaped the transmission of the text and that the earliest reading may be without significant manuscript support.

By the middle of the twentieth century, most of the standard works acknowledged that scribes did sometimes alter the text of the NT for theological and doctrinal considerations.[36] Prominent among these

---

28. J. Rendell Harris, *Side-Lights on New Testament Research*, Angus Lectures for 1908 (London: Kingsgate, n.d.), 29–35. Harris discusses examples of dogmatic alterations in the writings of Marcion and Tatian as well as Luke 4.16; 22.43–44; and 23.34.

29. Wilbert F. Howard, "The Influence of Doctrine upon the Text of the New Testament," *London Quarterly and Holborn Review* 6, no. 10 (1941): 1–16.

30. Frederick C. Conybeare, "Three Early Doctrinal Modifications of the Text of the Gospels," *HibJ* 1 (1902): 96–113.

31. Kirsopp Lake, *The Influence of Textual Criticism on the Exegesis of the New Testament* (Oxford: Parker and Sons, 1904).

32. Howard, "Influence of Doctrine upon the Text of the New Testament," 12.

33. Conybeare, "Three Early Doctrinal Modifications of the Text of the Gospels," 96–113.

34. Frederick C. Conybeare, "The Eusebian Form of the Text Matth. 28, 19," *ZNW* 2 (1901): 275–88. Conybeare misread the Eusebian citation and argued that "in my name" represents the earliest text of Matt 28.19, despite the fact that this reading has no MS support. He proposed that the earliest reading was altered by orthodox scribes who sought to align it with orthodox Trinitarianism.

35. Lake, *Influence of Textual Criticism*.

36. Maurice Goguel, *Le texte et les éditions du Nouveau Testament grec* (Paris: E. Leroux, 1920), 64–67; Daniel Plooij, *Tendentieuse Varianten in den Text der Evangeliën* (Leiden: Brill, 1926); Kirsopp Lake, *The Text of the New Testament*, rev. Silva New, 6th ed. (London: Rivingtons, 1928), 6; Léon Vaganay, *Initiation á la critique textuelle néotestamentaire* (Paris: Bloud et Gay, 1934), 53–54; C. S. C. Williams, *Alterations to the Text of the Synoptic Gospels and Acts* (Oxford: Blackwell, 1951), 5; Leon E. Wright, *Alterations of the Words of Jesus as Quoted in the Literature of the Second Century* (Cambridge, MA: Harvard University Press, 1952), 58–68; Alexander Souter, *The Text and Canon of the New Testament*, rev. Charles Stephen Conway Williams, 2nd ed. (London: Duckworth, 1954), 106; Heinrich J. Vogels, *Handbuch der Textkritik des Neuen Testaments*, 2nd ed. (Bonn: P. Hanstein, 1955), 178–82; Jacob H. Greenlee, *Introduction to New Testament Textual Criticism* (Grand Rapids: Eerdmans, 1964), 68; M. R. Pelt, "Textual Variation in Relation to Theological Interpretataion in the New Testament" (PhD diss., Duke University,

was Bruce Metzger, who identified two groups of alterations: (1) "those which involve the elimination or alteration of what was regarded as doctrinally unacceptable or inconvenient"[37] and (2) "those which introduce into the Scriptures 'proof' for a favorite theological tenet or practice."[38]

C. S. C. Williams described these "tendencious, reverential and doctrinal alterations" as highlighting some of "the most fascinating problems in the whole field of the textual criticism of the New Testament."[39] What is most notable about Williams's description is his commitment to recognize the goodwill of the scribes. He held that the changes these scribes introduced into the textual tradition were not sourced in malice, deceit, or agenda but, rather, derived from reverence for Christ. Metzger, while wrestling with the difficulties alterations raised in his *Textual Commentary on the Greek New Testament*, likewise noted the suppression of certain readings "for reverential considerations,"[40] the omission of doctrinally difficult words,[41] and secondary improvements "introduced from a sense of reverence for the person of Jesus."[42] Peter M. Head deemed these "reverential alterations" as evidence of "the scribe's involvement in his work understood as an act of devotion to the divine Christ."[43]

Orthodox Corruption of Scripture

As Ehrman has pointed out, the last forty years have seen significant developments in postulating the role of theology in connection with the transmissional history of the NT.[44] The first major development came in 1966, in Eldon Epp's masterful study on the theological tendency of Codex Bezae in Acts, in which he determined that 40 percent of the variant readings were anti-Judaic.[45] This finding was

---

1966); Eberhard Nestle, *Einführung in das griechische Neue Testament*, 2nd ed. (Göttingen: Vandenhoeck und Ruprecht, 1899), 161–62; Bruce M. Metzger, *The Text of the New Testament*, 2nd ed. (Oxford: Oxford University Press, 1968), 201.

37. Metzger, *Text of the New Testament*, 2nd ed., 201. Prior to Bart Ehrman's involvement in *The Text of the New Testament*, Metzger acknowledged the reality of orthodox corruption. These comments are repeated in Metzger and Ehrman, *Text of the New Testament*, 4th ed., 266.

38. Metzger, *Text of the New Testament*, 2nd ed., 201; Metzger and Ehrman, *Text of the New Testament*, 266.

39. Williams, *Alterations to the Text of the Synoptic Gospels and Acts*, 5.

40. Bruce M. Metzger, *A Textual Commentary on the Greek New Testament*, 2nd ed. (Stuttgart: Deutsche Bibelgesellschaft, 1994), 56, note on Matt 27.16–17.

41. Ibid., 51–52, note on Matt 24.36; cf. 164–66, "Note on Western Non-Interpolations."

42. Ibid., 200, note on John 11.33.

43. Head, "Christology and Textual Transmission," 129.

44. Metzger and Ehrman, *Text of the New Testament*, 283.

45. Eldon J. Epp, *The Theological Tendency of Codex Bezae Cantabrigiensis in Acts*, Society for New Testament Studies Monograph Series 3 (Cambridge: Cambridge University Press, 1966), 171.

Philip M. Miller

significant because it seemed to indicate that the scribe of Codex Bezae or his tradition was anti-Judaic and that bias intentionally or unintentionally found its way into the text as it was copied.[46] This conclusion called into question a scribe's ability to remain objective in transcription.

The second major development occurred in 1993, with the publication of Ehrman's *The Orthodox Corruption of Scripture*,[47] in which he argued that "scribes occasionally altered the words of their sacred texts to make them more patently orthodox and to prevent their misuse by Christians who espoused aberrant views."[48] His masterpiece is the most thorough treatment to date of theologically motivated alterations in the text of the NT. However, significant critiques of Ehrman's method and conclusions remain.[49]

In *The Orthodox Corruption of Scripture*, Ehrman began his argument by summarizing Bauer's view of early Christianity: that early Christianity was diverse, full of competing views, especially as it relates to Christology.[50] Ehrman reasoned that the scribes, who were aware of and possibly embroiled in the debated Christological issues, occasionally altered the text as they copied it, making it more patently orthodox and less subject to abuse by their opponents.[51] When orthodoxy "won," he argued, the scribes naturally gave preference to the most orthodox readings,[52] and thus the most orthodox readings came to dominate the textual tradition. The implicit conclusion

---

46. Metzger and Ehrman, *Text of the New Testament*, 284.

47. Bart D. Ehrman, *Orthodox Corruption of Scripture: The Effect of Early Christological Controversies on the Text of the New Testament* (Oxford: Oxford University Press, 1993).

48. Ehrman, *Orthodox Corruption*, xi. Again on p. 4, Ehrman claimed that "theological disputes, specifically disputes over Christology, prompted Christian scribes to alter the words of Scripture in order to make them more serviceable for the polemical task. Scribes modified their manuscripts to make them more patently 'orthodox' and less susceptible to 'abuse' by the opponents of orthodoxy."

49. For reviews of Ehrman's *The Orthodox Corruption of Scripture*, see J. Neville Birdsall, *Theology* 97, no. 780 (1994): 460–62; J. K. Elliott, *NovT* 36, no. 4 (1994): 405–6; Gordon D. Fee, *CRBR* 8 (1995): 203–6; Michael W. Holmes, *RelSRev* 20, no. 3 (1994): 237; Bruce M. Metzger, *PSB* 15, no. 2 (1994): 210–12; David C. Parker, *JTS* 45, no. 2 (1994): 704–8. See also Stratton Ladewig, "An Examination of the Orthodoxy of the Variants in Light of Bart Ehrman's *The Orthodox Corruption of Scripture*" (ThM thesis, Dallas Theological Seminary, 2000);Ivo Tamm, "Theologisch-christologische Varianten in der frühen Überlieferung des Neuen Testaments?" (Magisterschrift, Westfälische Wilhelms-Universität Münster, 2001); Daniel B. Wallace, "The Gospel according to Bart: A Review Article of *Misquoting Jesus* by Bart Ehrman," *JETS* 49, no. 2 (2006): 327–49.

50. Ehrman, *Orthodox Corruption*, 4, 7–11; cf. Walter Bauer, *Rechtgläubigkeit und Ketzerei im ältesten Christentum*, Beiträge zur historischen Theologie 10 (Tübingen: J. C. B. Mohr [Paul Siebeck], 1934).

51. Ehrman, *Orthodox Corruption*, 3–4.

52. Ibid., 8, 27.

---

from Ehrman's assertions is that when multiple readings exist for a Christologically significant passage, the reading that is least orthodox is most likely to be the earliest reading.

There were two primary reasons for this conclusion. First, only the least orthodox reading could have given rise to the widely divergent views of Christology found in the first three centuries, while the orthodox reading would have strongly supported the orthodox position only. Second, the orthodox scribes would be more likely to alter unorthodox and suborthodox readings so that they reflected an orthodox position, rather than the other way around.[53] Ehrman attempted to demonstrate his case by giving examples where he believed the orthodox scribes altered Scripture to clearly affirm orthodoxy over and against the Adoptionists, Separationists, Docetists, and Patripassianists.[54] Thus, he maintained, the orthodox scribes created variants that "*establish the orthodox character of the text*, either by promoting more fully an orthodox understanding of Christ or by circumventing the heretical use of a text in support of an aberrant teaching."[55]

In a more recent statement about his textual-critical approach, Ehrman advises in a 2009 web posting, "I think it is important to be very clear about methodology. At any point where there is textual variation, one has to decide what the earliest form of the text is and what the latter changes (corruptions) were. Only once that decision is made can you go on to consider whether theological debates were involved in making the corruption."[56] This is the two-step method Ehrman sought to employ in *The Orthodox Corruption of Scripture*: (1) establish the oldest reading using accepted text-critical methods and (2) only then inquire about

---

53. Ibid., 27.
54. In *Orthodox Corruption*, Ehrman addressed anti-adoptionistic corruptions of Scripture in chapter 2 (47–118), anti-separationist corruptions in chapter 3 (119–80), anti-docetic corruptions in chapter 4 (181–261), and anti-patripassianist corruptions in chapter 5 (262–73).
55. Ehrman, *Orthodox Corruption*, 28 (italics mine).
56. Ehrman, "RE: Greenlee's strawman (??) in The Text of the NT." In a subsequent reply to the same thread (see n. 4), Ehrman continues to identify some of the reasons for his two-step method:

> When I wrote *The Orthodox Corruption of Scripture*, I wanted to be very very careful not to argue in a circle, that orthodoxy affected scribes, that's why they changed the text, as we can see in places where orthodoxy affected the readings they created. Instead I wanted to argue **on other grounds** what the oldest form of the text was, and **then** to see, once that was established, whether the reason for the change may have been theological debates affecting the scribes. I thought then, and still think now, to use orthodoxy as a criterion would involve presupposing my conclusions. If it is widely accepted that there were such forces at work, however, I suppose I could see the possibility of using the question of orthodoxy as a criterion. But I would be very very careful in doing so, as there were often lots of other factors at work.

theological influence. Maintaining the order of this method is essential to Ehrman's line of argument. At issue is how faithfully this two-step method has been applied.

As is shown within the history of textual criticism, Ehrman is not alone in his thesis that theologically motivated alterations to the text of Scripture occurred; the "canon of unorthodoxy" has been discussed for centuries. Nevertheless, Ehrman seems to have taken this idea to a new level, arguing that orthodox corruption is both more extensive and more significant than previously understood. He also implied that significant doctrines of orthodoxy were at stake when he wrote that textual variation raised "such questions as whether the Gospels could have been used to support either an 'adoptionisic' Christology . . . or one that was 'anti-docetic' . . . , whether Luke has a doctrine of the atonement . . . , whether members of the Johannine community embraced a gnostic Christianity . . . , and whether any of the authors of the New Testament characterizes Jesus as God."[57] Ehrman has proposed that significant issues of orthodoxy are on the table for discussion in light of these variants, including whether Jesus is *ever* characterized as God by *any* of the NT authors. Ehrman apparently has entertained these possibilities because of his increasing commitment to the canon of unorthodoxy.

While Ehrman is not alone in viewing doctrinal considerations as playing a role in the rise and transmission of variant readings, he distinguishes himself in at least two ways. First, he appears to give strong preference to the least orthodox reading. When there are multiple readings of varying levels of orthodoxy, Ehrman seems to choose the least orthodox reading almost by default. He gives the impression that orthodox readings are guilty until proven innocent. Second, Ehrman allows the canon of unorthodoxy high priority in his text-critical methodology, as the next section will demonstrate.

THE CANON OF UNORTHODOXY DEMONSTRATED
IN EHRMAN'S METHODOLOGY

Ehrman's acceptance of the canon of unorthodoxy (*the least orthodox reading is to be preferred*) is observed by a careful examination of his text-critical methodology. Though the select textual problems discussed in this section are intended not to represent the totality of Ehrman's methodology, they seem to reflect instances where the canon of unorthodoxy has clear influence. The examination of each textual problem will consist of three steps: (1) a summary of Ehrman's thesis on the problem, (2) a discussion of both the external and internal evidence

---

57. Metzger and Ehrman, *Text of the New Testament*, 284–85 n. 32; cf. Ehrman, *Orthodox Corruption*, 276–77.

regarding the problem, and (3) an analysis of Ehrman's methodology in light of the evidence.

Matthew 24.36

In the Olivet Discourse, when commenting on the timing of his return, Jesus stated, "But as for that day and hour, no one knows it, not even the angels in heaven, *nor the Son*, but only the Father."[58] Ehrman's argument here is that orthodox scribes omitted the words οὐδὲ ὁ υἱός, "nor the Son," from Matthew 24.36[59] because "it suggests that the Son of God is not all-knowing and could therefore be used by Adoptionists to argue that Jesus was himself not divine."[60] Adoptionists believed that Jesus was born a human and that at some point, usually identified as his baptism, he was adopted as the Son of God. Ehrman argues that this "phrase in Matthew was seen as problematic by Christian scribes"[61] who "appear to have taken umbrage at the notion that Jesus was not all-knowing or spiritually perfect."[62] Thus, he maintains, scribes dropped the words οὐδὲ ὁ υἱός from the text because "if Jesus does not know the future, the Christian claim that he is a divine being is more than a little compromised."[63]

There are two relevant readings present in Matthew 24.36, and these readings may be translated as follows:

> But as for that day and hour, no one knows it, not even the angels in heaven, nor the Son [οὐδὲ ὁ υἱός], but only the Father.

> But as for that day and hour, no one knows it, not even the angels in heaven, but only the Father.

There are two possibilities for this variant: either (1) οὐδὲ ὁ υἱός was original to the text and was later omitted, or (2) οὐδὲ ὁ υἱός was not original to the text but was added later. Ehrman argues that οὐδὲ ὁ υἱός was the earliest form of the text and was later omitted by orthodox scribes who were troubled by the implication that Jesus did not know the timing of his own return. Others have argued that οὐδὲ ὁ υἱός was added to the text out of a desire to harmonize the Matthean account with Mark 13.32, which includes the phrase οὐδὲ ὁ υἱός.

---

58. All Scripture quotations are my own translations unless noted otherwise.
59. Ehrman discussed Matt 24.36 in *Orthodox Corruption* (91–94) and *Misquoting Jesus* (95, 203–4).
60. Ehrman, *Orthodox Corruption*, 92.
61. Ibid.
62. Ibid., 94.
63. Ehrman, *Misquoting Jesus*, 204.

FIGURE 2.1: SUPPORT FOR TWO READINGS IN MATTHEW 24.36	
οὐδὲ ὁ υἱός	ℵ*, 2vid B D Θ*f*[13] 28 1505 *l* 547[1/2] it[a, aur, b, c, d, (e), f, ff[1], ff[2], h, q,] r[1] vg[mss] syr[pal] arm eth geo[1, B] Diatessaron[arm] Irenaeus[lat] Origen[lat] Chrysostom Cyril (Hesychius); Hilary Ambrose Latin mss[acc. to Jerome] Augustine Varimadum
OMIT	ℵ[1] L W Δ *f*[1] 33 157 180 205 565 579 597 700 892 1006 1010 1071 1241 1243 1292 1342 1424 *Byz* [E F G H Σ] *Lect* it[g[1], l] vg syr[s, p, h] cop[sa, meg, bo] geo[A] Didymus[dub]; Phoebadius Greek mss[acc. to Ambrose] Jerome Greek mss[acc. to Jerome]

The external evidence largely supports Ehrman's contention for the inclusion of οὐδὲ ὁ υἱός. Some important witnesses support this reading, including such early Alexandrian and Western manuscripts as ℵ*, 2vid B D Θ*f*[13] pc it vg[mss] Ir[lat]. However, the exclusion of οὐδὲ ὁ υἱός also bears support from ℵ[1], as well as L W *f*[1] 33 *Byz* vg sy cop. On the basis of external evidence, the inclusion of οὐδὲ ὁ υἱός certainly possesses better support, although the evidence is divided.

The solution to this textual problem must primarily rely on the strength of the internal evidence. Ehrman argues, "[N]ot only is the phrase οὐδὲ ὁ υἱός found in our earliest and best manuscripts of Matthew, it is also *necessary* on internal grounds."[64] This necessity is derived from Ehrman's conviction that this is a clear example of orthodox corruption. He reasons that scribes were uncomfortable with Jesus' ignorance of his own return and therefore omitted this embarrassing text. This is a persuasive explanation, especially in light of the fact that the interpretation of this passage continues to be debated.[65] However, it is notable that οὐδὲ ὁ υἱός is solidly preserved in the parallel text in Mark 13.32:

> But as for that day and hour, no one knows it, not even the angels in heaven, nor the Son, but only the Father.

Only X *pc* vg[ms] omit the words οὐδὲ ὁ υἱός in Mark 13.32. If the idea of Jesus' ignorance about the timing of his return was so embarrassing to the orthodox scribes, one begins to wonder how Mark 13.32 escaped

---

64. Ehrman, *Orthodox Corruption*, 92 (italics mine).
65. Metzger proposed another line of reasoning in support of the longer reading. He proposed that the two οὐδέ were best understood as correlative within the sentence structure and therefore that the internal evidence supported the longer reading (*Textual Commentary*, 2nd ed., 51–52). However, this does not completely close the case, since οὐδέ may be used in the simple sense of "not even," in which case the shorter reading is tenable.

with such a clean pedigree.[66] It seems inconsistent to construct a historical setting in which orthodox scribes intentionally modified Matthew out of embarrassment yet left the identical embarrassing material in Mark intact. Although the scribes were hardly consistent, for such a theologically significant issue we would expect at least some consistency on the part of a few scribes. Furthermore, the variant reading in Matthew 24.36 can be accounted for differently.

The other possibility is that οὐδὲ ὁ υἱός was added to the text out of a desire to harmonize Matthew 24.36 with the parallel statement in Mark 13.32.

FIGURE 2.2: HARMONIZING MATTHEW 24.36 WITH MARK 13.32			
Mark 13.32	οὐδὲ οἱ ἄγγελοι ἐν οὐρανῷ	οὐδὲ ὁ υἱὸς	εἰ μὴ ὁ πατήρ
Matthew 24.36	οὐδὲ οἱ ἄγγελοι τῶν οὐρανῶν μόνος		εἰ μὴ ὁ πατὴρ

The inclusion of οὐδὲ ὁ υἱός in Matthew 24.36 can be easily explained by harmonization; the scribe could have harmonized these passages either through unintentional or intentional alteration. If the alteration was unintentional, the scribe's familiarity with the text of Mark did him a disservice when he copied Matthew, for he added to the verse without realizing it. If it was intentional, the scribe may have sought to eliminate an apparent inconsistency in the recorded words of Jesus by harmonizing the statements. However, intentional change seems less likely, since the word μόνος is found in Matthew but not in Mark. If this were intentional harmonization to eradicate an apparent inconsistency in the recorded words of Jesus, these statements would likely be changed in both Gospels. Since they are not, it seems reasonable that unintentional harmonization may have given rise to the addition of οὐδὲ ὁ υἱός in Matthew 24.36.[67] In addition, because Matthew generally softens Mark's harsh statements as he incorporates material into his own Gospel, it is likely that Matthew himself dropped the phrase οὐδὲ ὁ υἱός and added μόνος. In doing this, Matthew would have kept true to the *ipsissima vox*

---

66. Matthew was copied and used more frequently than Mark, but this hardly accounts for the great disparity in the external evidence if Ehrman is correct that orthodox scribal corruption gave rise to this reading. Since both Gospels were viewed as authoritative by the early church, the Adoptionists would have been able to prove their case in Mark as well as in Matthew.

67. Harmonization of Matthew to Mark seems to be the better explanation, despite the tendency in the MSS for Mark to conform to Matthew, rather than the other way around.

of Jesus, while softening Mark's harsh statement regarding Jesus' ignorance of his return.[68]

In discussing the textual problem of Matthew 24.36, Ehrman begins to reveal the role of the canon of unorthodoxy in his text-critical methodology in a number of ways (though it should be acknowledged that Ehrman is in good company in regard to this textual problem, since many textual critics believe οὐδὲ ὁ υἱός is the earliest reading):[69]

1. When Ehrman says that οὐδὲ ὁ υἱός is "necessary on internal grounds,"[70] he seems to be overstating his case. The internal evidence does not *necessitate* the originality of οὐδὲ ὁ υἱός. This is a debated text, a fact that Ehrman's word choice does not reflect.

2. Ehrman overstates the importance of this passage to historic orthodoxy. Ehrman claims that "if Jesus does not know the future, the Christian claim that he is a divine being is more than a little compromised."[71] Yet orthodoxy flourished despite the identical statement's solid presence in Mark 13.32.

3. Because viable, alternate explanations exist for the textual evidence, Ehrman's thesis is unconvincing in this passage.

4. Ehrman has indicated his desire to follow a two-step methodology: (1) establish the oldest reading using accepted text-critical methods and (2) only then inquire after theological influence. He has stayed true to this approach in that he has identified the strong external evidence for the inclusion of οὐδὲ ὁ υἱός. However, based on external evidence alone, it is difficult to establish this reading as the oldest reading. In some sense, Ehrman has strayed from his two-step method by placing the bulk of his argument on the notion of scribal embarrassment over Jesus' ignorance of his own return. At the very least, this reveals his methodological tendencies.

---

68. An alteration of this kind by an evangelist is distinct from scribal alterations, because of the authorial role. An author's role is to *create* new material and to *redact* existing materials, while a scribe's role is *transmission* of material. Thus, if Matthew softened the statement previously recorded by Mark, he would be exercising his role as an author and evangelist. Gospel redaction is not analogous to scribal activity.

69. UBS[4] and NA[27] both include οὐδὲ ὁ υἱός in their respective texts. UBS[4] gives this reading a "B" rating (*The Greek New Testament*, 4th ed. [Stuttgart: Deutsche Bibelgesellschaft, 1993], 95; cf. Metzger, *Textual Commentary*, 2nd ed., 51–52).

70. Ehrman, *Orthodox Corruption*, 92.

71. Ehrman, *Misquoting Jesus*, 204.

In the end, Ehrman's confidence in the necessity of the reading of οὐδὲ ὁ υἱός in Matthew 24.36 is derived from the fact that it aligns well with the canon of unorthodoxy, not because of overwhelming textual evidence. In light of the fact that this textual problem is debated, it is significant that Ehrman chooses to speak of the necessity of οὐδὲ ὁ υἱός. It appears that Ehrman finds this reading "necessary" precisely because he holds that *the least orthodox reading is to be preferred.*

John 1.18

The textual problem in John 1.18[72] is notoriously difficult and has been the subject of sharp disagreement. John 1.18 can be translated,

> No one has ever seen God, but *the unique one, himself God,* who resides in the Father's bosom, has made him known.

Scholars have long debated the textual evidence for whether the reading should be μονογενὴς θεός, which can be translated as "the unique one, himself God" or "the unique God,"[73] or ὁ μονογενὴς υἱός, "the unique Son." However, most textual critics are swayed by the strength of the external evidence in favor of μονογενὴς θεός, as Ehrman concedes.[74]

Nevertheless, Ehrman states that "the variant reading of the Alexandrian tradition, which substitutes God for Son, represents an orthodox corruption of the text in which the complete deity of Christ is affirmed."[75] Ehrman claims that orthodox and gnostic scribes corrupted this text to prevent its use by the Adoptionists, who taught that Jesus was not God but merely a man adopted by God.[76] Ehrman affirms, "For the scribe who created this variant, Christ is not merely portrayed as the 'unique Son.' He himself is God, the 'unique God,' who is to be differentiated from God the Father, in whose bosom he resides, but who nonetheless is his co-equal."[77] He writes that "now [after the alteration] Christ is not merely God's unique Son, he is the unique God himself!"[78] Thus, he concludes, "this Alexandrian reading derives from an anti-adoptionistic context, and therefore represents an orthodox corruption."[79]

---

72. Ehrman discussed John 1.18 in *Orthodox Corruption* (78–82) and *Misquoting Jesus* (161–62).
73. Ehrman translated μονογενὴς θεός as "the unique God." It is better to translate μονογενὴς as a substantival adjective. See Wallace, "Gospel according to Bart," 344–46.
74. Ehrman, *Orthodox Corruption*, 79.
75. Ibid., 78.
76. Ibid., 82.
77. Ibid.
78. Ehrman, *Misquoting Jesus*, 162.
79. Ehrman, *Orthodox Corruption*, 82.

There are five readings for this textual problem in John 1.18. For this discussion, the first three readings are most relevant. The first two readings differ in that one has the article while the other does not. Both readings support the translation "No one has ever seen God, but *the unique one, himself God* [μονογενὴς θεός // ὁ μονογενὴς θεός], who resides in the Father's bosom, has made him known." The third reading supports the translation "No one has ever seen God, but *the unique Son* [ὁ μονογενὴς υἱός], who resides in the Father's bosom, has made him known." The fourth reading is a conflation of the first two readings with the third, resulting in "the unique Son of God" (μονογενὴς υἱὸς θεοῦ) which gives mild support to the third reading. The fifth reading omits "Son" and "God" entirely and is translated substantively as "the unique one" (ὁ μονογενής).

FIGURE 2.3: FIVE READINGS IN JOHN 1.18	
μονογενὴς θεός	𝔓[66] ℵ* B C* L syr[p, h(mg)] geo[2] Origen[gr 2/4] Didymus Cyril[1/4]
ὁ μονογενὴς θεός	𝔓[75] ℵ[2] 33 cop[bo] Clement[2/3] Clement[from Theodotus 1/2] Origen[gr 2/4] Eusebius[3/7] Basil[1/2] Gregory-Nyssa Epiphanius Serapion[1/2] Cyril[2/4]
ὁ μονογενὴς υἱός	A C[3] W[supp] Δ Θ Ψ 0141 *f*[1] *f*[13] 28 157 180 205 565 579 597 700 892 1006 1010 1071 1241 1243 1292 1342 1424 1505 *Byz* [E F G H] *Lect* it[a, aur, b, c, e, f, ff2, 1] vg syr[c, h, pal] arm eth geo[1] slav Irenaeus[lat 1/3] Clement[from Theodotus 1/2] Clement[1/3] Hippolytus Origen[lat 1/2] Letter of Hymenaeus Alexander Eustathius Eusebius[4/7] Serapion[1/2] Athanasius Basil[1/2] Gregory-Nazianzus Chrysostom Theodore Cyril[1/4] Proclus Theodoret John-Damascus; Tertullian Hegemonius Victorinus-Rome Ambrosiaster Hilary[5/7] Ps-Priscillian Ambrose[10/11] Faustinus Gregory-Elvira Phoebadius Jerome Augustine Varimadum
μονογενὴς υἱὸς θεοῦ	it[q] Irenaeus[lat 1/3]; Ambrose[1/11 vid]
ὁ μονογενής	vg[ms] Ps-Vigilius[1/2]

The external evidence for this textual variant is inconclusive, but it strongly favors the first or second readings of μονογενὴς θεός // ὁ μονογενὴς θεός. Noteworthy support includes the earliest and best witnesses, such as 𝔓[66] ℵ* B C* // 𝔓[75] ℵ[1] 33. Ehrman concedes, "[I]t must be acknowledged that the first reading [μονογενὴς θεός] is the one found in the manuscripts that are the oldest and generally considered to be the best—those of the Alexandrian textual family."[80] Again he writes, "[T]he Alexandrian reading is more commonly preferred by textual critics, in no small measure because of its external support."[81] However, the reading ὁ μονογενὴς υἱός does have support from Codex Alexandrinus, which reflects the Byzantine text type in the Gospels, and from the majority of the witnesses, especially the later Byzantine manuscripts C³ Θ Ψ f¹, ¹³ *Byz* lat.

Like most of the textual problems that Ehrman discusses, the internal evidence is crucial to his thesis, for it is in this evidence that he believes "the real superiority of ὁ μονογενὴς υἱός shines forth."[82] Ehrman argues that the earliest form of the text read "the unique Son" but that orthodox and gnostic scribes altered it to read "the unique God," thus inscripturating a high Christology in John 1.18 and preventing the Adoptionists from having a textual foothold.

The alternate argument is that μονογενὴς θεός was original[83] and that a scribe changed it to ὁ μονογενὴς υἱός because it fits well with Johannine style. The title ὁ μονογενὴς υἱός is a Christological title unique to John (John 3.16, 18; 1 John 4.9). A scribe familiar with John's language could have been transcribing on "mental autopilot" and simply supplied the Johannine Christological title. Given the scribes' tendency to move in the direction of the author's style rather than away from it, μονογενὴς θεός is the harder reading, which is generally to be preferred. In contrast, it is difficult to see why a scribe would change ὁ μονογενὴς υἱός to μονογενὴς θεός, since the phrase μονογενὴς θεός occurs nowhere else in the Bible. In contrast, μονογενὴς υἱός appears elsewhere in Johannine material (John 3.16, 18; 1 John 4.9). Therefore, since μονογενὴς θεός is the harder reading, it would seem to be preferred.

Ehrman, however, argues that this reading is much too hard, for two main reasons. First, he contends that although some translations understand μονογενής as a substantival adjective in apposition to θεός, an adjective is never used substantivally when it immediately precedes a noun of the same inflection.[84] On this point and counter to Ehrman, Daniel B. Wallace has presented seven clear examples where an adjective is used substantivally when preceding a noun of the same inflection.[85]

Ehrman's second argument is that even though μονογενὴς θεός possesses the stronger support, it "is virtually impossible to understand

---

80. Ehrman, *Misquoting Jesus*, 161–62.
81. Ehrman, *Orthodox Corruption*, 79.
82. Ibid.
83. The articular θεός is almost certainly a scribal emendation to the anarthrous θεός; θεός without the article is a much more difficult reading.
84. Ehrman, *Orthodox Corruption*, 81.
85. Wallace, "Gospel according to Bart," 344–46.

Philip M. Miller

within a Johannine context."[86] He asserts that the reading μονογενὴς θεός must be translated "the unique God," resulting in a modalistic equation of the Son with the Father. Ehrman writes, "The problem, of course, is that Jesus can be the *unique* God only if there is no other God; but for the Fourth Gospel, the Father is God as well. Indeed, even in this passage the μονογενής is said to reside in the bosom of the Father. How can the μονογενὴς θεός, the unique God, stand in such a relationship to (another) God?"[87]

Interestingly, despite Ehman's objections, the translators that prefer the reading μονογενὴς θεός have not found it impossible to understand within a Johannine context. They translate μονογενής as a substantival adjective in apposition to θεός,[88] hence as "the unique one, himself God."[89] Even Ehrman concedes elsewhere that the context of the first chapter of John demands that a distinction between the person of the Father and the person of the Son be maintained, both of whom John indicates to be fully God. John 1.1 states, "In the beginning was the Word, and the Word was with God, and the *Word was God*," demonstrating that the Word was *with* God, thus distinct from God, and also fully *God*.[90] This distinction is seen again in 1.14: "And the Word became flesh and took up residence among us. We saw his glory—the glory of the one and only who came from the Father, full of grace and truth." The Word is *from* the Father and therefore not the same as the Father. Again, as Ehrman has noted, 1.18 itself does not allow for a confusion of the members of the Godhead, for Jesus is declared to be distinct from the Father since he is at the Father's side: "the unique one, himself God, who resides in the Father's bosom, has made him known." Thus, given the strong contextual distinction between the Father and the Son in the first chapter of John, the reading μονογενὴς θεός does not necessarily lead to a modalistic understanding of the Godhead. This reading is therefore the harder reading, but not an impossible reading as Ehrman has indicated.

---

86. Ehrman, *Orthodox Corruption*, 79.
87. Ibid., 80.
88. For a defense of understanding μονογενής as a substantival adjective, see Wallace, "Gospel according to Bart," 344–46.
89. E.g., the NET reads, "No one has ever seen God. *The only one, himself God*, who is in closest fellowship with the Father, has made God known" (italics mine); the NIV reads, "No one has ever seen God, but *God the One and Only*, who is at the Father's side, has made him known" (italics mine); with slight variation, the ESV reads, "No one has ever seen God; *the only* God, who is at the Father's side, he has made him known" (italics mine), and it offers in the footnotes, "the only One, who is God."
90. It is preferable to understand θεός as qualitative in John 1.1c. See Daniel B. Wallace, *Greek Grammar beyond the Basics: An Exegetical Syntax of the New Testament* (Grand Rapids: Zondervan, 1996), 266–69.

Ehrman's discussion of John 1.18 demonstrates more of how the canon of unorthodoxy functions in his methodology:

1. It is worth noting that Ehrman relies heavily on internal evidence, which brings with it a greater degree of subjectivity.

2. Ehrman paints the textual decision in John 1.18 as the choice between two *unorthodox* variants. On the one hand, Ehrman suggests that the earliest reading, ὁ μονογενὴς υἱός, was understood as adoptionistic. On the other hand, Ehrman indicates that ὁ μονογενὴς θεός would result in a modalistic reading incompatible with Johannine theology. According to Ehrman's perspective, no matter how the text is reconstructed, the text is less than orthodox or at least lends itself to supporting heterodox Christology. If Ehrman is correct that an orthodox scribe was responsible for the changes in the text of John 1.18, then regardless of which reading is original, an orthodox scribe was responsible for producing a less than orthodox reading.

3. Ehrman confuses a reading that contains a strong orthodox statement of Christ's deity in John 1.18 with modalistic theology. At best, this seems to indicate a lack of evenhandedness in his exegetical method given the wider context of John's Gospel.

4. As quoted earlier, Ehrman speaks of the hypothesized orthodox corruption of this passage as factual, when it is, in fact, debated. This presentation of the data overstates the conclusiveness of his case.

5. Given the chance to argue for either an anti-adoptionistic or anti-modalistic corruption, Ehrman has chosen to argue for the former. This is no doubt partly due to the early dating of 𝔓⁶⁶ and 𝔓⁷⁵, manuscripts that cannot possibly represent fully developed Modalism. However, one can imagine that Ehrman could have easily argued that ὁ μονογενὴς υἱός was an anti-gnostic or anti-patripassianistic orthodox corruption.[91] What is significant is that here, like elsewhere, Ehrman has argued for the reading with the lowest Christology.

6. In terms of following his two-step methodology, Ehrman seems to fall short of the mark. While he offers a number of arguments to support his favored reading, it is only when he turns to his thesis of orthodox corruption that "the real superiority of ὁ μονογενὴς υἱός shines

---

91. See Ehrman's discussion of the flexibility of categorizing these corruptions in *Orthodox Corruption*, 282 n. 16.

Philip M. Miller

forth."[92] In making this move—a move more severe than the one made in Matthew 24.36—Ehrman trades his preferred method for a questionable one. However, this trade is necessary if he is to offer a compelling case for orthodox corruption in John 1.18.

Ehrman's confidence that ὁ μονογενὴς υἱός is the reading of choice seems to stem not from the conclusiveness of the evidence but from its coherence with the canon of unorthodoxy: *the least orthodox reading is to be preferred.*

Hebrews 2.9b

In his discussion of Hebrews 2.9b,[93] Ehrman maintains that the proto-orthodox and Gnostics were debating during the second century over the significance of Jesus' death.[94] The Gnostics argued that the divine element "Christ" had left the man Jesus prior to the crucifixion and therefore that Jesus died without "Christ."[95] In contrast, the orthodox affirmed that Jesus and the Christ were one and the same, both in life and in death.[96] With this backdrop, Ehrman argues that Hebrews 2.9b originally said that Jesus would experience death "apart from God" (χωρὶς θεοῦ) on behalf of everyone:[97] "The Gnostics could readily take the original text to mean that the divine element within Jesus had already left him prior to his death, so that he died 'apart' from God, that is, abandoned by that divine being who had sustained him during his ministry."[98] Ehrman concludes, "[I]t appears that the scribes of the second century who recognized the heretical potential of the phrase χωρὶς θεοῦ changed it by making the simple substitution of . . . χάριτι θεοῦ ["by the grace of God"], thereby effecting an orthodox corruption that came to dominate the textual tradition of the New Testament."[99]

There are two readings offered for Hebrews 2.9b:

> . . . *by God's grace* [χάριτι θεοῦ] he would experience death on behalf of everyone.

---

92. Ehrman, *Orthodox Corruption*, 79.
93. Ehrman discusses Hebrews 2.9b in *Orthodox Corruption* (146–50) and *Misquoting Jesus* (144–48).
94. Ehrman, *Orthodox Corruption*, 150.
95. Ibid. This understanding of the crucified Jesus being separated from the immortality of the divine is represented well in the Apocalypse of Peter (James M. Robinson, *The Nag Hammadi Library*, rev. ed. [San Francisco: HarperCollins, 1990]).
96. Ehrman, *Orthodox Corruption*.
97. Ibid., 149.
98. Ibid., 150.
99. Ibid.

. . . he would experience death *apart from God* [χωρὶς θεοῦ] on behalf of everyone.

FIGURE 2.4: TWO READINGS IN HEBREWS 2.9b	
χάριτι θεοῦ	𝔓[46] ℵ A B C D Ψ 075 0150 6 33 81 104 256 263 365 424* 436 459 1175 1241 1319 1573 1739[v. r. vid] 1852 1881 1912 1962 2127 2200 2464 Byz [K L P] *Lect* it[ar, b, comp, d, v] vg syr[p, h, pal] cop[sa, bo, fay] arm eth geo slav mss [acc. to Origen] Origen[gr] Athanasius Didymus Chrysostom mss [acc. to Theodore] Cyril Theodoret[1/2] Ps-Oecumenius; Faustinus Jerome
χωρὶς θεοῦ	0243 (0121b) 424[cvid] 1739[txt] vg[ms] syr[pmss] Origen[gr v r, lat] mss[acc. to Origen] Theodore Nestorians[acc. to Ps-Oecumenius] Theodoret[1/2; lem]; Ambrose mss[acc. to Jerome] Vigilius Fulgentius

The external evidence for the first reading is nearly conclusively in favor of χάριτι θεοῦ as the preferred reading. This is one of the reasons the UBS[4] committee gave χάριτι θεοῦ an "A" rating, "indicating that the text is certain."[100] Not only are the earliest and best witnesses, such as 𝔓[46] ℵ A B, united in their support of this reading, but nearly *all* manuscripts support this reading. The reading Ehrman proposes, however, has external support from only three Greek witnesses from the tenth century and later.[101] Of these three, the only significant witness is Codex 1739, which is a copy of an early and important manuscript. This reading is also discussed by several church fathers and given support by one Vulgate manuscript and some copies of the Syriac Peshitta. In discussing this problem, Daniel B. Wallace notes, "[W]ith external evidence this weak many textual critics would dismiss this reading entirely."[102] Ehrman acknowledges the difficulty in entertaining this poorly attested variant when he writes that in "the case of Hebrews 2:9 there is a direct clash between these two kinds of evidence [external and internal]. Although the surviving documents are *virtually uniform* in stating that Jesus died for all people 'by the grace of God' (χάριτι θεοῦ), the force of the internal evidence *compels* us to accept as original the *poorly attested* variant reading, which states that Jesus died 'apart from

---

100. For an explanation of the letter rating system used by the UBS[4] committee, see n. 115.
101. Ehrman identified only MSS 0121b and 1739 in support of his favored reading (*Orthodox Corruption*, 146), although he acknowledged the presence of MS 424[cvid] in an endnote (176 n. 132).
102. Wallace, "Gospel according to Bart," 337.

　　　　　　　　　　　　　　　　　　Philip M. Miller

God' (χωρὶς θεοῦ)."[103] Compellingly strong internal evidence can outweigh strong external evidence. In this case, Ehrman finds the internal evidence to be compelling and decisive.

Concerning the internal evidence, Ehrman is wise to probe for some explanation for the reading χωρὶς θεοῦ, since it is the harder reading and is fairly early, as evidenced by the patristic quotations and Codex 1739.[104] There are three proposed explanations for how these readings arose. The first explanation proposed by Ehrman offers that the original reading, χωρὶς θεοῦ, was modified by orthodox scribes to read χάριτι θεοῦ because the original reading seemed to affirm a heterodox belief that Jesus was separated from the divine Christ prior to his death.[105] Ehrman is confident that "the external evidence notwithstanding, Hebrews 2:9 *must have originally said* that Jesus died 'apart from God.'"[106]

However, there are two other viable solutions to this textual problem that call into question Ehrman's certainty. A second explanation is that χάριτι was copied as χωρίς due to scribal lapse or carelessness.[107] This view is easier to understand when the text is seen in majuscule script: ΧΑΡΙΤΙΘΥ//ΧΩΡΙCΘΥ. Thus the change between χάριτι and χωρίς may be accidental.

A third and more persuasive explanation is that the phrase χωρὶς θεοῦ was a marginal note on Hebrews 2.8b that was confused by a later scribe as a correction for χάριτι θεοῦ in 2.9b.[108] Hebrews 2.8b quotes from Psalm 8.6 when it says, "when he subjected all things to him, he left nothing that is not subject to him." A similar passage is found at 1 Corinthians 15.27–28, which also quotes from Psalm 8.6: "For 'he has put everything in subjection under his feet.' But when it says 'everything' has been put in subjection, it is evident that this does not include the one who put everything into subjection to him. And when all things are subjected to him, then the Son himself will be subjected to the one who subjected everything to him, so that God may be all in all." In other words, Paul argues that all things will be subject to Jesus except for the Father. The theologian reading Hebrews 2.8b—"when he subjected all things to him, he left nothing that is not subject to him"—may have re-

---

103. Ehrman, *Orthodox Corruption*, 146 (italics mine).
104. Krista Miller has demonstrated that the patristic evidence, which is often cited as a basis for entertaining χωρὶς θεοῦ as a viable variant, actually offers stronger support for the reading χάριτι θεοῦ upon close examination (Krista M. Miller, "Evaluating the Reading Χωρὶς Θεοῦ in Hebrews 2:9 in Light of Patristic Evidence" [ThM thesis, Dallas Theological Seminary, 2010]).
105. Ehrman, *Orthodox Corruption*, 150.
106. Ibid., 149 (italics mine).
107. Metzger, *Textual Commentary*, 2nd ed., 594.
108. Ibid.; F. F. Bruce, *The Epistle to the Hebrews*, rev. ed., New International Commentary on the New Testament (Grand Rapids: Eerdmans, 1990), 32, 70–71.

Philip M. Miller

membered 1 Corinthians 15.27–28 and written χωρὶς θεοῦ, "except for God," as an interpretive comment in the margin. When a scribe copied the manuscript with the marginal notation, he may have understood it to be a correction for χάριτι θεοῦ in the following verse. A simple error in substitution can therefore explain the rise of χωρὶς θεοῦ as a secondary reading in this passage.[109]

In his analysis of Hebrews 2.9b, Ehrman reveals how determinative the canon of unorthodoxy is for his methodology.

1. As Ehrman himself acknowledges, he is placing the burden of his decision on the internal evidence, over and against solid external evidence to the contrary. In the end, this continued reliance on internal evidence makes Ehrman's methodology increasingly subjective.

2. While Ehrman cites this passage as a clear example of orthodox corruption, there are two other plausible explanations for the textual evidence. Hebrews 2.9b is therefore not as clearly in support of Ehrman's thesis as he seems to portray.

3. Ehrman's confidence level seems improper given the textual merits supporting the other reading. As quoted earlier, Ehrman uses words like "compels" and "must" to affirm a reading that many textual critics deem untenable in light of the overwhelming external and internal evidence to the contrary.[110]

4. Ehrman overestimates the theological importance of this variant to historic orthodoxy. Elsewhere, when arguing for χωρὶς θεοῦ as the best reading, Ehrman notes that it fits well with the picture of Jesus in Hebrews that "repeatedly emphasizes that Jesus died a fully human, shameful death, totally removed from the realm whence he came, the realm of God. His sacrifice, as a result, was accepted as the perfect expiation for sin. Moreover, God did not intervene in his passion and did nothing to minimize his pain. Jesus died 'apart from God.'"[111] This description of Christ offered by Ehrman is in complete accord with historic orthodoxy.

5. With regard to his two-step method, Ehrman simply falls flat in Hebrews 2.9b. Ehrman seems to find evidence for orthodox corruption there precisely because he is looking for it. In studying this

---

109. Metzger, *Textual Commentary*, 2nd ed., 594; Bruce, *Epistle to the Hebrews*, 32, 70–71; Hans-Friedrich Weiss, *Der Brief an die Hebräer*, Kritisch-exegetischer Kommentar über das Neue Testament 13 (Göttingen: Vandenhoeck und Ruprecht, 1991), 200–202.

110. Metzger, *Textual Commentary*, 2nd ed., 594.

111. Ehrman, *Orthodox Corruption*, 149.

textual variant, it is unlikely that someone would conclude that the orthodox scribes systematically purged the original reading from all but three tenth-century Greek manuscripts. It seems that in his desire to find orthodox corruption, Ehrman ferrets out passages that illustrate his point.[112] This may be a case of "begging the question," a logical fallacy in which the proposition to be proven is assumed implicitly or explicitly in one of the premises. In this case, Ehrman's premise is that orthodox corruption occurred in this passage. This premise is what allows him to see merit for the reading χωρὶς θεοῦ despite its paltry support. Once this reading is given credence, he can argue for its originality. His argument for its originality then becomes the basis for his conclusion that orthodox corruption has occurred in this passage. His argument is circular. He has presupposed his conclusion. In proving his case for orthodox corruption in Hebrews 2.9b, Ehrman must presume that it did take place. Otherwise, a variant like χωρὶς θεοῦ would never have the internal evidence to muster consideration. In this example, it appears that Ehrman has deviated from his method of choice.

Ehrman's confident dismissal of the almost conclusive evidence against his favored reading indicates that he has embraced the canon of unorthodoxy. Affirming that the least orthodox reading is to be preferred, Ehrman is able to dismiss the strength of the external evidence in favor of the canon that is more dominant for him. The canon of unorthodoxy holds such influential sway over Ehrman's methodology that he can dismiss the evidence for χάριτι θεοῦ that the USB[4] committee found to be persuasive to the point of certainty.

Other Texts with Extended Treatment

The limits of this chapter do not permit an exploration of all the textual variants Ehrman discusses in the *Orthodox Corruption of Scripture*. However, the methodological patterns mentioned here are present in many of Ehrman's discussions. The following table shows the passages to which Ehrman gives specific and extended treatment in *Orthodox*

---

112. Wallace calls this "Ehrman's overall agenda of exploiting the apparatus for orthodox corruptions, regardless of the evidence for alternative readings" ("Gospel according to Bart," 338 n. 40). However, Wallace has softened his stance on Hebrews 2.9b, in part because the father of reasoned eclecticism, Günther Zuntz, prefers this reading (Zuntz, *The Text of the Epistles: A Disquisition upon the Corpus Paulinum* [Oxford: Oxford University Press, 1953], 34–35). Zuntz bases some of his preference off the patristic evidence, which has been recently examined and found to better support χάριτι θεοῦ (Miller, "Evaluating the Reading Χωρὶς Θεοῦ in Hebrews 2:9").

Corruption.[113] While dozens of additional passages receive ample attention, these seem to be prominent in Ehrman's argumentation.

FIGURE 2.5: PASSAGES WITH TEXTUAL VARIANTS DISCUSSED IN *ORTHODOX CORRUPTION*			
Textual Problem[114]	Least Orthodox Reading Preferred by Ehrman?	NA[27]/UBS[4] Agreement with Ehrman?	UBS[4] Rating[115]
Luke 3.22	*Yes*	*No*	*B*
Mark 1.1	*Yes*	*No*	*C*
1 Timothy 3.16	*Yes*	*Yes*	*A*
John 1.18	*Yes*	*No*	*B*
1 John 4.3	*Yes*	*No*	*Unrated*
Mark 15.34	*Yes*	*Yes*	*B*
Hebrews 2.9b	*Yes*	*No*	*A*
Luke 22.43–44	*Yes*	*Yes*	*A*
Luke 22.19–20	*Yes*	*No*	*B*
Luke 24.12	*Yes*	*No*	*B*
Luke 24.51–52	*Yes*	*No*	*B*

In light of the tabulated results of Ehrman's text-critical methodology, some key observations are apparent.

---

113. This table contains all textual discussions that bear their own textual heading, denoting the prominent place they hold in Ehrman's discussion.
114. These textual problems are arranged according to the order in which Ehrman discusses them in *Orthodox Corruption* on the following pages, respectively: 62–67, 72–75, 77–78, 78–82, 125–35, 143–75, 146–50, 187–94, 198–209, 212–17, 227–32.
115. The UBS[4] committee explains the letter grades used to indicate their level of confidence in the reconstructed text as follows: "The letter A indicates that the text is certain. The letter B indicates that the text is almost certain. The letter C, however, indicates that the Committee had difficulty in deciding which variant to place in the text. The letter D, which occurs only rarely, indicates that the Committee had great difficulty in arriving at a decision" (*The Greek New Testament*, 4th ed. [Stuttgart: Deutsche Bibelgesellschaft, 1993], 3*). Thus the letter assignment in column 4 of fig. 2.5 corresponds to the reading accepted by the UBS committee in column 3; a "No" in the third column indicates that the UBS committee's preferred reading is different from Ehrman's, and the letter assignment signifies the level of certainty the committee had in their decision. The higher their certainty is, the more significant Ehrman's dissent is.

Philip M. Miller

1. Ehrman uniformly argues for what he believes is the least orthodox reading. This is to be expected, since Ehrman is arguing for the orthodox corruption of Scripture. However, this shows the consistency with which Ehrman is applying the canon of unorthodoxy.

2. In over 72 percent of these examples, Ehrman's textual decisions are in *disagreement* with the NA[27]/UBS[4] text. While this text form is far from definitive, it does represent mainstream NT text-critical scholarship. Of note is the fact that the late Bruce Metzger, whom Ehrman regarded as "the world's leading expert in the field,"[116] was influential in the shaping of the NA[27]/UBS[4] text. It appears that Ehrman's increasing commitment to the canon of unorthodoxy may be disassociating him from the NA[27]/UBS[4] text and from the views of his mentor.

3. Not only does Ehrman frequently disagree with the NA[27]/UBS[4] text, but he dissents from one "Unrated," one "A," five "B"s, and one "C" rated decisions. This means that in 63 percent of these examples, Ehrman disagrees with what the UBS[4] committee considered to be readings that were "certain" or "almost certain."[117] If Ehrman's methods are regularly resulting in textual decisions that are at odds with the NA[27]/UBS[4] text, especially "A"- and "B"-rated readings, it calls into question the value and legitimacy of that methodology.

4. In every case that Ehrman disagrees with the NA[27]/UBS[4] text, there are compelling reasons for choosing the more orthodox reading, which happens to be the reading found in the NA[27]/UBS[4] text. Furthermore, in each case where Ehrman is listed in agreement with the NA[27]/UBS[4] text, there are alternate explanations for the textual evidence aside from orthodox corruption.[118]

Ehrman's application of the canon of unorthodoxy not only estranges him from the widely accepted NA[27]/UBS[4] text but also fails to prove his thesis. To be sure, Ehrman discusses passages where theologically motivated alterations played a role in the transmission of Scripture. However, these passages are not nearly as significant as one might expect. The confidence of Ehrman's conclusions is derived not primarily

---

116. Ehrman, *Misquoting Jesus*, 7.
117. For calculation purposes, the "Unrated" reading is considered as an "A"-rated reading, since the UBS[4] committee did not consider the problem worthy of discussion because of its certainty.
118. 1 Tim 3.16 could be understood as an unintentional error, rather than an orthodox corruption, although I consider this explanation dubious. Mark 15.34 does not appear to be an issue of orthodoxy at all. The text of Luke 22.43–44 could be noncanonical historical material that found its way into the text independent of theologically motivated alterations.

from the force of the evidence but from the presupposed canon of unorthodoxy. For Ehrman, it appears that the least orthodox reading is to be preferred and that this presupposed canon often results in textual decisions that are at odds with the mainstream reconstruction of the text.

THE CANON OF UNORTHODOXY:
INITIAL CRITIQUE, VALUE, AND ROLE

In light of the evidence that Ehrman utilizes the canon of unorthodoxy in his assessment of textual data, this third section offers an initial critique of his canon and an assessment of its value and role within NT textual criticism. This critique will focus, first, on Ehrman's thesis and, second, on the canon of unorthodoxy itself.

A Critique of Ehrman's Thesis

To argue that the canon of unorthodoxy should be accepted, several tenets must be demonstrated to be valid.

1. A compelling sociohistorical setting in which scribes were persuaded to alter the NT texts must be established historically.

2. The textual problems in question must prove themselves to be significant, even central, to the Christological debates.

3. These variant readings must be demonstrated to be the result of *intentional* scribal activity with a *theological agenda*, rather than of unintentional or alternate sources of variation.

4. Theologically motivated alterations must account for a *significant* number of variants in order for the canon of unorthodoxy to carry substantial weight in navigating text-critical problems.

If the canon of unorthodoxy is to be accepted, all four of these tenets must be shown to be probable. This initial critique centers on these four tenets and is followed by a critique of the canon itself.

1. The first area of critique relates to the proposed sociohistorical setting in which orthodox corruption is said to have taken place. Because orthodox Christology involves truths held in tension (e.g., the hypostatic union), there are many ways to assemble the NT teachings incorrectly, resulting in unorthodox doctrine. The first three centuries are replete with discussion of these doctrinal tensions as well as the errors

associated with the overemphasis of one truth to the neglect of another. This time frame of conflicting theologies provides Ehrman with a rich supply of options for postulating a sociohistorical setting to explain the textual data. If the variant affirms the deity of Christ, Ehrman can call it anti-adoptionistic. If it affirms his humanity, Ehrman can call it anti-docetic. If it affirms the Son's oneness with the Father, Ehrman can call it anti-separationist. If it affirms the distinction between the Father and the Son, Ehrman can call it anti-patripassianistic. In the end, there is always a hypothetical, sociohistorical setting to which Ehrman can appeal. No matter to which side of the scale a variant seems to weigh, Ehrman can tip the scales in favor of orthodox corruption.

However, the convenience of this historical setting can cut the other way,[119] as Ehrman acknowledges.[120] If the presumed opposing party changes, the result is an opposite reconstruction of the data[121]; a good example is John 1.18. There are always opportunities for finding orthodox corruptions in a sociohistorical setting where orthodoxy is in the middle, holding the truth in tension between two opposing parties. Ehrman has offered a compelling case that a sociohistorical setting existed in which there is a *possibility* of intentional scribal alterations in the direction of orthodox theology; whether he has shown its widespread *probability* is another matter.

2. The second area of critique relates to Ehrman's ability to show that these passages are significant, even central, to the Christological debates. The most obvious way in which this can be proven is to find these passages or variants quoted in defense of a particular view by either the church fathers or their opponents. At times, Ehrman does just this; yet where many of his examples assume that a given passage was the subject of debate, evidence sufficient to affirm that it was or was not is simply unavailable. What further complicates this issue is that it is unnecessary to assume that these various groups appealed to the NT Scriptures as the primary basis for their theological positions. Differing groups may have primarily found their theological perspective in philosophy, the Old Testament, mystery religions, or sociological movements. They may not have appealed to the NT as the primary basis for their theological position. If this is the case, it is less likely that the orthodox would be compelled to modify the Scriptures they held in such esteem. Ehrman has argued persuasively that some passages

---

119. Adam G. Messer, "Patristic Theology and Recension in Matthew 24.36: An Evaluation of Ehrman's Text-Critical Methodology" (ThM thesis, Dallas Theological Seminary, 2009), 34, 45–46.
120. Ehrman, *Orthodox Corruption*, 282 n. 16.
121. Ibid.

were central to the Christological debates, and he simply assumes the centrality of other passages.

3. Concerning the third tenet, there are many cases in which Ehrman has not presented enough compelling evidence to conclude that intentional scribal alteration is the best possible explanation for the textual data. It is hardly valid to deduce that a scribe must have intentionally altered the text for theological reasons when the textual evidence is reasonably explained by alternate hypotheses. Ehrman's conclusions are inconclusive in many cases. The best evidence for this is seen in his frequent dissent from the NA[27]/UBS[4] text. As we have seen, Ehrman expresses a surprising degree of certainty in dissenting from the choices made by the UBS[4] committee. Gordon Fee poignantly states, "[U]nfortunately, Ehrman too often turns mere *possibility* into *probability*, and probability into *certainty*, where other equally viable reasons for corruption exist."[122]

4. The fourth postulate is the most difficult to demonstrate, since it rests on the validity of the preceding tenets. Since Ehrman has not demonstrated the first three tenets adequately, the fourth is also in question. At this point, the examples proffered by Ehrman are insufficient to conclude that the least orthodox reading is to be preferred. It does not appear that theologically motivated alterations plague the NT textual tradition to nearly the same degree as other sources of textual variants. Ehrman acknowledges that theologically motivated variants most likely number only in the dozens.[123] The small number of conclusively demonstrated instances of orthodox corruption provides an inadequate basis for asserting that the canon of unorthodoxy ought to be accepted.

A Critique of the Canon of Unorthodoxy

Concerning the merits of the canon of unorthodoxy itself, several critiques can be offered.

1. The canon that *the least orthodox reading is to be preferred* is too universal and needs to be nuanced carefully, for the least orthodox reading is *not* to be preferred in most cases, in light of the textual evidence. As demonstrated earlier, Ehrman's application of this canon seems to have taken him beyond the evidence at times.

---

122. Fee, review of *The Orthodox Corruption of Scripture*, 204 (italics his).
123. Ehrman, *Orthodox Corruption*, 46 n. 124; however, Ehrman entertained the idea that they may number into the hundreds.

Philip M. Miller

2. The canon of unorthodoxy seems properly to be understood not as an independent canon but as a specific extension of Bengel's canon that *the harder reading is to be preferred*. This is interesting, because Ehrman at times argues for the least orthodox reading over and against the harder reading (e.g., John 1.18). Since the canon of unorthodoxy seems to be a derivation of the canon of the harder reading, they should not conflict.

3. A strong emphasis on the canon of unorthodoxy fits best within rigorous eclecticism. Ehrman's employment of the canon of unorthodoxy frequently overrides compelling external evidence. He appears to be granting increasing weight to the internal canon of unorthodoxy while decreasing the weight of external evidence, especially the date and character of witnesses. As Ehrman begins to increasingly emphasize internal evidence, his approach appears to be moving toward a more rigorous eclectic approach to textual criticism.

4. The canon of unorthodoxy rests on the premise of widespread orthodox corruption. Ehrman has demonstrated that extensive orthodox corruption is possible, but its probability seems unlikely.

5. Placing a high value on the canon of unorthodoxy as a premise seems to bias the textual decision prior to a complete examination of the evidence. Ehrman frequently argues for the originality of variants that fit his sociohistorical model of transcription well but suffer from poor attestation and little likelihood of going back to the original. If Ehrman did not place a high value on the canon of unorthodoxy, it is unlikely that many of the variants he chooses would be considered as viable.

In the end, the canon of unorthodoxy appears to be presuppositionally driven. The fact that the UBS[4] committee and Ehrman come to widely different conclusions at so many points is an indication that different methods are being used to analyze the textual data. It has been the goal of this chapter to show that the difference is in the application of the canon of unorthodoxy, which Ehrman implicitly holds to while the UBS[4] committee does not. As noted earlier, the UBS[4] committee acknowledges the reality of theologically motivated corruptions.[124] However, the committee does not appear to be guided by the canon of unorthodoxy in the same way that Ehrman is. It seems that the difference in textual conclusions derives less from the weighing of textual data and more from Ehrman's commitment to the canon of unorthodoxy. The result is that Ehrman finds orthodox corruption in a far greater number of passages than does the UBS[4] committee. That Ehrman does not see himself as allowing presuppositions to enter into

---

124. Metzger, *Textual Commentary*, 2nd ed., 52, 56, 164–66, 185, 200.

his methodology is made clear when he writes, "[T]o use orthodoxy as a criterion would involve presupposing my conclusions."[125] However, it seems that "orthodoxy as a criterion" is exactly what Ehrman is employing in at least some of the cases discussed in this chapter. Martin Hengel's warning about the danger of allowing presuppositions to drive methodology comes to mind. Hengel warned of the danger of both "an uncritical, sterile apologetic fundamentalism" and the "no less sterile 'critical ignorance'" of radical liberalism.[126] In both cases, the *approaches* are the same; it is the *presuppositions* that set them apart. This critique does not fully apply to Ehrman, but his textual decisions seem to indicate a methodology shaped by presupposition.

> One of the perennial dangers that confront scholars in every discipline is the tendency to become one-sided and to oversimplify the analysis and resolution of quite disparate questions. In textual criticism, this tendency can be observed when a scholar, becoming enamored of a single method or criterion of textual analysis, applies it more or less indiscriminately to a wide variety of problems.[127]

CONCLUSION

Ehrman's thesis concerning orthodox corruption of Scripture, while innovative and thought provoking, still remains hypothesis. Where he has persuasively argued for it, the texts in question are not as central to the message of the NT or to orthodox theology as Ehrman indicates. As Wallace concludes, "Regarding the evidence, suffice it to say that significant textual variants that alter core doctrines of the NT have not yet been produced."[128] In the end, it seems that Ehrman's conclusions extend beyond the evidence and may have distorted his perspective of the textual transmission. In addition, the canon of unorthodoxy itself appears to be inadequate due to the lack of evidence supporting it and the distorting force it appears to apply to textual analysis.

In conclusion, two seemingly divergent positions must be affirmed. On the one hand, theologically motivated alterations are a reality and are the best explanation for some textual variants.[129] These theologically

---

125. Ehrman, "RE: Greenlee's strawman (??) in The Text of the NT."
126. Martin Hengel, *Studies in Early Christology* (Edinburgh: T&T Clark, 1995), 57–58.
127. Metzger and Ehrman, *Text of the New Testament*, 304.
128. Wallace, "Gospel according to Bart," 346–47 (italics his). While Ehrman has produced a fascinating survey of theologically motivated alterations, when it comes to the key evidence to cement his argument, Ehrman still has not found what he is looking for.
129. Possible examples include Matt 24.36; 27.16–17; Mark 1.41; Luke 2.33; 2.38; 8.3; 11.4; 22.43f; 24.51; 24.53; John 3.13; 11.33; Acts 1.14; 2.41; 4.24; 5.32; 9.22; 15.29; Rom 9.4; Gal 1.3; 1 Peter 1.22.

Philip M. Miller

motivated alterations are best accounted for in Bengel's maxim that *the more difficult reading is to be preferred*.[130] The harder reading for orthodox scribes would indeed have been unorthodox or suborthodox readings.[131] Although the importance Ehrman ascribes to these alterations has been overstated, he is correct that theologically motivated alterations occurred on occasion. On the other hand, the canon of unorthodoxy seems to move beyond the evidence.

How, then, can these alterations be understood? It seems best to affirm that orthodox scribes were inclined toward reverence for Christ and were committed to their faith. At times, that reverence and commitment influenced their scribal activity, introducing alterations into the textual tradition. For the most part, these alterations do not appear to be sourced in malice, deceit, or agenda. These corruptions do not "establish the orthodox character of the text"[132] but, rather, *clarify* and *confirm* that character. While important questions remain, it is significant to note that no cardinal doctrine of orthodoxy is at stake in light of the variants presented by Ehrman. He concedes that most cases of textual variation do not affect the orthodox understanding of the physical resurrection and deity of Jesus Christ.[133]

In the end, we can conclude that the least orthodox reading, by itself, is *not* a viable canon for determining the preferred reading.

---

130. Johann Albrecht Bengel, *Η ΚΑΙΝΗ ΔΙΑΘΗΚΗ: Novum Testamentum Graecum ita adornatum ut Textus probatarum editionem medullam, Margo variantium lectionum in suas classes distributarum locorumque parallelorum delectum, apparatus subjunctus criseos sacrae Millianae praesertim compendium limam supplementum ac fractum exhibeat*, ed. Johann Albrecht Bengel (Tübingen: I. G. Cottae, 1734), 433.

131. Head, "Christology and Textual Transmission," 109.

132. Contra Ehrman, *Orthodox Corruption*, 28.

133. In the final Question & Answer session at the fourth annual Greer-Heard Point-Counterpoint Forum ("The Textual Reliability of the New Testament: A Dialogue between Bart Ehrman and Daniel Wallace," April 4–5, 2008), I had the following recorded exchange with Ehrman:

     Miller: "Dr. Ehrman, at this point in scholarship does the . . . in your opinion, does the earliest reconstructible form of the text portray an orthodox understanding of, say, the resurrection and the deity of Christ?"

     Ehrman: "I'm not sure what the orthodox understanding of . . . You mean that Jesus was physically raised from the dead and that he was God?"

     Miller: "That Jesus was bodily raised from the dead and then that he's both God and man."

     Ehrman: "I don't think that the . . . I don't think that the text . . . the texts affect that one way or the other. I think . . . My own view is that the biblical authors thought that Jesus was physically raised from the dead. My own view is that most of the biblical authors did not think that Jesus was God. The Gospel of John does. I think Matthew, Mark, and Luke do not think that Jesus was God. It's hard to know what Paul's view about Jesus' divinity is, in my opinion. So I think different authors had different points of view, but I don't think . . . in most cases I don't think that it's affected by textual variation."

3

THE LEGACY OF A LETTER

Sabellianism or Scribal Blunder in John 1.1c?

Matthew P. Morgan

Regarding the study of NT transmission, it has been observed that "manuscripts have many more stories to tell if you listen closely to the sounds of the details they preserve for today's world."[1] Although the study of manuscripts has a rich heritage, the smaller, often more obscure stories, contained in every manuscript, remain untold; deservedly, the majority of attention has focused on the character, date, and quality of text preserved in a particular manuscript.[2] Thus the majority of these investigations seldom deal with the historical perspective contained in the transmission of a given document; instead, their greater

---

1. Thomas J. Kraus and Tobias Nicklas, "The World of New Testament Manuscripts: 'Every Manuscript Tells a Story,'" in *New Testament Manuscripts: Their Texts and Their World*, ed. Thomas J. Kraus and Tobias Nicklas, Texts and Editions for New Testament Study 2 (Leiden: Brill, 2006), 4.
2. See, e.g., Ernest Cadman Colwell, *Studies in Methodology in Textual Criticism of the New Testament*, New Testament Tools and Studies 9 (Leiden: Brill, 1969); Colwell, "Genealogical Method: Its Achievements and Its Limitations," *JBL* 66 (1947): 109–33; Colwell, "The Significance of Grouping of New Testament Manuscripts," *NTS* 4 (1957–58): 73–92; Eldon Jay Epp and Gordon D. Fee, eds., *New Testament Textual Criticism: Its Significance for Exegesis; Essays in Honor of Bruce Metzger* (New York: Oxford University Press, 1981); Eldon Jay Epp, *Perspectives on New Testament Textual Criticism: Collected Essays, 1962–2004*, Supplements to Novum Testamentum 116 (Leiden: Brill, 2005); Gordon D. Fee, "Textual Criticism of the New Testament," in *Studies in the Theory and Method of New Testament Textual Criticism*, ed. Eldon Jay Epp and Gordon D. Fee (Grand Rapids: Eerdmans, 1993), 3–44; Bart D. Ehrman, "Methodological Developments in the Analysis and Classification of New Testament Documentary Evidence," *NovT* 29, no. 1 (1987): 22–45; Kurt Aland and Barbara Aland, *The Text of the New Testament: An Introduction to the Critical Editions and to the Theory and Practice of Modern Textual Criticism*, trans. Erroll F. Rhodes, 2nd ed. (Grand Rapids: Eerdmans, 1989); Bruce M. Metzger and Bart D. Ehrman, *The Text of the New Testament: Its Transmission, Corruption, and Restoration*, 4th ed. (New York: Oxford University Press, 2005); Brook Foss Westcott and Fenton John Anthony Hort, *The New Testament in the Original Greek: Introduction [and] Appendix* (London: Macmillan, 1882).

concern is its contribution or place in the broader pursuit of the "original" text.

Although the study of scribal habits provides a personalized look at individual manuscripts, it is often limited to significant early manuscripts or families of manuscripts.[3] In addition, work on scribal habits typically pursues the historical nature of the transmission process with the aim of forming helpful canons of transcriptional probability. As a result, little attention is given to the role and testimony of individual manuscripts and even some of the unique readings they record.

Within the transmissional history of John 1.1, a single variant emerges from the vast array of manuscripts containing this sacred text.[4] More specifically, this lone variant does not stem from a deviation consisting of a phrase, a word, or even a collection of letters. Instead, its origin is the addition of a single letter, the article, so that the phrase καὶ θεὸς ἦν ὁ λόγος reads καὶ ὁ θεὸς ἦν ὁ λόγος in two eighth-century witnesses, Codex Regius (L [019]) and the first quire of Codex Freerianus (W^S [032-S]).[5]

If considered original, this reading with the article has serious implications for Christology. As the grammarian A. T. Robertson rightly pointed out, "It is true also that καὶ ὁ θεὸς ἦν ὁ λόγος (convertible terms) would have been Sabellianism."[6] If correct, this reading threatens the assertion that evangelical doctrine is unaffected by *any* variant.[7] At the same time, if the evidence shows that it preserves the

---

3. Ernest Cadman Colwell, "Method in Evaluating Scribal Habits: A Study of 𝔓⁴⁵, 𝔓⁶⁶, 𝔓⁷⁵" and "Hort Redivivus: A Plea and a Program," in *Studies in Methodology in Textual Criticism of the New Testament* (Leiden: Brill, 1969); James R. Royse, *Scribal Habits in Early Greek New Testament Papyri*, New Testament Tools, Studies, and Documents 36 (Leiden: Brill, 2008).

4. At first glance, it would appear that no variant exists in this verse, since the standard Greek texts, NA²⁷ and UBS⁴, do not list a single variant until John 1.3. Another critical text (Constantinus Tischendorf, *Novum Testamentum Graece*, 8th ed. [1869; repr., Graz: Akademische Druck-u. Verlagsanstalt, 1965], loc. cit.) gives several citations from the church fathers but lists only one variant for the entire verse. In a recent publication (U. B. Schmid, W. J. Elliott, and D. C. Parker, eds., *The New Testament in Greek IV: The Gospel according to St. John*, vol. 2, *The Majuscules*, New Testament Tools, Studies, and Documents 37 [Leiden: Brill, 2007], 189), this same variant is found along with the absence of the *nomen sacrum* in 1.1b, where the abbreviation θν has been replaced by θεόν in the ninth-century manuscript Codex M (021).

5. The date for W^S is debated. For a more detailed discussion, see "The Place of Codices Regius and Freerianus in Transmission History" below.

6. A. T. Robertson, *A Grammar of the Greek New Testament in the Light of Historical Research*, 4th ed. (Nashville: Broadman, 1934), 767–68.

7. Metzger and Ehrman noted that Johann Albrecht Bengel "came to the conclusions that the variant readings were fewer in number than might have been expected and that *they did not shake any article of evangelical doctrine*" (Metzger and Ehrman, *Text of the New Testament*, 158; italics mine). More recently, this view is echoed in

remnant of an early Sabellian ancestor, it also poses a clear challenge to the more recent claim that evangelical doctrine is immune to any *viable* variant.[8] As a result, to determine the legacy of this loaded letter in these two manuscripts, it is necessary to listen carefully to their stories.

THE APPROACH OF THIS STUDY

Three different perspectives inform the legacy and heritage of these two eighth-century manuscript witnesses and the text of John 1.1c:

1. The historical use of John's Gospel will be examined in the polemical environment of Sabellianism and its corollaries.[9] From this survey, the date and significance of this particular passage in the debates will be determined. As the dust settles on the issue of chronology, it is then possible to evaluate the potential threat of scribal influence during the period of greatest textual turbulence.

2. Scribal behavior and tendencies will reveal the nature and quality of transmission. If the legacy in this variant lies in a Sabellian Christology, this theological bias should be manifest throughout both manuscripts. Thus, as Hort aptly stated, "KNOWLEDGE OF DOCUMENTS SHOULD PRECEDE FINAL JUDGMENT UPON READINGS."[10] Subsequently, both Colwell[11] and, more recently, Royse[12] have continued the rich tradition pioneered by Hort. Royse wrote, "As Hort's own comments make clear, knowledge of the sorts of errors that a particular scribe tended to make, and of his overall method and accuracy of copying, is an essential portion of this 'knowledge of documents.'"[13] That being the case, it is important to examine this loaded letter through the eyes of the two eighth-century scribes who produced the two manuscripts. Through a detailed analysis of their unique scribal proclivities, their legacy will become apparent.

D. A. Carson and Douglas J. Moo, *An Introduction to the New Testament*, 2nd ed. (Grand Rapids: Zondervan, 2005), 31.

8. J. Ed Komoszewski, M. James Sawyer, and Daniel B. Wallace, *Reinventing Jesus: How Contemporary Skeptics Miss the Real Jesus and Mislead Popular Culture* (Grand Rapids: Kregel, 2006), 117.

9. Hurtado wrote, "Particularly in the christological disputes of the early centuries, it [Gospel of John] was unexcelled as the favorite arsenal of textual ammunition (often by both sides of the disputes!)" (Larry W. Hurtado, *Lord Jesus Christ: Devotion to Jesus in Earliest Christianity* [Grand Rapids: Eerdmans, 2003], 349).

10. Westcott and Hort, *New Testament in the Original Greek*, 31.

11. Colwell, "Redivivus," 148–71.

12. Royse, *Scribal Habits*.

13. Ibid., 1.

3.   Finally, given the grammatical nature of the variant καὶ ὁ θεὸς ἦν ὁ λόγος, its story touches the historical use of predicate nominative constructions in the NT. Looking at normative patterns for the addition of the article in similar constructions in the NT may show whether its origin resulted from an intentional theological change.

THE USE OF SCRIBAL HABITS AS A "HISTORICAL LENS"

A popular facet in mainstream textual criticism is the study of readings that show evidence of potential theological motivation. Initially, Hort and, to a degree, Colwell resisted the notion that textual variants point to the history of theology.[14] However, there is a growing consensus that many variants are helpful barometers for seeing the theological contours prevalent in the early church. As a result, the notion of an "original text" is jettisoned in favor of a moving canon contained within individual manuscripts.[15] The primary source of this perspective is the limited "window of opportunity" presented by the lack of con-

---

14.   Westcott and Hort do not deny theology as a possible influence on textual changes (Jeff Miller, "(Mis)Understanding Westcott and Hort," *ResQ* 41 [1999]: 155–62). However, they clearly reject the notion that theological changes were made to cover up competing doctrines by altering the sacred text. Colwell wrote, "The current enthusiasm for manuscript variations as contributions to the history of theology has no solid foundation" ("Redivivus," 150). Colwell, a pioneer in the field of textual criticism, denies not the presence of theologically motivated variants but, rather, their ability to reflect the state of historical orthodoxy. However, Metzger and Ehrman boldly denied Hort's claim that "even among the numerous unquestionably spurious readings of the New Testament there are no signs of deliberate falsification of the text for dogmatic purposes" (Metzger and Ehrman, *Text of the New Testament*, 282).

15.   Some examples will be given here to show the attention this concept is receiving. Bart Ehrman is perhaps the most outspoken in this regard (Bart D. Ehrman, "The Text as Window: New Testament Manuscripts and the Social History of Early Christianity," in *The Text of the New Testament in Contemporary Research: Essays on the Status Quaestionis*, ed. Bart D. Ehrman and Michael W. Holmes [Grand Rapids: Eerdmans, 1995], 361–79; Bart D. Ehrman, *The Orthodox Corruption of Scripture: The Effect of Early Christological Controversies on the Text of the New Testament* [New York: Oxford University Press, 1993]). See also Eldon Jay Epp, "The Multivalence of the Term 'Original Text' in New Testament Textual Criticism," *HTR* 92 (1999): 245–81; D. C. Parker, *The Living Text of the Gospels* (Cambridge: Cambridge University Press, 1997). For Parker, theological variants are representatives of a developing canon, so an original text is present in the individual variants (*Living Text*, 207–13). Similarly, Epp argued that individual variants should be viewed as proliferations of canon, so that "the same fluidity that can be observed in textual variation carries over to canonicity" ("Multivalence," 278). Therefore, according to both Epp and Parker, the NT canon is not a fixed body related to an "original" text but, rather, a moving target that accommodates the multiplicity of variants. In a milder manner, Peter Head noted, "The scribe of the New Testament was a participant in the life and faith of the church, and this life and faith clearly influenced the process of transmission" (Peter M. Head, "Christology and Textual

---

Matthew P. Morgan

trolled copying during the second century.[16] Although both Codices L (019) and W^S (032-S) fall outside the time frame of certain theological debates, it is still possible that they were copied from an early source. As a result, it is worthwhile to grapple with the relationship of these two eighth-century manuscripts to much earlier Christological disputes.

A HISTORICAL SURVEY OF SABELLIANISM

The Roots and Rise of Sabellianism

The variant in John 1.1c may spring from the historical seeds that later sprouted into the teaching of Sabellius and his closest followers. Beginning with the offshoot of Gnosticism in Proconsular Asia, the school of modalistic Monarchianism[17] first emerged toward the end of the second century.[18] The central figure for this school of thought in its infant stages was Noetus of Smyrna, followed later by Praxeas. Eventually, this view of Christ was given a more systematic and philosophical structure by Sabellius,[19] producing Sabellianism in the East and a nuanced form called Patripassianism in the West.[20]

Transmission: Reverential Alterations in the Synoptic Gospels," *NovT* 35 [1993]: 128).

16. For a treatment of the transmissional process prior to the fourth century, see Royse, *Scribal Habits*, 19–27; Fee, "Textual Criticism," 9–10; Head, "Christology and Textual Transmission," 106; Metzger and Ehrman, *Text of the New Testament*, 282–87. Ehrman specifically acknowledged this issue while addressing anti-patripassianistic corruptions, stating that "in the early third century, the textual tradition of the New Testament, as we have seen, had already begun to solidify" (*Orthodox Corruption*, 264).

17. For further discussion of the terminology employed here, see William G. Rusch, ed., *The Trinitarian Controversy* (Philadelphia: Fortress, 1980), 8–9; J. N. D. Kelly, *Early Christian Doctrines*, 5th rev. ed. (New York: Continuum, 1977), 119–22; Hubertus R. Drobner, *The Fathers of the Church*, trans. Siegfried S. Schatzmann (Peabody, MA: Hendrickson, 2007), 116; Adolf Harnack, *History of Dogma*, trans. Neil Buchanan, 3rd German ed., 7 vols. (New York: Dover, 1961), 3:52–53; T. E. Pollard, *Johannine Christology and the Early Church* (New York: Cambridge University Press, 1970), 52; R. P. C. Hanson, *The Search for the Christian Doctrine of God: The Arian Controversy, 318–381* (Grand Rapids: Baker Academic, 2005), 310.

18. John Henry Newman, *The Arians of the Fourth Century* (London: Gilbert and Rivington, 1871), 120.

19. For further discussion of the role and teaching of Sabellius, see Kelly, *Early Christian Doctrines*, 121–22; Rusch, *Trinitarian Controversy*, 9; Harnack, *History of Dogma*, 3:52–83; Newman, *Arians of the Fourth Century*, 211.

20. Some historians make reference to this geographical distinction (cf. Harnack, *History of Dogma*, 3:52–53; Hanson, *Doctrine of God*, 310). Since the origin and study of text types tends to be geographical in nature, this observation could potentially have a bearing on the presence of a given reading in the Alexandrian tradition as opposed to the Western text.

Sabellianism opposed the "orthodox" position in several ways.[21] The unifying characteristic of modalistic Monarchianism was the "denial of the distinctions of Persons in the Godhead."[22] Within this system, adherence to strict monotheism was essential, and the distinction of Christ from the Father was labeled blasphemy and considered to be the worship of two Gods (δίθεοι).[23] The logical extension of this theology was Patripassianism, which taught "the idea that it was the Father who suffered and underwent Christ's other human experiences."[24] Although debatable,[25] it seems best to merge these doctrines, given their strong logical relationship.[26]

Critical to the idea of a pro-Sabellian influence on the text of John is the time frame and impact these views had on the church. In the bigger picture, the conflict was both severe and widespread. As one historian wrote, "This much is certain, however, that in the East the fight against Monarchianism in the second half of the *third century* was a violent one, and that even the development of the Logos Christology (of

---

21. The term *orthodox* here refers primarily to the expressions of Origen, Hippolytus, Eusebius, and Tertullian, whose views were later refined and solidified in the great creeds of the fourth and fifth centuries. The language of Origen, with its tendency toward subordinationism, was not sufficient for later scholars and required further development to be considered orthodox in the sense that we now conceive of it. Hanson's comments on this development of doctrine are most helpful here: "The story is the story of how orthodoxy was reached, found, not of how it was maintained. . . . It was only very slowly, as a result of debate and consideration and the re-thinking of earlier ideas that the doctrine which was later to be promulgated as orthodoxy arose" (Hanson, *Doctrine of God*, 70). In a similar manner, Moule has presented a helpful analogy by contrasting the "evolutionary" view of history and doctrine, where the end product looks nothing like the initial life-form, with a "developmental" view, where "they are not successive additions of something new, but only the drawing out and articulating of what is there" (C. F. D. Moule, *The Origin of Christology* [New York: Cambridge University Press, 1977], 3). Only later, after the dangers and shortcomings of these initial orthodox expressions had been exposed to rigorous attacks, did more definitive and precise statements begin to emerge. This definitive understanding of the Father's relationship to the Son is evident by the time of Athanasius, as it becomes merely a "presupposition" in his arguments (Pollard, *Johannine Christology*, 136–37).
22. Newman, *Arians of the Fourth Century*, 124.
23. See Kelly, *Early Christian Doctrines*, 119; Harnack, *History of Dogma*, 3:55. This shows that the conflicts of modalistic Monarchianism came about not as the result of competing Christianities but, rather, through the difficulty and struggle of trying to articulate the reality of Christ's deity from a monotheistic framework.
24. Kelly, *Early Christian Doctrines*, 120.
25. For a slightly different perspective, see M. Slusser, "The Scope of Patripassianism," in *Studia Patristica*, vol. 17, ed. Elizabeth A. Livingstone (Oxford: Pergamon, 1982), 169–80.
26. The reasons for this are twofold: (1) because the logical relationship is so strong that it is unlikely most people within the church would be able to distinguish these doctrines and (2) to keep consistency with Ehrman (*Orthodox Corruption*, 270 n. 6).

Matthew P. Morgan

Origen) was directly and lastingly influenced by this opposition."[27] At the same time, the issue of Christ's relationship to the Father does not begin to demand serious attention until the early to mid-third century at the very earliest.[28] This last point is particularly significant since the manuscript tradition had already gained greater stability prior to this time period.

The Reaction of the Church Fathers

The weight and nature of the Sabellian controversies can be seen from a brief survey of the writings of those men charged with upholding the apostolic tradition, particularly in their response to Noetus and others who carried the theological torch after him.

Hippolytus (ca. 189–235)[29]

Perhaps the earliest defense of orthodoxy can be found in the writings of Hippolytus.[30] It is here that the orthodox position and the growing popularity of Sabellianism within the Roman church became apparent.[31] The pivotal work in these modalistic debates was *Adversus Noetus*, preserving the primary historical record of the initial teachings put forward by Noetus. Hippolytus defended orthodoxy with an appeal to philosophy rather than Scripture,[32] resulting in a crude framework labeled the

---

27. Harnack, *History of Dogma*, 3:82 (italics added). See also Kelly, *Early Christian Doctrines*, 119; Pollard, *Johannine Christology*, 52.
28. Harnack indicated that with the presence of Origen in Egypt, the earliest this schism could have occurred would be 230–40 CE (*History of Dogma*, 3:83). Similarly, Slusser pointed to the lack of trustworthy evidence after 250 CE ("Scope of Patripassianism," 169). Even Ehrman acknowledged this problem, stating, "When these distinctions [between God and the Son] *did* gain in importance for orthodoxy at large, in the early third century, the textual tradition of the New Testament, as we have seen, had already begun to solidify" (Bart D. Ehrman, *The New Testament: A Historical Introduction to the Early Christian Writings* [New York: Oxford University Press, 1997], 264).
29. Drobner, *Fathers of the Church*, 122–24.
30. Harnack, *History of Dogma*, 3:62.
31. Other primary figures were the bishops Zephyrinus and Callistus, whose leadership spanned the late second and early third centuries. From Hippolytus's polemical language and his record of Callistus's later excommunication of Sabellius as a "cover-up" for his own doctrinal problems, there appears to be an *internal political conflict* involved in these writings as well (Ehrman, *Orthodox Corruption*, 262–63).
32. For Hippolytus, the language and structure are concerned more with philosophical frameworks than with key Scripture citations (Raymond B. Williams, "Origen's Interpretation of the Gospel of John" [PhD diss., University of Chicago, 1966], 247). His contribution lies more in the connection of a "universal monad," the ancient philosophy taught by Heracleitus, than with Sabellian views (Kelly, *Early Christian Doctrines*, 121).

"economic trinity,"[33] where God's unity was seen in his power, while his diversity was found in his economy or manifestation.[34] This primitive formulation became an initial spark that would later burst into open flames as the groups worked to express the relationships within the Trinity.

Tertullian (ca. 160–240)[35]

Little is known about the identity of Tertullian's opponent Praxeas;[36] however, the presence of his Sabellian teaching in Africa is evident in Tertullian's strong response in *Adversus Praxeam* (ca. 213).[37] According to Tertullian's claim in this writing, Praxeas taught that the Father and Son were one identical person.[38] Tertullian approached the problem much like Hippolytus, only with greater sophistication. He stated that God was "three in degree, not condition; in form, not substance; in aspect, not power."[39] Arguably his greatest Christological contribution was the proposal of "the twofold state, which is not confounded but conjoined in one person—Jesus, God and man."[40] In Tertullian's approach, the dawn of the third century had arrived, and a primitive orthodox articulation of the Trinity was beginning to take shape, but a formal and concerted appeal to John 1.1 remained absent from the nucleus of the debates.

Origen (ca. 185–254)[41]

While earlier church fathers made philosophical arguments, Origen firmly staked his view of Christ's relationship to the Father on the opening verse of John's Gospel. As a serious textual critic, he

---

33. Kelly pointed out that this formulation of the Trinity was the catalyst that threatened the unity of the Godhead and produced the extreme response found in modalistic monarchian theology (*Early Christian Doctrines*, 109).
34. Alexander Roberts and James Donaldson, eds., *Hippolytus, Cyprian, Caius, Novatian, Appendix*, vol. 5 of *Ante-Nicene Fathers: The Writings of the Fathers Down to A.D. 325* (1886; repr., Peabody, MA: Hendrickson, 2004), 226. See also the comments in Ehrman, *Orthodox Corruption*, 264.
35. Drobner, *Fathers of the Church*, 153.
36. Newman, *Arians of the Fourth Century*, 120–24; Kelly, *Early Christian Doctrines*, 121; Drobner, *Fathers of the Church*, 163–64.
37. Regarding the date of *Adversus Praxeam*, both Kelly and Drobner place this work in the early third century (ca. 213) (Kelly, *Early Christian Doctrines*, 121; Drobner, *Fathers of the Church*, 163).
38. The technical language was *vox et sonus oris*, reflecting the view that the Word had "no independent subsistence" (Kelly, *Early Christian Doctrines*, 121).
39. Ehrman, *Orthodox Corruption*, 264.
40. Drobner, *Fathers of the Church*, 164. The corresponding Latin phrase in *Adv. Prax.* 27.11 is *Videmus duplicem statum, non confusum sed coniunctum in una persona, deum et hominem Iesum.*
41. Drobner, *Fathers of the Church*, 136–48.

also preserved extensive testimony to the exclusivity of the anarthrous reading of θεός within the Alexandrian manuscript tradition,[42] as the following segment from his commentary on John shows:

> We next notice John's use of the article in these sentences. He does not write without care in this respect, nor is he unfamiliar with the niceties of the Greek tongue. In some cases he uses the article, and in some he omits it. He adds the article to the Logos, but to the name of God he adds it sometimes only. He uses the article, when the name of God refers to the uncreated cause of all things, and omits it when the Logos is named God.[43]

In addition, Origen's understanding of the Trinity, with the Father alone as αὐτόθεος, was dependent on the description of the Son as θεός and not ὁ θεός in John 1.1c.[44] As a result, Origen, a credible third-century textual critic, becomes a pivotal historical witness to the *exclusion* of the article in John 1.1c.[45]

Chronologically, if Sabellianism was unable to make inroads while Origen was in Alexandria, it is doubtful it could wield any influence on textual transmission prior to ca. 231, when the textual sheriff was forced to leave for Caesarea.[46] The sequence of these events is significant, as it makes dubious, at best, the likelihood of a pro-Sabellian textual tradition in Alexandria during the first quarter of the third century.

---

42. For a study of the textual awareness of Origen, see the listing in Bart D. Ehrman, Gordon D. Fee, and Michael W. Holmes, *The Text of the Fourth Gospel in the Writings of Origen*, vol. 1, Society of Biblical Literature: The New Testament in the Greek Fathers 3 (Atlanta: Scholars Press, 1992), 38–42.
43. Allan Menzies, "Origen's Commentary on John," in *The Ante-Nicene Fathers: Translations of the Writings of the Fathers Down to A.D. 325*, ed. Allan Menzies, vol. 10 (Grand Rapids: Eerdmans, 1962), 323. Taken from Origen, *Comm. Jo.* 2.2.13–14, which reads: Πάνυ δὲ παρατετηρημένως καὶ οὐχ ὡς ἑλληνικὴν ἀκριβολογίαν οὐκ ἐπιστάμενος ὁ Ἰωάννης ὅπου μὲν τοῖς ἄρθροις ἐχρήσατο ὅπου δὲ ταῦτα ἀπεσιώπησεν, ἐπὶ μὲν τοῦ λόγου προστιθεὶς τὸ ὁ, ἐπὶ δὲ τῆς θεὸς προσηγορίας ὅπου μὲν τιθεὶς ὅπου δὲ αἴρων. Τίθησιν μὲν γὰρ τὸ ἄρθρον, ὅτε ἡ θεὸς ὀνομασία ἐπὶ τοῦ ἀγενήτου τάσσεται τῶν ὅλων αἰτίου, σιωπᾷ δὲ αὐτό, ὅτε ὁ λόγος θεὸς ὀνομάζεται. Portions of this Greek text from Origen's commentary also appear in Tischendorf's critical apparatus for John 1.1c (Tischendorf, *Novum Testamentum Graece*, loc. cit.).
44. Kelly, *Early Christian Doctrines*, 129–32; Pollard, *Johannine Christology*, 93–94. With regard to the concept of αὐτόθεος, my limited investigation found Origen's perspective in Origen, *Comm. Jo.* 2.2.17–20.
45. Although willing to entertain the possibility of the article in John 1.1c, Ehrman acknowledged the strength of Origen's comments in Origin, *Comm. Jo.* 2.2.17–18]) against such a notion (Ehrman, *Orthodox Corruption*, 179 n. 87).
46. Drobner, *Fathers of the Church*, 137.

Eusebius (ca. 260/64–340)[47]

Following in Origen's footsteps, Eusebius provided an even more pointed discussion of the text of John 1.1c. He clearly asserted what John's Gospel does not say:

> Not saying, "and the word was the God" [καὶ ὁ θεὸς ἦν ὁ λόγος], with the appended article, so that it is not the one that will define "the One over all" [τὸν ἐπὶ πάντων], . . . therefore it says, "and the word was God" [καὶ θεὸς ἦν ὁ λόγος], so that we might see God, "the One over all," with whom was the Word, and the Word himself was God.[48]

Like Origen, Eusebius provided additional textual attestation to the lack of the article with θεός in John 1.1c, continuing the textual tradition of his predecessor.[49] From this point forward, the distinction between the Father and the Son in the midst of their unity is clearly defined by the *absence of the article* in John 1.1c. Equally important was the continued presence of the anarthrous θεός, extending into the fourth century and beyond the Council of Nicea (325).

The Historical Viability of Sabellian Influence on the Textual Transmission of the New Testament

We have already seen the sociohistorical climate that gave birth to the teachings known as Sabellianism. On one level, both the geographical spread and the intensity of this conflict certainly had the potential to influence Christians during the later portion of the third century. Therefore, it is conceivable that certain orthodox scribes may have had some theological impetus to alter the text of John 1.1c, given its explicit use by Origen, Eusebius, and possibly others. To advance the mere possibility of this influence into a likely explanation, certain variables must be in place:

1. Sabellianism's polemical influence must be strong enough to cause numerous pious scribes to alter the sacred text by universally eradicating the presence of the article. A fundamental challenge to this notion was the use of allegorical interpretation by Sabellians to deny the Logos concept in the prologue of John's Gospel. As a result, "they did

---

47. Ibid., 223–24.
48. This is my own translation of the Greek text listed as Eus[mcell 121] in Tischendorf's critical apparatus for John 1.1c (Tischendorf, *Novum Testamentum Graece*, loc. cit.). I was unable to locate this exact statement in Eusebius but found similar expressions in *Eccl. theol.* 2.14.3 and 2.17.1–2.
49. See Pollard, *Johannine Christology*, 282.

Matthew P. Morgan

not regard that book [John's] as justifying the introduction of a Logos, and the bestowal on him of the title Son of God."[50] Instead, their core appeal was to passages emphasizing Jesus' unity with the Father (cf. John 10.30; 14.8–10).[51] Therefore, Sabellians would be more prone to avoid John 1.1 than to alter its content, given their preference for other texts that better articulated their view. It seems doubtful that the Sabellian approach to John 1.1 would trigger theological sensitivity among even the most licentious scribe.

2. The strength of the controversy needs to have its greatest impact during the early second century, when manuscript production was scattered and vulnerable. Since the orthodox arguments were not related to the text of John 1.1c prior to Origen in the third century, the timing of Sabellianism does not fit. Likewise, in its earliest forms, the debate addresses philosophical frameworks and not the prologue to John's Gospel. Consequently, it is difficult to posit theological motivations to a text that the Sabellians preferred to set aside.

3. Finally, it would be reasonable to expect some hesitancy in references about the lack of the article in John 1.1c if competing manuscripts existed. However, the voices of both Origen and Eusebius boldly deny the presence of the article within the early manuscript tradition while explicitly affirming the anarthrous reading in John 1.1c.

In conclusion, the historical evidence indicates that whatever theological tensions may have existed, their role in the textual legacy of John 1.1 was nonexistent. Without earlier roots, the Sabellian conflicts would have been unable to produce the fruits of their teachings during the most vulnerable period of NT transmission. So, with

---

50. Harnack, *History of Dogma*, 3:63.
51. Multiple scholars affirm John 10.30 and 14.8–10 as key "proof texts" utilized by the patripassianists: see Kelly, *Early Christian Doctrines*, 120; Pollard, *Johannine Christology*, 52; Harnack, *History of Dogma*, 3.63; Drobner, *Fathers of the Church*, 163. Though much of what we know comes through the polemical writings of the orthodox camp, the available evidence gives at least four reasons to doubt their impact on the textual transmission of John 1.1. First, the debates took place primarily *within* the church, where Scripture was held in high regard and was less likely to be manipulated. Second, as fierce as the debates were, the Sabellians did not turn to John 1.1 or even the prologue of John's Gospel as part of their defense. Since the distinction between the Father and Son is undeniably evident in 1.1b, even if 1.1c included the articular θεὸς, the earlier portion of the verse would have presented even greater challenges. This best explains the use of allegorical interpretation in John 1.1–18. Third, these writings focus on either monotheistic passages from the Old Testament (Deut 6.4) or clear statements by Jesus of His unity with the Father (John 10.30; 14.8–10). Fourth, the time period when these debates were at their pinnacle happens *after* the time frame when "uncontrolled" transmission was more plausible.

regard to the sociohistorical context, the likelihood that early scribes would have seen the transmission of John 1.1c in polemical terms quickly evaporates. At the same time, the wealth of historical evidence demands a truly exceptional historical reconstruction in order to propose any Sabellian influence on the textual transmission of John 1.1c.

AN ANALYSIS OF SCRIBAL HABITS
IN CODICES REGIUS AND FREERIANUS

Terms and Methodology

Following, at the macro and micro level, the methodology of E. C. Colwell for determining scribal behavior,[52] "we wish to find a way to characterize the habits of scribes that will avoid, as far as possible, both any question-begging assumptions about scribal behavior and any controversial presuppositions about the history of the text."[53] In this way, we can create a scribal rap sheet that can be used to assess the quality and character of Regius's testimony with regard to John 1.1c.[54] In addition, this analysis will rest on my own collation of Codex Regius and the first quire of Freerianus against the Robinson-Pierpont Majority Text (2005)[55] of John's Gospel.[56] These variants, individually classified and categorized, provide a more detailed quantitative analysis that is able to shed light on the character and background of the manuscript as a whole.[57]

Before continuing, it is necessary to establish how the language of the discipline will be applied throughout the remainder of this presentation.[58] Of particular interest for the determination of scribal

---

52. Colwell, "Redivivus," 160.
53. Royse, *Scribal Habits*, 31.
54. The pivotal nature of studying the scribal habits of entire MSS can be seen in Colwell, "Redivivus," 160; James R. Royse, "Scribal Tendencies in the Transmission of the Text of the New Testament," in Ehrman and Holmes, *Text of the New Testament in Contemporary Research*, 245; and James D. Yoder, "The Language of the Greek Variants of Codex Bezae," *NovT* 3 (1959): 241–42.
55. Maurice A. Robinson and William G. Pierpont, *The New Testament in the Original Greek: Byzantine Textform* (Southborough, MA: Chilton, 2005).
56. This personal collation has been compared against the extensive collation found in Schmid, Elliott, and Parker, *New Testament in Greek IV*, 189–553. The justification for using the MT rather than the TR as a collating base is found in Daniel B. Wallace, "The Majority Text: A New Collating Base?" *NTS* 35 (1989): 609–18.
57. Royse, *Scribal Habits*, 42–44.
58. For cogent definitions, see Gordon D. Fee, "On the Types, Classification, and Presentation of Textual Variation," in *Studies in the Theory and Method of New Testament Textual Criticism*, ed. Eldon Jay Epp and Gordon D. Fee (Grand Rapids: Eerdmans, 1993), 67.

habits are the singular readings of a manuscript. For Colwell, a singular reading was "a reading that had no Greek support in the critical apparatus of Tischendorf's 8th edition."[59] Recently, textual criticism has pushed for an updated investigation where a singular reading is preserved in several major critical texts.[60] In keeping with Royse's expansion of Colwell's method, singular readings in this study were examined against NA[27], Tischendorf's eighth edition, and the recently published IGNT for John's Gospel.[61] Therefore, a singular reading in this study includes any variant that is preserved in *only* one Greek manuscript according to NA[27], Tischendorf's eighth edition, and IGNT.[62] Unless otherwise noted, subsingular readings will conform to the definition given by Fee: "The meaning of 'sub-singular readings' is a non-genetic, accidental agreement in variation between two MSS which are not otherwise closely related."[63] Finally, a nonsense reading will be defined as "words unknown to grammar or lexicon, words that cannot be construed syntactically, or words that do not make sense in the context."[64]

Key evidence in uncovering the legacy of any manuscript is the nature and quality of its singular and subsingular readings. In these peculiar strokes are found the slips and secrets that form a personalized portrait of the human instruments used to copy each manuscript. To a large degree, the story of every manuscript is the story of the individual whose diligent labor produced it. For our variant in John 1.1c, its testimony hinges on the lives of two scribes, to whose stories I now turn.

---

59. Colwell, "Scribal Habits," 108.
60. Royse, *Scribal Habits*, 65–67. Royse recommended consulting NA[27], Tischendorf[8], von Soden, Clark, Legg, and the recently published IGNT volumes on Luke and John. Other works following a similar approach are Peter M. Head, "The Habits of New Testament Copyists: Singular Readings in the Early Fragmentary Papyri of John," *Bib* 85 (2004): 400–401; and Juan Hernández, *Scribal Habits and Theological Influences in the Apocalypse: The Singular Readings of Sinaiticus, Alexandrinus, and Ephraemi* (Tübingen: Mohr Siebeck, 2006), 45.
61. There are a few instances where a reading is listed as singular by Tischendorf but the broader collection of evidence in the IGNT proves otherwise. This observation should present caution in only utilizing a single older work when determining singular readings. My personal analysis of the singular readings in Codices L and W[S] begins with Tischendorf's reading but is refined by the data available in IGNT. The text of John 1.1c is a good example of the added rigor of this method. In almost all of the critical additions recommended by Royse, the article with θεός stands as a singular reading found only in Codex Regius. However, IGNT lists this as a subsingular reading with two witnesses, L and W[S] (032-S) (Schmid, Elliot, and Parker, *New Testament in Greek IV*, 189).
62. An exception to this are certain orthographic variants that are difficult to determine since spelling was not always standardized, leading most critical texts to exclude these variants.
63. Fee, "Types, Classification, and Presentation," 67.
64. Colwell, "Scribal Habits," 111.

The Place of Codices Regius and Freerianus in Transmission History

Codex Regius (L [019])

Codex Regius (L [019]), a Gospels manuscript, is universally re-garded as from the eighth century. With regard to text type, it serves as a primary representative of the secondary Alexandrian[65] text.[66] The sig-nificance of this genealogical history is its frequent alignment with the major and early Alexandrian witnesses Codex Vaticanus (B) and Codex Sinaiticus (א).[67] At the same time, there is also a notable intrusion of Byzantine readings, producing a polluted form of the Egyptian text.[68] In some sense, the textual history of Regius can be likened to a teenager whose biological heritage comes from early Alexandria (B א) but whose most influential friends are primarily Byzantine, resulting in a mixture of these two forms.

Of significance to the present study is the strong relationship this manuscript has with the "proto-Alexandrian" text form found in the combination of Vaticanus (B) and $\mathfrak{P}^{75}$ dated as early as the second cen-tury CE.[69] This past heritage presents the possibility that Regius pre-serves a more primitive text deliberately removed by previous orthodox scribes. If this is the case, it is possible to argue that L somehow pre-served the "original text." Yet there is a tension between the genealogical quality of this manuscript and the scribe who recorded it. Thus Metzger and Ehrman noted, "Though badly written by a scribe who committed many ignorant blunders, its type of text is good, agreeing frequently with Codex Vaticanus (B)."[70] For that reason, a detailed assessment of scribal proclivity must be compared against the prestigious heritage of this manuscript to better discern the legacy it leaves behind.

---

65. For a helpful history behind the transition from the term "late Alexandrian" prior to Westcott and Hort to the more recent "secondary Alexandrian," see Carlo M. Martini, "Is There a Late Alexandrian Text of the Gospels?" NTS 24 (1978): 285–96.
66. This date and type are affirmed in Metzger and Ehrman, Text of the New Testament, 77; and Aland and Aland, Text of the New Testament, 334–35.
67. For a quantitative analysis and subsequent profile of Codex Regius, see Aland and Aland, Text of the New Testament, 332–37. For more details regarding the signifi-cance and limitations of this method, see Colwell, "Genealogical Method," 109–33; Colwell, "Significance of Grouping," 73–92.
68. See Aland and Aland, Text of the New Testament, 332–37. Fee noted this in his analysis of Origen's text (Gordon D. Fee, "Origen's Text of the New Testament and the Text of Egypt," NTS 28 (1982): 350). Elsewhere, he also showed how L, 33, and Cyril, considered neutral texts, have begun to assimilate the character of standard Byzantine readings (Gordon D. Fee, "The Text of John in Origen and Cyril of Alex-andria: A Contribution to Methodology in the Recovery and Analysis of Patristic Citations," Bib 52 (1971): 370–71).
69. Martini, "Late Alexandrian Text," 291.
70. Metzger and Ehrman, Text of the New Testament, 277. For further support, see Parker, Living Text, 83.

Matthew P. Morgan

Codex Freerianus (W [032-S])

Codex W (032), as a whole, is considered to be a late fourth- or early fifth-century manuscript representing the "Western" order of the Gospels (Matthew, John, Luke, Mark).[71] According to Metzger and Ehrman, "The type of text is curiously variegated, as though copied from several manuscripts of different families of text."[72] Regarding John 1.1, Metzger and Ehrman also noted, "The text of John 1.1–5.11, which fills a quire that was added about the seventh century, presumably to replace one that was damaged, is mixed, with some Alexandrian and a few Western readings."[73] Significant is the recognition that this opening portion of John's Gospel was the creation of a different scribe during a later time period than the remainder of the manuscript. Similarly, the IGNT clearly distinguishes this portion as supplemental (032-S). Although Sanders proposed a rather elaborate reconstruction, dating John 1.1–5.11 before the remainder of the manuscript,[74] most scholars

---

71. Metzger and Ehrman, *Text of the New Testament*, 80; NA[27]. The *Kurzgefasste Liste* is more specific in dating the MS in the fifth century (Kurt Aland, *Kurzgefasste Liste der griechischen Handschriften des Neuen Testaments* [Berlin: Walter De Gruyter, 1963], 40). Sanders went even further, dating all but John 1–5.11 no later than the fifth century and probably in the fourth century due to the Diocletian persecutions in 303 (Henry A. Sanders and Freer Gallery of Art, *The New Testament Manuscripts of the Freer Collection* [New York: Macmillan, 1918], 135–39; Henry A. Sanders, *Facsimile of the Washington Manuscript of the Four Gospels in the Freer Collection, with an Introduction by Henry A. Sanders*, copy 390 of 435 [Ann Arbor, MI: University of Michigan, 1912], v).
72. Metzger and Ehrman, *Text of the New Testament*, 80; cf. also Sanders, *New Testament Manuscripts*, 133.
73. Metzger and Ehrman, *Text of the New Testament*, 80.
74. Sanders, *New Testament Manuscripts*, 134–39. One reason for this chronological placement is the omission of John 5.12 in the later witnesses Γ (036 [tenth century]) and Λ (039 [ninth century]), which he attributed to a relationship with the parent document that this quire is replacing (128–30, 136). The freshness of the superscription on the first page compared with the rest of the writing (136), as well as the low quire number (137), contribute to his view that the first page of the MS "probably did not include Matthew and may have contained only John" (137). Later, he pointed to various peculiarities (e.g., enlarged letters, punctuation, and ornamental dots) from the first quire that are also found throughout the MS (139). Thus he concluded, "The first quire of John is slightly older than the rest of the MS" (139). However, this explanation is unwarranted for four reasons. First, arguing for an early date on the basis of a connection with later MSS (Γ, Λ) is inconclusive at best. Second, it is implausible that a scribe who apparently rewrote the rest of the Gospels *by copying other fragmentary texts* would wrap four Gospels around one quire and would *not* rewrite that one quire. If such was his pattern for the rest of the MS—as Sanders himself articulated—why would he not rewrite the quire at the beginning of John? (This idea was proposed by Daniel B. Wallace during a review of the paper on which this chapter is based [February 24, 2009].) Third, the various common traits can also indicate harmonization with the larger portion of the MS, rather than a core around which the rest of the MS was crafted (this idea was first

do not find this argument tenable.[75] Instead, a more plausible view considers John 1.1–5.11 to be "a later (probably eighth-century) replacement quire that bears no relation to the rest of the manuscript and made up for the (presumably) lost original portion."[76] Therefore, until further evidence can be provided, the assessment of Royse and Goodspeed should be adopted, dating W^S to sometime in the eighth century.[77]

Given an eighth-century date for W^S, its production falls within the same general time frame as Codex Regius. So how does this close chronological connection influence the possible relationship between these two manuscripts? It is at least plausible to suggest that their story is intertwined in some way. In fact, could their harmony in John 1.1c serve as the lone remnants of an earlier Sabellian ancestor?

Codex Regius's Scribal Profile

A collation of John's Gospel in Regius against the Robinson-Pierpont Majority Text (2005)[78] produced a total of 1,321 variants. From this virtual sea of evidence, a total of 209 (15.8%) singular readings remain, but if we remove insignificant orthographic fluctuations,[79] the field narrows to 145 variants (11%) worthy of more detailed consideration.[80] Within the confines of these 145 unique recordings lays

---

presented by J. Bruce Prior in a personal email on February 20, 2008). Fourth, the presence of various lengthening devices on the last page of the first quire cause it to strategically end at 5.11. This points to a later, rather than earlier, creation (J. Bruce Prior, email, February 20, 2008).

75. E.g., see Metzger and Ehrman, *Text of the New Testament*, 80–81; James R. Royse, "The Corrections in the Freer Gospels Codex," in *The Freer Biblical Manuscripts: Fresh Studies of an American Treasure Trove*, ed. Larry W. Hurtado (Atlanta: Society of Biblical Literature, 2006), 186; Edgar J. Goodspeed, "The Freer Gospels," *AJT* 17 (1913): 599.

76. Royse, "Corrections in the Freer Gospels," 186.

77. Goodspeed, "Freer Gospels," 599.

78. Robinson and Pierpont, *New Testament in the Original Greek*.

79. The most common orthographic fluctuations involved changing ι to η in 16 instances. So μαρτυρια is spelled μαρτυρηα in John 8.13, John 10.31 has λιθασωσιν as λιθασωσην, and φοινικων is spelled φοινηκων in John 12.13. The change from ε to αι occurred 12 times. So με is written μαι in John 1.33, and ημεραις is spelled ημαιραις in John 2.19. The inverse of both these alterations were equally popular, but the replacement of ω with ο frequently produced singular readings (5). Thus ουπω reads ουπο in John 7.30, and two changes are found in John 17.2, with καθως written as καθος and εδωκας spelled εδοκας.

80. For an extensive discussion of the issues and complexity of orthographic errors, see Chrys C. Caragounis, *The Development of Greek and the New Testament: Morphology, Syntax, Phonology, and Textual Transmission* (Grand Rapids: Baker Academic, 2006), 339–96, 475–564. Not only is the issue difficult due to our limited understanding and historical distance from the Koine Greek language, but the common acceptance of "itacisms" makes determining a unique spelling like finding a needle in a haystack. Therefore, these variants will not be included in the

Matthew P. Morgan

the legacy of the scribe who produced Codex Regius. More specifically, they illuminate any potential theological motivation that might permeate the transmission process.[81]

Regius's Copying of Units

One component of the scribal profile is the method of copying observed in the singular readings. Given the later date of the manuscript and the high number of orthographic mistakes, it seems probable that Regius was the product of a scriptorium.[82] In addition, this scribe appears to have copied one or two letters at a time, in short syllables, rather than words or phrases. This conclusion is sustained by the pattern of errors, with over half (88 [60.7%]) involving a single letter, while a significantly smaller number (17 [11.7%]) take place at the syllable level.[83]

---

general pool of singular readings but will be reserved to support other conclusions along the way. For a defense of this approach, see Royse, "Scribal Tendencies," 239. Also see T. C. Skeat, "The Use of Dictation in Ancient Book Production," in *The Collected Biblical Writings of T. C. Skeat*, ed. J. K. Elliott, Supplements to Novum Testamentum 113 (Leiden: Brill, 2004), 3–32.

81. Royse, *Scribal Habits*, 51–56.

82. Certainly the date of this manuscript makes its production in a scriptorium more likely, since that became the standard method when Christianity became the national religion in the fourth century (Royse, *Scribal Habits*, 29–30; Metzger and Ehrman, *Text of the New Testament*, 25–30). It also falls prior to the ninth century, when evidence of stricter controls in the monastic community, including severe punishment for careless errors, began to occur (Metzger and Ehrman, *Text of the New Testament*, 30). With regard to Codex Regius, the volume of nonsense readings involving orthographic confusion lends support to this conclusion, since there are a large number of orthographic mistakes that produce lexically viable words that make no sense in context. E.g., in John 17.14, εισιν has become ησιν. Likewise, there are seven instances where τις is mistakenly written της, producing nonsense in the context (2.25; 3.3, 5; 6.51; 7.20; 16.30; 21.12). As these test cases reveal, it appears as though the scribe only hears the letters either in his head or in a scriptorium and then hurriedly tries to reproduce them in short syllables. Furthermore, if the copy was produced by sight, we should expect fewer cases where orthographic confusion produces a lexically viable word. The conditions described here fit Skeat's argument for dictation (Skeat, "Dictation," 25). The virtual absence of unique transpositions can also be explained by a scribe who was copying in units of letters and/or syllables. Based on the nature of his orthographic mistakes, our general impression is that this manuscript was copied orally in a scriptorium.

83. A handful of phrases (4) are not listed here. In terms of total variants, the second largest grouping is words (36). At first glance, this would seem to go against the assertion that this scribe was copying short units by sound. However, in the sorting of the data, there were a number of instances where a variant was counted as a word when it could also be classified as a syllable. E.g., there were 8 additions involving a word. Of these 8 singular readings, 6 consisted of three or less letters. Similarly, 6 of the 7 omissions classified as a word involved variants containing three or fewer letters. Therefore, it seems that many of the word variants function phonetically like syllables but are considered words due to their syntactical function.

Matthew P. Morgan

This tendency is further reinforced by the large volume and quality of orthographic variations found throughout this manuscript.[84] As the statistical dust settles, Regius's scribe emerges as one whose distinctives are most often shown in either a letter or a single syllable.

Corruption Trends and Observations

With a better grasp of the copying methods, it is necessary to stage the camera over the shoulder of our scribe and observe his tendencies. Figure 3.1 gives a breakdown of the major categories into which his singular readings fall.

FIGURE 3.1: BREAKDOWN OF REGIUS'S SINGULAR READINGS	
Substitutions	62 (29.7%)
Transpositions	2 (1.0%)
Additions	23 (11.0%)
Omissions	58 (27.8%)
Orthographic[85]	64 (30.6%)

For a manuscript filled with "many ignorant blunders,"[86] the presence of only two transpositions is striking; yet it further confirms the probability that this particular scribe possessed a limited grasp of Greek grammar and was so focused on short sounds that he almost never alters the order. In addition, these adjustments to word order can best be explained by a skipping of the initial word, which was then added back later.[87]

At this point, the scribal story behind Codex Regius is beginning to emerge. Understanding the scribal proclivities and activities that distinguish our main figure, we can now proceed to the story within the story.

---

84. Significant in Regius are 94 singular readings produced purely by the confusion of vowel sounds. Furthermore, in approximately 30 instances, this phonetic variation produces a valid Greek word that makes absolutely no sense in the context.
85. Purely orthographic variants listed here are those where a common vowel substitution has occurred but the meaning and intention of the word is clearly the same.
86. Metzger and Ehrman, *Text of the New Testament*, 77.
87. The two instances found in Regius's copy of John appear within a span of four verses (John 6.23, 27), so the close proximity of these variants may suggest that the scribe was getting rather weary at this point or had his concentration disrupted for a period of time.

Matthew P. Morgan

For this particular scribe, does the meat of his textual transmission indicate a theological legacy or legend?

Quality of Transmission

A critical look at both the integrity and motivations behind the frequency and distribution of errors reveals the potential for theological variants. Those readings whose nature and character reveal no careless, transcriptional errors may be our window into the theological world of our scribe.

The first step in the analysis is to examine the quantity and type of "nonsense" readings evident in Codex Regius. Metzger and Ehrman have already speculated that a fair number of singular readings would fit this category, but the actual data are overwhelming. Of the 145 singular readings, 87 (60%) are guilty of producing nonsense on the written page. Figure 3.2 represents a detailed breakdown.

FIGURE 3.2: BREAKDOWN OF REGIUS'S NONSENSE SINGULAR READINGS	
Substitutions	18 (20%)
Transpositions	0
Additions	17 (20%)
Omissions	52 (60%)

Clearly our scribe was prone to erratic behavior with regard to letters, particularly orthographic confusion. This serves as the primary culprit behind many of these nonsensical variants. For example, in John 6.22, the article τη becomes τι, so that the temporal phrase "on the next day" (τῇ ἐπαύριον) becomes the contextually nonsensical question "What tomorrow?" (τί ἐπαύριον). Similarly, in John 3.18, the adverb ηδη becomes the subjunctive verb ιδη according to Regius. This variant turns the temporal statement of judgment "condemned already" (ἤδη κέκριται) into "he would see he is condemned" (ἴδη κέκριται).[88] More evidence could be brought forward, but it should suffice here to say that in the copying of short words (e.g., prepositions, relative pronouns, articles, etc.), orthographic mistakes that produce nonsense in the word written on the page abound. A similar wildness is also evident in the substitution of words. Thus, in John 5.2, "five porticoes" (πέντε στοάς) becomes "five mouth" (πέντε στόμα).

---

88. The reading of Regius does not mean "he would see *that* he is condemned," which would require something like ἴδη ἑαυτὸν κέκρισθαι.

In fairness to this scribe, several of his readings do reflect more deliberation and thought. For example, John 8.20 seems to be a clear instance of harmonization. In this case, the pluperfect "it had come" (ἐληλύθει) is modified to the aorist "it came" (ἦλθεν) to match the tense of the previous verb (ἐπίασεν). However, the most intriguing variant in John's Gospel occurs in 12.34, where "this saying" (ὁ λόγος οὗτος) replaces "the son of man" (ὁ υἱὸς τοῦ ἀνθρώπου).[89]

As we saw earlier, this scribe's primary characteristic is the production of variants when dealing with individual letters. A detailed breakdown of all the singular omissions and additions (in figs. 3.3 and 3.4) confirms this observation.

FIGURE 3.3: BREAKDOWN OF REGIUS' S OMISSIONS BY TYPE	
Letters	45 (78.9%)
Syllables	5 (8.8%)
Words	7 (12.3%)

FIGURE 3.4: BREAKDOWN OF REGIUS' S ADDITIONS BY TYPE	
Letters	10 (43.5%)
Syllables	5 (21.7%)
Words	8 (34.8%)

When weighed on the basis of these variants' contribution to the sense of a passage, virtually all of them make little to no contribution. For instance, the only omissions that ever produce a significant reading are those that consist of, at least, a syllable or, more typically, a word. When it comes to omitting individual letters, *the scribe of Codex Regius is unable to produce a single sensical reading in 45 instances.* In fact, some of these blunders are so bad they are laughable. Thus, in John 1.30, he wrote "after me comes air" (ὀπίσω μου ἔρχεται ἀήρ) for "after me comes a man" (ὀπίσω μου ἔρχεται ἀνήρ). On another occasion, in John 8.45, he changes the conjunction "that" (ὅτι) to "the" (ὁ), which even Tischendorf labels "careless" (*ex incuria excidit*).[90] As for additions, *the only case in all 55 of this scribe's singular readings where*

---

89. See "Variant Analysis in Christologically Significant Passages" below.
90. Tischendorf[8], *Novum Testamentum Graece*, loc. cit.

a single letter produces a potentially meaningful variant is in John 1.1c,[91] *in the case of the article with* θεός.

Given the carelessness of the scribe, it seems likely that any textual variant involving a single letter is an ignorant blunder.[92] The addition of a single letter, the article with θεός, does create a sensical reading, but as Hort recognized,

> Singular readings which make good sense and therefore need imply no clerical error, but which might also be easily explained as due to a kind of clerical error already fixed upon the scribe by undoubted examples, are rendered by the presence of possible clerical error as *versa causa* more doubtful than they would otherwise be.[93]

In the end, the claim that ὁ θεός somehow preserved a Sabellian exemplar appears to contain more legend than legacy; our scribe has no proclivity for premeditated theological alterations. Instead, he is just incapable of the skill and care necessary to make such a fine distinction in a single letter.

Variant Analysis in Christologically Significant Passages

For the majority of the Christologically significant variants in John's Gospel, the testimony is completely unified. At most, only one singular reading in Codex Regius has any Christological bearing.[94] Thus, both in the classic proof texts for Sabellians, John 10.30 along with 14.9–11, and in the other Christological bookend to the Gospel,[95] John 20.28, no singular or subsingular readings were created by the scribe of Regius.[96]

---

91. Two other instances involving syllables, John 5.3 and 7.8, produce sensical variants. However, in John 5.3, the addition of the article το before πληθος is arguably nonsense, because it creates awkward grammar in the relationship of this noun to the following anarthrous adjective (πολυ). In John 7.8, the addition of και at the beginning of the verse is an insignificant variation.

92. Metzger and Ehrman, *Text of the New Testament*, 77.

93. Westcott and Hort, *New Testament in the Original Greek*, 233.

94. In John 12.34, Codex Regius reads "this saying" (ὁ λόγος οὗτος) instead of "this son of man" (οὗτος ὁ υἱὸς τοῦ ἀνθρώπου). One possible explanation is harmonization with John 7.36, which also contains the phrase τίς ἐστιν ὁ λόγος οὗτος (much thanks to Dr. Hall Harris III for his input on the use of this expression in John's Gospel).

95. Several scholars have noted the *inclusio* formed by John 1.1 and 20.28: see Raymond E. Brown, *The Gospel according to John*, vol. 1, *I–XII*, Anchor Bible (Garden City, NY: Doubleday, 1966), 5; William Loader, *The Christology of the Fourth Gospel: Structure and Issues* (New York: Peter Lang, 1989), 167; Hurtado, *Lord Jesus Christ*, 369.

96. There is a variant in John 20.28 involving the omission of the article with the divine name θεός, which Tischendorf listed in two witnesses (D, 46ᵉᵛ). Though Ehrman called this an "anti-Patripassianist corruption" (*Orthodox Corruption*, 266), he still affirmed that John 10.30 and 20.28 were key texts that speak of Jesus deity (Bart D.

An assessment of the theological legacy or legend in Codex L would be incomplete without examining John 1.18, where the external evidence is more evenly divided. There, three different textual options appear, which have been proposed as a chronologically linked progression of theologically motivated changes.[97] A detailed treatment of this textual problem is not fitting here,[98] but figure 3.5 highlights a possible theological progression and the motivations that generated different readings.

FIGURE 3.5: POSSIBLE PROGRESSION OF VARIANT READINGS IN JOHN 1:18[99]	
ORIGINAL:[100]	ὁ μονογενὴς υἱός
FIRST CORRUPTION:[101]	ὁ μονογενὴς θεός (anti-adoptionistic)
SECOND CORRUPTION:[102]	μονογενὴς θεός (anti-Sabellian *found in L*)

If this reconstruction is correct, the following alternatives about Regius's scribe emerge:

1. the scribe holds inconsistent theology,
2. he faithfully copies a conflicted *Vorlage*, or
3. he is completely ignorant of its theological significance.

Ehrman, *Misquoting Jesus: The Story behind Who Changed the Bible and Why* [San Francisco: HarperSanFrancisco, 2005], 161).

97. Ehrman, *Orthodox Corruption*, 265–66; Ehrman, *Misquoting Jesus*, 161–62.

98. For a detailed discussion, see Kenneth Willis Clark, "The Text of the Gospel of John in Third-Century Egypt," *NovT* 5 (1962): 19–20; Murray J. Harris, *Jesus as God: The New Testament Use of Theos in Reference to Jesus* (Grand Rapids: Baker, 1992), 74–83; Stratton L. Ladewig, "An Examination of the Orthodoxy of the Variants in Light of Bart Ehrman's *The Orthodox Corruption of Scripture*" (ThM thesis, Dallas Theological Seminary, 2000), 1–80; Raymond E. Brown, *Jesus: God and Man* (Milwaukee: Bruce, 1967), 12–13; Paul R. McReynolds, "John 1:18 in Textual Variation and Translation," in *New Testament Textual Criticism: Its Significance for Exegesis: Essays in Honour of Bruce M. Metzger*, ed. Eldon Jay Epp and Gordon D. Fee (New York: Oxford University Press, 1981), 105–18; Bart D. Ehrman, Gordon D. Fee, and Michael W. Holmes, *Text of the Fourth Gospel*, 60 n. 12; Bart D. Ehrman, "Heracleon and the 'Western' Textual Tradition," *NTS* 40 (1994): 166.

99. This table does not reflect the view of the author but shows the possible progression of variants as proposed by Bart Ehrman (*Orthodox Corruption*, 265–66; *Misquoting Jesus*, 161–62).

100. Witnesses for this reading are A C³ Wˢ ᐩΘ Ψ 𝔐 *f*¹, ¹³ lat syrᶜ, ʰ.

101. Witnesses for this reading are 𝔓⁷⁵ ℵ¹ 33 *pc*.

102. Witnesses for this reading are 𝔓⁶⁶ ℵ* B C* syrʰᵐᵍ.

Assuming intentionality in L's alterations in John 1.18, the singular reading ὁ θεός in John 1.1c potentially represents a *pro*-Sabellian Christology. Yet in the span of only seventeen verses, the same person produces an equally motivated *anti*-Sabellian reading in John 1.18. Given the history of textual changes in 1.18, the potential for theological influence on the transmissional process is much greater due to the early manuscript evidence;[103] but if 1.18 is our window into the *Vorlage* of Regius, we should expect a text that has removed any hint of Sabellian influence. Consequently, it is unlikely that an internal theological conflict existed in the exemplar of L, eliminating the preceding option 2.

Thus the origin of this variant lies squarely on the shoulders of this eighth-century scribe. This brings us back to two possible explanations: either his personal motivations were easily conflicted, or he was oblivious to the theological implications of the reading he produced. When combined with his general ineptitude regarding individual letters, *the best explanation for the addition of the article in John 1.1c once again lies in a careless mistake on the part of the scribe rather than in any theological predisposition.*

In retelling the story of Codex Regius from the standpoint of scribal habits, with special attention given to theological motivations, all roads lead to a common destination: *the reading* καὶ ὁ θεὸς ἦν ὁ λόγος *stands as the exception to every identifiable pattern of behavior (i.e., singular readings and theologically significant variants) in this entire eighth-century manuscript's transmission of John's Gospel.*

Codex Freerianus's Scribal Profile

Although somewhat obscure over the last hundred years,[104] the additional witness preserved in the replacement quire of Codex Freerianus (only John 1.1–5.11) forms another story within the textual history of John 1.1c. The limited length and scope of this quire makes the discovery of detailed scribal behavior more difficult; however, given its chronological relationship to Codex Regius, it is important to analyze how these stories intersect. The primary avenue for this investigation is the subsingular readings shared only by L and W^S, along with other textual variants involving a few key witnesses (e.g., ℵ [01] B [03] $\mathfrak{P}^{66}$ $\mathfrak{P}^{75}$ etc.).[105] From this angle, we can explore the degree of dependence

---

103. Ehrman also stresses this point (*Orthodox Corruption*, 271 n. 23) to show the certainty of an early third-century date corresponding to the time period when this heresy was prominent (see Figure 3.5).

104. See the appendix at the end of this chapter for a survey of the history of W^S in the critical editions.

105. This investigation does not perform a detailed quantitative analysis but provides a simple exploration of the 53 instances where both L and W^S agree against the

between these two documents and the likelihood that their combined witness has legitimate roots extending back to the early Sabellian controversies. Five key points emerge:

1.   A look at the subsingular readings involving only Codex L and Codex W^S reveals that John 1.1c is the only *meaningful* variant produced exclusively in both manuscripts.[106] Even though W^S does not contain a large portion of John's Gospel, it is striking that there are no other places where a sensical variant is recorded only in these eighth-century witnesses. Furthermore, that none of these variants can even be found in the apparatus of NA^{27}/UBS^4 casts further doubt on the quality of their legacy. This lack of overlap also demonstrates that *these readings are isolated and not derived from one another.*

2.   There are 50 variants where L and W^S join forces against the MT. A good majority of these (42 [84%]) involve some relationship to the key witnesses ℵ (01) and B (03).[107] The strong presence of ℵ and B (25 variants [60%])[108] in places where these manuscripts intersect is striking. As was noted earlier, both of these are parental figures in the Alexandrian heritage for Codex L.[109] Combined with Metzger and Ehrman's analysis that W^S contains some Alexandrian and Western readings,[110] these variants probably represent the common Alexandrian ancestry shared by both eighth-century manuscripts.

---

reading of the Robinson-Pierpont Majority Text (2005). This group of variants in John 1:1–5:11 produced some patterns that provide clues to possible relationships with other MSS. From these initial observations, a more thorough profile of both L and W^S in John's Gospel is necessary to gain greater confidence in textual relationships that may exist for these particular MSS.

106. There are a total of 4 subsingular readings, but the other 3 (John 1.19, 39, 47) all involve insignificant orthographic variants: απεστειλαν is spelled απεστιλαν by both L and W^S in John 1.19, οψεσθε is spelled οψεσθαι in John 1.39, and 1.47 replaces ιδε with ειδε.

107. Though orthographic variants were included in the analysis of subsingular readings shared by L and W^S, they have been thrown out for the remainder of the discussion, as they do not further our understanding of the relationship between MSS (cf. n. 105). Therefore, the total number of variants where L and W^S stand against the tide of the MT is 50.

108. These statistics do not reflect a pure quantitative analysis or family profile but denote how frequently ℵ and B both agree with L and W^S against the MT.

109. This observation is all the more striking given Fee's conclusion that ℵ's text type found in John 1–8 is primarily Western, based on its frequent alignment with D [06] (Gordon D. Fee, "Codex Sinaiticus in the Gospel of John," *NTS* 15 [1968–69]: 23–44). This snapshot seems to show that L and W^S find agreement through a different gene pool than the predominantly Western character of ℵ. In fact, there was not a single alignment of L and W^S against the MT where the witness D [06] was involved. Therefore, it is difficult to see how there is any Western influence on variants where our two MSS argue against the MT.

110. Metzger and Ehrman, *Text of the New Testament*, 80.

3.   Looking at these 50 variants from another vantage point, there are 19 instances where both L and W^S find support from a broader range of early manuscripts in their agreement against the MT.[111] Within this demographic, 12 instances (63%) involve the early Alexandrian witness B (03). There are also 10 (53%) that are supported by the papyri tandem of $\mathfrak{P}^{66}$ and $\mathfrak{P}^{75}$, with 3 others containing at least one of these early papyri.[112] From the standpoint of quality, less than half (9) attest to the accepted reading in the NA^{27} text.[113] Digging deeper into the accepted readings, 5 contain the triad of B $\mathfrak{P}^{66}$ $\mathfrak{P}^{75}$,[114] but *all* include at least B. At the same time, 5 (28%) of the variants in this category went *against* the reading supported by ℵ (01).[115]

4.   There are 23 instances where the reading of W^S appears with a *few* other witnesses.[116] Within this grouping, 6 were included in the NA^{27} text, and all were no doubt adopted due to the presence of more noble ancestry (ℵ B C D $\mathfrak{P}^{66}$ $\mathfrak{P}^{75}$).[117] There were 8 readings attested only in MSS dating from the eighth century or later.[118] From this entourage, there was not a single reading warranting inclusion in the NA^{27} text. The observation that W^S cannot stand without help from other early Alexandrian or Western witnesses deals a critical blow to the possibility that its reading in John 1.1c preserves a unique legacy from early in the manuscript tradition.

5.   A survey of the variants in this replacement quire for W revealed two nonsense errors involving *nomina sacra* of the divine names. In John 4.24, the articular *nomen sacrum* for θεός was written οϲ rather than ο θϲ. Similarly, in the next verse, 4.25, Χριστός was spelled χρ instead of χϲ. Then, in 4.48, the article was removed from Ἰησοῦς, producing a singular reading in W^S. Similarly, at the end of the quire, 5.12, the

---

111. John 1.19, 20, 37, 49*bis*; 2.15*bis*, 18; 3.3, 4; 4.1, 5, 34, 36, 37, 38, 45, 52; 5.10.
112. Of the 12 readings attested by B, 6 of them are supported by both $\mathfrak{P}^{66}$ and $\mathfrak{P}^{75}$ as well.
113. John 1.49; 2.18; 3.3; 4.34, 36, 37, 45, 52.
114. The three exceptions are John 2.18, 4.37, and 4.52.
115. John 1.49*bis*; 3.3; 4.36, 37. It is interesting to note that John 1.49 plays a significant role in the articulation and development of Colwell's rule (E. C. Colwell, "A Definite Rule for the Use of the Article in the Greek New Testament," *JBL* 52 [1933]: 12–21, esp. 13).
116. John 1.44; 2.4, 17, 24; 3.21, 23, 28; 4.14, 17, 23, 25, 27, 30, 31, 35, 42*bis*, 43, 46; 5.2, 9, 11*bis*.
117. John 3.23; 4.14, 25, 42, 43, 46. All of these readings contain at least 2 of the 6 witnesses previously listed, and 2 of them (John 4.25, 43) appear in 5 of the 6 witnesses.
118. John 1.44; 2.4, 24; 3.21; 4.17, 27, 35, 42. The variant in 1.44 is the most interesting. It involves the omission of the article ο with the proper name Φίλιππος and is only supported by the corrector of Codex F (09) and Codex 047, which are dated in the ninth and eighth centuries, respectively. The substitution in 3.21 changes from εστιν to εισιν only in W^S and Ψ (044), which are both late witnesses.

entire verse 12 is missing to make a clean fit with the adjoining section of the book. Though limited, these tendencies further the notion that the scribe of this quire was not cautious when copying the divine name. Such a trait casts further doubt on the credibility of his legacy contained in John 1.1c.

In conclusion, this survey of the quality and type of readings found in W^S affirms three important things pertaining to Codex Regius and John 1.1c:

1. There is no evidence to establish a *direct relationship* between these two eighth-century manuscripts. As a result, the occurrences of the article with θεός found in John 1.1c in both MSS should be considered isolated readings.

2. Alignment of Codex L and W^S never merits inclusion in the accepted text of NA^{27} *without support* from other key MSS (ℵ B C D 𝔓^{66} 𝔓^{75}).

3. There are *no known instances* where a combination of W^S with a single other witness finds credibility as a potentially "original" reading.

Therefore, the inclusion of W^S as a subsingular reading in John 1.1c does not negate the egregious nature of the scribal behavior in Codex L, and it further demonstrates that this combination possesses insufficient testimony to consider the reading καὶ ὁ θεὸς ἦν ὁ λόγος to be a plausible original.

The Impact of Scribal Behavior on the Variant in John 1.1c

Despite the lengthy and often complex stories of Codices Regius and Freerianus, the possible conclusions are more straightforward. Does the tale of these two eighth-century manuscripts and the scribes that produced them point to a rich, almost extinct theological legacy or to an innocent blunder mistaken as a theological legend? The answer lies in the individual scribes and the potential relationship between these two ancient documents.

In the case of Codex Regius, we entered the world of its scribe to determine whether this variant faithfully reflects an earlier original or finds its origin in a mindless slip of the scribe's pen. Describing the possibilities, Hort noted, "One MS will transmit a substantially pure text disfigured by the blunders of a careless scribe, another will reproduce a deeply adulterated text with smooth faultlessness."[119] For the scribe of

---

119. Westcott and Hort, *New Testament in the Original Greek*, 36.

Matthew P. Morgan

Codex Regius, the addition of a single letter fits the description of his most common blunders like a glove. So, although a theological reading seems legitimate on the surface, placing this variant in the company of similar variants exposes its careless character. As a result, the addition of the article in John 1.1c in Regius faithfully preserves the story of a scribe whose wildness desecrated the purity of his exemplar, rather than an early Sabellian legacy.

The story of John 1.1c in Codex Regius becomes more complex with the addition of W^S as a witness. Outside of John 1.1c, there is not a single meaningful variant found only in L and W^S. Also, the textual reliability of these eighth-century manuscripts is weak at best, requiring reinforcement by multiple witnesses, particularly the pillars of the manuscript tradition ($\aleph$ B C D $\mathfrak{P}^{66}$ $\mathfrak{P}^{75}$). Although the story of the article's origin in W^S remains somewhat obscure, it has no demonstrable relationship to the transmission of Regius, and its ability to reflect a pristine early text is irrevocably marred by its company with the equally late and poorly copied Regius text.

THE GRAMMATICAL VIABILITY
OF THE TEXTUAL VARIANT IN JOHN 1.1C

The History and Significance of Colwell's Rule in John 1.1c

At times, the heavy clouds of history seem to restrict the clarity and definitiveness of the story preserved in Codices L and W^S, but a look at the grammatical character of the variant καὶ ὁ θεὸς ἦν ὁ λόγος goes a long way in removing the fog. The rationale for this approach can be found in the opening remarks of Middleton's magnum opus on the Greek article:

> The student in Theology cannot fail to have remarked, that the exposition of various passages of the New Testament is by Commentators made to depend on the presence or the absence of the Article in the Greek original.[120]

When dealing with the text of John 1.1c, the weight of Middleton's comments has been shown in the wealth of scholarship that has sought to understand the meaning of the anarthrous θεός. The foremost concern of previous grammatical analysis has been in determining whether this noun should have a qualitative, definite, or indefinite force. As a result, few have addressed the significance of the preverbal anarthrous predicate

---

120. T. F. Middleton, *The Doctrine of the Greek Article*, ed. J. Scholefield, 2nd ed. (Cambridge: J. and J. J. Deighton, 1841), xii.

construction with regard to the textual problem in John 1.1c.[121] By adding the article, this reading makes both the subject and the predicate explicitly definite. Semantically, it also places the two nouns in a convertible proposition that would explicitly support a Sabellian or modalistic theology.[122]

The modest goal in this section is twofold: first, to determine how the grammar and semantics of predicate nominative constructions in the NT relate to the presence or lack of the article; second, to scrutinize the grammatical viability of the specific textual variant found in our two eighth-century manuscripts. As a result, normative grammatical patterns will be used to shed light on the potential legacy of the article in the two manuscript testimonies.

An Examination of Predicate Nominative Constructions Using Εἰμί in the New Testament

Since it was first published, [123] Colwell's rule has received much criticism due to some serious methodological flaws in its formulation.[124] Appropriately, the approach taken here will first categorize the use of numerous predicate nominatives in the NT on the basis of word order and the inclusion or omission of the article. Once the usage has been arranged according to these factors, it will be further evaluated in terms of the type of proposition it creates, either subset or convertible. The final analysis will then seek to compare the viability of both variants in John 1.1c on the basis of normative usage in the NT.

The Methods and Limitations of this Study

This study will only examine predicate nominative constructions that occur with the verb εἰμί.[125] Excluded from the present treatment is the force (e.g., qualitative, indefinite, definite) of the predicate

---

121. Philip B. Harner, "Qualitative Anarthrous Predicate Nouns: Mark 15:39 and John 1:1," *JBL* 92 (1973): 85. Harner noted this variant in Codex L but quickly dismissed it on the basis of the theological contradiction it poses with 1.1b.

122. Robertson, *Grammar of the Greek New Testament*, 767–68.

123. Colwell, "Definite Rule," 12–21.

124. For a detailed history of Colwell's rule in NT studies, see Matthew P. Morgan, "The Legacy of a Letter: Sabellianism or Scribal Blunder in John 1:1c?" (ThM thesis, Dallas Theological Seminary, May 2009), 53–69.

125. Other verbs that utilize predicate nominative constructions are γίνομαι, ὑπάρχω, and εὑρίσκω, along with the passive form of the verbs οἰκοδομέω, ὀνομάζω, καλέω, and ἑρμηνεύω. Of these verbs, BDAG only explicitly mentions the use of predicate nominatives with the passive form of ὀνομάζω (ad loc.), although the examples listed with the passive of καλέω (ad loc.) also show its use of the predicate nominative. However, due to length and scope (John 1.1c), these were not considered at this point.

nominative as a primary factor in the presence of the article. In addition, it will largely ignore cases where the equative verb occurs with relative pronouns and proper names, since they do not directly apply to the situation in John 1.1c. Although some consideration will be given to other semantic influences on the article (e.g., monadic nouns, genitive modifiers, etc.), word order and function (i.e., subject versus predicate) will form the structure of this investigation.

Overview of Predicate Nominative Constructions Using Εἰμί in the New Testament

Postverbal Anarthrous Constructions[126]

For the purposes of the present study, this structural category has no bearing on either the nature or the semantics of the readings in question. Though there are a fair number of instances in the NT (53), the fact that ὁ λόγος is uncontested among known manuscripts removes its voice from the grammatical discussion of John 1.1c. In addition, the lack of the article with the predicate produces fertile soil for subset, rather than convertible, propositions.[127]

Preverbal Arthrous Constructions[128]

If ὁ θεός in John 1.1c functions as the predicate nominative,[129] it should conform to normative patterns of other preverbal arthrous predicates in the NT. There are at least two instances (Matt 6.22; Luke 11.4) that would seem to affirm the possibility of a postverbal articular subject

---

126. For a more detailed analysis, see Morgan, "Legacy of a Letter," 36–37, 70.

127. Daniel B. Wallace, *Greek Grammar Beyond the Basics: An Exegetical Syntax of the New Testament* (Grand Rapids: Zondervan, 1996, 41–46. Wallace stated that a convertible proposition occurs "when both substantives meet one of the three qualifications for S" (Wallace, *Exegetical Syntax*, 45). Since one of the criteria for determining the subject is the presence of the article, it is often the case that the predicate will be anarthrous. In instances where this occurs, the most likely semantic relationship is a subset proposition where the predicate "describes the class to which the subject belongs" (Wallace, *Exegetical Syntax*, 41). Within this category, just over half of the qualified applicants fit this caricature by forming subset relationships.

128. For a more detailed analysis, see Morgan, "Legacy of a Letter," 37–39, 70.

129. Based on well-documented rules (Lane C. McGaughy, *Toward a Descriptive Analysis of ʾEINAI as a Linking Verb in New Testament Greek*, SBL Dissertation Series 6 (Missoula, MT: Society of Biblical Literature for the Linguistics Seminar, 1972), 53–54), this condition would not be the case. However, as will be argued later, this is not a viable option for other reasons. Its treatment here accommodates those who would label it as predicate in order to avoid even greater problems that arise when ὁ θεός becomes the subject.

(ὁ λόγος). However, this support dwindles to only one unique case containing other influential factors that best explain the arthrous predicate.[130] Furthermore, in keeping with less debatable examples,[131] the preferred placement of ὁ λόγος would be before the verb, with the predicate ὁ θεός on the same side.[132]

Looking at the semantic situation, *every* instance involving a nominative subject[133] forms a convertible proposition indicating an "identical exchange"[134] between them.[135] If the reading καὶ ὁ θεὸς ἦν ὁ λόγος is squeezed into this structural category, it would find further semantic support as a convertible proposition, or, as Robertson points out, Sabellianism.[136]

However, the barriers to placing the variant within this camp are insurmountable. First, this structural category as a whole is extremely rare, making it unlikely that a scribe would intentionally consider it. Second, to squeeze into this framework, the variant must swim against the current of normative word order. Finally, it fails to adopt conventional word order that places both nominatives before the verb. As a result, it is difficult to embrace a diagnosis that renders the reading καὶ ὁ θεὸς ἦν ὁ λόγος as a viable grammatical option within this classification.

Postverbal Arthrous Constructions[137]

I now turn to the category that best fits the reading καὶ ὁ θεὸς ἦν ὁ λόγος in John 1.1c. Here the roles will be reversed, with ὁ θεός being the subject and ὁ λόγος the predicate.[138] Of all of the potential structural matches, at least one of the nominatives is impersonal and carries a distinctively qualitative force. Though the pool of examples is quite

---

130. The text in Matthew reads ὁ λύχνος τοῦ σώματος ἐστιν ὁ ὀφθαλμός, and the only difference in Luke is the genitive modifier attached to the subject: ὁ λύχνος τοῦ σώματος ἐστιν ὁ ὀφθαλμός σου. Thus these two texts are identical in terms of how they arrange the subjects and predicates. It should be pointed out that the lexical nature of the predicate is impersonal (ὁ λύχνος) as well as figurative. Also, both of these examples contain arthrous genitive modifiers that demand an article for their nominative counterpart in accordance with Apollonius's canon.

131. John 6.63*bis*; 15.1; 1 Cor 11.3, 25; 2 Cor 3.17.

132. It is interesting that none of the potential constructions Harner proposed for John 1.1c include this possibility (Harner, "Predicate Nouns," 84).

133. This statement excludes nominative pronouns, since they do fit the construction in John 1.1c and are clear in expressing the subject.

134. Wallace, *Exegetical Syntax*, 41.

135. Matt 6.22; Luke 11.34; John 15.1; 1 Cor 11.3, 25; 2 Cor 3.17.

136. Robertson, *Grammar of the Greek New Testament*, 767–68.

137. For a more detailed analysis, see Morgan, "Legacy of a Letter," 39–41, 70.

138. This distinction is in keeping with the rule that makes word order the determining factor for the subject when both nominatives have the article (McGaughy, *Descriptive Analysis*, 53–54).

shallow, when an articular subject and predicate are split across the verb, at least one *prefers* to be impersonal.

Initially, the variant καὶ ὁ θεὸς ἦν ὁ λόγος appears to be in good semantic and structural company when ὁ θεός is the subject. On the surface, then, the semantic "equal sign" formed by the convertible proposition appears to favor a pro-Sabellian reading; but since the variant καὶ ὁ θεὸς ἦν ὁ λόγος contains two personal nominatives, Revelation 18.23 presents the *only* structural parallel within the confines of convertible propositions. Still, the type of equivalence found in the variant for John 1.1c involves two individuals, not two groups or classes of people, like those in Revelation 18.23. So, within the scope of the limited examples in the NT, the reading καὶ ὁ θεὸς ἦν ὁ λόγος represents *the only clear case* where two *personal singular nominatives* are placed in a convertible proposition. As a result, both the rarity and the nuances of these constructions place the reading καὶ ὁ θεὸς ἦν ὁ λόγος in a league of its own.

Preverbal Anarthrous Constructions[139]

So far, the focus has been on the variant reading in John 1.1c compared against other parallel NT constructions, but now I turn to focus on the text as it appears in NA[27]. Statistically, this structural pattern is the overwhelming favorite. This confirms Colwell's general conclusion that preverbal predicates *normally* omit the article without the baggage of assuming their definiteness. The reading καὶ θεὸς ἦν ὁ λόγος not only forms a textbook structural example but also fits the most popular form of equative constructions.

The reading καὶ θεὸς ἦν ὁ λόγος can be shown to fit perfectly within the grammatical boundaries and tendencies of the NT. From this analysis, it appears that *when the subject occurs opposite an anarthrous predicate and after the verb, unless it is a pronoun, it prefers the article.* In the case of John 1.1c, the subject (ὁ λόγος) comports perfectly with this tendency.

Although this category of predicates contains fertile soil for producing equative constructions, it yields only a paltry harvest of convertible or subset propositions.[140] Based on the limited crop of examples, the overwhelming majority involve singular nouns in subset propositions. Similarly, the reading καὶ θεὸς ἦν ὁ λόγος is a classic example of a subset proposition where "the word" is classified in the broader category of God.[141]

---

139. For a more detailed analysis, see Morgan, "Legacy of a Letter," 41–42, 71.

140. Pronouns are not included in the idea of nominatives here because they strip away any ambiguity regarding the semantic relationship (i.e., convertible or subset).

141. Wallace, *Exegetical Syntax*, 45.

Most often, singular nominatives forming a subset proposition *prefer* to place *both* the subject and predicate *before* the verb. This leaves only 7 instances where the semantic situation fits the contours of John 1.1c.[142] By hiding the subject behind the verb, these contructions lay additional stress on the class indicated by the predicate, while clearly specifying the subject with the article.[143] This nuance fits the context of John 1.1c nicely, balancing the earlier distinction from God (1.1b) with a strong statement emphasizing the Word's existence in the category of θεός. As a result, the reading καὶ θεὸς ἦν ὁ λόγος not only conforms to its grammatical peers but also provides the best reading within the context of John 1.1 as a whole.

Although the reading καὶ ὁ θεὸς ἦν ὁ λόγος represents the most natural way to convey a convertible relationship between two nominatives, if authentic, it would stand as the only clear instance where two singular personal nouns are interchangeable in the NT.

Grammatical Implications for the Textual Problem in John 1.1c[144]

As an expert in textual criticism, Colwell formulated his rule to determine whether the addition or omission of an article should be "original." Likewise, the present investigation has sought to determine whether the story of the variant καὶ ὁ θεὸς ἦν ὁ λόγος finds harmony among its grammatical peers. When the rules and nuances of nominatives used with εἰμί are unpacked, the plausibility of this variant holds very little promise; and in terms of both structure and semantics (i.e., convertible or subset proposition), its species is virtually extinct in the NT. More pointedly, it *represents the only construction of its kind*, equating two singular personal nominatives without

---

142. Matt 12.8; Mark 2.28; Luke 6.5 (these first 3 are synoptic parallels); John 1.1c; Acts 28.4; Rom 1.9; 1 Tim 6.10.

143. To illustrate this point, consider the difference between Acts 22.26 and 28.4. The subject in both is "this man" (ὁ ἄνθρωπος οὗτος), making the only distinction in the orientation relative to the verb. Though the predicate nouns are different, both appear without any modifiers or other grammatical influences. The construction in Acts 22.26 is typical of the majority (20) of the subset propositions involving singular nouns that seek to lay stress on the subject. In the context of this passage, both the soldier and the tribunal (22.27) are stressing their amazement that the person they are about to flog is a Roman. Meanwhile, in Acts 28.4, Paul has a viper latched onto his hand, causing the people of Malta to classify him as a murderer. Therefore, in this instance, the predicate "murderer" (φονεύς) is moved forward to stress the class that Paul's recent circumstance reveals. In conclusion, these two examples illustrate the semantic function of different subset propositions and how they influence the word order and emphasis in the context.

144. For a discussion of the grammatical nuances of λόγος and θεός in the NT and their influence on the textual problem in John 1.1c, see Morgan, "Legacy of a Letter," 43–45.

involving a proper name.[145] Meanwhile, the reading καὶ θεὸς ἦν ὁ λόγος does not face a single grammatical challenge to its integrity. For these reasons, the tale of an early Sabellian reading in John 1.1c grows taller under the scrutiny of normative grammatical usage in the NT.

CONCLUSION

This study began on a quest to listen carefully to the shouts and whispers of two eighth-century voices with regard to the text of John 1:1c. Although numerous scholars draw attention to the possibility of theologically motivated corruptions, they rarely move beyond the realm of speculation to discern the source of these readings (i.e., individual MSS, patristic evidence, syntax/internal evidence). During each step along the winding road of history, this search has sought to discern whether the reading καὶ ὁ θεὸς ἦν ὁ λόγος speaks of a mostly hidden Sabellian legacy that has almost vanished from transmissional history. This task involved muting those voices that represent a mythical legend rather than a theological landmark. To this end, our pursuit sequestered three streams of evidence: the roots and rise of Sabellianism, the scribal character of Codices L and W^S, and the normative grammatical constitution of equative constructions in the NT. Three conclusions result:

1. The most likely scenario for an early Sabellian text and subsequent orthodox cover-up would be front-page news about this heresy during the early second century. This allows for the polemical heat to rise to the surface of the transmissional process in its most vulnerable period. Furthermore, this polemical environment would likely include strong disagreement centered on John 1.1, but if we listen carefully to the voice of history, the story does not line up.

2. The evidence from the ancient scribes who produced the reading καὶ ὁ θεὸς ἦν ὁ λόγος is compelling. With Codex Regius, the addition of a single letter fits the scribe's most common foibles to a tee, so the extra article in John 1.1c best demonstrates sloppy habits rather than an early Sabellian legacy.

Although W^S does not leave sufficient information to form solid scribal tendencies, its presence deserves some attention. The natures and dates of Regius and W^S raise the possibility of at least one earlier

---

145. For an extensive investigation regarding the use of proper names in equative constructions, see Mario Cerda, "Subject Determination in Koine Greek Equative Clauses Involving Proper Nouns and Articular Nouns" (ThM thesis, Dallas Theological Seminary, May 2005), 1–123.

parent, but no dependency can be established between these two manuscripts. They also appear feeble and frail when left on their own, only garnering serious consideration when they echo the voice of much stronger manuscripts (‭א‬ B C D 𝔓⁶⁶ 𝔓⁷⁵). As a result, it seems very unlikely that W^S has preserved a Sabellian legacy.

3. Another voice in the halls of history is that of comparable grammatical usage in the NT. As with both of the other perspectives, the reading καὶ ὁ θεὸς ἦν ὁ λόγος heads into unchartered territory. The addition of the article changes the semantics from a subset relationship to a convertible proposition, making θεός equivalent to λόγος. Though structurally sound, it represents the only place in the NT where two singular personal nouns are made interchangeable. At the same time, its counterpart, καὶ θεὸς ἦν ὁ λόγος is the epitome of a typical equative construction. Consequently, I conclude that the notion that the article with θεός supports an earlier Sabellian reading is an unsightly myth.

The fascinating story of these two eighth-century manuscripts, with a single letter that they alone record, has only one ending. To argue that the reading of John 1.1c originally included the article with θεός and preserves a Sabellian Christology is to violate the historical context, the scribal and transmissional story, and the demonstrable norms of NT Greek syntax. Such a feat is more than two questionable eighth-century manuscripts can bear. Rather, their tarnished voice can only join the chorus of countless others that boldly proclaim that Jesus is God (καὶ θεὸς ἦν ὁ λόγος).

APPENDIX[146]
THE HISTORY OF W^S IN THE CRITICAL EDITIONS

At the beginning of this study, a few years ago, there was almost unanimous confirmation that the reading καὶ ὁ θεὸς ἦν ὁ λόγος was found only in the eighth-century manuscript Codex Regius (L [019]). Looking at standard critical texts such as NA²⁷, Tischendorf's eighth edition, Swanson, and UBS⁴, there was no place where the supplement to Codex Freerianus (W^S [032-S]) appeared.[147] The only critical texts showing Codex W^S in support of this variant were the editions done by Hermann von Soden and Augustinus Merk.[148] Most recently, the

---

146. Special thanks go to J. Bruce Prior and T. A. E. Brown, whose kind attention and interaction strengthened the contents of this appendix.

147. In all publications prior to James R. Royse's *Scribal Habits* (65), the reading of Codex L in John 1.1c was more than qualified to stand as a singular reading.

148. Hermann Freiherr von Soden, *Die Schriften des Neuen Testaments in ihrer Ältesten erreichbaren Textgestalt hergestellt auf grund ihrer Textgeschichte* (Göttingen:

release of the IGNT presented the first indication that the supplement of Codex W also supported the articular θεός in John 1.1c.[149]

This shift in textual support led to my interaction with Larry Hurtado, an expert on Codex W, and with two of his colleagues, J. Bruce Prior and T. A. E. Brown, who have special access to several series of recent digital images of the manuscript, have had access to the manuscript itself, and were responsible for the transcription of W[S] used in the IGNT. Along with seeking other expert opinion, my own personal investigation sought to make sense of the inconsistent record found in this survey of critical Greek texts. After studying Sanders' facsimile of the manuscript,[150] it seemed possible that the faint presence of an omicron in John 1.1c was due to bleed-through from the verso side of the leaf or offset from the end of Matthew.[151] During this process, Brown was able to draw my attention to some images that have been made available to the public since 2006 and that conclusively ruled out the possibility of bleed-through or offset as an explanation for the article.[152] As a result, all three scholars that were consulted affirm the presence of the omicron in John 1.1c as "incontrovertible."[153]

Important in this discussion is the history of the Freer Gospel manuscripts and how their acquisition and public availability fit chronologically with the publication of several Greek texts. The story begins in 1906, when Charles Freer purchased the manuscripts in Cairo, Egypt. Approximately one year later, they were brought to the attention of Henry A. Sanders at the University of Michigan, where they were first analyzed by scholars.[154] Along with Sanders, one of the first to publish a collation of the manuscript was Edgar J. Goodspeed in 1913.[155] Until that publication, textual scholars were largely unaware of this manuscript.

Vandenhoeck und Ruprecht, 1911), 390; Augustinus Merk, *Novum Testamentum: Graece et Latine*, 11th ed. (Romae: Sumptibus Pontificii Instituti Biblici, 1992), 307.

149. Schmid, Elliott, and Parker, *New Testament in Greek IV*, 189.

150. Sanders, *Facsimile of the Washington Manuscript*, 113.

151. The main reasons for this were (1) the clear indication of offset seen in the title of John's Gospel onto the last page of Matthew; (2) severe water damage on the top portion of the page containing John 1; and (3) the location of the ρ in αρχη above the omicron in question, which gave the distinct impression in the facsimile that another letter was impressed on top of it.

152. These images addressed two things that could not be adequately seen in the Sanders facsimile. First, a digital overlay of the recto and verso sides showed that none of the surrounding omicrons aligned with the letter in John 1.1c. Second, the enhanced digital images of the omicron give strong indication that this was included in the creation of the page and not part of later water damage.

153. This quotation came from Prior in an email of February 20, 2008, where he wrote, "As far as I am concerned, the reading with the article before ΘΣ in W[S] is incontrovertible." Along the same lines, Brown wrote in an email of February 16, 2008, that he was "certain the article was present." Hurtado also affirmed the presence of an omicron in an email of February 15, 2008.

154. Hurtado, "Introduction," in *The Freer Biblical Manuscripts*, 1–3.

155. Goodspeed, "Freer Gospels," 599–613.

Considering that Tischendorf died in 1874, it was obviously impossible for him to know of the additional evidence of W^S supporting the inclusion of the article with θεός in John 1.1c. Similarly, the completion of Hermann von Soden's massive work, combined with his death in 1914, made inclusion of such breaking information rather remarkable.[156]

More difficult to explain are the recent versions that could have accessed the collations of Sanders and Goodspeed. For instance, Swanson seems to have missed the omicron in his survey of the manuscript while using a "photographic film negative."[157] Similarly, the apparatus of NA^{27} was produced without resources like the Prior and Brown transcription. According to Prior, discussions are underway with Klaus Wachtel in Münster to include this information in the forthcoming NA^{28} text. My own personal examination of the Sanders facsimile confirmed that the extent of the water damage and resolution of the text around John 1.1c make any judgment of its reading tenuous at best. However, the numerous digital photographs taken by the Freer and Sackler Galleries and reviewed by Prior and Brown conclusively affirmed the inclusion of the article in W^S.

---

156. Credit for the historical backdrop of this section must be given to J. Bruce Prior. During numerous email interactions, he carefully and extensively answered many questions regarding the history of scholarship pertaining to this manuscript.
157. J. Bruce Prior, email, February 20, 2008.

Matthew P. Morgan

PATRISTIC THEOLOGY AND RECENSION IN MATTHEW 24.36

An Evaluation of Ehrman's

Text-Critical Methodology

Adam G. Messer[1]

The many differences in the biblical manuscripts seem to dim the lit beacon of God's Word, forcing us to ask, is the light emanating from the text of Scripture the brilliance of a sacred message, or is it merely the flames of a dying faith? It has been acknowledged for some time that alterations in the manuscript tradition were not due merely to accidental slips of the senses. In fact, the fathers of modern textual

---

1. This chapter is dedicated to my wife Alicia, who suffered the effects of HG, a debilitating and potentially life-threatening pregnancy disease, with our firstborn child. Every day for four months, she wasted away a little more, seemingly beyond hope; yet she trusted in the Lord to bring her through it, and he surprised us with his provision.

It is also dedicated to a woman who offered her aid even while losing her husband and to a man who has been steadily losing his wife to an evil illness yet still wears the garment of trust and affection for his Lord and others. The strength of my wife and friends makes hearts flutter in expectation of what awaits those who are partakers of the divine nature.

My parents have continually shown me unconditional love and incredible generosity, and I could not recompense them for their sacrifices of time and resources. Their actions have exemplified for me the overwhelming and nonreciprocal love of God through Christ.

My mentor Dan Wallace has exemplified an exceptional desire to nurture the next generation of Christian thinkers and researchers. I thank him for his time and energies, for his endearing quirkiness that makes our time together lively, and especially for his concern for my wife.

My appreciation goes to Michael Svigel for his valuable insight into the first several Christian centuries and for the extra effort he invested in this chapter, strengthening its argumentation and improving its tone.

criticism,[2] Westcott and Hort, admitted intentionality, though they presumably asserted that no alterations were made on account of doctrinal biases.[3] More recently, others have disagreed, finding ample changes made from theological motivation.

Some purport, for example, that Matthew 24.36 was changed for theological reasons. In this verse tucked away in the middle of the Olivet Discourse, Jesus sobers his listeners with a discussion about signs present at the end of the age but pleads ignorance about the specific time of the return. Such ignorance is peculiar to readers who come to the text with presuppositions of his divinity. Why would Jesus, himself a member of the Godhead, not know the time of his own return? Some feel that this theological conundrum is precisely the reason the phrase οὐδὲ ὁ υἱός ("nor the Son") was stricken from a number of manuscripts and that such an alteration indicates the undoing of a sacred text's veracity.

Among those whose writings have called into question the textual reliability of the NT is Bart Ehrman, whose basic stance is that there are obvious examples of tampering by orthodox scribes and no basis for finding the original buried beneath an excess of a quarter million other variants.[4] Although the predominant interaction with Ehrman throughout this work assumes his credibility as a scholar—a respect earned through his

---

2. Cf. Jacobus H. Petzer, "The History of the New Testament—Its Reconstruction, Significance, and Use in New Testament Textual Criticism," in *New Testament Textual Criticism, Exegesis, and Early Church History: A Discussion of Methods*, ed. Barbara Aland and Joël Delobel (Kampen: Pharos, 1994), 12; J. Harold Greenlee, *Introduction to New Testament Textual Criticism*, 2nd ed. (Peabody, MA: Hendrickson, 1995), 72.

3. F. J. A. Hort, *Introduction to the New Testament in the Original Greek* (New York: Harper and Brothers, 1882), 282. But see now Jeff Miller, "(Mis)understanding Westcott and Hort," *RestQ* 41, no. 3 (1999): 155–62.

4. Although Ehrman would overtly argue that the great variety of alternative readings in the manuscript record and the wild copying of the early centuries make it impossible to ever know if our reconstructed copies resemble the original text, this *overt* argument would not do justice to his actual claims. While traditional textual criticism recognizes these factors and acknowledges that absolute certainty over every word of our reconstructed text is not possible, it still sees no insurmountable obstacle to a faithful reconstruction, for throughout long centuries, we see reliable copying in general and can identify and correct most unintentional orthographic alterations. However, Ehrman argues that since the orthodox emended the text from theological bias, a faithful reconstruction is implausible. It is no stretch to enumerate the resulting impressions. First, if the orthodox have made innumerable *intentional* alterations, they were not as concerned with preserving the original wording as previously regarded. Second, this makes the long centuries of the orthodox transmission increasingly enigmatic, because theologically motivated changes could be introduced without any mechanism for recovery. Third, this encourages a conspiratorial view of the church's use of Scripture, which not only has the undesirable effect of shifting the onus of reliability away from the church's faithful preservation of its text but consequently empties modern Christian truth claims of both authenticity and historical congruity.

Adam G. Messer

engaging writing style and valuable contribution to the disciplines of textual criticism and religious studies—his recent works have shown a tendency, in my estimation, to overemphasize the tentative nature of certain conclusions from his seminal work *The Orthodox Corruption of Scripture*. For certain conclusions to bear the weight of several of Ehrman's recently published views, the supporting historical evidence needs more rigorous enumeration and demonstration for any single example used to support his primary contention. Here, I wish to highlight with one example what I feel is an incongruity between the amount of attention given to the historical evidence and the implications Ehrman draws from the conclusions in *Orthodox Corruption*. Because no method can remain forever sufficient nor engender absolute confidence, caution should be exercised toward sensationalizing results that may unnecessarily be construed to run contrary to the NT's textual reliability—particularly when conclusions draw support from a highly publicized example for which less scrutiny has been applied than what is required.

Most concede that there have been theologically motivated changes in the manuscript tradition, given the thousands of diverse manuscripts in diverse periods. From among all of these, Ehrman chooses Matthew 24.36 as his case in point. He elaborately introduces it in *Orthodox Corruption of Scripture*.[5] It riddles his popular work *Misquoting Jesus*, where he says, "The reason [for the omission] is not hard to postulate; if Jesus does not know the future, the Christian claim that he is a divine being is more than a little compromised."[6] It makes the cut in his *Introduction to the New Testament*[7] as the example of theologically driven changes. It is called "the most famous example of doctrinal alteration" in his *Studies in the Textual Criticism of the New Testament*,[8] and it also appears in the fourth edition of the standard *Text of the New Testament*,[9] which he coauthored with the late Bruce Metzger.

---

5. Bart D. Ehrman, *The Orthodox Corruption of Scripture: The Effect of Early Christological Controversies on the Text of the New Testament* (Oxford: Oxford University Press, 1993), 91–92, 117 nn. 220–21.

6. Bart D. Ehrman, *Misquoting Jesus: The Story behind Who Changed the Bible and Why* (San Francisco: HarperSanFrancisco, 2005), 204. He mentions Matt 24.36 in these places: 95, 110, 204, 209, 223 n. 19, 224 n. 16 (Daniel B. Wallace, "The Gospel according to Bart: A Review Article of *Misquoting Jesus* by Bart Ehrman," *JETS* 49 [2006]: 327–49). This list contains two relevant references (95 and 204), two irrelevant references (110 and 209), and two footnotes with faulty mappings (223 n. 19 and 224 n. 16).

7. Bart D. Ehrman, *The New Testament: A Historical Introduction to the Early Christian Writings*, 4th ed. (New York: Oxford University Press, 2008), 494.

8. Bart D. Ehrman, *Studies in the Textual Criticism of the New Testament*, New Testament Tools and Studies 33 (Leiden: Brill, 2006), 333.

9. Bruce Manning Metzger and Bart D. Ehrman, *The Text of the New Testament: Its Transmission, Corruption, and Restoration*, 4th ed. (New York: Oxford University Press, 2005), 267.

Given that Matthew 24.36 is Ehrman's example *par excellence*, it may be worth seeing if the lens of church history will provide a clearer view. The patristic evidence may show how the church fathers viewed this troublesome concept of the Son's ignorance and could explain both the time frame and extent of the alterations to the text. Such information may help in explaining the specific text-critical problem in Matthew 24.36 and in evaluating Ehrman's conclusions on the verse. From a broader perspective, if Ehrman's analysis of the leading example of orthodox corruption is flawed, his whole edifice may require significant alteration.

PERSPECTIVE ON MATTHEW 24.36

Outline of the Problem

Modern Bibles are largely based on the NA[27] reading of Matthew 24.36: "Concerning that day and hour no one knows, not the angels in heaven nor the Son, except the Father alone." But this was not always the rendering; past critical editions often excluded the phrase οὐδὲ ὁ υἱός ("nor the Son"), because prior to the Alexandrian discoveries of Sinaiticus and early papyri, a textual stream that lacked οὐδὲ ὁ υἱός blossomed into the Byzantine tradition. This text type shaped the church for over a millennium, undergirding the King James Version, which, in turn, dominated the English-speaking world for centuries. The omission is strongly attested in the majority of manuscripts, mostly Byzantine, but also with a significant Alexandrian link. The presence of οὐδὲ ὁ υἱός is attested in important Western manuscripts and our best Alexandrian exemplars. Further, several versions attest each reading, and the patristic evidence is split. This textual problem has been difficult to decide with any ecumenical finality, and critical editors, all aware of the variant readings, have made different textual decisions.[10] Recent editions have tended to favor the inclusion of οὐδὲ ὁ υἱός, yet if they are correct, how do we explain the manuscript and patristic evidence attesting to the omission?

Bart Ehrman, among others, has suggested that scribes had problems with Christ's ignorance and so struck οὐδὲ ὁ υἱός from their copies of Matthew, in response to adoptionistic influences. Although scholars prior to Ehrman advanced the notion that theological changes affected the textual tradition, *Orthodox Corruption* is arguably the most influential book on the topic. However, whereas *Orthodox Corruption* sought primarily to argue the case that it happened, Ehrman's more recent works have reflected a more radical perspective. He has argued in

---

10. Scrivener, von Soden, and Merk attest to the omission, while Lachmann, Tischendorf[8], Legg, NA[27], and UBS[4] contain the phrase.

these that since orthodox emendation happened, our text, by implication, cannot be established; he contends that since the originals are forever lost, the hopes for accurate reconstruction lie buried far beneath a mountain of pious alteration and unchecked fideism.

Methodology

The majority of scribes were not the intellectual giants of their day, so they would likely derive their understandings of a particular passage (and the perceived difficulty thereof) from the leading theologians of the period.[11] If the major teachers of the church had problems with a text, it is probable that scribes in their region likewise had issues with it. Such a situation would offer the necessary motivation for omitting οὐδὲ ὁ υἱός during the transcription process.

My method for this analysis included perusing every reference within BP for Matthew 24.36 and its parallel in Mark 13.32 to enumerate the fathers' testimonies.[12] The Greek texts come from several

---

11. The merit of this assertion is also corroborated by Brogan, who takes it a step further by arguing that even if their leaders had a theological problem with a passage, the scribes probably did not introduce the corruptions; rather, their role would have been limited to the reproduction (perhaps unknowing) of the alterations made by prominent leaders (John J. Brogan, "Another Look at Codex Sinaiticus," in *The Bible as Book: The Transmission of the Greek Text*, ed. Scot McKendrick and Orlaith O'Sullivan [London: British Library and Oak Knoll Press, 2003], 25). The Alands implicitly acknowledge an analogous idea (i.e., that alterations were not the provenance of the scribe) when they speak of the origins of the Western text type: "Wherever we look in the West, nowhere can we find a theological mind capable of developing and editing an independent 'Western text'" (Kurt Aland and Barbara Aland, *The Text of the New Testament: An Introduction to the Critical Editions and to the Theory and Practice of Modern Textual Criticism*, trans. Erroll F. Rhodes, 2nd ed. [Grand Rapids: Eerdmans, 1989], 54).

12. This includes a broad corpus of ancient literature but omits the testimony of certain fathers (e.g., Jerome, Ambrose, Augustine, etc.) who also referenced Matt 24.36 in their works. Jerome, in particular, has often been the subject of modern inquiries surrounding this verse: cf. Émile Bonnard, *Saint Jérôme, Commentaire sur S. Matthieu*, vol. 1, Sources Chrétiennes 242 (Paris: Les Éditions du Cerf, 1977); Dennis Brown, *Vir Trilinguis: A Study in the Biblical Exegesis of Saint Jerome* (Kampen: Peeters, 1992); J. K. Kitchen, "Variants, Arians, and the Trace of Mark: Jerome and Ambrose on 'Neque Filius' in Matthew 24:36," in *The Multiple Meaning of Scripture: The Role of Exegesis in Early-Christian and Medieval Culture*, ed. Ineke van 't Spijker (Leiden: Brill, 2009). For Ambrose, cf. A. Bludau, *Die Schriftfälschungen der Häretiker: ein Beitrag zur Textkritik der Bibel* (Münster, 1925); Kitchen, "Variants, Arians and the Trace of Mark"; Craig Alan Satterlee, *Ambrose of Milan's Method of Mystagogical Preaching* (Collegeville: Liturgical Press, 2002). While not minimizing the fruit of these and other analyses, distinct evidence from the anterior (and contemporaneous) period has sometimes been overlooked when drawing conclusions. The present work has striven to supplement the discussion by focusing on this other early testimony.

---

critical texts (where available), MPG, and TLG. All renderings are personal translations unless otherwise noted. From this collection of references, the most poignant examples of the patristic ways of thinking are shown for purposes of illustration.

Effort was made to ascertain a particular father's form of Matthew based on the four Greek differences with the text of Mark. First, Matthew uses a TSKS construction for "day" and "hour" (τῆς ἡμέρας καὶ ὥρας) that Mark does not (τῆς ἡμέρας ἢ τῆς ὥρας). Second, Matthew uses the conjunction καί where Mark uses ἤ. Third, the grammatical case of "heaven" is genitive plural in Matthew (τῶν οὐρανῶν) and dative singular in Mark (ἐν οὐρανῷ). Finally, Matthew has the word μόνος at the end, while Mark lacks it. The fathers seemed to have little difficulty with small morphological variation surrounding articles and conjunctions in the first half of the verse and even in the form of "heaven." So I classify the verses with the following hierarchical method:

1. If the father identifies his source, I take him at his word.

2. Since the Markan transmission of this verse appears remarkably unadulterated, texts without οὐδὲ ὁ υἱός are generally assumed to be Matthean.

3. Preference is shown to identifying the source of a reference containing μόνος as Matthean[13] because the presence or absence of μόνος has significantly greater rhetorical impact than alterations to the case and number of "heaven," "day," or "hour." Consequently, the fathers would have been more likely to preserve μόνος in their quotations and memory, and this fact *should* weigh as a heavier indicator of the source than less rhetorically significant differences in form.[14]

In some cases, a father wrote in Latin, or our only access is through extant Latin translations. In such cases, it is noteworthy that Latin

---

13. This assumption seems plausible because no extant manuscripts of Mark from the first four centuries contain μόνος. In fact, of the few listed in Tischendorf's apparatus, none are earlier than the ninth century, and some are much later. This amount of time (at least five centuries) would create a situation more fertile for a harmonization from Matthew to Mark, due to a significantly longer time frame and increased frequency of manuscript duplication.

14. The form of "heaven" will be weighed less than the presence of μόνος but greater than the other two differences in form. However, enough variation occurs that situations might be construed that would upset a rigid application of this hierarchical method. The classification is somewhat of an art and may be interpreted differently by others more or less qualified. In deference to such endeavors, effort was taken to footnote the original Greek and Latin texts from which my classifications were made.

versions essentially preserve the differences in the Greek,[15] so *tentative* judgments may be offered.

Caution must be exercised in how the data of patristic evidence is applied to the textual reconstruction of Matthew 24.36. The assumption that a father's intention was to perfectly quote a verse is demonstrably false, and each father is subject to a fallible memory, even as their writings are subject to the same challenges of transmission as the NT. Despite these caveats, some conclusions are possible. Further, whereas the challenge to reconstruct the perfect form of a given verse from patristic evidence may prove insurmountable, the determination of what *ingredients* they saw in that verse pays remarkable dividends. Whatever the *exact* original words were, the fathers can help us see what *concepts* existed in their text, which offers an important angle for textual reconstruction by highlighting which variants included those concepts and which did not.[16]

In addition to researching explicit references to Matthew 24.36 and Mark 13.32, I noted the views of the early church on the Son's ignorance, hopefully illuminating the transmission of this theological doctrine when there is no explicit reference made to the verses in question and in cases where the references do not speak to the issue.

Textual Problem

Although a comprehensive portrait of textual problems in Matthew 24.36 is of secondary importance to the theme of this chapter, manuscript witnesses, versional testimony, and internal criteria must be added to patristic evidence in determining the final text. The omission is strongly attested in the majority of manuscripts,[17] predominantly Byzantine, but not merely so; there is also a smattering of manuscripts from the Alexandrian and debated "Caesarean" text types, none prior to an early corrector to Codex Sinaiticus.[18] Several versions—namely, the Old Latin,

---

15. The Latin equivalents are (1) *illa et* vs. *illo vel* for καί vs. ἢ τῆς, (2) *caelorum* vs. *in caelo* for τῶν οὐρανῶν vs. ἐν οὐρανῷ, and (3) Latin *solus* for Greek μόνος.

16. Establishing the exact form of the fathers' manuscripts can help us in our reconstruction of the original because it can help compare the purity of one transmission stream to another in the *conceptual* realm (*cf.* Bart D. Ehrman, "The Use and Significance of Patristic Evidence for NT Textual Criticism," in Aland and Delobel, *New Testament Textual Criticism*, 119–20, 134–35).

17. ℵ[1] L W *f*[1] 33 𝔐 et al.

18. The early corrector appears to be contemporaneous with its original production (H. J. M. Milne, T. C. Skeat, and Douglas Cockerell, *Scribes and Correctors of the Codex Sinaiticus* [London: British Museum, 1938], 40). Jongkind affirms Milne and Skeat's conclusions regarding the time of these corrections (Dirk Jongkind, *Scribal Habits of Codex Sinaiticus*, Text and Studies, 3rd ser., 5 [Piscataway, NJ: Gorgias, 2007], 39).

Syriac,[19] Coptic,[20] and Georgian—attest to the omission. The exclusion has the patristic support of Didymus, Phoebadius, Ambrose, and Jerome. The presence of the phrase, however, has a strong pedigree, including Alexandrian and Western witnesses.[21] The Diatessaron, Armenian, Ethiopic, and Georgian[22] versions contain it, as well as several fathers, including Irenaeus, Origen, and Chrysostom.[23]

A few internal considerations enliven the discussion. When the transcriptional possibilities are evaluated for instances of accidental orthographic omission in Greek,[24] a few unlikely candidates present themselves.[25] The most interesting involves a novice scribe overlooking a faded overbar above the *nomen sacrum* for "son" (ΥC) and misconstruing the phrase to read "nor the boar." The resulting verse would read, "But of that day and hour no one knows, not the angels of heaven, *nor the boar*, but the Father alone." In such a scenario, a pious neophyte might remove the sacrilegious phrase, under the notion that some tired or careless scribe had accidentally added it or that a mischievous copyist had inserted it for sport. Several other scenarios may be invoked by an appeal to novice, secular, or illiterate scribes, but these are improbable. Since the chances for accidental errors of sight to occur are small, it is more likely that if an accidental error occurred, it was an error of memory.

One such explanation for inclusion involves harmonization.[26] The absence of οὐδὲ ὁ υἱός may be original to the Gospel of Matthew. This possibility is bolstered by a recognizable tendency in Matthew, using Mark as a literary source, to smooth out the Markan reading in favor of a higher Christology.[27] Matthew may have omitted the phrase οὐδὲ

---

19. The Syriac version has its own variety of readings. In support of the omission are the Sinaitic Old Syriac version (third/fourth century), the Peshitta (early fifth century), and the Harklean version (616 CE). The presence of "nor the Son" is attested in the Palestinian Syriac version (sixth century).
20. In support of the omission are the Sahidic, Bohairic, and Middle Egyptian forms of the Coptic text.
21. ℵ*,2 B D Θ *f*[13] et al.
22. The Georgian testimony is split. Some manuscripts support the omission, and others contain οὐδὲ ὁ υἱός.
23. A complete list is not enumerated because a more in-depth perusal will be subsequently laid out.
24. Options seem to be present in Aramaic and Coptic texts, but given the lack of scholarly consensus regarding an Aramaic Matthean original and the awkward construal of a social scenario allowing a Coptic variant to penetrate the Greek tradition, these unlikely possibilities are relegated to little more than thoughtful contemplation.
25. See appendix B.
26. Harmonizations can also be intentional.
27. Plummer mentions examples of Matthew's higher Christology across parallels: Mark 3.5 and Matthew 12.13, Mark 6.5–6 and Matthew 13.58, Mark 8.12 and Matthew 16.4, Mark 10.14 and Matthew 19.14, and statements removed from

ὁ υἱός in his gospel to portray his unique perspective of Jesus.[28] The parallel passage in Mark 13.32 contains the phrase οὐδὲ ὁ υἱός, and this reading remained remarkably fixed across the centuries.[29] If the phrase is not original to Matthew 24.36, could the early appearance of οὐδὲ ὁ υἱός reflect a harmonization to Mark? How likely was harmonization in this direction? One attempt to answer this question analyzed over sixty of "the most significant instances involving harmonization" between Matthew and Mark and calculated that Mark harmonized to Matthew around 70 percent of the time in these instances.[30] This would seem to indicate that it was less likely for a scribe to harmonize Matthew 24.36 to Mark 13.32.

If οὐδὲ ὁ υἱός is original to Matthew 24.36, could theological motivation be responsible for the disappearance of the phrase from various manuscripts? Might a scribe with a doctrinal preference for an omniscient Christ strike the phrase? In support of this, Metzger and Ehrman see the originality of the longer reading as a grammatical necessity,[31] but its absence would not create the grammatical inconcinnity they presume.[32] More germane to their argument is that the longer reading is more difficult. Further, given scribal tendencies to harmonize, had this phrase *not* existed in Matthew's original, Ehrman asserts that omitting the parallel phrase from Mark (due to Matthew's influence) would have been more likely than striking οὐδὲ ὁ υἱός from Matthew.[33] Metzger

---

Matthew's parallels pertaining to Jesus' perceived ignorance in Mark 5.9, 5.30, 6.38, 8.12, 8.23, 9.16, 9.21, 9.33, 14.14, etc. (Alfred Plummer, *An Exegetical Commentary on the Gospel according to S. Matthew* [Minneapolis: James Family Christian, 1909], xiv–xvi; cf. also Robert H. Stein, *Studying the Synoptic Gospels: Origin and Interpretation*, 2nd ed. [Grand Rapids: Baker Academic, 2001], 91–94). This prospect assumes the view (Markan priority) currently held by the majority of NT scholars.

28. He may also have simply recorded what Jesus said on another didactic occasion pertaining to the same general topic.

29. Only one tenth-century codex (Codex X) and apparently a random Latin manuscript of the Vulgate attest to the omission. The overwhelming majority of Vulgate manuscripts (as well as the critical determination) contains the phrase in Mark 13.32.

30. Powell indicated that the population of harmonizations between Matthew and Mark did not represent all possible instances but were "probable harmonizations" that involve "the major manuscripts" (Charles Powell, "The Textual Problem of Οὐδὲ Ὁ Υἱός in Matthew 24:36," http://www.bible.org/page.php?page_id=2478 [accessed January 25, 2009]).

31. Bruce Manning Metzger, *A Textual Commentary on the Greek New Testament*, 2nd ed. (Stuttgart: United Bible Societies, 1994), 52; Ehrman, *Orthodox Corruption*, 92.

32. Powell, "Textual Problem of Οὐδὲ Ὁ Υἱός." Central to his argument is the fact that Matthew has other instances that include just one οὐδέ (e.g., Matt 6.28, 21.32, 25.45, and 27.14), signifying that this word does not require a correlative pair.

33. This follows from two considerations. First, Matthew was more popular and thus copied more frequently than Mark. Second, Mark apparently harmonized to Matthew significantly more often than the reverse (Powell, "Textual Problem of Οὐδὲ

simply believed that the chances for a theologically motivated removal were greater than a harmonization to Mark 13.32.[34] Running counter to this idea are three considerations:

1. Why did the scribe(s) not also remove the phrase from Mark 13.32? Mark remains essentially untouched.

2. Scribal tendency was to conflate rather than remove, and it is not difficult to imagine that a phrase indicating a Messianic ignorance would be so vividly associated with this context ("nobody knows the day or hour") that the copyist would know this verse by memory. With such a pregnant phrase, it is easy to suggest a harmonization from Mark.

3. During a textual decision, the reading that differs from its parallel is ordinarily preferred, because an explanation is sought for the rise of the other variants.[35] This would make the omission a good candidate for originality, except that, as mentioned earlier, the presence of οὐδὲ ὁ υἱός is the harder reading in light of the doctrinal difficulties it may have presented. These key factors vie for precedence.

From another angle, that Mark seems to have an established transmission history (no manuscript evidence attests to the omission until the tenth century) seems difficult to explain apart from a text of Matthew that matched it for the predominant period in question; otherwise, we might have expected a number of manuscripts attesting to the omission in Mark. Even so, there are scholars who see in Matthew's higher Christology the tendency to literarily smooth out potentially denigrating perceptions of Christ found in Mark's Gospel and who thus prefer the originality of the shorter reading.[36] Suffice it to say at this point that most of the text-critical theories that favor weighted external

---

Ὁ Υἱός"; Ehrman, *Orthodox Corruption*, 92), a tendency, if true, that Ehrman believes is due to Matthew's comparatively greater notoriety (Ehrman, *Orthodox Corruption*, 92).

34. Metzger, *Textual Commentary on the Greek New Testament*, 52.

35. Metzger and Ehrman, *Text of the New Testament*, 314.

36. Daniel B. Wallace argued for its original exclusion in his fall 2007 class on textual criticism (for reasons outlined in the text), as do the notes in the NT translation for which he was an editor (NET Bible). John Wu's reinvigorated study of original readings within the Byzantine tradition reflects a preference for the shorter reading, on the basis that the Byzantine copyists went against their tendency to harmonize and conflate in Matt 24.36, to explicitly follow its archetype. He posited that the interpolation probably happened in the Western and Alexandrian texts early in the second century (Wei-Ho John Wu, "A Systematic Analysis of the Shorter Readings in the Byzantine Text of the Synoptic Gospels" [PhD diss., Dallas Theological Seminary, 2002], 60–64).

evidence[37] will prefer the longer reading,[38] while the variety of internal considerations will result in conflicting conclusions.

After surveying the possibilities, two options rise to the fore as most probable. Either οὐδὲ ὁ υἱός originally existed in Matthew and was stricken by a scribe due to theological difficulties presented by the verse, or the phrase did not exist in Matthew, in which case its presence in a large number of manuscripts resulted from a harmonization from Mark 13.32. If we assume that οὐδὲ ὁ υἱός was part of the original text, two problems must be explained:

1. What accounts for the theologically motivated omission?

2. How do we explain the predominance of the shorter reading in the manuscript tradition?

If we assume that the shorter reading is authentic, we must disagree with our earliest and best witnesses, and we must explain how οὐδὲ ὁ υἱός was added, in light of the fact that scribal harmonization of Matthew to Mark occurred less frequently.

Whereas some combination of external manuscript considerations and internal considerations tend to rule the day as far as establishing the original text, the patristic evidence finds its primary contribution in the realm of establishing the geographic and chronological transmission of the text and doctrines. Sometimes this plays an important part in the text-critical process. Whichever variant is original, it appears that both readings existed by the time the fourth-century Codex Sinaiticus was composed. Milne and Skeat suggest that before it ever left the scriptorium, a corrector had stricken οὐδὲ ὁ υἱός.[39] It was then "readded" by erasing the diacritical marks indicating its omission. This makes plain that some deliberation existed for the scribe(s) of Sinaiticus—presumably the result of multiple and contradictory exemplars at Matthew 24.36. In addition, the vitally important fourth-century Codex Vaticanus bears earmarks of disclosing this variant.[40] Because both variants are at-

---

37. Powell, "Textual Problem of Οὐδὲ Ὁ Υἱός"; Metzger, *A Textual Commentary on the Greek New Testament*, 51–52; Ehrman, *Orthodox Corruption*, 92, 117 n. 221.

38. They will do so on the basis of the dominant presence of οὐδὲ ὁ υἱός in the Alexandrian and Western traditions, generally thought to better reflect the original, especially when they agree.

39. Cf. n. 18.

40. Caroli Vercellone Sodalis Barnabitae and Iosephi Cozza Monachi Basiliani, eds., *Bibliorum Sacrorum Graecus Codex Vaticanus Auspice Pio IX. Pontifice Maximo* (Detroit: Brown and Thomas, 1868; repr., 1982), 35. Next to Matt 24.36 is a *distigma*. Miller concludes that *distigmai* (or what he calls "umlauts") represent variants (J. Edward Miller, "Some Observations on the Text-Critical Function of the Umlauts in Vaticanus, with Special Attention to 1 Cor 14.34–35," *JSNT* 26, no. 2 [2003]: 235). At the SBL conference in November 2009, Peter Head of Tyndale

tested in the manuscript tradition by the fourth century, patristic evidence that might play a role in tracking down the origin of this textual problem is delineated here by this general time frame.

THEOLOGICAL MOTIVATIONS IN MATTHEW 24.36

Background

Some comment is in order regarding *who* is responsible for the alteration in Matthew 24.36. Heretics made copies of the NT, often in light of concerns they had with the text.[41] A combination of factors—including the sometimes wild copying in early centuries, the multiplicity of languages into which the church was translating, the lack of centralized authority and proliferation, the resulting absence of accountability, the cost to create a manuscript and their consequent high value, the competing sub-Christian groups who self-identified as Christians, and the difficulty in verifying and/or regulating the content of new texts— all contribute to the very real possibility that manuscripts copied by heretics could end up being used for communal worship and as exemplars by later scribes.[42] Ehrman argues that competing Christian groups struggled for dominance in the first few centuries, each trying to pass their own traditions down and reflecting a valid form of Christianity.[43] While the latter claim deserves additional clarification, it is true that various groups of various sizes sought to proliferate their truth claims

---

House, Cambridge, argued that the *distigmai* were added about a thousand years after codex B was written. If so, then the fact of such a symbol here may only indicate that the phrase was not in the copies of the Vulgate current at the time these *distigmai* were added. However, the fact that no *distigma* is found at Mark 16.8 in B is problematic for this hypothesis.

41. Examples include Theodotus, Asclepiodotus, Hermophilus, and Appollonius (Eusebius, *Hist. eccl.* 5.28); Marcion (Heikki Räisänen, "Marcion," in *A Companion to Second-Century Christian "Heretics*," ed. Antti Marjanen and Petri Luomanen [Leiden: Brill, 2005], 113–16); Ebionites and their copy of Matthew (Eusebius, *Hist. eccl.* 6.17.1); and Valentinians (Irenaeus, *Against Heresies* 3.11.9).

42. This assertion is ambivalent toward the idea that the majority of copies "were made by and for individuals or, at the very least, for individual churches during the second and third centuries" (Kim Haines-Eitzen, *Guardians of Letters: Literacy, Power, and the Transmitters of Early Christian Literature* [Oxford: Oxford University Press, 2000], 6, 16). If true, this speaks only to the majority practice and not against the complicated nature of social history that would occasionally have "interbred" orthodox and heretical texts. In fact, if the lines between what *was* considered "Christian" in antiquity and what *was not* were truly as variegated as Ehrman has suggested, particularly in the thesis of *Lost Christianities*, we might presume this to have happened much more frequently than we would otherwise think.

43. Bart D. Ehrman, *Lost Christianities: The Battles for Scripture and the Faiths We Never Knew* (New York: Oxford University Press, 2003), ix, 4, 6–7.

Adam G. Messer

against the ancestors of Nicene theology, whom Ehrman calls the "proto-orthodox." As they attempted to pass their traditions and writings forward, the complicated process known as social life transpired, and manuscripts shifted hands, were recopied, and intermingled. Such a view is implicit in C. S. C. Williams's view of Marcion's influence on the textual transmission of Luke and various Pauline epistles: "Strange as it may seem, the readings adopted by the heresiarch [Marcion] were more than once reproduced by the copyists of the Church's text."[44] He spoke also to the *accuracy* of Marcion's copying: "Marcion did not find the original text either of the Epistles or of the Gospel of Luke quite adequate to support his teaching and he emended the texts of both."[45] That heretics altered the text has been acknowledged for some time; in fact, the accepted, if informal, scholarly position was that they were responsible for the majority of theologically motivated changes—until, perhaps, the 1993 publication of *Orthodox Corruption* and its overwhelming wake. The reason heretical alterations are important to mention is not that Ehrman or any other scholar would deny them but because it complicates our inquiry. There were periods in which there might have been orthodox motivation to change the text, but there were also times and places of heretical influence.

What reason for alteration will best account for the patristic evidence and manuscript history?[46] Attempting to surmise the time period during which the alteration occurred, who or what is responsible for it, and how it happened should give some insight into the reason for the alteration. Without simply assuming that the group(s) who would profit from a change to the text would necessarily be those responsible for them, I hope to offer reasoned conclusions, listing a number of options for the omission or inclusion in Matthew 24.36.

Who's On Trial?

Orthodox Corruption

What motivations might exist for the phrase οὐδὲ ὁ υἱός to be omitted by the proto-orthodox? To each heresy discussed in this section may also be apportioned the motivation to *add* the phrase οὐδὲ ὁ υἱός to support their theology had the phrase originally been lacking in Matthew.[47] Of the plethora of early heresies, a theologically motivated alteration would occur against heresies that (1) use the phrase οὐδὲ ὁ

---

44. C. S. C. Williams, *Alterations to the Text of the Synoptic Gospels and Acts* (Oxford: Basil Blackwell, 1951), 10–11.
45. Ibid.
46. I use the word *alteration* to mean either the removal of οὐδὲ ὁ υἱός or its addition, depending on Matthew's original state.
47. Such an addition would have been strategically imported from Mark 13.32.

υἱός or the idea behind it to support their theology, (2) are significant enough to be taken seriously,[48] and (3) overlap the time period in which the omission appears to have been made.

Since the omission was well attested by Jerome—it took over the basic Bible of the day by Jerome's time—and given that it appears in some versions with roots as far back as the third century CE (Syriac) and perhaps even the second (Sahidic Coptic),[49] this early period will be the target of investigation. Although many aberrancies litter these centuries, two stand as good candidates: Adoptionism and Arianism. The Adoptionists claimed that Jesus was only a man who was adopted by God at his baptism. The Arians, also called Eunomians, Anomœans, Anomeans, Heterousians, and Aetians at various points by patristic writers, believed Jesus was a created being who was not fully God. Against both perspectives, a phrase demonstrating a self-attested lack in Jesus' knowledge could present difficulties for the orthodox view that he was truly divine. Thus their adherents may have been motivated to remove οὐδὲ ὁ υἱός.

Adoptionism did not hit Rome until around 190 CE, and Epiphanius claims that its originator was Theodotus the Tanner.[50] It

---

48. It is rightly observed that even local heresies were considered of utmost concern to those leaders and churches they affected. Epiphanius's *Panarion* lists scores of heresies that could be examined in their particulars, yet I here narrow the list by assuming two things. First, heresies that were widespread and durative would have greater probabilities of causing manuscript alterations that would survive until the present times. Second, attention to these many heresies would no doubt further muddy the waters by greatly expanding the number of possible scenarios. It is, of course, reflective of good scholarship to mention fields ripe for future study; however, I lean on the following consideration to help choose which rocks to overturn first: the general consensus of the scholarly world in highlighting certain heresies no doubt corresponds with the heresies most often attacked by extant patristic writings. I assume that these represent the most fertile *initial* garden for study, and I acknowledge that this assumption is only as strong as (since it relies on) the assumption that our extant patristic manuscripts are generally representative of the total body of ancient ecclesiastical literature.

49. Bruce M. Metzger, *The Early Versions of the New Testament: Their Origin, Transmission, and Limitations* (Oxford: Clarendon, 1977), 127–32. Although Metzger mentions Horner's and Thompson's advocacy of a late second-century Sahidic text, he seems to inconspicuously align himself with Kasser's chronology of Coptic development, which suggests that the latter half of the third century is the most likely period from which to expect a full Sahidic version. Others have asserted that the earliest Sahidic manuscripts would have appeared within the time frame delineated by 250–350 CE and, perhaps more relevant, that the entrance of a standard version would be even later (350–450 CE) (Frederik Wisse, "The Coptic Versions of the New Testament," in *The Text of the New Testament in Contemporary Research: Essays on the* Status Quaestionis, ed. Bart D. Ehrman and Michael W. Holmes [Grand Rapids: Eerdmans, 1995], 134–35).

50. Epiphanius, *Panarion* 34. Theodotus the Tanner was active during the late second century. More precise dates for those considered heretics are sometimes unattainable. Approximate dates will be included when available. Epiphanius's discussion

soon exerted enough influence to elicit the reactions of concerned, orthodox apologists.[51] Whatever manuscript influence Adoptionists may have had would have been to stress Jesus' humanity to the exclusion of his deity. One group of Adoptionists, the Ebionites,[52] only used Matthew,[53] so perhaps an orthodox scribe omitted οὐδὲ ὁ υἱός to undermine their reliance on Matthew 24.36.[54] Some evidence exists that the Ebionites adjusted their own copies of Matthew to suit their beliefs.[55] If this is true, the orthodox adjustment of their manuscripts to address a deviant view derived from self-maintained, he-

---

of Theodotus from Byzantium is available for the English reader in Frank Williams, *The Panarion of Epiphanius: Books II and III (Sects 47–80, De Fide)*, Nag Hammadi and Manichaean Studies 36 (Leiden: Brill, 1994), 2, 72–77, 91.

51. Irenaeus against the Ebionites and Cerinthus et al. (*Against Heresies* 1.26.1–2; 3.11.7; 3.21.1; 4.33.4; 5.1.3), Hippolytus against the Ebionites and Cerinthus et al. (*Refutation of All Heresies* 7.21–22), Epiphanius against the Ebionites and other Adoptionists et al. (*Panarion* 30.1.1; 30.2.1–8; 30.3.7; 30.16.1; 30.26.1; 30.34.6; 65.1.5–10; 65.3.2–4), Eusebius against Cerinthus, Ebionites, and other Adoptionists et al. (*Hist. eccl.* 3.27–28; 5.28; 7.30), etc. Cerinthus is usually considered an early *Gnostic* influence, but his teaching about the origin of Jesus was, like other Gnostics (e.g., Basilides), essentially the same as the more formal Adoptionists. For modern summaries of ancient heresies, see Walter Bauer, *Orthodoxy and Heresy in Earliest Christianity*, ed. Robert A. Kraft and Gerhard Krodel, trans. the Philadelphia Seminar on Christian Origins (Philadelphia: Fortress, 1971); Harold O. J. Brown, *Heresies: Heresy and Orthodoxy in the History of the Church* (Peabody, MA: Hendrickson, 1984); Ehrman, *Lost Christianities*; Arland J. Hultgren and Steven A. Haggmark, eds., *The Earliest Christian Heretics: Readings from Their Opponents* (Minneapolis: Fortress, 1996); Marjanen and Luomanen, *Companion to Second-Century Christian "Heretics."*

52. Some scholars believe the Ebionites existed as early as the composition of the NT, stemming from an original Jewish following of Jesus (e.g., Robert H. Eisenman, *James, the Brother of Jesus: The Key to Unlocking the Secrets of Early Christianity and the Dead Sea Scrolls* [New York: Viking, 1997], 5–6). Others suggest they originated early in the second century from Jews disillusioned by repeated failures to reestablish the kingdom of God (e.g., James D. Tabor, *The Jesus Dynasty: The Hidden History of Jesus, His Royal Family, and the Birth of Christianity* [New York: Simon and Schuster, 2006], 302–3). Since the Ebionite stress on Jesus' humanity was similar to the Adoptionists, their influence may have provided the motivation for alterations even earlier than 190 CE, perhaps as early as the very beginning. They also appear to have existed in various places until the fourth century (Tabor, *Jesus Dynasty*, 302–3).

53. Irenaeus, *Against Heresies* 1.26.2.

54. This would make sense of why this alteration only happened in Matthew.

55. Ehrman, *Lost Christianities*, 102. The Ebionites use of Matthew and their vocal protest against Jesus' virgin birth—a problematic denial had they not altered the first two chapters (or subsections) of Matthew, which testify to it—make alterations to Matthew a strong likelihood. Eusebius (*Hist. eccl.* 6.17.1) also hints at this editorial work. Against this view, Häkkinen argues that the silence of another church father (Irenaeus) about Ebionite alteration of Matthew indicates that they apparently used the same version as the orthodox (Sakari Häkkinen, "Ebionites," in Marjanen and Luomanen, *Companion to Second-Century Christian "Heretics,"* 260–61). However, he earlier makes the case that Irenaeus was not personally acquainted

---

retical manuscripts might not be as good a fit as it would initially seem. Other Adoptionists, such as Asclepiodotus and Theodotus the Money-Changer,[56] were not as isolated as the Ebionites or limited to sectarian copies of Matthew. Adoptionism, most prominent in the years 190–275 CE if one includes the overlapping theology of Paul of Samosata (ca. 200–275 CE),[57] undoubtedly had earlier moorings in Jewish Christianity.

Arianism is the most logical heresy in which to look for an orthodox advantage because it became so popular and generated such a strong reaction. Since Arians saw Christ as a lower, created entity, one can readily see how an omission of οὐδὲ ὁ υἱός would benefit their *orthodox* opponents. Although the exact relationship between Arius (ca. 250–336 CE) and Arianism is in dispute,[58] it is certain that Arianism was a full-fledged controversy by 321 CE, necessitating the Great Council of Nicea just four years later. Thus strong orthodox motivation for striking οὐδὲ ὁ υἱός existed from perhaps 280 CE until Arianism's head was severed at Constantinople in 381 CE, and motivation may also have existed from about 190 CE, and possibly from the very roots of Christianity, through Jerome's inception of the Vulgate. Conversely, had Matthew originally not contained the phrase, the Arian groups would have been motivated to add it during this period.

Heretical Corruption

Could heretical movements such as Marcionism, Gnosticism, Docetism,[59] and Sabellianism[60] have been responsible for the removal of οὐδὲ ὁ υἱός? What would have been their motivation?

---

with the Ebionites and used inherited information to compose his short paragraph regarding them in *Against Heresies* 1.26.2 (ibid., 250).

56. These disciples of Theodotus the Tanner were active during the rule of Bishop Zephyrinus (198–217 CE) of Rome (Eusebius, *Hist. eccl.* 5.28.3).

57. Paul freely called Jesus "God." Whereas this might seem Sabellian, he redefined godhood to signify mere man infused with the divine. Cf. Brown, *Heresies*, 98.

58. R. P. C. Hanson, *The Search for the Christian Doctrine of God: The Arian Controversy, 318–381* (Grand Rapids: Baker Academic, 2007), 123–28. Hanson notes the curious affair that many of those dubbed "Arian" did not associate themselves with Arius. Some even disavowed such a thought. He concludes that Arius "was usually not thought of as a great man by his followers" (128). However, that his ideas were somewhat prominent should be inferred from, e.g., Athanasius's work entitled *Discourses against the Arians,* the interspersed mention of his name in Hilary's *On the Trinity* (e.g., "Arian fanatics" from 7.7), and the movement called "Arian madness" in Gregory of Nazianzus's *Orationes* 34.8.

59. Docetism shared characteristics with Gnosticism and was modalistic, and it technically falls under the category of Monarchianism (God as "one" entity).

60. Sabellianism, similarly known by the terms Modalism and Patripassianism, is also a form of Monarchianism.

Marcion (ca. 85–160 CE) may be ruled out as a direct candidate, not because of his theology or manner of readjusting Scripture, but because he seemed to only accept portions of Luke through Acts and various Pauline epistles as Scripture. However, his impact on later churches is worth examination. His Christology bore features of Modalism in that the pure God came in the form of (and was) Jesus.[61] Phrases assigning ignorance to Jesus would have been problematic for Marcionism, and its adherents might have been motivated to change the text. This possibility would have been bolstered in Matthew 24.36 by an equally problematic distinction between the Father and Son. Marcion's church prospered in the latter half of the second century and was still exerting influence as late as the fifth century in Syria.[62] Because of the complex interbreeding of ideas in the early centuries, some Marcionite churches may have begun using orthodox Gospels after the death of their forebear and been motivated to change them. Overall, the relative improbability of this scenario due to Marcionite's selective canon, combined with the infrequent reassimilation of these manuscripts into orthodox circles, makes alterations by Marcionism unlikely.

Gnosticism either had no united system of Christology or, if there was one, would typically conceive of Jesus, however near to an emanation of God, as nevertheless distinct from the Father.[63] So if the Gnostics are implicated by known tampering with Scripture,[64] perhaps they are exonerated by the difficulty in finding a certain advantage and consequent motivation to remove statements of Jesus' ignorance.

Reservations about a movement altering the text drain away with such modalistic expressions as Docetism, Sabellianism, and Patripassionism (hereafter referred to collectively as Modalism) because they would have been motivated to remove any apparent differentiation between the Father and Son.

Docetism was a very early strand of Gnostic presuppositions that drove the notion that Jesus only *appeared* to be a man (but was not). Seeds of this thinking began with the apparently convoluted and

---

61. Räisänen, "Marcion," 105.
62. Räisänen, "Marcion," 101.
63. Valentinus (ca. 115–65 CE) taught the utter unknowable transcendence of the Father (Brown, *Heresies*, 100–101). Gnostic thinkers such as Saturnilus (or Saturninus) of Syria, Basilides of Egypt (specifically Alexandria), and Valentinus of Rome/Alexandria would stress Christ's lack of humanity. Saturninus was Docetic and stressed that Christ was not really a man. Basilides theorized in the early second century that Christ was an emanation from the Father. He was apparently involved in the Christian church in Alexandria and had great influence on it by teaching in the schools.
64. Irenaeus charged the Valentinians of corrupting Scripture not only by reinterpretation but by *adding* to it (*Against Heresies* 3.11.9). The addition was not explicitly interpolation into the current Gospel narratives per se but the *creation* of new ones considered to be Gospels (e.g., the Gospel of Truth).

self-aggrandizing personality of Simon Magus. He claimed to be both the Son and the Father,[65] and he apparently invoked the challenge of the NT writers. The thread of Docetism that centered on Jesus (rather than Simon) was undergirded by a dichotomy between the good, spiritual realm and the bad, physical realm. Christ was heavenly and good and therefore could not have a physical body. Diminutive notions of the "Son" (for Simonites) and of "Jesus" (for all Docetists) that appeared to Docetists to be rooted in the material realm would have been problematic for their Christology. Further, those strains that equated Christ with the "chief of the Aeons" would have been further motivated to strike οὐδὲ ὁ υἱός.[66] Docetism incited the polemics of the apostle Paul, the apostle John,[67] Ignatius, Polycarp, Tertullian, Hippolytus, and others.[68] It appears to have remained in existence by evolving into (or clinging to) Manichaeism and its derivatives in certain sectors and even in a pure form as late as the fourth and fifth century in Spain.[69] However, we may assume its primary period of influence to overlap the period of extant orthodox contestation (ca. 70–230 CE). This lengthy period is somewhat mitigated by the difficulty in determining what proportion of Docetists would have been motivated to make an alteration to Matthew 24.36.

Docetism was subsequently overshadowed by Adoptionism (discussed earlier under *orthodox* motivations for alteration), and the Christo-diminutive conceptions inherent in Adoptionism nourished the impetus behind another heretical suspect, Sabellianism. Noëtus of Smyrna and his disciple Praxeas of Rome,[70] responding to Adoptionism

---

65. Acts 8.9–24; Justin, *Apology* 1.26; Irenaeus, *Against Heresies* 1.23.1–4. Simon was active during the first century, as is evident from his interaction with Philip, Peter, and John. Hultgren and Haggmark venture a date of 70 CE for his death (*Earliest Christian Heretics*, 15). Apparently, a statue was erected in his honor with the Latin epigraph *SIMONI DEO SANCTO*—which means, "To Simon the Holy God" (Justin, *Apology* 1.26). Ignatius of Antioch said that Simon, claiming to be God, should consequently be able to overcome death. Though Simon died, his followers existed at least to the time of Origen (Origen, *Against Celsus* 1.57).

66. As mentioned, forerunners of Docetism such as Simon Magus and Menander saw themselves as "the Son." These groups would have been motivated to remove diminutive references to "the Son" (e.g., Matt 24.36) to whatever extent they used NT writings.

67. Paul may refer to a form of Docetism in Col 1.19 and 2.9. The elder combats it in 1 John 1.1–3 and 4.1–4 and in 2 John 7.

68. Ignatius, *Trallians* 10; *Ephesians* 7, 18; *Smyrnaeans* 1–6; Polycarp, *Epistle to the Philippians* 7; Tertullian, *On the Flesh of Christ* 5; Hippolytus, *Refutation of All Heresies* 8.1.

69. John Arendzen, "Docetae," in *TCE*, vol. 5 (New York: Encyclopedia, 1913), 70–72.

70. Warren H. Carroll, *The Founding of Christendom*, vol. 1 of *A History of Christendom* (Front Royal, VA: Christendom College Press, 1985), 467. Praxeas was active in Rome at the very end of the second century onward, and Noëtus came sometime afterward (Brown, *Heresies*, 100–101). Some chronologies list Noëtus as Praxeas's successor because Noëtus came to Rome after Praxeas.

Adam G. Messer

as well as a strand of Gnosticism that saw Christ as a lesser Aeon, stressed Jesus' divinity to the exclusion of his personal uniqueness from God the Father. Although Praxeas repented and realigned with the orthodox, Noëtus's disciple Epigonus began a school attended by Sabellius, who ushered into full bloom the idea that the Son *was* the Father.[71] Such conceptions peaked in the early third century and were subjugated by Pope Callistus I (d. ca. 223 CE) sometime around 220 CE. These ideas influenced later Trinitarian formulations, particularly the recognition of the divinity of the Holy Spirit.[72] What we discover from this short rumination of early Christological diversity is a lengthy period for Docetist ideals, perhaps from 70 to 212 CE,[73] and sharp Sabellian influence for several decades, from 190 to 220 CE.[74]

Each of these heresies would have been motivated to strike οὐδὲ ὁ υἱός against developing orthodox theology. Against each heresy discussed in this section, orthodox scribes would have benefited by the addition of οὐδὲ ὁ υἱός had it been originally absent in Matthew. We can speculate about both *who* would be motivated to change the text and *when*, but given the substantial overlap of influence among these groups (many with polar opposite Christologies), it is difficult to implicate one group without embroiling another by extension of the arguments used. Patristic evidence may be helpful in sorting out the who and when of the omission in Matthew 24.36.

THE PATRISTIC EVIDENCE

At what point did the orthodox begin to become concerned with the notion that Jesus did not know the day or hour of his return?[75] Until

---

71. Carroll, *Founding of Christendom*, 467. Other historical accounts set up the relationships differently; e.g., Hippolytus saw Cleomenes, a follower of Epigonus, as the founder of the school (Hippolytus, *Philos.* 9.7).

72. Brown, *Heresies*, 103.

73. The date of 70 CE reflects the conviction that Simon Magus was the Simon from Acts 8. The date of 200 CE is more indirect. We can surmise that Ignatius wrote his letters against the Docetists ca. 110 CE, during a set of years constrained by his date of death somewhere in the reign of Trajan (98–117 CE). Although I sidelined Marcion's direct following, Tertullian was still writing against Marcion's ideas in *Adversus Marcionem* between 207 and 212 CE.

74. One who objects on the ground that such groups could not have altered manuscripts not in their possession should realize that (1) the complicated nature of manuscript transmission would allow for it, (2) the heretics were often inside the church ranks, and (3) one cannot have it both ways: either the orthodox controlled their manuscripts or they did not, and if they did, the claims of wild copying must be revisited.

75. Of the references listed in BP, one reference to Ambrose appears to be mismarked (Ambrose, *De fide* 5.4.54), and the Pseudo-Clementine reference is vague, but the author did not seem to have a problem with an alleged ignorance of Jesus. More important, if a reference in BP is not listed in the following examples, it is because

they are concerned with this, the motivation for alteration is difficult to assert. In accordance with Origen's solution, I distinguish between a theological problem with *pre*-resurrection ignorance and a problem with *post*-resurrection ignorance.[76] As the impact of Origen on later fathers was substantial, his differentiation between the levels of Christ's knowledge before and after the resurrection is a poignant issue when considering whether they would remove the phrase to alleviate his pre-resurrection ignorance, because the church fathers may have had a problem with one and not the other. Further, since the idea behind Mark 13.32 is identical to that of Matthew 24.36, it is important to determine, as often as possible, whether the verse quoted is indeed from Matthew. If we mistake the *source* for a patristic quotation wherein οὐδὲ ὁ υἱός is present to be from Matthew's Gospel when it is truly from *Mark*, we may falsely conclude that the church father in question used a version of Matthew containing the phrase. So I will seek to determine the form of Matthew a father is using by invoking the aforementioned method against the differences in the Greek.

Irenaeus of Lyon

The earliest patristic discussion about Matthew 24.36 is by Irenaeus of Lyon (ca. 130–200 CE). Irenaeus received the torch from Polycarp, who received it from the apostle John, and he was not afraid to invoke his heritage against Gnostics who were claiming that *their* truth was of apostolic origin. In addition to Irenaeus's early attestation to the symmetry between the *four* Gospels and the "four zones of the world . . . and four principal winds,"[77] we learn much about his theology in his five-volume treatise entitled *Adversus haereses* (*Against Heresies*), written to counteract Gnostic teaching. At one point, Irenaeus is addressing the Gnostic practice of using Scripture to serve their own ends, so he seeks to show the proper method of interpreting Scripture—particularly obscure passages and the multifarious interpretations of parables. He concludes that we should interpret these in light of what we know to be true about God and not vice versa. In contrast to the Gnostic emphasis on secret knowledge, Irenaeus argues that complete knowledge about every inquiry into divine Scripture cannot be obtained in this life, and he points to Christ as an example of ignorance to chastise those who claim to know the "unspeakable mysteries of God":

---

it either did not help discern a father's form of Matthew or did not appear to offer additional insight beyond those examples explicitly discussed.

76. Origen, *Commentary on Matthew* 55.
77. Irenaeus, *Against Heresies* 3.11.8.

　　　　　　　　　　　　　　　Adam G. Messer

Ye presumptuously maintain that ye are acquainted with the unspeakable mysteries of God; while even the Lord, the very Son of God, allowed that the Father alone knows the very day and hour of judgment. . . . If, then, the Son was not ashamed to ascribe the knowledge of that day to the Father only,... neither let us be ashamed to reserve for God those greater questions which may occur to us. For no man is superior to his master.[78]

Irenaeus gives no indications of struggle regarding Christ's ignorance; rather, he uses it as *instructive* for the Christian. It is difficult to discern what his Matthean text looked like, particularly since the Greek text is missing, but a Latin translation is extant. Because some of the verse is missing, he may be quoting from memory, but we can at least say that the presence of "alone" (*solus*), combined with the reality that Matthew was, in general, the most read of the synoptics, would favor the view that *if* he is recalling a verse to memory, it would be Matthew, in which case our phrase is present in his text.[79] Whatever the case, we find no evidence of the *omission* in Irenaeus.

Hippolytus of Rome

Assuming the authenticity of his work *Philosophumean*, Hippolytus of Rome (ca. 180–230 CE) had an intriguing career. While his mentor combated the heresy of Gnosticism, Hippolytus fought against the Theodotians (Adoptionism), on the one hand, and Noëtus and Sabellius (Modalism), on the other. When Pope Zephyrinus remained hesitant to condemn Modalism, Hippolytus declared him incompetent. When that pope died and Callistus, whom Hippolytus believed to be modalistic, took his place, Hippolytus withdrew and declared himself not only a rival pope but the antipope—that is, *against* the establishment and *as* the true apostolic successor. Historians are uncertain whether Hippolytus's objections against Zephyrinus or Callistus are fair, but several of his personal characteristics are evident. He was uncompromising and somewhat reactionary, was an eloquent and prolific writer, and had some association with Origen. At one point, he was banished from the Catholic Church, but he reconciled with it prior to his death and was possibly even martyred for the faith.[80]

---

78. Irenaeus, *Against Heresies* 2.28.6; translation from ANF 1:401.
79. The Latin of 2.28.6 appears to be a direct (albeit partial) quotation: *De die autem illa et hora nemo scit, neque Filius, nisi Pater solus* (Adelin Rousseau and Louis Doutreleau, eds., *Irénée de Lyon contre les Hérésies*, vol. 2, pt. 2, Sources Chrétiennes 294 [Paris: Les Éditions du Cerf, 1982], 282). Aside from leaving out "not the angels of heaven," its form matches *exactly* both the words and word order of the Vulgate's form of Matthew. It retains the functional equivalent of μόνος (*solus*).
80. Johann Peter Kirsch, "Saints Hippolytus," in *TCE*, vol. 7 (New York: Robert Appleton, 1910), 360–62.

Hippolytus understands Christ as an amalgam between both the human and divine traits, who acts in accordance with each nature at different times and does not refuse the limitations of humanity (which would seem to exclude foreknowledge):

> For it was not in mere appearance or by conversion, but in truth, that He became man. Thus then, too, though demonstrated as God, He does not refuse the conditions proper to Him as man, since He hungers and toils and thirsts in weariness, and flees in fear, and prays in trouble. And He who as God has a sleepless nature, slumbers on a pillow. And He who for this end came into the world, begs off from the cup of suffering. And in agony He sweats blood, and is strengthened by an angel.[81]

In his commentary on Daniel that references Matthew 24.36, we find these sentiments: "The disciples also sought to learn these things [the time of end] from the Lord, but he concealed the day from them, so that he might have people who watch [for it]."[82] Here is a difference between Hippolytus and Irenaeus; the former makes Jesus the *concealer* of the mystery. Although Hippolytus makes the assumption that Christ knew the time of the end *at some point* (since he is the concealer of it), he was probably referring to Acts 1.7, wherein it seems to be Christ's explicit intention to deny the disciples this information. Therefore, Hippolytus would probably have had a problem with the notion of post-resurrection ignorance. Since his references to Matthew 24.36 are only conceptual, no determination can be made about his form of the text.

Hippolytus lived in the late second and early third centuries, and he battled against heresies on opposite sides of the theological spectrum—both Adoptionism and Modalism. During this precise time frame when some have conjectured an orthodox alteration to Matthew 24.36,[83] church leaders were fighting heresies that would have *benefited* by the removal of οὐδὲ ὁ υἱός (the Modalists). Therefore, it seems unlikely that the orthodox would have made such a revision.

Tertullian of Carthage

Quintus Septimius Florens Tertullianus (ca. 160–220 CE), or Tertullian, is arguably the most important Latin father after Saint Augustine, and he is well known for shunning philosophy and yet coining the term *Trinity* in opposition to early Sabellians. His training in law, literature, and philosophy perhaps disillusioned him to the role philosophy could play in the spiritual life, even though he was not averse

---

81. Hippolytus, *Against Noetus* 17–18; translation from ANF 5:230.
82. Hippolytus, *Commentarium in Danielem* 4.16.2.
83. Ehrman, *Orthodox Corruption*, 91–92.

to employing it as a jurist and later as a priest. He alludes to Matthew 24.36 in three separate works. In *On the Resurrection of the Flesh*, he spends time making the point that Christians are not resurrected immediately upon death but must wait for the last day, known only to God the Father:

> Now, forasmuch as the seasons of our entire hope have been fixed in the Holy Scripture, and since we are not permitted to place the accomplishment thereof, as I apprehend, previous to Christ's coming, our prayers are directed towards the end of this world, to the passing away thereof at the great day of the Lord—of His wrath and vengeance—the last day, which is hidden (from all), and known to none but the Father.[84]

A second reference can be found in *De anime* (*A Treatise on the Soul*), which is about the inherent conflict between judgment and the transmigration of souls. In it, he makes a vague reference to Matthew 24.36 and affirms that only the Father knows the day of judgment:

> Accordingly, God's judgment will be more full and complete, because it will be pronounced at the very last, in an eternal irrevocable sentence, both of punishment and of consolation, (on men whose) souls are not to transmigrate into beasts, but are to return into their own proper bodies. And all this once for all, and on "that day, too, of which the Father only knoweth;" . . . in order that by her trembling expectation faith may make full trial of her anxious sincerity, keeping her gaze ever fixed on that day, in her perpetual ignorance of it, daily fearing that for which she yet daily hopes.[85]

In a context about the uncertain time of death, the fact that he brings in the Father's singular knowledge of the end rather than the minimum rhetorical idea needed (viz., that of the soul's ignorance) suggests that he has no conflict with Christ not knowing this same information.

In *Against Praxeas*, Christ's ignorance of the last day and hour exists in juxtaposition with reference to Christ's deity.[86] Tertullian also addresses the distinctness of the Son from the Father by listing a number of Jesus' unique characteristics, one of which is simply that "He is also ignorant of the last day and hour, which is known to the Father only."[87] Although it appears that Tertullian can hold Jesus' selective ignorance in a cohesive theological schema without any signs of

---

84. Tertullian, *On the Resurrection of the Flesh* 22; translation from ANF 3:560.
85. Tertullian, *A Treatise on the Soul* 33; translation from ANF 3:215.
86. Tertullian, *Against Praxeas* 26.
87. Ibid.

conflict, the polemical nature of this treatise would preclude the likelihood that he would express signs of conflict with this understanding while arguing against Modalists. Had he held such internal reservations, he might just as easily have left out this example without any violence to his argument. His importation of this idea into a treatise against the transmigration of souls seems to suggest that Tertullian had no problem with a pre-resurrection ignorance of Christ, if not also a post-resurrection lack of knowledge, but the latter is speculative. As far as his form of Matthew is concerned, no reference establishes it for certain, but the presence of "only" suggests that Matthew was the source and that Tertullian's copy contained the phrase.[88]

Origen of Alexandria

Origen of Alexandria (185–254 CE) was an astute textual critic, even compiling a massive work known as the *Hexapla*, which consisted of six columns comparing different versions of the OT for the purpose of establishing the original. Further, he discusses manuscript evidence in his homilies and commentary on the NT. For example, in his *Commentary on Matthew*, his discussion on Matthew 18.1 notes that some manuscripts use "in that hour" while others use "in that day." He then proceeds to establish what the original said.[89] Origen truly had an acumen for textual criticism that was extraordinary for the early third century, but despite claims to the contrary,[90] I was unable to find any discussion of this omission by Origen; rather, the extant Latin text from section 55 of his *Commentary on Matthew* attests to the presence of οὐδὲ ὁ υἱός,[91] and he says about this text,

---

88. Tertullian, *Against Praxeas* 26. The Latin is *ignorans et ipse diem et horam ultimam soli Patri notam*. The presence of *soli* reminisces of the same word *solus* in the Latin version of Matthew. See Hermann-Josef Sieben, ed., *Tertullian Adversus Praxean: Gegen Praxeas*, Fontes Christiani (Freiburg: Herder, 2001), 232; Ernest Evans, *Tertulliani Adversus Praxean Liber* (London: S.P.C.K., 1948), 123.

89. He states his intent: "Let us see if it is possible from them [the variants] to find a way to understand, as being necessary, the addition, 'in that day' or 'hour'" (Origen, *Commentary on Matthew* 2.13.14). If the production of the *Hexapla* and the preceding example are not enough to establish his interest, he is forthright why this enterprise is important to him, "But now it is clear that there are many differences in the manuscripts, whether from carelessness [ῥᾳθυμία] of various scribes, from the audacity of some wicked scribes, from the neglect of correctors of the Scriptures, and even from the supposition made by the corrector himself to add or take away [words]" (Origen, *Commentary on Matthew* 2.15.14). This statement references both a problem in Matthew and one in the OT.

90. Ehrman, *Orthodox Corruption*, 91–92.

91. The Latin is *de die autem illa et hora nemo scit, neque angeli caelorum, neque Filius, nisi Pater solus* (MPG). This is an exact match in word form and word order to the Vulgate, but with "nor the Son" (*neque Filius*).

Adam G. Messer

Just as Paul said, "So at that time the Son will be subjected to the Father"; not as one who was formerly independent, but as one whose members are not yet fully perfected. Similarly, Christ did not know that day or hour . . . according to the use of the word "know" in these passages, "the one who keeps the commands will not know stumbling," and, "the one who knew no sin was made sin on our behalf." In this way [we understand] what is meant by "nor the Son [knew]."[92]

Origen understands Jesus to be claiming that he does not have intimate knowledge of the affair, like the experience of Adam knowing Eve intimately. His reason for why the Son claimed ignorance was that, although he established the date prior to the incarnation, he had not fully grown into all knowledge prior to his resurrection. This explains why Jesus, during a post-resurrection occurrence in Acts 1.7, later changed his response to the same question to "It is not *for you* to know the day or hour."[93] Origen affirms this: "Because afterwards the Son also knew by receiving knowledge from the Father even over the day and the hour of the consummation, so that no longer would only the Father know, but also the Son."[94]

In summary, Origen does not appear to have a problem with Christ's pre-resurrection ignorance.[95] He often contemplated the limitations

92. Origen, *Commentariorum Series in Evangelium Matthaei* 126–27. An interpretive issue surrounds the phrase τὸ σῶμα τοῦ Χριστοῦ, which is here taken to refer to Christ himself ("*Christ* did not know") and not to a group of believers or his church ("*the body of Christ* did not know"). Although the immediately following lacuna prevents additional verification of this interpretative decision, the context is seeking to show what is meant by the phrase "neither the Son."

93. The emphatic placement of the pronoun in the verse brings legitimacy to the rhetorical stress indicated with italics. My appreciation goes to Dan Wallace for this observation.

94. Origen, *Commentary on Matthew* 55. This section is only extant in Latin: *Nam postea et Filius cognovit scientiam a Patre suscipiens, etiam de die consummationis et hora, ut jam non solum Pater sciret de ea, sed etiam Filius* (MPG).

95. Origen elsewhere entertains the notions that God has not even fixed the day of the return (Origen, *Commentary on Matthew* 55) or that possibly Christ was speaking on behalf of the church, to help its members realize that it is not for them to know the time (Origen, *Commentary on Matthew* 55). These notions may indicate that he was looking for reasons to avoid the implication that Jesus was ignorant, but it is more likely that they represent Origen's focus and passion. When one reads his works, what strikes the reader is his attention to detail and grasp of its implications. He explores issues from a great variety of angles and demonstrates a willingness to explore uncharted theological territory. He was truly an early Christian academic in this regard. This predilection would explain why Origen disclosed multiple theories, along with the fact that the fathers were not averse to seeing multiple senses to Scripture. Origen held to a threefold interpretation: a literal sense, a moral sense, and an allegorical-mystical sense (Robert M. Grant and David Tracy, *A Short History of the Interpretation of the Bible*, 2nd ed. [Minneapolis: Fortress, 1984], 59). He was particularly favorable to the allegorical sense, believing it to be preeminent.

listed in Scripture about Jesus, and yet his systematic works found no inconsistency between Jesus having ignorance while on earth and yet being deity. He did, however, believe that Christ acquired all knowledge after his resurrection. Of further interest, his great concern for properly establishing the text is valuable for the modern textual critic's understanding of what manuscripts Origen knew about in both Alexandria and Caesarea.

Eusebius of Caesarea

Eusebius of Caesarea (260–341 CE), the famous church historian of the fourth century, may have referenced Matthew 24.36 in a fragmentary work known as *Supplementa ad quaestiones ad Marinum*:

> He was able to attain the resurrection from the dead, according to which hour no one knew, and according to which time no one was told by the evangelists. And so one opportunely inquired, and to him was told everything concerning the end by what had [already] been said, "Concerning the day none knows, not even the angels of God." Therefore, the Savior, who has become the first fruits of the resurrection, according to which hour none knew, was raised, escaping the notice of everyone, and brought up in form out from the stone [grave] he had occupied.[96]

The possible reference to Matthew 24.36 has all distinguishing Greek features eradicated (probably because it is a recollection from memory), so there is no way to discern its source or his form of Matthew. Theologically, the verse appears to be associating the uncertainty of the day and hour to Christ's resurrection. There are no indications that Christ was ignorant, but given that other important parts, such as the Father's sole possession of this knowledge, is also absent, Eusebius's evidence is neutral at best.

Athanasius of Alexandria

Athanasius (ca. 290–373 CE) was a staunch defender of the doctrine of the Trinity, so much so that he earned the title "the Father of Orthodoxy." He records his thoughts on the matter in *Discourses Against*

As such, Origen was unalterably committed to finding in every piece of Scripture a spiritual nugget for the church. He is known to make even relatively mundane details applicable to his listeners (e.g., Origen, *Homilies on Luke* 47). In this light, it is entirely unsurprising that he would posit Jesus speaking as the church in Matt 24.36. However, we also find that he did write a systematic presentation of his beliefs called *De principiis* (On First Things) in which his language is less speculative, and his section on the end clearly states that only the Father knows the time (*De principiis* 1.6).

96. Eusebius, *Supplementa ad quaestiones ad Marinum* 985.

Adam G. Messer

the Arians. He addresses the Arian point of view in multiple ways, but one is hermeneutical—by referring to the canonical context:

> "But of that day and that hour knoweth no man, neither the Angels of God, nor the Son;" for being in great ignorance as regards these words, and being stupefied about them, they think they have in them an important argument for their heresy. . . . and the Son who knows the Father is said to be ignorant of an hour of a day; now what can be spoken more contrary to sense, or what madness can be likened to this? Through the Word all things have been made, times and seasons and night and day and the whole creation; and is the Framer of all said to be ignorant of His work? And the very context of the lection shews that the Son of God knows that hour and that day, though the Arians fall headlong in their ignorance.[97]

Athanasius argues that since other portions of Scripture indicate that Christ is the creator of all things, interpreters should allow this truth to inform less clear verses. For him, the question is not, did the Son know the day and hour? Instead, it is, given that the Son knows by virtue of other clear passages, why would he say he did not? His answer pertains to the nature of humanity:

> Now why it was that, though He knew, He did not tell His disciples plainly at that time . . . [of] this I think none of the faithful is ignorant, viz. that He made this as those other declarations as man by reason of the flesh. For this as before is not the Word's deficiency, but of that human nature whose property it is to be ignorant.[98]

Athanasius has a definite problem with the idea that Jesus was not omniscient, for he continues to give reasons, such as the following, for why Jesus did know the time of his return: (1) the absence of the Holy Spirit in Matthew 24.36 should clue us in that Jesus was not excluded from the knowledge, because if the Spirit had it, so must have the one on whom he depended;[99] (2) for him to express ignorance was to identify with humanity, even though he was much more;[100] (3) Christ set the proper example for how believers should not be negligent toward the end;[101] and (4) in context, Christ's admonition to keep watch "because you do not know on what day your Lord will come" does not say "because *I* do not know" (italics mine).[102] It is worth mentioning that these

---

97. Athanasius, *Discourses against the Arians* 3.42; translation from NPFS 4:416.
98. Ibid., 3.43; translation from NPFS 4:417.
99. Ibid., 3.44.
100. Ibid., 3.46.
101. Ibid., 3.49.
102. Ibid., 3.45. The context is Matt 24.42. Cf. Mark 13.33.

arguments by no means exhaust the arsenal of Athanasius, but they are sufficient to demonstrate his problem with an ignorant Christ even before the resurrection. It is also noteworthy that his version of Matthew does not contain the phrase οὐδὲ ὁ υἱός.[103]

Hilary of Poitiers

Hilary of Poitiers (d. 368 CE) was exiled to Phrygia during the first six of his final twelve years, for his steadfast stance against Arianism. This sojourn provided opportunity to study the ways in which the East and West used different vocabulary to refer to the same ideas. He discovered that some differences between the East's and West's Christologies lay not in their underlying ideas but in their phraseology. This insight and his sharp rhetoric allowed him to be an influence toward reconciliation between the Eastern and Western Trinitarian churches of the empire for the short remainder of his exonerated life. Another advantage of this banishment was the opportunity to write his *De Trinitate* (On the Trinity) and *De Synodis* (On the Councils). In Hilary we can see some of the sophistication with which these early fathers tackled the problem of Christ's ignorance, because much of Hilary's writing on this issue is extant. Whereas moderns may get involved in countering Arianism with linguistic arguments, the fathers, such as Hilary, typically offered *conceptual* rebuttals:

> The Son is ignorant, then, of nothing which the Father knows, nor does it follow because the Father alone knows, that the Son does not know. Father and Son abide in unity of nature, and the ignorance of the Son belongs to the divine Plan of silence, seeing that in Him are hidden all the treasures of wisdom and knowledge. This the Lord Himself testified, when He answered the question of the Apostles concerning the times, It is not yours to know times or moments, which the Father has set within His own authority. The knowledge is denied them, and not only that, but the anxiety to learn is forbidden, because it is not theirs to know these times. Yet now that He is risen, they ask again, though their question on the former occasion had been met with the reply, that not even the Son knew. They cannot possibly have understood literally that the Son did not know, for they ask Him again as though He did know. They perceived in the mystery of His ignorance a divine Plan of silence, and now, after His resurrection, they renew

---

103. Ibid., 28.472.47–52. His Greek text of Matt 24.34–36 is almost identical to NA²⁷, except for the omission of the phrase in question: Ἀμὴν, λέγω ὑμῖν, ὅτι οὐ μὴ παρέλθῃ ἡ γενεὰ αὕτη, ἕως ἂν πάντα ταῦτα γένηται. Ὁ οὐρανὸς καὶ ἡ γῆ παρελεύσεται, οἱ δὲ λόγοι μου οὐ μὴ παρέλθωσι. Περὶ δὲ τῆς ἡμέρας ἢ τῆς ὥρας οὐδεὶς οἶδεν, οὔτε οἱ ἄγγελοι τῶν οὐρανῶν, εἰ μὴ ὁ Πατὴρ μόνος.

Adam G. Messer

the question, thinking that the time has come to speak. And the Son no longer denies that He knows, but tells them that it is not theirs to know, because the Father has set it within His own authority. If then, the Apostles attributed it to the divine Plan, and not to weakness, that the Son did not know the day, shall we say that the Son knew not the day for the simple reason that He was not God?[104]

Here are Hilary's basic arguments:

1. Christ's assertion of his ignorance pertains to the divine economy rather than to true ignorance.[105]

2. The apostles understood that Jesus' words in Matthew 24.36 only indicated that it was not *yet* time to reveal the divine plan,[106] which is why they asked again in Acts 1.7.[107]

3. The ignorance is a means not to delude but to encourage in perseverance.[108]

4. That the Father alone knows does not exclude the Son from knowing, since he is one with the Father.

5. Jesus' ignorance was true of him as a man but not as God.[109]

6. Christ spoke of this ignorance to demonstrate, against Sabellianism, that Christ submitted to the prerogative of the Father, who held original initiative within himself.[110]

Did Hilary have problems with a genuine ignorance of Christ such that his thought influenced scribes toward the removal of οὐδὲ ὁ υἱός

---

104. Hilary, *On the Trinity* 9.75; translation from NPFS 9:181.

105. Ibid., 9.62.

106. Hilary saw the great challenge of Christ's life as the gradual impartation of a truth too big for the contemporary mind, particularly the contemporary Jewish mind. For this reason, Christ was restricted in what he could say and when he could say it, by his purpose to move a disbelieving people committed to monotheism into the true fabric of reality, which centers on a Trinitarian understanding of his person. This, he says, "is explained by a discrimination between gradual revelation and full expression of His nature and power. . . . Christ's true Godhead is no whit impaired because, to form the mystery of the Gospel faith, the birth and Name of Christ were revealed gradually, and under conditions which He chose of occasion and time" (ibid., 1.30; translation from NPFS 9:48).

107. Ibid., 9.63.

108. Ibid., 9.67.

109. Ibid., 9.75.

110. Ibid., 10.8.

from the manuscript tradition? All of the preceding explanations assume this difficulty, against which he offers additional counters: (1) the apostle Paul's declaration in Colossians 2.3 that all wisdom and knowledge is contained in the Son,[111] (2) the principle that overattention on a single word or phrase divorced from conceptual contexts is greatly dangerous,[112] (3) that we should understand the words of Matthew 24.36 in light of (a) what manner of questions he was answering, (b) at what time he was speaking, and (c) what knowledge he wished to impart at that time,[113] (4) that ignorance cannot defeat the "Lord of glory,"[114] and (5) Jesus' desire to serve as an example to his disciples.[115] Hilary dealt with the issue of Christ's ignorance on a conceptual level. Having said this, his version of Matthew did appear to have contained οὐδὲ ὁ υἱός.[116]

Epiphanius of Salamis

In 367 CE, Epiphanius[117] became the bishop of Salamis, a town on the east coast of Cyprus. He was intelligent and broadly studied, being called "five-tongued" for his learning in Hebrew, Syriac, Egyptian, Greek, and Latin. His work *Panarion* (Medicine Chest) deals with around eighty ancient heresies he traveled widely to squelch. He apparently even took issue with Origen and John Chrysostom. These factors, along with his ascetic background, probably made him well known, which means that his views were not parochial. He was an ardent defender of Trinitarian theology, not unlike Athanasius.

---

111. Ibid., 9.62.
112. Ibid., 1.32. He says, "[The heretics'] folly being as great as their blasphemy, they fail to mark that Christ's words, spoken under similar circumstances, are always consistent; they cleave to the letter and ignore the purpose of His words."
113. Ibid., 1.30.
114. Ibid., 9.60. This is a sophisticated argument based on 1 Cor 2.8, namely, that unless Christ participates in deity, how can he be glory's Master?
115. Ibid., 9.71.
116. Ibid., 1.29–30. The reference in Hilary's *On the Councils* (85) seems to quote from Mark, since it is lacking "only."
117. At least two men named Epiphanius are recorded in church history. They are actually over a hundred years apart, yet attribution of the works *Ancoratus* and *Panarion* is made to both. BP attributes these works to Epiphanius of Constantinople, a patriarch of this city in the early sixth century. Others attribute it to Epiphanius of Salamis, an ascetic who lived through most of the fourth century, including the Arian battles that accompanied this period. Interestingly, TLG attributes it to the patriarch of Constantinople and yet dates it as though it were the other. Without entering into this particular discussion, other than to note it, I assume the earlier Epiphanius of Salamis for two reasons: (1) this position seems to have broader support, and (2) he is strategically placed within the Arian controversies of the fourth century following the Nicene formulation (ca. 315–403 CE). Even more intriguing, Epiphanius of Salamis was born in Judea, and after his conversion from Judaism and sojourn as a monastic in Egypt, he returned to his birthplace and set up a monastery.

Epiphanius had a definite problem with the idea that the Son did not know the day and hour of his return. In his work *Ancoratus* (Well-Anchored), he paraphrases Matthew 24.36 and Mark 13.32, saying:

> For it is not said concerning angels [that] they examine the deep things of God, nor about archangels. "For no one knows the day or hour," the Son of God said, "not the angels of heaven nor the Son, except the Father." But the foolish who have not been adorned by the Holy Spirit [need to] consider [that] one is not in the Father who is not in the divinity of the Son. "For as the Father has life in himself, so also the Son has life in himself." And, "All that belongs to my Father is mine," said the holy Word of God himself. And as for the things which belong to the Father: What belongs to God the Father is also of the Son. The life of the Father, this also is of the Son.[118]

Here he argues that everything that the Father has, the Son also has—including all knowledge. An ambiguity exists in the fact that Epiphanius is speaking in the present tense, and this may refer to Christ's current estate. If a number of church fathers interpreted Christ's statement of ignorance as temporarily limited to his earthly sojourn prior to the resurrection (as Origen earlier brought out), even if they believed that Christ in his exalted state knew the day and hour, a scribe encountering Matthew 24.36 in the heat of controversy might have found reason to strike οὐδὲ ὁ υἱός from his copy. He may have reasoned that such ignorance was liable to misrepresent Christ's present actuality and abilities. Though this may not reflect a direct quotation, it uses a genitive for expressing "in heaven" (like Matthew) and omits μόνος. If it is a quotation, it is probably from Mark.

Within this same work, Epiphanius later references Matthew 24.36 twice[119] and adds two arguments to his arsenal. First, he argues that since the Son knows the Father fully and since knowledge of the Father is greater than knowledge of the day and hour, Christ must know the time of his return.[120] Second, he maintains that there are differing degrees of knowledge—namely, that of raw information and that of experience—and that Christ was only claiming ignorance of the latter.[121]

---

118. Epiphanius, *Ancoratus* 16.2–6. The candidate for quotation is οὐδεὶς γὰρ οἶδε τὴν ἡμέραν οὐδὲ τὴν ὥραν οὔτε οἱ ἄγγελοι τοῦ οὐρανοῦ οὔτε ὁ υἱός, εἰ μὴ ὁ πατήρ.

119. Epiphanius, *Ancoratus* 19.6–7. The candidate for quotation is οὐδεὶς οἶδε τὴν ἡμέραν καὶ τὴν ὥραν οὔτε οἱ ἄγγελοι οἱ ἐν τῷ οὐρανῷ εἰ μὴ μόνος ὁ πατήρ. Though this may not reflect a quotation, it uses a dative for expressing "in heaven" (like Mark), omits οὐδὲ ὁ υἱός, and includes μόνος. If it is a quotation, it is probably Matthew and would reflect the omission. The second reference is Epiphanius, *Ancoratus* 22.1–4, which is just a snippet: εἰ μὴ ὁ πατὴρ μόνος, οὔτε οἱ ἄγγελοι οὔτε ὁ υἱός.

120. Epiphanius, *Ancoratus* 17.1–4.

121. Ibid., 21.3–5.

Epiphanius's *Panarion* is built around a systematic attempt to dismantle ancient heresies, from Ebionite to Essene, from Stoic to Sebuaean, from Pepuzian to Pharisee. His discussion in *Panarion* argues that since the Father has entrusted all judgment to the Son, the Son would know the day.[122]

Some interesting observations surface. The first of note is that Epiphanius traveled widely throughout Judea, Egypt, and the region of Cyprus to battle heresies and makes no formal mention of differing versions of Matthew. Second, although he takes vehement issue with the idea that the Son did not know the time of his return, he may not have had an issue with the Son's pre-resurrection ignorance.[123] Third, five of Epiphanius's references to Matthew 24.36/Mark 13.32 (presented here with word order excepted) illustrate the difficulty in making a determination of what his form of Matthew looked like:

a.	τὴν ἡμέραν	καὶ	τὴν	ὥραν οὐδεὶς οἶδε
b. περὶ	τῆς ἡμέρας ἐκείνης	καὶ	τῆς	ὥρας οὐδεὶς οἶδεν
c. περὶ δὲ	τῆς ἡμέρας ἐκείνης	ἢ	τῆς	ὥρας οὐδεὶς οἶδεν
d. γὰρ	τὴν ἡμέραν	οὐδὲ	τὴν	ὥραν οὐδεὶς οἶδε
e.				

a. οὔτε οἱ ἄγγελοι	οἱ ἐν τῷ	οὐρανῷ		εἰ μὴ ὁ πατήρ μόνος
b. οὔτε οἱ ἄγγελοι	ἐν	οὐρανῷ	οὔτε ὁ υἱός,	εἰ μὴ ὁ πατὴρ μόνος
c. οὔτε οἱ ἄγγελοι			οὔτε ὁ υἱός,	εἰ μὴ ὁ πατὴρ μόνος
d. οὔτε οἱ ἄγγελοι	τοῦ	οὐρανοῦ	οὔτε ὁ υἱός,	εἰ μὴ ὁ πατήρ
e. οὔτε οἱ ἄγγελοι			οὔτε ὁ υἱός	εἰ μὴ ὁ πατὴρ μόνος

---

122. Epiphanius, *Panarion* 69.46.

123. Two indicators argue that he did not have a problem with at least some difference of knowledge between the Father and Son. Epiphanius's breakdown of knowledge into degrees allows him to maintain Jesus' omniscience, but it still highlights a difference between the Father's knowledge and the Son's (Epiphanius, *Ancoratus* 22.4). Second, all discussions seem to use present tense verbs ("the Son does not know") rather than past tense verbs. This may suggest that he is taking issue with those who say Christ *currently* does not know the time of his return. As mentioned, Origen differentiated Christ's knowledge before the resurrection with his knowledge afterward. Epiphanius was no friend of Origen, for his condemnations of Origen's writings led to synodal censure. So for Epiphanius and Origen to share this idea attests to its ingemination in patristic theology apparently across a diverse spectrum of points of view.

Adam G. Messer

No recognizable patterns truly emerge.[124] However, if the presence of μόνος is used as an indicator of Matthew's text, Epiphanius would attest to the reading with οὐδὲ ὁ υἱός. As it stands, the absence of certain phrases and forms in any single example indicates that he is likely operating primarily from memory—perhaps completely so. That no reference matches our critically reconstructed text does not help decide the case.

Amphilochius of Iconium

Amphilochius of Iconium (ca. 340–400 CE), a contemporary and member of the Cappadocian fathers, a friend to Gregory of Nazianzus, and a theologian in league with Basil of Caesarea, interacts in an interesting manner regarding the concept of the Son's ignorance. In response to such an idea, he argues that the Son was not making an emphatic statement about his ignorance of the second coming as much as he was asserting his dependence on his Father; that is, although Christ offers foresight about a number of things, he is concerned to stress the utter secrecy of the event. To support this assertion, Amphilochius makes a case, from similar constructions in both testaments, that the εἰ μή ("except") should be taken in this instance—as it is taken in other places, such as 1 Corinthians 2.11, Isaiah 1.9, and Psalms 93.17 and 123.2–3— as *not* meaning "without exception":

> And when it [our passage] says, "neither the Son, except the Father," it does not falsely allege an ignorance of the Son, but it explains an assertion about knowledge. For all things, as many as the Father has, are clearly *also* of the Son. Not that the Son has this knowledge unless (εἰ μή) the Father has this knowledge. But [what] the Father has, truly, [so] also does the Son similarly have. For Scripture has been known, on occasion, to put the εἰ μή in various places indeed, such as: no one knows the things of man except (εἰ μή) the Spirit of man which is in him—similarly also the things of God no one knows, except (εἰ μή) the Spirit which is from God [1 Cor 2.11]. But when εἰ μή is placed beside those things which are expected, then no longer does it assert what is presented in the apodosis. Take, for example, when it says, "Unless (εἰ

---

124. The Greek text appearing closest to direct quotation is περὶ δὲ τῆς ἡμέρας ἐκείνης ἢ τῆς ὥρας οὐδεὶς οἶδεν, οὔτε οἱ ἄγγελοι οὔτε ὁ υἱός, εἰ μὴ ὁ πατὴρ μόνος (Epiphanius, *Panarion* 69.15.5). The conjunction is from Mark, the μόνος from Matthew, and the angelic abode ("in heaven") is missing. The Greek in the other is περὶ τῆς ἡμέρας ἐκείνης καὶ τῆς ὥρας οὐδεὶς οἶδεν, οὔτε οἱ ἄγγελοι ἐν οὐρανῷ οὔτε ὁ υἱός, εἰ μὴ ὁ πατὴρ μόνος (Epiphanius, *Panarion* 69.43.1). The conjunction is taken from Matthew, while the TSKS is absent as in Mark; and the μόνος is from Matthew, while the dative ἐν οὐρανῷ is from Mark. Because of this mixture, it is difficult to discern which text he is quoting from—perhaps both.

μή) the Lord of the Sabbath had left to us a posterity, we would have become like Sodom, and would have resembled Gomorrah" [Isa 1.9; Rom 9.29]. Therefore, since he did leave for us a posterity, we have not become like Sodom nor truly resembled Gomorrah.[125]

Amphilochius understood the εἰ μή to reflect a less exclusive idea than "except." Rather, it would be used to mean, "No one knows the day or hour, and no one could know—not the angels in heaven nor the Son—if the Father didn't know." But since the Father knows, so also does the Son; nevertheless, it is information locked away by virtue of belonging exclusively to the divine realm. When Jesus brought the focus back to the Father, he was asserting not his own ignorance but the domain of God.

Basil of Caesarea

Basil of Caesarea (329–79 CE), arguably the most brilliant of the Cappadocian fathers, spent time as a youth in Pontus and was schooled in Caesarea, Constantinople, and Athens. He labored in arenas that the modern American church might find politically unfeasible. He worked to *exclude* "unfit candidates from the sacred ministry" and to deliver "bishops from the temptation of simony."[126] Later in life, he was influenced by his sister Macrina toward a more ascetic lifestyle and retraction of earthly attachments, and he visited monasteries in Egypt, Palestine, Coele-Syria, and Mesopotamia to gather information in order to start one in Pontus, in which he implemented his cenobitic form. His foci revolved around self-discipline, almsgiving, and avoiding the jealousy his superior administrative and intellectual giftedness roused in more established clergymen. He interacted not only with the Cappadocians but also with Athanasius.

Basil was a powerful player in the Trinitarian battle, and he took up our passage with these words:

> So now also, if anyone takes the fact of ignorance as applying to Him who had received all things according to the dispensation and was advancing in wisdom and grace with God and men, will not be carried beyond a conception consistent with piety. It would be a fitting task for your diligence to set forth the words of the Gospel and to compare those of Matthew and those of Mark with each other. For these alone appear to have agreed with each other on this passage. Now

---

125. Amphilochius, *Fragment 5 of Scr. Eccl.* 5. This reference is from TLG.
126. Joseph McSorley, "Saint Basil the Great," in *TCE*, vol. 2 (New York: Encyclopedia, 1913), 330–34. Basil and Gregory of Nazianzus compiled a work known as *Philocalia*, which contained excerpts of Origen's work.

Adam G. Messer

the reading in Matthew is as follows: "But of that day and hour no one knoweth, not the Angels of heaven, but the Father alone."[127] And Mark's is: "But of that day or hour no man knoweth, neither the angels in heaven, nor the Son, but the Father."[128] What, then, is worthy of note in these words? That Matthew said nothing about the ignorance of the Son, but seems to agree with Mark in meaning when he says: "But the Father alone." And we hold that "alone" was said in contradistinction to the angels, and that the Son is not included with His own servants in the matter of ignorance.[129]

There are a few things to notice here. Although Basil is fairly well-traveled, he does not make mention of manuscripts of Matthew that contain οὐδὲ ὁ υἱός. Rather, he declares it noteworthy that Matthew does not mention the ignorance of the Son but uses μόνος in contradistinction to the angels only.[130] He believed that the εἰ μή did not necessarily contain an exclusive idea but was here to be taken to mean that God alone was *preeminent*; that is, Christ was asserting not his ignorance but his dependence on the Father's knowledge as the source of his own. Beyond its interpretive implications, Basil's comment is also singularly interesting in light of the fact that Origen, who wrote his commentary on Matthew while he was in Caesarea around 246 CE, mentioned no awareness of its omission. Within 120 years, οὐδὲ ὁ υἱός apparently disappeared from the manuscript landscape available to Origen in Caesarea in his day.[131]

Basil references the Son's ignorance and our verse in other places as well, incorporating these additional arguments:

1. It would be strange for the creator of all to be selectively ignorant of something that he created.[132]

---

127. The Matthean Greek is Περὶ δὲ τῆς ἡμέρας ἐκείνης οὐδεὶς οἶδεν, οὐδὲ οἱ ἄγγελοι τῶν οὐρανῶν, εἰ μὴ ὁ Πατὴρ μόνος.

128. The Markan Greek is Περὶ δὲ τῆς ἡμέρας ἐκείνης ἢ ὥρας οὐδεὶς οἶδεν, οὐδὲ οἱ ἄγγελοι οἱ ἐν οὐρανῷ, οὐδὲ ὁ Υἱός, εἰ μὴ ὁ Πατήρ.

129. Basil *Letters* 236.1–2; translation from Roy J. Deferrari, *Saint Basil: The Letters*, vol. 3, Loeb Classical Library (Cambridge, MA: Harvard University Press, 1926).

130. The Markan parallel has no μόνος but uses an εἰ μή construction that can apparently be taken in a preeminent sense instead of merely an exclusive manner (Charles Edward Powell, "The Semantic Relationship between the Protasis and the Apodosis of New Testament Conditional Constructions" [PhD diss., Dallas Theological Seminary, 2000], 180–207).

131. Although Origen may have brought manuscripts from Alexandria with him, he has a penchant for comparing available manuscripts, and he establishes this practice within his *Commentary on Matthew* in at least these places: Matt 4.17, 16.20, 18.1, 21.5, 24.19, and 27.16–17 (Bruce M. Metzger, "References in Origen to Variant Readings," in *Historical and Literary Studies: Pagan, Jewish, and Christian*, New Testament Tools and Studies 8 [Grand Rapids: Eerdmans, 1968], 92–94).

132. Basil, *Adversus Eunomium* 696–98. This reference is from TLG.

2. The canonical context establishing "all things whatsoever the Father hath are mine" should be an overruling consideration.[133]

3. The interpretive flexibility of the Greek phrase εἰ μή can be further corroborated by listing other scriptural examples.[134]

The significance of these observations is that Basil has a problem with an assertion of the Son's ignorance. He does not explicitly mention whether he takes issue with a pre-resurrection or post-resurrection ignorance (Basil was very familiar with Origen's work). Yet it seems likely that he would take issue with even a pre-resurrection ignorance, given that he argues that this passage should be read in light of other passages that discuss the Son's *present* ownership of all that belongs to the Father.[135]

Gregory of Nazianzus

Fighting alongside Basil in the battle for the Son's coequality was a friend he made while he schooled in Athens, Gregory of Nazianzus[136] (ca. 325–89 CE). He composed orations wherein he addressed the Arian objection to the Son's *homoousian* with the Father:

> Their tenth objection is the ignorance [of Christ], and the statement that Of the last day and hour knoweth no man, not even the Son Himself, but the Father. And yet how can Wisdom be ignorant of anything—that

---

133. Basil, *Letters* 236.2.
134. Ibid., 236.1. He lists Matt 11.27 and Mark 10.18.
135. One cannot help but suspect that even had Matthew contained οὐδὲ ὁ υἱός, Basil would have interpreted it just like he does Mark, namely, with a hermeneutic dependent on a canonical context *and* a tradition that regarded the "rule of faith" (or "rule of truth") as a passed-down lens through which a correct reading of Scripture comes into focus. For Basil, this rule seems to have included Nicea (325 CE) and the Son's divinity.
136. Gregory was no stranger to Athens. He spent ten years there for school and met the future apostate emperor Julian, even then discerning Julian's true character and distrusting him. Torn between a desire toward the monastic life of Basil and the separate conviction that such was not in accordance with his reading of Scripture, he visited Basil on and off at the monastery during his period of reflection. His bishop and father finally forced him to take on the priesthood around 361 CE in Nazianzus. Gregory devoted his inheritance to the poor, refused the bishopric offered him, and retreated to a monastery in 375 CE. Yet he emerged four years later, upon invitation from persecuted Trinitarians, to minister to the arch city of Constantinople, which had fallen into the darkness of Arianism for three decades. Here he gave his celebrated treatises on the Trinity that earned him both fame and persecution. During this period, St. Jerome became his disciple; the eastern emperor Theodosius was converted and baptized; and the consequent First Council of Constantinople (381 CE) was convened, in which Gregory had considerable influence.

is, Wisdom Who made the worlds, Who perfects them, Who remodels them, Who is the Limit of all things that were made, Who knoweth the things of God as the spirit of a man knows the things that are in him? For what can be more perfect than this knowledge? How then can you say that all things before that hour He knows accurately, and all things that are to happen about the time of the end, but of the hour itself He is ignorant? For such a thing would be like a riddle.[137]

Gregory has essentially the same line of argumentation as his Cappadocian brothers, namely, an *a fortiori* argument: if Christ knows the greater, how much more should he know the lesser subset of it? Further, some things can be known as God while not being known as man. This paradox does not bother Gregory, but the controversies of Monophysitism and Monothelitism, although germinated, had not yet bloomed.

Gregory of Nyssa

Gregory of Nyssa (d. ca. 385 CE), Basil of Caesarea's brother, entered into the Christological controversies with argumentation similar to that of his brother and Gregory of Nazianzus. Like the other Cappadocian fathers, he had a problem with associating ignorance with Christ.[138] Notable to this discussion is the fact that his version of Matthew does not appear to have had οὐδὲ ὁ υἱός.[139]

Ambrose of Milan

Saint Ambrose (340–97 CE), beloved influencer of Saint Augustine, also mentioned our verse:

---

137. Gregory of Nazianzus, *Orationes* 30.15; translation from NPFS 7:315. The Greek text is not Matthew or Mark but reflects a conceptual parallel (καὶ τὸ μηδένα γινώσκειν τὴν τελευταίαν ἡμέραν ἢ ὥραν, μηδὲ τὸν υἱὸν αὐτόν, εἰ μὴ τὸν πατέρα).

138. "How [is it that] with everyone else the son does not know the day either—the one who has in himself the Father and himself is in the Father?" (Gregory of Nyssa, *Adversus Arium et Sabellium de patre et filio* 84–85).

139. Gregory of Nyssa, *Adversus Arium et Sabellium de patre et filio* 76. The Greek text is οὐδεὶς οἶδε τὴν συντελεστικὴν ἡμέραν καὶ τὴν ὥραν οὐδ' οἱ ἄγγελοι τῶν οὐρανῶν οὐδὲ ὁ υἱὸς ἐν τοῖς κατὰ Μάρκον εἰρημένοις, εἰ μὴ ὁ πατὴρ μόνος. The phrase ἐν τοῖς κατὰ Μάρκον εἰρημένοις can be taken in two ways. Either the whole verse is "according to Mark" (i.e., quoting Mark), or just οὐδὲ ὁ υἱός is according to Mark. I take it in the latter sense, because of Gregory's placement of the attribution to Mark and the verse's striking similarity in form with Matthew—note the genitive plural οὐρανῶν and the presence of καί and μόνος. The implication of this interpretation is that his copy of Matthew did not contain this phrase and that Gregory was bringing in Mark's emendation to address the principle behind it.

It is written, they say: "But of that day and that hour knoweth no man, no, not the angels which are in heaven, neither the Son, but the Father only." First of all the ancient Greek manuscripts do not contain the words, "neither the Son." But it is not to be wondered at if they who have corrupted the sacred Scriptures, have also falsified this passage. The reason for which it seems to have been inserted is perfectly plain, so long as it is applied to unfold such blasphemy.[140]

Like all the other fathers since the beginning of the fourth century that I have mentioned, Ambrose clearly had a problem with the Son's ignorance before his resurrection. He even introduces a new twist by asserting that none of the ancient Greek manuscripts (plural) contain the phrase "neither the Son." He even ponders that its *presence* is due to unorthodox corruption. Although he is writing in Latin, the fact that he specifically mentions "ancient Greek manuscripts" as testifying to the omission might suggest that *current* Greek manuscripts contained the phrase.[141]

Didymus the Blind

Didymus the Blind (ca. 310–95 CE) of Alexandria is so named because he lost his sight at the age of four. Yet such was his attention to oral learning and so acute his knowledge and wisdom that St. Jerome referred to him as "the Seer." Didymus may even have coined the phrase *treis hypostaseis, mia ousia* ("three Persons, one substance"). He has four works that reference the idea of the Son's ignorance. His arguments against it are similar to other fathers of the fourth century. Notable is his mention of Basil and interpreting the $\epsilon\grave{\iota}$ $\mu\acute{\eta}$ in the

---

140. Ambrose, *De fide* 5.192–93; translation from NPFS 10:308. We have two peculiarities here. First, Migne's numbering (5.193) is different than NPFS (5.192). Second, Migne or later editors of MPG believed that Ambrose was quoting from Mark 13.32, but he seems to be quoting from Matthew, because (1) his text bears all the earmarks of Matthew (*de die autem illo et hora nemo scit, neque angeli caelorum, nec Filius, nisi solus Pater*) and (2) he mentions ancient Greek witnesses without οὐδὲ ὁ υἱὸς (Mark's more stable text makes Matthew a more likely source).

141. This is, of course, not a necessary deduction. However, that he has knowledge of ancient Greek manuscripts suggests that he also has knowledge of current ones, which he would not have been reluctant to include in bringing forth evidence for the omission. He knew Greek very well, studied Greek authors such as Philo and Origen, and even exchanged letters with Basil of Caesarea (e.g., Basil, *Letters* 197). It is possible that Basil, whose manuscripts had the omission, told Ambrose of them, but one then must question Ambrose's use of "ancient," since Origen does not seem to have been aware of them while writing his *Commentary on Matthew* in Caesarea. Ambrose and Basil's relationship is imitable; in fact, some have asserted that had the East and West always had the ability to communicate as intimately as they did, the schism would never have happened (James Loughlin, "Saint Ambrose," in *TCE*, vol. 1 [New York: Encyclopedia, 1913], 383–88).

preeminent sense.[142] Didymus apparently had multiple manuscripts at his disposal, for his quotation of Matthew in *De Trinitate* is lacking οὐδὲ ὁ υἱός (384–92 CE), while it is present in his *Commentaries on Zechariah*.[143]

SUMMARY AND SYNTHESIS OF PATRISTIC FINDINGS

Despite their attendant issues, the patristic testimonies provide a historical understanding of why οὐδὲ ὁ υἱός was omitted or added in Matthew 24.36. Appendix A orders the fathers chronologically by the dates of their work, their provenance, whether or not they were aware of οὐδὲ ὁ υἱός or its absence in Matthew, and whether or not they had a theological problem with the idea of an ignorant Christ before and after his resurrection.

By the time Athanasius comes onto the scene around 350 CE, not only do we have unambiguous problems with an ignorance of Christ addressed in patristic writings, but many of the fathers, if not all, seem to explain the inclusion of οὐδὲ ὁ υἱός as indicative of a *pre-resurrection* ignorance.[144] At this same time, evidence of the omission begins to appear in their references to Matthew 24.36. There exists no incontrovertible evidence that the omission existed in the fathers' writings about Matthew 24.36 prior to about 350 CE, but there are hints of it in Ambrose.[145] Additionally,

---

142. Didymus, *De Trinitate* 920.

143. Ibid., 916–17. His Mark reads, Περὶ δὲ τῆς ἡμέρας ἐκείνης, ἢ τῆς ὥρας, οὐδεὶς οἶδεν, οὐδὲ οἱ ἄγγελοι οἱ ἐν οὐρανῷ, οὐδὲ ὁ Υἱὸς, εἰ μὴ ὁ Πατὴρ. His Matthew reads, Περὶ δὲ τῆς ἡμέρας ἐκείνης, ἢ τῆς ὥρας, οὐδεὶς οἶδεν, οὐδὲ οἱ ἄγγελοι τῶν οὐρανῶν, εἰ μὴ ὁ Πατὴρ μόνος. The other quotation of Matthew comes from Didymus, *Commentarii in Zacchariam* 5.78: Περὶ τῆς ὥρας καὶ τῆς ἡμέρας ἐκείνης οὐδεὶς οἶδεν, οὔτε οἱ ἄγγελοι οὔτε ὁ Υἱός, εἰ μὴ ὁ Πατὴρ μόνος.

144. Did Greek philosophy inform the fathers' view of Christ's omniscience? With Plato's theory of recollection, knowledge is recollected by the soul out of an invisible, eternal realm, often through reason (Plato, *Meno*). Such recollection is a process, and immediate knowledge is consequently not available. Did the fathers adopt a process-like view of recollecting knowledge whereby Christ could either exercise recollection to yield knowledge or intentionally leave it unemployed to remain in practical ignorance? Such a view has two interpretive strengths. First, it would shed light on the patristic claim that Christ knew the time of his return in his divinity but not in his humanity, because knowledge would only be selectively present for Christ at a conscious level. Second, it would draw together a few seemingly disparate reasons that the fathers choose over and over, namely, that in Jesus' refusal to perpetually employ his omniscience, he was identifying with humanity and serving as our model. Although later fathers such as Athanasius and Hilary are predominantly occupied with rejecting the notion that Christ is ignorant, it is difficult to determine if they would have had a problem with Christ's practical ignorance, because such is not their milieu—they are reacting against Arian claims that Jesus was inherently not omniscient.

145. Ambrose may not have had direct knowledge of ancient exemplars omitting οὐδὲ ὁ υἱός. He and Basil corresponded by letter—Ambrose's rare Greek knowledge being

the geographic arrangement of their appearance raises questions. By this time, its absence is the *assumed* correct reading in some sectors, and no knowledge of its *presence* appears to exist in others. This suggests that the omission existed prior to the Arian controversies of the fourth century, and our writers understandably gravitated toward those manuscripts that were lacking the phrase.

We have several lines of geographical evidence to consider. In Alexandria, Origen, Athanasius, and Didymus inform our discussion, but our conclusions depend largely on the assumptions we make about Origen. His *Commentary on Matthew* (ca. 246 CE), normally noting where textual variants existed, is silent on this point. In fact, Origen never alludes to knowing about variants in Matthew 24.36, and it may be difficult to reconcile his penchant for textual criticism with him not knowing about a textual problem in this verse, though such a perspective may assume too much.[146] Although Origen mentions variants in his *Commentary on Matthew*, which was written from Caesarea, we do not know whether or not he had Alexandrian exemplars. If he did and if those exemplars differed, it would be a fair assumption that he would mention the issue. If we can also assume that Origen either had or could recall to memory Alexandrian forms of Matthew, then since he does not mention any variants, manuscripts attesting the omission must appear sometime after Origen (246 CE) but before Athanasius (357 CE). Whenever it appeared, Didymus (381–98 CE) seems aware of both readings. The omission thus may have made its way into Egypt sometime during the century 250–350 CE.[147] If Origen did not have and could not remember

---

an asset to East-West relations. It seems entirely conceivable that Basil, who was *only* aware of the omission, informed Ambrose of the state of his exemplars. If true, this sets limits on understanding Ambrose's modifier "ancient," because the manuscripts to which Basil would have referred, if dated too early, would have conflicted with the manuscripts available to Origen when he wrote his *Commentary on Matthew* in Caesarea. So "ancient" may mean documents written within 120 years or less.

146. Origen's memory was apparently voluminous, and he had an eye for manuscript variation. Had he brought no manuscripts to Caesarea (which is by no means certain), would he have forgotten how his Alexandrian exemplars, over which he had pored for many years, read? Origen may not have known about every manuscript in Alexandria or Caesarea, but some confidence can be garnered by the fact that had other manuscripts existed and been used, he would likely have encountered this discrepancy and was unlikely to have forgotten it. Further, he had earlier (220–30 CE) referenced Matt 24.36 in *De principiis* 1.6, wherein he mentions that only the Father knows the time (technically he uses "God," but it is done in a context where Christ is referred to separately).

147. This might help explain the confluence of factors we see within Sinaiticus, namely, that the correctors seemed to be undecided whether or not to include the phrase οὐδὲ ὁ υἱός. According to the work of Milne and Skeat (1938) as well as Jongkind (2007), the first round of corrections happened before the manuscript left the scriptorium (NA²⁷, in light of the work of Tischendorf and Lake, places the

exemplars from Alexandria that attested the omission, it is possible that manuscripts without the phrase existed there from the very beginning.

In Caesarea, Origen had multiple exemplars from which he wrote his commentary on Matthew, and he attests directly to the presence of οὐδὲ ὁ υἱός. Thus the omission seems to have entered Caesarea after 246 CE and to have obliterated all traces of οὐδὲ ὁ υἱός, according to Basil's testimony in 370 CE, so we can suggest the omission becoming standard between 275 and 325 CE.[148] This concurrence between Alexandria and Caesarea is not all that surprising, since they are very near to each other relative to the greater Roman Empire (less than four hundred miles) and, being major cities, would have had many travelers between them, particularly given that Alexandria was the most important center for trade in the empire.[149]

In France, both Irenaeus and Hilary were quoting (in ca. 185 and 359 CE, respectively) from a version containing the phrase. In Greece, Epiphanius knew of both readings (377 CE). Pseudo-Clement, thought to be of third- or fourth-century Rome, seemed to attest to οὐδὲ ὁ υἱός. Ambrose, twenty years after Hilary, said his Italian manuscripts were without the phrase as were the ancient Greek manuscripts, yet he was aware of those that still had the phrase (379 CE). If we take Ambrose's statements to mean that ancient Greek manuscripts *in Italy* attested the omission, we have an omission existing at least by the late third century, if "ancient" is to mean anything at all.[150] How do we explain the appearance of the omission in distant geographical precincts (Alexandria, Caesarea, and Italy) by the late third century? One of the following might have happened:

---

first correction in either the fourth or sixth century). This initial indecision by the scribes of Sinaiticus is consistent with our theory of the coexistence of exemplars with and those without the phrase. It would also explain the oddity of a stricken phrase that was readded: the readdition (by erasure of the diacritical dots) could have happened later. Due to scribal evidence indicating time spent in Caesarea (earlier noted by Lake), Milne and Skeat have asserted a Caesarean *origin* for Sinaiticus (Milne and Skeat, *Scribes and Correctors of the Codex Sinaiticus*, 69). If this is true, the manuscripts present within Alexandria at the time of the manuscript's creation would obviously be irrelevant. However, Jongkind undermines the Caesarean hypothesis (Jongkind, *Scribal Habits of Codex Sinaiticus*, 252–54).

148. Of course, Caesarea was large, and there may have been multiple scriptoria. If so, manuscripts attesting the omission may have existed alongside manuscripts attesting otherwise.

149. Cornelius Clifford, "Saint Athanasius," in *TCE*, vol. 2 (New York: Encyclopedia, 1913), 35–40.

150. Although Ambrose was qualified to speak to the state of the Greek texts, he was also in correspondence with Basil, who may have told him of the omission in Caesarea. This would have been a relevant topic of discussion during the Arian controversies.

1. An unrecorded edict influenced the orthodox to alter the manuscripts all in the same way.

2. Scribes uniformly, but *randomly*, struck the phrase across the empire.

3. The omission truly happened much earlier and naturally disseminated over the decades, a fact not advertised until it was convenient during the heresies of later centuries.

There are problems with each option. The first suffers from a lack of any direct evidence. Further, why would the proposed ecclesiastical edict not address Mark's parallel phrase? Even worse, any such "edict" during the fourth century could hardly have escaped attention, and this strategy runs across the grain of the interpretive strategies employed by the fathers.

Option 2 is not without issues either. It is not difficult to conjecture that a scribe, fearing the potential of misinterpretation, altered the text to relieve this tension. But why would a scribe remove the phrase οὐδὲ ὁ υἱός and leave the word μόνος intact? Would this truly alleviate the problem? Further, why would such a scribe remove the problem from Matthew and forget to remove it in Mark? Would it not have been easier to simply remove μόνος to make the Matthean account match Mark? There are several reasons why this would have been better:

a. Any hermeneutical explanation found for Mark could likewise be applied to Matthew.

b. A scribe would not have to remove a divine, personal reference.

c. A scribe could have removed one word rather than three.

d. There would consequently be no need to find an explanation for the exclusive μόνος still present.[151]

Given that there were better or at least multiple ways to alter the text, it is oddly peculiar that when a variant occurs, it always occurs in the same way in this verse—by removing οὐδὲ ὁ υἱός. None of the

---

151. To believe otherwise would require that the scribe either did not believe Mark to be a problem or had no opportunity to change Mark. Scribes sometimes cooperated to finish manuscripts, so it is possible that the offending scribe was not able to also change Mark. This possibility lessens as we move earlier into history, for as Christianity became more organized, manuscript production was sometimes collaborative. Another possibility is that, since Matthew was used and therefore copied more often, the goal may just have been to transcribe Matthew.

Adam G. Messer

other options for alleviating the potential confusion were exploited. These factors make highly unlikely the theory that scribes in different sections of the empire who were having problems with the phrase randomly removed it from their respective manuscripts, for one would have expected to see other solutions employed to assuage the theological dilemma.

With the challenge to option 2 of how to get the omission across the empire, option 3 seems better.[152] Whether or not the change was intentional, this dissemination would take some time. An early third-century *or prior* archetypal omission is the best time frame to allow its proliferation to foreign lands. If it is in reaction to adoptionistic influences, we might even tentatively suggest the time frame of 190–225 CE. If it is in reaction to modalistic influences (a point taken up shortly), we might likewise suggest a late second-century alteration in the West.

EVALUATION OF EHRMAN'S METHODOLOGY

This chapter has been an assessment of Ehrman's thesis applied to one concrete example (Matt 24.36), but our findings revolve around two broader critiques that apply to his work as a whole. With the evidence now available to us of a great diversity of points of view about Christ in the first four centuries, it appears that there is always a reason to postulate an orthodox corruption. As succulent as this is to our critical taste, an unqualified application of this approach should leave some distaste.

There are several general problems with the type of approach that maps every variant to a theologically motivated *orthodox* alteration. Not only does it fail to give ample respect to the level of reverence most scribes within the tradition gave to the words being copied, but this approach also fails to take into account the scribal habits of individual scribes.[153]

Ehrman has asserted that the change in Matthew 24.36 represents an anti-adoptionistic alteration at least as early as the late second century. He ascertains this time frame from the idea that the Diatessaron

---

152. This follows unless we want to posit a champion of the shorter reading to speed the dissemination, but this is unwarranted for any historical personality prior to Athanasius in the fourth century. Athanasius himself may be a good candidate (Brogan, "Another Look at Codex Sinaiticus," 20).

153. One example is Ehrman's postulate that a scribe purposely added an article to an ancestor of Codex Regius, an eighth-century manuscript, in John 1.1c. As Morgan concludes, the most probable reason for the presence of this "Sabellian" article resides in the sporadic habits of the scribe, not in any theological agenda (Matthew P. Morgan, "The Legacy of a Letter: Sabellianism or Scribal Blunder in John 1.1c?," in this volume).

and Origen testify to the omission of οὐδὲ ὁ υἱός, as do a range of versional witnesses.[154] Several comments are in order.

There are a number of different versions of the Diatessaron (e.g., Syriac, Persian, Latin, Armenian, Arabic, Middle Dutch, etc.), with a complex interrelationship.[155] There are three reasons to conclude that the Diatessaron does, contrary to Ehrman's claim, attest to the phrase οὐδὲ ὁ υἱός.

1. Several, if not all, versions attest it: the Armenian version of Saint Ephrem's commentary, the Chester Beatty Syriac manuscript 709,[156] and at least one strand of the Arabic version.[157]

2. Peterson outlines a process by which one may settle on an original Diatessaronic reading.[158] Because both readings in Matthew 24.36 have attestation in Greek and Latin texts, which could have influenced the transmission of the Diatessaronic text, one could never, in Peterson's estimation, have full confidence that the omission is attested in the Diatessaron.

3. Tatian's Diatessaron was a *harmony*, and it was carefully crafted from all four Gospels.[159] It is unlikely that Tatian would have missed οὐδὲ ὁ υἱός in Mark.[160]

Given these three factors, it is unlikely that the Diatessaron attests to the omission.

What about the versional witnesses? The Latin manuscripts it[g1] (eighth/ninth century) and it[l] (thirteenth century) and the Vulgate were born in the aftermath of the Arian controversies of the fourth century. In fact, with the exception of the Sahidic Coptic version and perhaps the Syriac Sinaitic version (third/fourth century), the Middle Egyptian Coptic (fourth/fifth century), Bohairic (fourth century), popular Peshitta (fourth/fifth century), and Harclean (seventh century)

---

154. Ehrman, *Orthodox Corruption*, 92.
155. Carmel McCarthy, *Saint Ephrem's Commentary on Tatian's Diatessaron*, Journal of Semitic Studies Supplement 2 (Oxford: Oxford University Press, 1993), 4, 8–9.
156. Ibid., 278–79.
157. ANF 10:35, 108–9. This translates Vatican Arabic MS 14. It is also referenced by the apparently nonstandardized label "Section 42."
158. William Lawrence Petersen, *Tatian's Diatessaron: Its Creation, Dissemination, Significance, and History in Scholarship* (Leiden: Brill, 1994), 373–74.
159. McCarthy, *Saint Ephrem's Commentary on Tatian's Diatessaron*, 7.
160. One argument for this possibility might be construed from Tatian's possible participation in Encratism, which is believed to have affected the readings of the Diatessaron in thirteen places. However, the Encratites were primarily known for beliefs that would not have motivated a change in Matt 24.36, namely, strict asceticism and sexual continence (Hultgren and Haggmark, *Earliest Christian Heretics*, 123).

versions find their origin in the Arian controversies of the fourth century or later, including the Georgian text (fourth century).[161] Further, they are not monolithic testimonies but have dissenting readings. For example, the Palestinian Syriac version (sixth century), the Diatessaron, various Georgian manuscripts, and a number of Old Latin and Vulgate manuscripts contain οὐδὲ ὁ υἱός. Although our earliest manuscripts of the Sahidic Coptic version are from the early fourth century, it may originate in the late third century, and it does not offer mixed testimony. Although we would not expect the Coptic tradition to be any more immune from theological alteration than the Greek one,[162] this may enable us to push the shorter reading back to the period just prior to the fourth century.[163] Nevertheless, the implication of this information is that, contrary to the opinion of Ehrman, there is no clear reason to push the origin of the omission back to the late second century based on the versional testimony.

All references to Matthew 24.36 listed in BP were researched, including all those in Origen's writings. Contrary to Ehrman's assertion, no instances were found where Origen was aware of manuscripts attesting to the omission.[164] There is, however, indirect evidence indicating so. Jerome states in his *Commentary on Matthew*, "In some Latin manuscripts is added: 'nor the Son,' though in the Greek copies, and especially those of Adamantius and of Pierius, this addition is not

---

161. Our earliest Georgian evidence supporting the omission comes from a tenth-century revision of the Georgian version (UBS[4], 28*–29*, with dates in the insert). Apparently, other manuscripts from this same revision differ at this point from those that attest to the omission.

162. Indeed, it introduces the possibility of unintentional orthographic alterations, one of which might occur by skipping from one Sahidic ⲉ to the next (or even from ⲏⲩⲉ to ⲏⲣⲉ). An intriguing possibility revolves around an apparent lacuna in Matt 24.36 surrounding the word ⲉⲓⲙⲏⲧ ("alone"). Although this observation needs verification by a good Sahidic apparatus, perhaps the Sahidic synonym ⲟⲩⲱⲧ ("alone") was used instead. If so, a pregnant possibility would involve skipping from one ⲉⲟⲩ to the next: ⲛ̄ⲙ̄ⲡⲏⲩⲉⲟⲩⲧⲉⲡϣ̄ⲏⲣⲉⲟⲩⲱⲧⲡⲉⲓⲱⲧ. These examples would cleanly skip over ⲟⲩⲧⲉⲡϣ̄ⲏⲣ ("nor the Son"). The text used as the Sahidic exemplar is taken from Rudolph Kasser, *Papyrus Bodmer XIX: Evangile de Mattieu XIV, 28–XXVIII, 20 Epitre aux Romains I, 1–II, 3 en Sahidique* (Geneva: Bibliotheca Bodmeriana, 1962). These possibilities require additional erudition to determine their validity, but they demonstrate a field ripe for study.

163. There are other Greek manuscripts that support the omission: L (019) from the eighth century; W (032) from the fourth/fifth century; *f*[1] (Family 1), whose earliest manuscript (MS 1582) dates from the tenth century (949 CE); and 33 from the ninth century. None of these help establish a second-century entrance of the omission.

164. Neither NA[27], UBS[4], Tischendorf[8], Legg, von Soden, Swanson, Lachmann, Scrivener, or Merk listed Origen in support of the shorter reading. Likewise, in his work dedicated to this topic, Metzger does not mention Origen's awareness of this variant (Metzger, "References in Origen to Variant Readings," 88–103).

---

found."[165] According to Jerome, Origen knew of manuscripts lacking the phrase,[166] but the fact that Jerome implies that *all* (or at least the majority) of Origen's manuscripts were missing the phrase seems, in light of modern evidence to the contrary, to leave a bewildering number of possibilities in its wake. Was Jerome unaware of the texts of Origen we currently have? Was he mistaken in mentioning Origen? Did the intervening church add the phrase into Origen's Greek manuscripts as they were transmitted?[167] Jerome's mention of two witnesses adds credence to his claim.[168] However, Jerome's writings were no less immune from ecclesiastical tampering than the biblical manuscripts, and a strategic interpolation recalling that Origen's manuscripts were lacking the phrase would have strengthened a claim for an original shorter reading.

If Origen did know about the omission, as Jerome has suggested, it would mean that the shorter reading was attested by the late second century. Although few would claim that our manuscript evidence is comprehensive, it seems strange that Origen does not mention manuscripts attesting the absence of the phrase in his *Commentary on Matthew*. This perplexity warrants the exercise of caution when suggesting a second-century origination of the omission on the basis of Origen's testimony. Since the case is not as settled as Ehrman makes it appear, one is left with a temporally unanchored variant that cannot be established apart from other lines of evidence.

In *Orthodox Corruption*, Ehrman slices the early period into differing heresies and then puts a number of Christologically significant NT variants in juxtaposition to the theology of the heresies. Of course, most variants in Christologically significant verses can be construed to favor some heresy, so it is fairly easy to find several good fits. He then concludes that since the proto-orthodox would have benefited by altering their manuscripts to combat that heresy, they therefore did. He estimates that there are five or six dozen examples.[169]

Even if Ehrman's assertions about Christologically significant verses were correct, we do not have manuscript evidence from the first three

---

165. Jerome, *Commentary on Matthew* 4.24.36; translation from Saint Jerome, *Commentary on Matthew*, trans. Thomas P. Scheck, Fathers of the Church 117 (Washington, DC: Catholic University of America Press, 2008), 277.

166. Adamantius is Origen—to be distinguished from a later Adamantius of Alexandria (fourth/fifth century).

167. As earlier mentioned, an intentional alteration of this sort is not good, since there would not have been motivation to do so after the height of the Arian controversies. A later harmonization to the text of Mark, however, still remains a viable option.

168. Pierius was contemporaneous with the bishopric of Theonas (who ruled between 283 and 301) and apparently died in Rome sometime after 309 CE (Michael Ott, "Pierius," in *TCE*, vol. 12 [New York: Encyclopedia, 1913], 79).

169. Ehrman, *Orthodox Corruption*, 281.

centuries to prove them—a fact he plainly acknowledges.[170] Apart from the patristic testimony (itself subject to tampering), it is very difficult to date at what point these "corruptions" materialized. Thus, unless we find definitive discussion by the fathers on the matter, Ehrman's examples each could have transpired at any time during those first three centuries. The significance of this fact is that during most of this time, opposite heresies were struggling against the proto-orthodox. So Ehrman's theory is a double-edged sword. For every alleged orthodox motivation that existed, an equally possible heretical motivation existed, sometimes in conjunction with a less reverent attitude toward the text. With no clear rubric for preferring orthodox or heretical tampering, Ehrman's book may just as easily have been entitled *The Unorthodox Corruption of Scripture.*

THE LIKELIHOOD OF THEOLOGICAL MOTIVATION

Ehrman has used Matthew 24.36 as a key element in most of his discussions of orthodox corruption; however, he has to make three basic assumptions in order for orthodox corruption to stand:

1. Οὐδὲ ὁ υἱός must originally exist in Matthew.

2. The alteration must be more likely to have been performed by orthodox scribes than by heretical ones.

3. No accidental orthographic options must present themselves.

If any of these assumptions are upset, so is his claim about Matthew 24.36. I here offer comment on the first two assumptions. As for the third, although room disallows a perusal, several possibilities do present themselves among the exemplars from several languages that, despite traditional reservations, have potential for mutual interaction in the early period (e.g., Greek, Aramaic, and Coptic). Nevertheless, their improbability campaigns against them.

Whatever was the case for the Matthean manuscripts of the fathers, their Markan reading was fixed.[171] If the orthodox responded to adoptionistic or Arian use of Scripture by changing the text for Matthew 24.36, not only would we *expect* issues with Mark,[172] but we would an-

---

170. Ibid., 28.
171. Wallace notes that Ehrman neglects to share this counterbalancing information in *Misquoting Jesus* and *Orthodox Corruption* (Wallace, "Gospel according to Bart," 343).
172. Some believe that the Arians primarily used Mark 13.32 to support their contention (Kevin Madigan, "*Christus Nesciens?* Was Christ Ignorant of the Day of Judgment? Arian and Orthodox Interpretation of Mark 13:32 in the Ancient Latin

ticipate similar alterations to places where Jesus could be construed as limited in body or mind.[173] Such verses include Matthew 26.39 ("let this cup pass from me"), Mark 10.18 ("no one is good except for God alone"),[174]

West," *HTR* 96, no. 3 (2003): 258; Hanson, *Search for the Christian Doctrine of God*, 107). Since Matthew was read more often and contained the phrase οὐδὲ ὁ υἱός, the presence of μόνος would have made Arian use of Matthew more advantageous, but they may have used Mark due to mixed manuscript evidence in Matthew. However tidy this argument might be for our purposes, Hanson offers no corroborating evidence to support the assertion; in fact, when he makes the claim that Mark was predominantly used, he quotes a verse *containing* μόνος. Such an observation introduces the suspicion that either proper discernment was not exercised in making this attribution or such attribution was irrelevant to his purposes. Madigan probably relied on Hanson's claim.

173. Interestingly, in Ehrman's anti-adoptionistic section, he spends the majority of his space on alterations that made Christ's deity explicit (Matt 3.3; Mark 1.3; Luke 3.5; John 1.18; 10.33; 12.41; Acts 20.28; 1 Cor 10.5; Gal 2.20; 1 Tim 3.16; 1 Pet 5.1; 1 John 3.23; etc.). This angle does not truly bear the force of his argument, because many of these texts already implied what was made explicit. Further, the motivation behind these changes may be attributed to simple devotion or Docetic alterations. More pertinent would be verses that present *problems* for Christ's divinity. His applicable list is much shorter—he mentions only eight. Three deal with clarifying that Jesus was not merely a man (John 19.5; 1 Cor 15.47; Col 1.22). All three examples suffer from problems unmentioned in *Orthodox Corruption*. In John 19.5, an article before "man" is removed in Vaticanus, and the resulting translation seems to support an anti-adoptionistic meaning, but no mention is made of another omitted article before another substantive in the same verse—such that an investigation of scribal habits/tendencies is warranted prior to drawing conclusions, for these habits may offer greater explanatory power than theological motivation. Further, the translation need not carry the angle Ehrman asserts, nor does the alteration truly alleviate the difficulty in seeing Jesus as a man. In 1 Cor 15.47, the interpolations are as easily devotional as reactionary; in fact, their intents all seem to clarify the referent (the Lord Jesus) or to express reverence, rather than to destress his humanity (ἄνθρωπος is not excised). Ehrman asserts that the removal of the possessive pronoun αὐτοῦ from Col 1.22 in certain manuscripts changes the meaning in such a way as to disassociate Jesus with a negative Pauline connotation of σάρξ ("flesh"). While such a meaning is *possible* when the pronoun is removed, the context (particularly v 20) necessitates that the referent be Jesus' body, making αὐτοῦ unnecessary and redundancy a greater motivation for intentional change. The article (in this case before σαρκός) sometimes signifies that an idea of possession is present, particularly when human anatomy is in view (Daniel B. Wallace, *Greek Grammar beyond the Basics: An Exegetical Syntax of the New Testament* [Grand Rapids: Zondervan, 1996], 215). Of the eight aforementioned examples, three others represent clarification against a misconstrual of the text, which is reason enough for the change, without positing any antiheretical influence (Heb 1.3, 2.18, 10.29). The final two seem most relevant. One is Luke 2.40, which may just represent a harmonization to Luke 1.80, and the other is the primary text of this chapter—Matt 24.36.

174. This verse's parallel in Matt 19.16–17 underwent scribal harmonization by orthodox scribes to match Mark and Luke. Wallace discusses an implication of this fact, namely, that since the resulting Matthean text posed greater difficulty to an orthodox Christology than Matthew's original, this example demonstrates that harmonization could take precedence over a high Christology as a motivation for

Mark 15.34 ("my God, my God, why have you forsaken me?"), Luke 2.52 ("Jesus increased in wisdom and maturity"), John 12.27 ("Father, save me from this hour"), John 14.28 ("the Father is greater than I"), John 17.3 ("in order that they might know You, the only true God, and Jesus Christ whom You sent"), and John 20.17 ("my God and your God"). No Christologically significant variants for these verses exist within our manuscript record prior to the fifth century.[175]

We do see attempts by church fathers to deal with problematic passages through a hermeneutical grid; that is, they tended to clarify their theology rather than change their texts. We see this in Hilary's argument for a preeminent understanding of εἰ μή, in Athanasius' argument that Christ was exemplifying true humanity for us, and in Basil's argument that Christ had already asserted that all things that were of the Father were also of the Son.[176] In fact, all the fathers were found to argue from the greater canonical context of Scripture. This raises a pertinent question: if the leaders of the churches tended to deal with apparent problems in Scripture using interpretive means, why would we expect Christian scribes, by and large, to do otherwise?

A related observation surfaces. The idea of Jesus as "the Concealer" of the mystery appears in Hippolytus. Slightly later, Origen's assorted interpretations of the Son's ignorance initiates (or continues the earlier

---

textual emendation (Daniel B. Wallace, "Lost in Transmission: How Badly Did the Scribes Corrupt the New Testament Text?," in this volume). His observation validates by illustration what we might similarly deduce from a statistical comparison between the frequency of scribal harmonizations and the number of alterations resulting from an orthodox Christological bias. The significantly greater frequency of the former supports Wallace's contention that "narrative harmonization was a stronger impetus [for alteration] than a high Christology" (ibid., 52). By way of corollary, one should generally prefer the explanatory power of harmonization over a high Christology (all else being equal), in light of the relative prevalence of harmonization—a prevalence Ehrman describes with pizzaz by judging this scribal tendency to be "ubiquitous" (*Misquoting Jesus*, 97).

175. Two variants from NA[27] (post-fourth century) may be construed as Christologically significant. In John 20.17 ("your God and my God"), two fifth-century manuscripts and a ninth-century manuscript remove "and my God" from Jesus' words. In Mark 15.34 ("forsaken" [ἐγκαταλείπω]) is found as "reviled" (ὀνειδίζω) in several manuscripts—none prior to the fifth century. Ehrman interprets the latter as an anti-separatist corruption (*Orthodox Corruption*, 143–45) and would probably construe the former as anti-adoptionistic. He also views anything found in later manuscripts as primarily reflective of changes made during the first three centuries (ibid., 28), but as I will later argue, this assumption needs to be revisited.

176. O'Keefe and Reno make the case that the fathers of this period, specifically Athanasius among others, knew that many scriptural passages presented problems to any theological system, but they strove for "a reading that maximizes the number of unstrained interpretations of individual words, verses, and episodes" (John J. O'Keefe and R. R. Reno, *Sanctified Vision: An Introduction to Early Christian Interpretation of the Bible* [Baltimore: Johns Hopkins University Press, 2005], 61); that is, they did not reword, they retheologized.

initiation of) an exegetical tradition from which later authors would draw and on which they would expand. This growing body of interpretive commentary, ever widening in scope and geographical proliferation, would have served to *diminish* the motivation to omit οὐδὲ ὁ υἱός in Matthew 24.36.[177] Instead, Christians would have drawn on the hermeneutical tradition to understand the verse and dismantle heretical misinterpretation. These considerations would tend to argue for an origination of the variant in the centuries prior to an established exegetical tradition surrounding Matthew 24.36.

The evidence from the fourth century suggests an earlier time frame for the removal of οὐδὲ ὁ υἱός. This would leave two good possibilities for corruption: (1) the orthodox removed the phrase to combat Adoptionism, or (2) Modalists removed the phrase to combat orthodoxy. Which of these groups more likely did it? To answer that, we must assess which group would benefit more (strength of motive) and which group's theology would be better served by the change (usefulness of strategy).

The orthodox would have had some reason to remove the phrase, since Adoptionism was plaguing the scene from 190 to 275 CE. Yet Modalism also affected the proto-orthodox from as early as 70 to 220 CE and even until Nicea. If the orthodox omitted the phrase to counter diminutive Christologies, the change would have *aided* the position of those on the opposite side of the spectrum. This dilemma would have had a mitigating influence on any willingness to make alterations. Modalists, in comparison, would only have benefited from the omission against *any* opposing theology.

Might the actual alteration itself tell us anything about its employer? A Modalist who came to Matthew 24.36 would find one clear way to alter it for benefit—he would remove οὐδὲ ὁ υἱός. An orthodox scribe would come to the same verse, notice the stark contrast between the Father and Son devised by the presence of μόνος, and find several options advantageous:

1. Strike οὐδὲ ὁ υἱός.

2. Strike μόνος.

3. Strike both οὐδὲ ὁ υἱός *and* μόνος.

4. Strike the whole verse.

5. Try any number of additive options.

---

177. My appreciation goes to Michael Svigel for this observation.

Adam G. Messer

Option 1 has the disadvantage of catering to Sabellian claims. Options 3 and 4 would suffice but have the disadvantage of striking more words than would be necessary. Option 5 is fascinating but probably requires too much planning and pretension.[178] Option 2 would be the most strategic, because it would guard against Modalism, enact the least possible violence to the text, have a greater chance of going undetected (since comparing to Mark would raise no flags), prevent the deletion of a divine reference, and allow whatever interpretive explanation existed for Mark to apply equally to Matthew. Even more significant, if scribes were having problems with this idea of the Son's ignorance, one would expect manuscripts to appear with some variation of the preceding possibilities. They do not.

Contemplation of this fact alone suggests greater significance than might at first appear. If οὐδὲ ὁ υἱός is original and if orthodox scribes had problems with this phrase, why did every other remedial alternative remain untapped? Why do they appear to have chosen *and never deviated from* and option that (1) was not the most strategic,[179] (2) left open the same conflict they were trying to resolve,[180] and (3) happens to be a model example of what an early harmonization to Mark would look like? Without alternative manuscript scenarios, we seem left with a vacuity. Perhaps a solitary scribe omitted this phrase so early that its propagation was the *introduction* of the gospel in various other regions, a situation becoming increasingly impossible to evidentially differentiate from an aboriginal lack of the phrase. Or perhaps we have to devise a way for the omission to propagate *against* the exemplars of the known world. This latter scenario would require an interesting paradox: it would show a simultaneous *use and eschewal* of the change process. In other words, the deviation from their exemplars in transcription would reflect a willingness to change, an inclination that is difficult to reconcile with their dogged refusal to alter their text *in other strategic ways*. Either we adopt this somewhat convoluted theory of the variant's propagation,[181] or we

---

178. Ehrman concluded that scribes were more likely to correct than to interpolate notions previously nonexistent (*Orthodox Corruption*, 277).

179. As already mentioned, since orthodox alteration against one heresy would benefit another heresy on the opposite side of the theological spectrum, it would often not be strategic for the orthodox to make any Christologically significant changes. Further, if the orthodox *were* inclined to omit text in order to combat a diminutive Christology, two different alterations would have proven superior to the omission of οὐδὲ ὁ υἱός: (1) the removal of just μόνος and (2) the removal of both μόνος and οὐδὲ ὁ υἱός.

180. Basil's interpretation of εἰ μή in a preeminent sense was not employed until a century *after* the alleged omission. Prior to this, hermeneutical factors that allowed εἰ μή to mitigate the inherent contrast presented by μόνος did not exist, so a contrast would have naturally existed between the Father and the speaker (the Son) whether or not our phrase was present.

181. It is patently obvious that history can be, at times, very convoluted. However, taking our cue from Ockham, we will at least look for a simpler explanation, if not

are driven back to the possibility that Matthew never contained οὐδὲ ὁ υἱός in the first place.

The absence of οὐδὲ ὁ υἱός in the original would easily account for what we see in the manuscript tradition. Instead of postulating a complex social scenario for how the omission was transported around the empire, we would expect random scribes in random places to frequently harmonize this verse to Mark, all in exactly the same way and without collusion. This alleviates any need for a mechanism of transport. It would also offer a reason for why the fathers almost constantly mix aspects of the two in their quotations of Matthew 24.36. It would explain why the phrase is missing from some early versional evidence, such as the Sahidic Coptic and the Sinaitic Syriac versions (fourth century).[182] It may do justice to Ambrose's intent in using the word "ancient" (*veteres*) of manuscripts in 380 CE.[183]

What we do with Origen is key in this patristic discussion. He is crucial because he represents the earliest unambiguous evidence for Greek manuscripts attesting οὐδὲ ὁ υἱός, but there are multiple reasons to doubt his testimony in both Caesarea and Alexandria. Did Origen have manuscripts available to him in Caesarea from Alexandria? Were the multiple exemplars in Caesarea even complete? Did he feel compelled to mention every variant or just variants for those texts that he could find a parenetic purpose? Did he, as Jerome states, attest to the shorter reading in works not extant? The relevant Greek text is missing from his *Commentary on Matthew* for Matthew 24.36, which is extant only in Latin. In short, there are too many unknowns to be dogmatic about this lone stronghold for the attestation of the οὐδὲ ὁ υἱός. When we get to a time period where we find multiple testimonies about Matthew 24.36 against which we can compare, we find *both* variants attested.

As mentioned earlier, if Matthew originally did not have οὐδὲ ὁ υἱός, it would require comment on two resulting problems. First, such a position requires us to ignore our earliest and best witnesses. Second, scribal harmonization of Mark to Matthew was much more likely to occur than vice versa. In response to the first problem, I offer these insights:

---

prefer it. This is precisely what Ehrman does when he argues for theological motivation in Matt 24.36.

182. The Middle Egyptian (Coptic), Bohairic (Coptic), Peshitta (Syriac), Harclean (Syriac), and Georgian versions also attest to the omission, but all these versions or at least their manuscript evidence find their origin in the Arian controversies of the fourth century or later (dates from Metzger, *Early Versions of the New Testament*), so they are far less significant in impact.

183. The Latin word *vetus* has a range of meanings from "old" to "ancient," but for Ambrose to appeal to these manuscripts, they must have been of an age worthy of referral.

Adam G. Messer

1.   We must acknowledge that our manuscript testimony is some-what limited from the first few centuries of the church.

2.   This type of variant would be of the type of alteration that would readily require almost no time to occur, particularly given the less rigorous methods of transcription known to have dominated the early centuries and in conjunction with early efforts at harmonizing all the Gospels into one (e.g., Tatian's Diatessaron in ca. 170 CE). In fact, no manuscript evidence exists for this text for three centuries, and even then, both of our earliest manuscripts (Sinaiticus and Vaticanus) may be from the same provenance—a provenance that was, based on the corrections of Sinaiticus, itself struggling with the text of Matthew 24.36. Finally, Jerome was also a textual critic; perhaps the decision he made in the Vulgate at this juncture reflects more than just an anti-Arian bias.

In response to the second problem, pertaining to the likelihood of the direction of the harmonization, the only consideration really posing any form of issue is exemplified by the statistics calculated by Powell. He figured that for 70 percent of the instances when there was a harmonization between Matthew and Mark, Mark was harmonizing to Matthew.[184] It is here where statistics can easily lead us astray. In this case, they only reflect what an author was likely to do, not what any given text is likely to be; that is, they describe rather than prescribe, and to make it otherwise fails to take into account the character of the individual instances. In fact, it seems commandingly sufficient to know that there were any cases where Matthew was harmonized to Mark, because this instance alone is enough to conjecture it. For the specific instance of Matthew 24.36, the proper perspective of the fact that it did happen with some frequency should be not that the statistics make the chances of harmonizing Matthew to Mark unlikely but that such harmonizations set a precedent within which our instance fits nicely.[185]

CONCLUSION

This chapter has addressed two main issues. First, did the theology of the fathers and their practices make a theological motivation likely in Matthew 24.36? If so, who most likely did it and in which time period?

---

184. Powell, "Textual Problem of Οὐδὲ Ὁ Ὑιός."
185. Powell's argument that Matthew never harmonized to Mark in places where Mark contained Christo-diminutive verses is specious, because it is unfair to equate the situations. All of his examples were instances were Matthew did not even contain the verse. It is much less likely for long segments of text (an entire verse) to be harmonized from memory than for harmonization to occur with a short phrase that is in the same verse and made memorable by its alliteration in Mark (οὐδὲ ... οὐδέ).

If not, how do we account for the omission? Second, does the testimony of the fathers have anything to say to the text-critical problem?

It seems likely that if the omission is the result of a theologically motivated change, it was most probably removed by Modalists, who would have had no conflict of interest in doing so and whose theology would strategically have warranted *precisely* this change—as opposed to the mixed results that the employment of such a strategy would have caused for the orthodox. Given the paucity of early manuscript evidence and the dearth of incontestable patristic witnesses, a time frame is currently too difficult to resolve with certainty, but a late second-century omission is as close as we can surmise. The omission might be best traced to the West, perhaps to Rome, where Praxean and Sabellian schools were in force at this time.

While a theologically motivated alteration is entirely possible, it is more probable that οὐδὲ ὁ υἱός never existed in Matthew 24.36, given the distribution of patristic evidence and the singular form of the alleged theologically motivated textual remedy; that is, I feel that the *geographical* and *temporal* distribution of the variants, in both our patristic writings and the manuscript evidence, along with the manuscripts' *singular* manner of alteration, preclude the likelihood that οὐδὲ ὁ υἱός is original, a stance commemorating Jerome's text critical work,[186] done from a vantage point a millennium and a half closer to the original.

Although a late second-century adoptionistic influence may have motivated the orthodox to remove οὐδὲ ὁ υἱός as Ehrman posits, the aforementioned historical alternatives better explain the confluence of factors in the testimony of the fathers and manuscript evidence. These alternatives are grounded on a conscientious exploration of the competing motivations within orthodoxy as well as an analysis of the geographic and temporal distribution of the variants. In light of these alternatives, if the omission is either original or the result of heretical alteration, the exoneration of the orthodox should correspondingly detract from the marketed impression that the orthodox irretrievably corrupted the text.

As the church was emerging during its first centuries with this burgeoning, yet not fully realized, notion of the hypostatic union of Christ and his relation to the Father, the church wavered between two opposing points of view: denigrating Christ's identity and confusing him with the Father. The pendulum began swinging. Perhaps most aboriginal was confusing him with God without true flesh (Docetism), followed by confusing him with mere man (Adoptionism), followed thereafter by

---

186. Jerome asserted that only the original text of the Scriptures were inspired and without error. As a result, he sought to determine whether there had been alterations. See Louis Saltet, "Saint Jerome," in *TCE*, vol. 8 (New York: Encyclopedia, 1913), 341–43.

confusing him again with God the Father enfleshed (Modalism), followed yet later by confusing him with a godlike entity who was not coequal with the Father (Arianism). To be sure, this oversimplification ignores the fact that all these incomplete and false theologies coexisted throughout the period leading up to Nicea, where the Great Council pushed them to the fringe by embracing all opposing emphases, namely, declaring Christ's deity *and* humanity *and* distinctness from the Father. Interlaced throughout were ripe opportunities by both orthodox and heretic for textual emendation.

I have suggested that Adoptionism was most prevalent from 190 to 275 CE and may have existed from the very beginning. Docetism and Modalism existed from 70 to 220 CE and Arian influence from 318 to 381 CE (with earlier roots). The significance of the dates corresponding to the heresies is that with the exception of a few intervening decades, from the end of the first century until the end of the fourth century and even after, one heresy or another was attacking the church, often several simultaneously. Although some of these groups may have found the removal of οὐδὲ ὁ υἱός in Matthew 24.36 to be advantageous against the orthodox view, others would have been hindered in their lesser Christologies by its removal. These heresies fell on both sides of the orthodox fence, each with varying levels of deviation from the truth and requiring a response by the church to settle the matter in accordance with the most biblical and historically conscious understanding as possible. These heresies revolved around the doctrine of Christ, of God, and of the Holy Spirit for at least the first four centuries.

This means that no matter what textual problem relating to the central theme and soul of the Bible (i.e., the Trinitarian God) may be found in the manuscript tradition amid the first centuries—themselves already characterized by a great diversity of variants due to a lack of centralization, various persecutions, and a predominantly illiterate populace—one can always postulate a motivation for an orthodox corruption, whether or not it is probable. This disingenuous method can be applied because no matter whether an article is left off or added, a word slightly shifted or removed, due to orthographic errors or any other unintentional type, it often changes the meaning just enough that there is bound to be a heresy that would contemn the change. If an article is missing, it may seem that the unity of the Godhead is in danger. If the article is present, it may appear to threaten their distinct personalities. If a phrase exemplifying Jesus' humanity is removed, it was obviously to combat the heresy of Adoptionism. If it is added, it was obviously to combat the heresy of Sabellianism. Realizing that hundreds and perhaps thousands of variants can be construed to favor the orthodox against *some* heresy, the orthodox can be incriminated with impunity. This raises a bemused inquiry: has discrimination moved from the ethnic and socioeconomic realms into the theological arena?

In each scenario, the orthodox are characterized as underhandedly altering the text to counter whatever heresy would seem to benefit by its anterior reading. This unfortunate but convenient state of affairs allows one to posit an orthodox corruption for any given Christologically significant variant. But when critics capitalize on the prevalence of alleged doctrinal alterations to sow distrust in the NT's transcriptional fidelity, an important consideration is often overlooked: namely, such a point of view surreptitiously carries the assumption that these changes, though intentional, actually corrupted the meaning of the text instead of clarifying it. Although any change is a deviation from the original, the difference in a clarification is that it typically better preserves the meaning and buttresses it against heretical counterfesance.[187]

Christian orthodoxy, itself given contours by passages of Scripture in tension, is like a razor. Readers of Scripture will feel the sharpness of its edge—the conundrum that this scriptural tension creates. To avoid the pain of being cut, those predisposed against mystery allow this tension to force them to one side or the other—an easy theological position, but one without the sharpness and vitality of truth. In response to the heretic's plea to pick a side or be torn asunder, the orthodox prayer is, Though I be torn asunder, yet will I trust him.

---

187. Ehrman acknowledges this (*Orthodox Corruption*, 276).

Adam G. Messer

APPENDIX A: PATRISTIC CHART

This appendix contains a chart outlining the basic findings from my examination of the patristic writings listed in BP. It shows each father's approximate lifespan; the works in which he discusses Matthew 24.36; whether his version of Matthew 24.36 attested to the omission or the presence of οὐδὲ ὁ υἱός, along with an indication of my confidence level in this judgment; and two columns indicating whether or not he had a theological problem with Christ's ignorance regarding the day and hour of his second coming—both prior to and after the resurrection.

As for confidence levels, a "low" designation usually means that we are dealing with an indirect reference. A "medium" designation typically means that a father's form of the verse matches two of the three primary Greek differences (mimicked in Latin) between Matthew and Mark. A "high" designation usually means that we are dealing with a direct Greek quotation, and "high–" means that the direct quotation is in Latin and therefore that some caution is in order.

In the columns associated with ascertaining a father's comfort level with an ignorance belonging to Jesus, I use the following four designators:

Y yes
L likely
P possibly
N no

When an asterisk attends a "possibly" (i.e., "P*"), it means that it is difficult to determine on the basis of present tense verbs in the surrounding context. For example, we may read a phrase like "of course the Son of God knows the time and hour he will return." Such discourse immediately informs us that the writer in question has a definitive problem with a post-resurrection ignorance, but it does not necessarily mean that he has a corresponding problem with a pre-resurrection lack of knowledge. The chart[188] offers boundaries around which we can quickly survey and summarize early patristic evidence surrounding this issue, but it also allows the reader to peer into some of the complexities inherent in this study.

---

188. The question mark behind Pseudo-Clement of Rome, while explicitly indicating that we don't know the provenance for sure, is because, although it self-attests to being written by Clement of Rome, its nature and dating make this unlikely if not implausible. For Eusebius's work, the question marks simply mean that we don't know (or at least that I wasn't able to find) what date he wrote that work. For Athanasius, the question mark next to the year indicates that some attempt has been made to verify the year, but it is not real solid. The rest of the question marks simply mean that we don't have enough information to fill in the blanks.

FATHER	DATES (ca.)	RELEVANT WORK(S)
Irenaeus of Lyon	130–200	*Against Heresies* (182–88)
Hippolytus of Rome	180–230	*Commentary on Daniel* (204)
Tertullian of Carthage	160–220	*Against Praxeus* (213)
Origen of Alexandria	185–254	*Commentary on Matthew* (246)
Pseudo-Clement of Rome?	N/A	*Recognitiones* (third/fourth century)
Eusebius of Caesarea	260–341	*Gospel Questions and Solutions to Marinus* (??)
Athanasius of Alexandria	290–373	*Discourses against the Arians* (357) *Disputes against Arius* (357?)
Hilary of Poitiers (France)	300–368	*On the Council* (359) *On the Trinity* (360)
Epiphanius of Salamis	310–403	*Ancoratus* (374) *Panarion* (377)
Basil of Caesarea	329–379	*Epistula* (370–78)
Amphilochius of Iconium	340–400	*Fragmenta* (370–80)
Gregory of Nazianzus	325–389	*Orationes* (379–81)
Ambrose of Milan	340–397	*De fide ad Gratianum* (377–80) *Exposito Evangelii secundam Lucam* (377–89)
Didymus the Blind of Alexandria	313–398	*On the Trinity* (381–92) *Commentaries on Zechariah* (398)
Gregory of Nyssa	335–385	*Antirrheticus adversus Apollinarem* (385) *Adversus Arium et Sabellium de patre et filio*

Adam G. Messer

READING (OMISSION/ PRESENCE)	HOW SURE?	ISSUE WITH IGNORANCE?	
		PRE	POST
Presence	High–	N	??
??	N/A	P	Y
Presence	Low	N	??
Presence	High–	N	Y
??	??	N	??
??	N/A	??	??
Omission	High	L	Y
Presence	High-	Y	Y
Presence	Med	P*	Y
Omission	Low		
Omission	High	L	Y
??	N/A	P*	Y
??	N/A	P*	Y
Both	High	Y	Y
Both	High	P	Y
Omission	Low	L	Y

APPENDIX B: ACCIDENTAL
ORTHOGRAPHIC CORRUPTIONS

This appendix outlines ways in which the Greek text may have become unintentionally corrupted from its original form.

POSSIBILITY 1

There is the possibility that the overbar above the *nomen sacrum* for "son" (ΥC) was faded to the degree that a novice or secular scribe may have taken the text to say,

English: "Concerning that day and hour no one knows, not the angels in heaven, nor the boar, except the Father."

Greek: ΠΕΡΙΔΕΤΗCΗΜΕΡΑCΕΚΕΙΝΗCΚΑΙΩΡΑCΟΥΔΕΙCΟΙΔΕΝΟ
ΥΔΕΟΙΑΓΓΕΛΟΙΤΩΝΟΥΡΑΝΩΝΟΥΔΕΟΥCΕΙΜΗΟΠΑΤΗΡΜΟΝΟC.

Note that the Greek text may have been intact enough to alert the scribe to an obvious (and sacrilegious) error, which he promptly removed.[189]

ΟΥΔΕΙCΟΙΔΕΝΟΥΔΕΟΙΑ
ΓΓΕΛΟΙΤΩΝΟΥΡΑΝΩΝ
ΟΥΔΕΟΥCΕΙΜΗΟΠΑΤΗ
ΡΜΟΝΟCΩCΠΕΡΓΑΡΑΙ

POSSIBILITY 2

The Greek text that the fathers used often had slight changes. For instance, Epiphanius seemed to have a version of Matthew that read,

ΟΥΔΕΙCΟΙΔΕΤΗΝΗΜΕΡΑΝΚΑΙΤΗΝΩΡΑΝΟΥΤΕΟΙΑΓΓΕΛΟΙΟΙΕ
ΝΤΩΙΟΥΡΑΝΩΙΕΙΜΗΜΟΝΟCΟΠΑΤΗΡ.[190]

---

189. A secular or novice scribe is postulated because they would be less likely to immediately recognize a *nomen sacrum* (particularly if *nomina sacra* are indeed Christian phenomena), but any scribe working under very tiring conditions could likewise have stumbled into this error, particularly under conditions of poor light.

190. This type of text-critical work is highly dependent on the exact form of the verse, and here is where value judgments about whether a father was quoting verbatim or not *really* matter and precisely where the most care ought to be shown. For this reason, conclusions must remain tentative where a particular "version" of Matthew is invoked for orthographic analysis. In this case, 24.36 is embedded sporadically within surrounding commentary, so it is also possible that it represents Mark or

Adam G. Messer

Such small changes introduce the real possibility of orthographic errors that otherwise seem more remote.

The primary criteria for any of these orthographic errors to work would be the presence of a scribe who does not know Greek well. Using Epiphanius's version of Matthew for our exploration of accidental changes, we could postulate the following two-stage textual error from Epiphanius's text (or one like it):[191]

... ΟΥΔΕΙϹΟΙΔΕΤΗΝΗ
ΜΕΡΑΝΚΑΙΤΗΝΩΡΑΝΟΥΤΕ
ΟΙΑΓΓΕΛΟΙΟΙΕΝΤΩΙΟΥΡΑΝ
ΩΙΟΥΤΕΟΥΙΟϹΕΙΜΗΜΟΝΟϹ
ΟΠΑΤΗΡ ...

Upon reaching the first "IO," the scribe accidentally drops down to the "IO" on the next line (the third instance), omitting everything in between (haplography). This would result in the reading, "no one knows the day and hour, not the angels <u>who</u> except the Father alone?"[192] At a later point, a more learned copyist recognized that the relative pronoun "who" did not belong and struck it. This would make sense of why some versions of the text appear to be missing "in heaven" and why its case is sometimes genitive and sometimes dative. It is also possible that the first scribe copied until the second "IO" and skipped past the third, resulting in this text: "no one knows the day and hour, not the angels in heaven who except the Father alone." Again, a later scribe could have removed the relative pronoun.

It is admittedly a more difficult conjecture to explain a variant by positing a double corruption in a location. However, it likely happened a few times within the manuscript tradition. Perhaps our reluctance to explore this possibility is the reason this problem seems more likely to be attributed to an intentional change.

POSSIBILITY 3

Another option would work with our NA[27] critical text. A non-Greek-speaking scribe may have committed an error of haplography

---

even an amalgam between the two gospels. However, even though the lack of οὐδὲ ὁ υἱός leans strongly toward a reference to, if not quotation of, Matthew, the main point is that we are simply positing *possibilities* for the unintentional introduction of the omission into the historical record.

191. His text would actually be the first stages of corruption. These corruptions do not struggle for credibility (given that Matthew and Mark's accounts were divided over case), so this type of minimal harmonization is definitely possible.

192. Here is the punctuated equivalent in minuscule: οὐδεὶς οἶδε τὴν ἡμέραν καὶ τὴν ὥραν οὔτε οἱ ἄγγελοι ὃς εἰ μὴ μόνος ὁ πατήρ.

with the iota (instance 1) or the omicron (instance 2), resulting in the same nonsense relative pronoun, which was subsequently stricken.

Instance 1

... ΟΥΔΕΙCΟΙΔΕΝΟΥΔΕΟΙ
ΑΓΓΕΛΟΙΤΩΝΟΥΡΑΝΩΝ
ΟΥΔΕΟΥΙΟCΕΙΜΗΟΠΑΤ
ΗΡΜΟΝΟCΩCΠΕΡΓΑΡΑ ...

Instance 2

... ΟΥΔ
ΕΙCΟΙΔΕΝΟΥΔΕΟΙΑΓΓΕΛΟΙΤΩΝΟ
ΥΡΑΝΩΝΟΥΔΕΟΥΙΟCΕΙΜΗΟΠΑΤ
ΗΡΜΟΝΟCΩCΠΕΡΓΑΡΑ ...

 Adam G. Messer

5

TRACKING THOMAS

A Text-Critical Look at the
Transmission of the Gospel of Thomas

Tim Ricchuiti[1]

Since its discovery over sixty years ago,[2] the Gospel of Thomas has excited the minds of scholars[3] and the public alike.[4] It has proved a malleable work, transforming from a primarily Gnostic[5] and apocryphal[6] text to a more theologically neutral work esteemed on a level

---

1. I thank Dr. Daniel B. Wallace for his initial thoughts on the transmission of the Gospel of Thomas that pushed me to take up this subject in the first place, his guidance through the initial stages of the formulation of the argument of the paper on which this chapter is based, and his consistent availability in pursuing the resulting project through to its completion. Additionally, many thanks go to Stazsek Bialecki, Adam Messer, Philip Miller, and Matt Morgan, my σύνδουλοι, without whose thoughts, criticisms, and encouragement I would be in the tall grass. Finally, I would like to thank my lovely wife, Angel, who has put up with many cancelled evenings through the completion of this work.
2. Technically speaking, though the Coptic manuscript was discovered approximately sixty years ago, Thomas has been known to scholars in one form or another since the late nineteenth century. See J. K. Elliott and M. R. James, *The Apocryphal New Testament: A Collection of Apocryphal Christian Literature in an English Translation* (Oxford: Oxford University Press, 1994), 128–29, for additional information.
3. So says Stevan Davies in *The Gospel of Thomas: Annotated and Explained* (Woodstock, VT: Skylight Paths, 2002), xxvii: "For those interested in Jesus of Nazareth and the origins of Christianity, the *Gospel of Thomas* is the most important manuscript discovery ever made."
4. R. McL. Wilson's English translation appeared just before Christmas 1959. It sold in excess of forty thousand copies, undoubtedly providing more than a few puzzling looks at the Christmas tree that morning (Stephen J. Patterson, James M. Robinson, and Hans-Gebhard Bethge, *The Fifth Gospel: The Gospel of Thomas Comes of Age* [Harrisburg, PA: Trinity, 1998], 2).
5. See Robert M. Grant and William R. Schoedel, *The Secret Sayings of Jesus* (Garden City, NY: Doubleday, 1960), for the strongest point of view in this direction.
6. "[The Gospel of Thomas] is an apocryphal Gospel, and in no way can it enter the canon as 'the Fifth Gospel'" (Joseph A. Fitzmyer, "The Oxyrhynchus Logoi of Jesus and the Coptic Gospel according to Thomas," in *Essays on the Semitic Background of the New Testament* [London: Geoffrey Chapman, 1971], 419]).

with the four New Testament Gospels,[7] contributing, in the process, to the demise of more than a few trees. Indeed, Thomas has suffered its fair share (and then some) of abuses at the hands of idle scholars. Nevertheless, I humbly request that it suffer one more.

Of the extensive bibliographies one could produce for the Gospel of Thomas,[8] one discipline that seldom pops up is textual criticism.[9] More often than not, any textual criticism accomplished in relation to Thomas occurs within a framework of replacing lacunae in order to translate the Greek fragments, the Coptic manuscript, or both. This is due to a number of foreseeable elements:

1. Unlike the case of the New Testament, external evidence plays next to no part at all in the discussion of Thomas. Therefore all decisions must be made on the basis of more subjective, internal considerations.

2. Those decisions must also be made on the basis of two dead languages, with uncertainty as to the relationships between the manuscripts and as to the provenance of the text.

3. Being a much more particular subject than the New Testament, the Gospel of Thomas resists the level of comprehensive treatment to which New Testament textual criticism lends itself (i.e., no one is going to produce a whole volume on Thomasine textual criticism).[10]

It is my purpose here, however, to devote some energy to exploring Thomasine textual criticism, in part to answer some questions scholars raise about the reliability of the transmission of Thomas.

---

7. Or even esteemed above the other Gospels in some cases. See especially Robert Funk, Roy W. Hoover, and the Jesus Seminar, *The Five Gospels: The Search for the Authentic Words of Jesus: New Translation and Commentary* (New York: Macmillan, 1993).

8. They have been legion. Ernst Haenchen's "Literatur zum Thomasevangelium" (*TRu* 27 [1961]: 147–78) represents scholarship leading up to 1960. Fitzmyer's "Oxyrhynchus Logoi" (420–33) takes over from there, cataloguing the next (extremely fruitful) decade. Since then, there have been many additions to the scholarship, and two recent works by April DeConick are about as comprehensive as can realistically be expected: her *Recovering the Original Gospel of Thomas: A History of the Gospel and Its Growth* (Library of New Testament Studies 286 [London: T&T Clark, 2005]) contains a nice overview of the field, with particular emphasis on the background of the Thomas community, while her *The Original Gospel of Thomas in Translation: With a Commentary and New English Translation of the Complete Gospel* (Library of New Testament Studies 287 [London: T&T Clark, 2006]) features selected works for each logion.

9. The explicit exception to this is Miroslav Marcovich's, "Textual Criticism on the Gospel of Thomas" (*JTS* 20 [1969]: 53–74), though, as shown in the previous notes, there are many implicit exceptions.

10. Yet.

Peter Head, for example, in his 1993 article on the tendency toward theological corruption in the NT, asserts about the transmission of apocryphal works:

> It is noteworthy that in the scribal tradition this "adaptation" [as observed in the article] is much more conservative than in the production of apocryphal gospels. The scribes were interested in "transmission" of texts, rather than in the creation of new texts.[11]

Larry Hurtado tackles Thomas's role more explicitly, stating, "[I]t is important to note, however, that the Greek fragments indicate that GThomas was transmitted with a noticeable fluidity in contents and arrangement."[12] Finally, Nicholas Perrin makes similar comments, though a bit more neutrally, when he observes:

> What is particularly striking on any comparison between the Greek fragments and the later discovered Coptic text is that, even accounting for the obvious fact that the two recensions are in different languages, there are dissimilarities in wording. At points the Greek text is more expansive; at other places, it is more abbreviated than its Coptic counterpart.[13]

What I wish to accomplish first here, therefore, is an exhaustive comparison of the Greek to the Coptic.[14] Secondly, I will assess the "dissimilarities" by utilizing some universally recognized principles of textual criticism, ultimately offering a conclusion on the matter of the primacy of either the Greek or Coptic manuscripts. Thirdly, I will attempt to ascertain whether or not scholars are correct in their representation of Thomas's fluidity and what that fluidity means, both in light of the communities that produced Thomas and in the broader stream of early Christian backgrounds.

---

11. Peter M. Head, "Christology and Textual Transmission: Reverential Alterations in the Synoptic Gospels," *NovT* 35 (1993): 128.
12. Larry W. Hurtado, *The Earliest Christian Artifacts: Manuscripts and Christian Origins* (Grand Rapids: Eerdmans, 2006), 34. Here, Hurtado cites an extended discussion of Thomas in another of his works, *Lord Jesus Christ: Devotion to Jesus in Earliest Christianity* (Grand Rapids: Eerdmans, 2003), 425–79.
13. Nicholas Perrin, *Thomas, the Other Gospel* (Louisville: Westminster, 2007), 8.
14. Comparisons such as this are not without precedent. Though I hope to contribute something new to this discussion (in format if nothing else), I recognize that I am walking on well-tread ground. DeConick's *Original Gospel of Thomas in Translation* and Uwe-Karsten Plisch's *The Gospel of Thomas: Original Text with Commentary* (trans. Gesine Schenke Robinson [Stuttgart: Deutsche Bibelgesellschaft, 2009]) come to mind in terms of recent studies, but this comparison has also been undertaken by Fitzmyer ("Oxyrhynchus Logoi") and Marcovich ("Textual Criticism"), among others.

There are any number of things that we cannot know in the process of analyzing and comparing the Greek fragments to the Coptic manuscript: whether and which of the fragments are reliable transmissions of the "original" text,[15] whether the eventual Greek manuscript that served as the exemplar for the translation to Coptic maintained such reliability, and whether the line of transmission from that initial translation to the extant manuscript was commensurately reliable. Indeed, any study on the textual support of the Gospel of Thomas must necessarily be full of caveats. Perrin, for one, notes the source of such a problem:

> [T]he Coptic text is probably only a translation of other texts which in turn were presumably copies. The date of the original composition of each of these texts must have been still earlier, perhaps considerably earlier.[16]

The limited nature of the evidence requires that we extrapolate from these meager beginnings and accept that the evidence can only go so far in supporting a level of conclusiveness with which scholars are comfortable. For that reason, I take to heart the instructions of Harold Attridge, who, in his excellent survey of the Greek papyri, points out that "[with respect to Thomas] caution is required in drawing text-critical inferences,"[17] a notation that shall here be my mantra.

With those qualifications in place, however, it is my desire to conduct just such an analysis of the text of the four extant manuscripts of this gospel. I hope to demonstrate, as cautiously as possible, the relative merits and faults of the three scribes who copied the Greek text,

---

15. Indeed, if there was, at any point, what we would consider an original text, or, more accurately, what we would consider an original text in the sense of the original NT documents. I realize that even the NT usage of the term *original* is not without controversy. Cf. E. J. Epp, "The Multivalence of the Term 'Original Text' in New Testament Textual Criticism," *HTR* 92 (1999): 245–81; D. C. Parker, *The Living Text of the Gospels* (Cambridge: Cambridge University Press, 1997). DeConick (*Recovering the Original Gospel of Thomas*, 38–63) writes of the problems with determining an original text of Thomas. Because I am persuaded by much of DeConick's research (though, as will become clear, not all), I use the term *original* cautiously. Sometime in the mid-second century, it appears likely that the text of Thomas gained stability (see chart 1 of DeConick, *Original Gospel of Thomas in Translation*, 10). Whether that stability stems from the original composition of Thomas with redaction and dependence on the Gospels and other traditions or from a concretizing of the community that had been adjusting and molding Thomas over a period of about one hundred years is an issue I will leave to other scholars. My primary interest here is the question of what the transmission history reflects *once the text gained stability*, so it is in that sense that I am using the term *original*.
16. Perrin, *Thomas, the Other Gospel*, 8.
17. Harold W. Attridge, "Appendix: The Greek Fragments," in *Nag Hammadi Codex II, 2–7: Together with XIII,2*, Brit. Lib. Or. 4926(1), and P. Oxy. 1, 654, 655*, ed. Bentley Layton, Nag Hammadi Studies 20 (New York: Brill, 1989), 103.

Tim Ricchuiti

as well as those of the Coptic scribe. The method will be first to conduct the comparison previously mentioned and note the differences between the texts. In that comparison, I will make a determination as to which reading is more likely to be original. My fundamental criterion is simple enough: where there is variation and where the variation is not nonsensical,[18] the reading that best explains the rise of the other is probably authentic. This criterion will be expressed through two corollaries: (1) the shorter reading is usually "original," and (2) the more difficult reading is usually "original."

For that second canon, the Gospel of Thomas presents a special challenge: what exactly is the more difficult reading in the case of a noncanonical text? To the best of my ability, I will utilize that canon *only when it is clear that a particular reading is more difficult to the worldview of the manuscript in question.*[19] There will, of course, be times when these criteria do not apply or when they conflict with each other. In those situations, I will either leave the case open or attempt to make a determination on other grounds. It is my belief that such an analysis will yield results in favor of the conclusion that *the Greek fragments represent an earlier strain of the Gospel of Thomas.*

Certainly, this result would not be unexpected. Considering the fact that the latest of the Greek fragments (probably P. Oxy. 655, ca. 250 CE) is about one hundred years senior to the Coptic manuscript (ca. 350 CE), it appears eminently reasonably that scholars would assume this position.[20] Indeed, this is the default position of virtually every scholar who tackles the question, and very few stray from those beginnings.[21]

---

18. In cases where the variation is nonsensical, involves misspellings, and so forth, it will be classified inauthentic. This decision is a difficult one to make, yet I have made it for the sake of consistency (both within this work and within the text-critical field). It is certainly true that a nonsensical reading can yet point to an earlier form of the text. That did not happen to occur in this analysis.

19. As will be taken up in further detail in this chapter, the worldview of Thomas is a bit difficult to establish. Generally, however, the strongly noticeable elements in Thomas include an elevation of knowledge (*gnosis*), particularly for salvation, with Christ as mediator to that knowledge. There are also a number of logia that feature a reconciliation of dualisms (22, 87, 106, 112), but quite a few more that do not feature such reconciliation—specifically, logia regarding the earthly versus heavenly realms (3, 27, 57, 76, 82, 109).

20. As does, e.g., Helmut Koester in "The Gospel according to Thomas: Introduction," in Layton, *Nag Hammadi Codex II*, 38.

21. This is a slightly different question from one of composition. On that end, James M. Robinson represents the majority opinion rather boldly when he states, without exception, "All [of the Nag Hammadi texts] were originally written in Greek and translated into Coptic" (*The Nag Hammadi Scriptures*, ed. Marvin W. Meyer [New York: HarperCollins, 2007], xi). For another scholarly affirmation of this opinion, similar thoughts are echoed by Marvin Meyer a few pages later in the same volume,

The next step in my method will be to determine what patterns exist among the variations (essentially attempting to describe the scribal habits behind each manuscript). Put most basically, are the changes evidence of random accretions and deletions due to the degradation of time, or do they represent a slightly more consistent character toward a particular theological point of view? Fitzmyer did not shy away from such characterizations, stating:

> Though it is possible that another Greek recension existed, of which the Coptic is a faithful rendering, it is much more likely that the Coptic version is an adapted translation—most likely with adaptations made to suit some of the theologoumena of the Gnostics who used or translated the Gospel.[22]

Presumably, he would be among those scholars Meyer pointed to as deluded or unduly influenced by the historical record of rejection of such texts as Thomas due to their heretical character.[23]

As we may be entering more controversial waters, let me be clear about what I do and do not mean. I am not resurrecting the blanket assumption that Thomas represents full-blown Gnosticism. Nor do I care to get into a debate regarding whether the text is fully Gnostic or is, rather, a gospel too often misinterpreted as Gnostic.[24] It will be enough for our purposes to see if the alterations move discernibly toward a Gnostic worldview[25] or meander about more haphazardly. On this matter, Head has already argued for this kind of noncanonical theological alteration: "This type of activity can be seen in other forms of Gospel-redaction: in the Gospel of Peter, the Gospel of

---

as he states a bit more softly, "The texts included [in this volume] were translated into Coptic . . . though they were likely composed in Greek" (1).

22. Fitzmyer, "Oxyrhynchus Logoi," 416.
23. Meyer, *Nag Hammadi Scriptures*, 6–7.
24. Koester's affirmation that "[e]lements of gnostic theology are present in these passages" ("Introduction," 44) represents well the cautious note I attempt to strike herein.
25. April DeConick has written a series of posts on her blog (*The Forbidden Gospels*, http://forbiddengospels.blogspot.com [accessed April 1, 2009]) entitled "Transtheism or Supratheism?," "Transtheism/Supratheism follow up," and "Transtheism it is." In this series, she moves away from the terms *Gnostic* and *Gnosticism*, because of their abuse, and prefers to use *Transtheism* instead to denote "groups of religious people in the ancient world that worship a god who is spatially beyond our universe and who is not identified as the immediate creator and ruler of our universe. Instead, these roles are attributed to subordinate powers who are not being worshiped." However, as she herself continues to affirm that there were Gnostics in the early centuries of Christianity ("My reason for [changing terminology] is not that I do not think that gnosticism existed in the ancient world—in fact I do"), I feel I am on solid ground in continuing to speak of a "Gnostic worldview."

Tim Ricchuiti

Thomas, and to some extent in Tatian's redaction of the Diatessaron."[26] Once again, I note Perrin's thoughts on the minefield we are getting ourselves into:

> While I agree that "Gnostic" and "Gnosticism" makes for a pretty un-wieldy rug under which to sweep all those sects that are not ostensibly proto-orthodox, the term has its place, at least if defined accurately enough. All the same, I disagree with those who say that the *Gospel of Thomas* is Gnostic. To be sure, the sayings in the gospel shares many elements with purported Gnostic texts (elements of anti-Judaism, hatred of the body, secret knowledge, etc.), but there is no hint that Thomas's Creator God is the same sadistic deity or pompous idiot that we meet in the Gnostic materials. Lacking these features, Thomas must be judged to be non-Gnostic.[27]

Contra Perrin and, to a certain extent, DeConick,[28] I contend that Thomas, either as it is now or as it existed "originally," need not be clas-sified either as Gnostic or non-Gnostic.[29] Instead, I intend to explore whether or not the alterations to Thomas, subtle though they were, were such that lent themselves toward Gnostic thought, leading to the inclu-sion of Thomas in the Nag Hammadi materials. Meyer makes a similar distinction, carefully qualifying the extent to which Thomas is Gnostic, saying, "the *Gospel of Thomas* may most appropriately be considered a sayings gospel with an incipient Gnostic perspective."[30] So I submit that *the additions, omissions, and substitutions of material between the Greek fragments and the Coptic manuscript represent, in at least some cases, theological corruption of the text.*

---

26. Head, "Christology and Textual Transmission," 128.
27. Perrin, *Thomas, the Other Gospel*, 12–3.
28. April D. DeConick, *Seek to See Him: Ascent and Vision Mysticism in the Gospel of Thomas*, Supplements to Vigiliae Christianae 33 (Leiden: Brill, 1996), 11–27.
29. Obviously, there are myriad studies that tackle just this question, though many of them remain agnostic on it. There is, of course, DeConick's early work (ibid.), which comes down in favor of a Jewish Apocalyptic model, as well as her later work (*Recovering the Original Gospel of Thomas*), which represents a maturation/evolution of that earlier view. A recent ThM thesis at Dallas Seminary (Christo-pher Scott Geyer, "Is Thomas Gnostic? A Comparison of Doctrines in the Gospel of Thomas to Early Gnosticism" [2007]) also engages in a comparison between Jewish Apocalyptic and Gnostic doctrines (the author splits the difference). Be-yond those comprehensive works, there are more particular studies into various aspects of Thomasine theology (cf. Stevan Davies, "The Christology and Protology of the 'Gospel of Thomas," *JBL* 111 [1992]: 663–82). Indeed, an important part of the debate is to remember that the Gospel of Thomas was not produced in isola-tion, and other Thomasine works can help shed light on, at the very least, where the community that produced Thomas was headed.
30. Meyer, *Nag Hammadi Scriptures*, 133.

THE MANUSCRIPT ATTESTATION
TO THE GOSPEL OF THOMAS

Thomas is preserved in four manuscripts (three of which are merely fragments), composed within 100 and 150 years of each other, in two different languages.[31] The three Greek fragments were discovered in Oxyrhynchus during the late nineteenth century[32] and were initially published separately[33] within a collection of the findings, as ΛΟΓΙΑ ΙΗΣΟΥ (P. Oxy. 1, dated shortly after 200 CE), "The New Sayings of Jesus" (P. Oxy. 654, dated to the mid-third century), and "Fragments of a Lost Gospel" (P. Oxy. 655, dated somewhere between the beginning and middle of the third century).[34] Not until the Nag Hammadi discovery in 1945,[35] some fifty years later, would scholars recognize the connection between these works.[36]

The Nag Hammadi finding revealed a Coptic manuscript identified as "The Gospel according to Thomas" (ⲡⲉⲩⲁⲅⲅⲉⲗⲓⲟⲛ ⲡⲕⲁⲧⲁ ⲑⲱⲙⲁⲥ: Nag Hammadi Codices [NHC] II 2.51.27–28; dated to some time before the middle of the fourth century),[37] containing 114 logia, some of which were subsequently revealed to match up with ancient attestation of the Gospel of Thomas as well as the discovery half a century earlier from Oxyrhynchus. That attestation (by numerous church fathers between the early third century and the eleventh century[38]) had always interested scholars, and here, for the first time, was the discovery of a truly "lost" gospel. To be sure, Thomas is not a gospel in the sense that we understand the genre from the four canonical Gospels. It is largely devoid of narrative material and instead consists mainly of sayings, usually

---

31. Attridge, "Greek Fragments," 96–99.
32. Elliott and James, *Apocryphal New Testament*, 128.
33. P. Oxy. 1: Bernard P. Grenfell and Arthur S. Hunt, *The Oxyrhynchus Papyri*, vol. 1 (London: Egypt Exploration Fund, 1898). P. Oxy. 654 and 655: Bernard P. Grenfell and Arthur S. Hunt, *The Oxyrhynchus Papyri*, vol. 4 (London: Egypt Exploration Fund, 1904).
34. Attridge, "Greek Fragments," 96–99.
35. Davies (*Gospel of Thomas*, ix) places discovery of the site in 1945, and Perrin tells the tale of that discovery in *Thomas, the Other Gospel*, 1–2, 15.
36. White (H. G. Evelyn White, *The Sayings of Jesus from Oxyrhynchus* [Cambridge: Cambridge University Press, 1920]) and Grenfell and Hunt both felt the connections between the two sayings collections (P. Oxy. 1 and 654), but they could not be expected to realize the nature and scope of the connections (and the connection to P. Oxy. 655) without the Coptic manuscript.
37. See Koester, "Introduction," 38, for more information on the dating. It is a rather difficult question to answer, as there is the problem of dating the initial translation from Greek to Coptic and then attempting to figure out how far down that line this manuscript is.
38. Attridge, "Greek Fragments," 103–9.

Tim Ricchuiti

introduced by "Jesus said" (ⲡⲉϫⲉ ⲓ̅ⲥ̅).[39] Some of these would be recognizable to the average Sunday school class, having close verbal and thematic parallels in the Synoptic Gospels, but many of them would defy the modern Christian conception of Christ (not always to the scholar's dismay).[40] The discovery nonetheless raised the possibility that we now had in possession more material pointing back to the historical Jesus than ever before.

The relationship of these four manuscripts to each other is difficult to work out.[41] Marcovich attempted one such explanation,[42] hypothesizing three separate recensions, but his attempt was unpersuasive to Attridge, who noted that "it is methodologically unsound to construct a stemma illustrating conjectured relationships among the witnesses to the text of the *GTh*. . . . Such a construction simply goes beyond the available evidence."[43] All of the Greek fragments are earlier than the Coptic manuscript, and none of them overlap with each other. It is impossible to know whether any of the Greek fragments, in their fuller form, would have contained the same basic content as the eventual Coptic manuscript or if the Coptic represented a vast expansion from the original text. At the same time, the fragments do come in roughly the same order as the Coptic manuscript, so it is best that our presumption regarding the transmission from Greek to Coptc not be too negative. Ultimately, I do not here intend to present such a reconstruction of the relationship between the witnesses, choosing instead to merely work out the relative merits of each manuscript in comparison with each other.

---

39. Most translators (Davies in *Gospel of Thomas* and DeConick in *Original Gospel of Thomas*, to name just a few) take this introductory formula as the aforementioned "Jesus said." A few, however (cf. Marvin W. Meyer and Harold Bloom, *The Gospel of Thomas: The Hidden Sayings of Jesus* [San Francisco: HarperCollins, 1992]; Plisch, *Gospel of Thomas*), take both the Coptic and Greek to be historical presents. It is an interesting problem, particularly because historical presents normally occur in narrative material, which for the most part Thomas is not. It is also a problem beyond the scope of the present study. For more, see Peter Nagel, "ⲡⲉϫⲉ ⲓ̅ⲥ̅—Zur Einleitung der Jesuslogien im Thomasevangelium," *Göttinger Miszellen* 195 (2003): 73–79.
40. See, e.g., Andrew Harvey's foreword to Davies, *Gospel of Thomas*.
41. Richard Valantasis (*The Gospel of Thomas* [New York: Routledge, 1997], 4) observes, "The Coptic sayings comparable to the Greek do not seem to be a direct translation of the same Greek text, and the Greek seems to witness to another version of the gospel than the one on which the Coptic translation is based. So there is not really a singular gospel, but two divergent textual traditions. This situation makes a precise and well-delineated description of the *Gospel of Thomas* problematic, because the *Gospel of Thomas* may refer to a number of different elements in its textual history."
42. Marcovich, "Textual Criticism."
43. Attridge, "Greek Fragments," 101.

COMPARISON OF THE COPTIC
THOMAS TO THE GREEK FRAGMENTS

The Greek papyri have here been placed roughly in order relative to the occurrence of their content in the Coptic manuscript. The accompanying English translations have been completed with a word-for-word equivalence in mind. I checked the Coptic text against Layton's scholarly text,[44] as well as that of Meyer.[45] The text for the Greek fragments was based on Grenfell and Hunt's text.[46] Both texts were then corrected as necessary against Plisch,[47] Fitzmyer,[48] Attridge,[49] Aland,[50] and DeConick.[51] The symbols function as follows:

( )	An abbreviation (usually *nomina sacra*) or otherwise omitted text has been supplied. *Text in parentheses would not have been in the original manuscripts and is supplied for the ease of the reader.*
[ ]	Lacunae in the manuscript and any emendations proposed to fill in those lacunae.
Black on gray	Text not present in the corresponding Greek or Coptic logion (i.e., in *addition* to what is present in the corresponding logion).
White on black	Greek and Coptic phrases being used in each other's place (i.e., in *substitution* of each other)
Wavy line	Text missing from the corresponding Greek or Coptic logion, usually due to lacunae, and without proposed emendations.

---

44. Layton, *Nag Hammadi Codex II*, 52–93.
45. Meyer and Bloom, *Gospel of Thomas: The Hidden Sayings of Jesus.*
46. Grenfell and Hunt, *Oxyrhynchus Papyri*, vols. 1 and 4.
47. Plisch, *Gospel of Thomas.*
48. Fitzmyer, "Oxyrhynchus Logoi."
49. Attridge, "Greek Fragments."
50. *Synopsis Quattuor Evangeliorum: Locis Parallelis Evangeliorum Apocryphorum et Patrum Adhibitis*, ed. Kurt Aland, 15th rev. ed. (Stuttgart: Deutsche Bibelgesellschaft, 1996).
51. DeConick, *Original Gospel of Thomas in Translation.*

Tim Ricchuiti

P. Oxy. 654—Prologue	
NHC II 2.32.10–12	*P. Oxy. 654.1–5*
ⲚⲀⲈⲒ ⲚⲈ ⲦⲘϢⲀⲬⲈ ⲈⲐⲎⲠ ⲈⲚⲦⲀ	οὗτοι οἱ οἱ λόγοι οἱ [ἀπόκρυφοι οὓς
ⲓ(ⲎⲤⲞⲨ)Ⲥ ⲈⲦⲞⲚϨ ⲬⲞⲞⲨ ⲀⲨⲱ	ἐλά]λησεν Ἰη(σοῦ)ς ὁ ζῶν κ[αὶ
ⲀϤⲤϨⲀⲒⲤⲞⲨ ⲚϬⲒ ⲆⲒⲆⲨⲘⲞⲤ	ἔγραψεν Ἰούδα ὁ] καὶ Θωμᾶ
Ⲓ̈ⲞⲨⲆⲀⲤ ⲐⲱⲘⲀⲤ	
These are the hidden words that the	*These are the hidden words that the*
living Jesus spoke and Didymos	*living Jesus spoke and Judas Thomas*
Judas Thomas wrote.	*wrote.*

The prologue to the first saying is identical in all but the name of the recipient of Jesus' words.[52] The Greek fragment clearly has "Thomas" (Θωμᾶ/ⲐⲱⲘⲀⲤ),[53] but its lacuna would be unable to fit both "Didymos" (Δίδυμος/ⲆⲒⲆⲨⲘⲞⲤ) and "Judas" (Ἰούδα/Ⲓ̈ⲞⲨⲆⲀⲤ). This text plays rather nicely into our first canon: the shorter text of the Greek is most certainly the earlier form. The scribal tendency toward explicitness (and, indeed, harmonization with other traditions)[54] asserts itself here in the longer name of the disciple.[55] This also illustrates our general principle rather well: it is more likely that the shorter Greek text would give rise to the longer Coptic text (through the aforementioned scribal expansion) than it is that a longer and more explicit Coptic text (or Greek forbearer to that text) would lead to a deletion. It is, of course, possible that the scribe would have deleted Δίδυμος from the forbearer to his copy, but absent any compelling evidence for such a deletion, I will not entertain the possibility.

---

52. Ignoring the easy-to-detect dittography (οὗτοι οἱ οἱ λόγοι οἱ) occurring at the beginning of the logion, an unintentional scribal error.

53. Most commentators are unconcerned by the lack of a final ς in P. Oxy. 654. Marcovich ("Textual Criticism," 53) passed it over fairly easily with a reference to its "common enough" nature, pointing, for attestation, to E. Mayser, *Grammatik der griechischen Papyri aus der Ptolemäerzeit*, 3 vols. (Berlin: Walter de Gruyter, 1926), 1:205.

54. A. F. J. Klijn ("John XIV 22 and the Name Judas Thomas," in *Studies in John Presented to Professor Dr. J. N. Sevenster on the Occasion of His Seventieth Birthday*, Supplements to Novum Testamentum 24 [Leiden: Brill, 1970], 271–78) goes into detail on the series of Thomasine works (Gospel of Thomas, Acts of Thomas, Book of Thomas) that feature "Judas the twin" and on the traditions from which they stem. Marvin W. Meyer ("The Beginning of the Gospel of Thomas," *Semeia* 52 [1990]: 161–73) also comments a bit on the ascription.

55. While it is by no means certain that the scribe of *this particular* Coptic manuscript was the one who originally made the addition (indeed, it is rather doubtful that he is), that is not really our concern. I will here be treating the Coptic manuscript representatively for the Coptic tradition.

P. Oxy. 654—Logion 1

NHC II 2.32.12–14	*P. Oxy. 654.3–5*
ⲁⲩⲱ ⲡⲉⲭⲁϥ ϫⲉ ⲡⲉⲧⲁϩⲉ	καὶ εἶπεν· [ὃς ἂν τὴν ἑρμηνεί]αν τῶν
ⲉⲑⲉⲣⲙⲏⲛⲉⲓⲁ ⲛⲛⲉⲉⲓϣⲁϫⲉ ϥⲛⲁϫⲓ	λόγων τούτ[ων εὕρῃ, θανάτου] οὐ
ϯⲡⲉ ⲁⲛ ⲙⲡⲙⲟⲩ	μὴ γεύσηται.
And he said, "Whoever finds the	And he said, "Whoever finds the
meaning of these words will not	meaning of these words will not taste
taste death."	death."

There are no significant differences between the Greek and Coptic in logion 1.

P. Oxy. 654—Logion 2

NHC II 2.32.14–19	*P. Oxy. 654.5–9*
ⲡⲉⲭⲉ ⲓ(ⲏⲥⲟⲩ)ⲥ ⲙⲛⲧⲣⲉϥⲗⲟ ⲛϭⲓ	[λέγει Ἰη(σοῦ)ς]· μὴ παυσάσθω ὁ
ⲡⲉⲧϣⲓⲛⲉ ⲉϥϣⲓⲛⲉ ϣⲁⲛⲧⲉϥϭⲓⲛⲉ ⲁⲩⲱ	ζη[τῶν τοῦ ζητεῖν ἕως ἂν] εὕρῃ, καὶ
ϩⲟⲧⲁⲛ ⲉϥϣⲁⲛϭⲓⲛⲉ ϥⲛⲁϣⲧⲣⲧⲣ ⲁⲩⲱ	ὅταν εὕρῃ [θαμβηθήσεται, καὶ
ⲉϥϣⲁⲛϣⲧⲟⲣⲧⲣ ϥⲛⲁⲣ ϣⲡⲏⲣⲉ ⲁⲩⲱ	θαμ]βηθεὶς βασιλεύσει, κα[ὶ
ϥⲛⲁⲣⲣⲣⲟ ⲉϫⲙ ⲡⲧⲏⲣϥ	βασιλεύσας ἀναπα]ήσεται.
Jesus said, "Do not let the one who	Jesus said, "Do not let the one who
seeks stop seeking until he finds. And	seeks stop seeking until he finds. And
when he finds, he will be troubled;	when he finds, he will be amazed;
and when he is troubled, he will be	and when he is amazed, he will rule;
amazed. And he will rule over	and when he rules, he will rest.
everything.	

Logion 2 illustrates well the difficulty of a textual comparison span-
ning two languages. Despite overlap at the edges, there are four distinct additions within the text—two in Coptic and two in Greek. We will
deal with the last two first, as they are significantly easier to sort out.
Internally, Thomas is familiar with "rest" as a final stage in the spiritual
journey (l. 90). Externally, the text has many parallels, both themati-
cally and verbally. We find thematic parallels among wisdom literature
recommending the pursuit of knowledge as a method to achieve peace
(Sir 51.13–14; Wisd Sol 1.1–2; 6.12–14).[56] Therefore, we are on solid
ground when it comes to accepting the Greek reading καὶ βασιλεύσας
ἀναπαήσεται as original. However, verbal parallels to logion 2 (such
as Gos Heb 4)[57] do not contain the final Coptic addition (ⲉϫⲙ̄ ⲡⲧⲏⲣϥ),
making it quite likely that the Coptic scribe expanded the text, possibly
for clarity, possibly for some sort of theological reason. Bammel posits
that the Coptic is actually *less* Gnostic than the Greek,[58] but DeConick
dismisses such an interpretation out of hand.[59]

Indeed, what is going on with the first two additions is much harder
to work out. At first glance, it appears that the Coptic ϥⲛⲁϣⲧⲣⲧⲣ̄ ⲁⲩⲱ
ⲉϥϣⲁⲛϣⲧⲟⲣⲧⲣ̄ ("he will be troubled, and when he is troubled") is parallel to the Greek θαμβηθήσεται, καὶ θαμβηθεὶς ("he will be amazed,
and when he is amazed").[60] However, the Coptic verb ϣⲧⲣⲧⲣ̄ ("to be
troubled/disturbed") does not match up well to the Greek θαμβέω ("to
be astounded/amazed"). If this were the end of the story, making an
evaluation as to whether or not they represent a scribal corruption
of the text or just a very loose translation would be next to impossible.[61] In this case, however, I think I can offer an explanation. The
Greek represents the original text, with a certain process toward elevation (seek→find, find→be amazed, be amazed→rule, rule→rest).
The Coptic has inserted another step early in the process (find→*be
troubled, be troubled*→be amazed) and deleted a step at the end
(~~rule→rest~~) to maintain symmetry in the steps. There does not appear to be a compelling theological motivation for adding and deleting
those particular steps, but that does not mean that there is not one.

---

56. Stevan Davies, *The Gospel of Thomas and Christian Wisdom* (New York: Seabury, 1983), 38–39.
57. As found in Clement of Alexandria, *Stromata* 2.9.45 and 5.14.96.
58. Ernst Bammel, "Rest and Rule," *VC* 23 (1969): 88–90.
59. DeConick, *Original Gospel of Thomas in Translation*, 49–50.
60. Plisch (*Gospel of Thomas*, 41) does see this as a possibility but does not wholly endorse it, preferring instead to simply recognize that the original Thomas would have had *some* multistep process toward salvation.
61. In other cases such as this at first appears to be, it will here be my philosophy to give the scribe the benefit of the doubt, particularly in semantic and lexical consid- erations. Only where there is compelling evidence that the exemplar would have had a different word at some point in the transmission history will I discuss the possibility of textual corruption.

P. Oxy. 654—Logion 3

NHC II 2.32.19–33.5

ⲡⲉⲭⲉ ⲓ(ⲏⲥⲟⲩ)ⲥ ⲭⲉ ⲉⲩϣⲁⲝⲟⲟⲥ

ⲛⲏⲧⲛ̄ ⲛ̄ϭⲓ ⲛⲉⲧⲥⲱⲕ ϩⲏⲧⲧⲏⲩⲧⲛ̄ ⲭⲉ

ⲉⲓⲥϩⲏⲏⲧⲉ ⲉⲧⲙⲛ̄ⲧⲉⲣⲟ ϩⲛ̄ ⲧⲡⲉ ⲉⲉⲓⲉ

ⲛ̄ϩⲁⲗⲏⲧ ⲛⲁⲣ̄ϣⲟⲣⲡ ⲉⲣⲱⲧⲛ̄ ⲛ̄ⲧⲉ ⲧⲡⲉ

ⲉⲩϣⲁⲛⲝⲟⲟⲥ ⲛⲏⲧⲛ̄ ⲭⲉ ⲥϩⲛ̄

ⲑⲁⲗⲁⲥⲥⲁ ⲉⲉⲓⲉ ⲛ̄ⲧⲃⲧ ⲛⲁⲣ̄ϣⲟⲣⲡ

ⲉⲣⲱⲧⲛ̄ ⲁⲗⲗⲁ ⲧⲙⲛ̄ⲧⲉⲣⲟ

ⲥⲙ̄ⲡⲉⲧⲛ̄ϩⲟⲩⲛ ⲁⲩⲱ ⲥⲙ̄ⲡⲉⲧⲛ̄ⲃⲁⲗ

ϩⲟⲧⲁⲛ ⲉⲧⲉⲧⲛ̄ϣⲁⲛⲥⲟⲩⲱⲛ ⲧⲏⲩⲧⲛ̄

ⲧⲟⲧⲉ ⲥⲉⲛⲁⲥⲟⲩⲱ(ⲛ) ⲧⲏⲛⲉ ⲁⲩⲱ

ⲧⲉⲧⲛⲁⲉⲓⲙⲉ ⲭⲉ ⲛ̄ⲧⲱⲧⲛ̄ ⲡⲉ ⲛ̄ϣⲏⲣⲉ

ⲙ̄ⲡⲉⲓⲱⲧ ⲉⲧⲟⲛϩ ⲉϣⲱⲡⲉ ⲇⲉ

ⲧⲉⲧⲛⲁⲥⲟⲩⲱⲛ ⲧⲏⲩⲧⲛ̄ ⲁⲛ ⲉⲉⲓⲉ

ⲧⲉⲧⲛ̄ϣⲟⲟⲡ ϩⲛ̄ ⲟⲩⲙⲛ̄ⲧϩⲏⲕⲉ ⲁⲩⲱ

ⲛ̄ⲧⲱⲧⲛ̄ ⲡⲉ ⲧⲙⲛ̄ⲧϩⲏⲕⲉ

Jesus said, "If those who lead you

say to you, 'Behold, the kingdom is in

heaven,' then the birds in the sky will

come before you. If they say to you,

'It is in the sea,' then the fish will

P. Oxy. 654.9–21

λέγει Ἰ[η(σοῦ)ς. . . .[62] ἐὰν] οἱ ἔλκοντες

ἡμᾶς [εἴπωσιν ὑμῖν· ἰδοὺ] ἡ βασιλεία

ἐν οὐρα[νῷ, ὑμᾶς φθήσεται] τὰ

πετεινὰ τοῦ οὐρ[ανοῦ· ἐὰν δ' εἴπωσιν

ὅ]τι ὑπὸ τὴν γῆν ἐστ[ιν,

εἰσελεύσονται] οἱ ἰχθύες τῆς

θαλά[σσης προφθάσαν]τες ὑμᾶς· καὶ

ἡ βασ[ιλεία τοῦ θεοῦ] ἐντὸς ὑμῶν

[ἐς]τι [κἀκτός. ὃς ἂν ἑαυτὸν] γνῷ,

ταύτην εὑρή[σει, καὶ ὅτε ὑμεῖς]

ἑαυτοὺς γνώσεσθα[ι, εἴσεσθε ὅτι

υἱοί] ἐστε ὑμεῖς τοῦ πατρὸς τοῦ

ζ[ῶντος· εἰ δὲ μὴ] γνώσθε ἑαυτούς,

ἐν [τῇ πτωχείᾳ ἐστὲ] καὶ ὑμεῖς ἐστε ἡ

πτω[χεία].

Jesus said, "If those who lead you

say to you, 'Behold, the kingdom is in

heaven,' then the birds in the sky will

come before you. If they say to you,

'It is under the earth,' then the fish

---

62. DeConick (*Original Gospel of Thomas in Translation*, 51) suggests that Attridge's reconstruction is wanting here, as the Greek manuscript has room for another "five to eight" characters. She tentatively proposes something like αὐτοῖς but correctly notes that any such proposal "would be purely conjecture, since there is no parallel

come before you. Rather,[63] the kingdom is inside of you and outside of you. When you know yourselves, then you will be known, and you will realize that you are the children of the living father. But if you will not know yourselves, then you are in poverty, and you are that poverty.

will come before you. Indeed, the kingdom of God is inside of you and outside of you. Whoever knows himself will find it, and when you know yourselves, you will realize that you are the children of the living father. But if you will not know yourselves, then you are in poverty, and you are that poverty.

One of the five variants in logion 3 is easily explainable: the occurrence of γνώσθε for what should be γνώσεσθε is due to unintentional scribal error (haplography of the -σεσ-). From there, however, the road gets significantly more winding. The initial substitution of ⲭⲉ ⲥⲅ̄ⲛ̄ ⲑⲁⲗⲁⲥⲥⲁ for ὑπὸ τὴν γῆν is likely another place where the Coptic scribe or translator was attempting to make sense of a difficult passage. The Greek ὑπὸ τὴν γῆν—the more confusing, though still sensical, reading[64]—has parallels in early literature[65] and is likely original. The addition of a modifier following ἡ βασιλεία presents an interesting problem, not least because the modifier is lost to us. Some have proposed τοῦ οὐρανοῦ to fill the lacuna, noting that it is

---

in the Coptic to aid us." Such an addition would likely be inauthentic, but due to the uncertainty on all ends, I remain agnostic on the matter and have elected not to include the possible variant in any count.

63. Note the differing translations at this point due to a slight difference in the Coptic and the Greek (ⲁⲗⲗⲁ for καί). I decided that it was best to interpret this difference not as a variant (for which there would appear to be little motivation) but as a case where the syntax of a particular term (in this case καί) could not be replicated in the recipient language. So another, more appropriate term was chosen. Dieter Mueller ("Kingdom of Heaven or Kingdom of God?," *VC* 27 [1973]: 271) argues that the alteration would have been intentionally clarifying the "feeble 'and.'"

64. Indeed, the fact that it is confusing is a point in its favor. It is easy to see a scribe reading "If they say to you, 'It is under the earth,' then the fish will come before you" and thinking that the original must surely have read something more like "It is in the sea." It is much more difficult to see a scribe altering an internally coherent phrase ("If they say to you, 'It is in the sea,' then the fish will come before you")—one with well-attested parallels (see n. 65)—to something nearly nonsensical.

65. Mueller ("Kingdom of Heaven or Kingdom of God?") notes the parallel to Job 12.7–8. T. F. Glasson ("The Gospel of Thomas, Saying 3, and Deuteronomy xxx.11–14," *ExpTim* 78 [1977]: 151–52) notes the parallel to Deut 30.11–14.

a much more common phrase within the gospel[66] and fills out the space more fully.[67] Mueller demonstrates a compelling case that τοῦ θεοῦ ought to fill the lacuna.[68] Logion 27 uses the same modifier for "kingdom," and the Coptic redactor appears to exhibit a tendency toward replacing other instances of ἡ βασιλεία τοῦ θεοῦ (cf. l. 54, where Luke 6.20 has been altered just slightly). As with other places in Thomas, a conclusion cannot be stated too strongly due to the number of factors up in the air. However, I favor an original reading of ἡ βασιλεία τοῦ θεοῦ, making this a probable case of theological alteration.

The other two expansions of the text (ⲧⲟⲧⲉ ⲥⲉⲛⲁⲥⲟⲩⲱ(ⲛ) ⲧⲏⲛⲉ, "then/when you will become known"; ὃς ἂν ἑαυτὸν γνῷ, ταύτην εὑρήσει, "whoever knows himself will find it") represent yet another special problem in this logion. Regarding the Coptic addition, the phrase awkwardly interrupts a sequence similar to what we just saw in logion 2. It is so awkwardly worded that Mueller suggests it might have originated as a marginal note.[69] Regarding the Greek addition, we could argue that the addition bears similarity to that same sequence in logion 2 that the secondary Coptic addition interrupts— and so is original. But we could just as easily argue that it is because of that similarity that the phrase is likely a secondary expansion from an overzealous scribe. A third possibility is that the two additions are not actually independent, instead being in corrupted transposition of each other. In lieu of any significant evidence to illuminate the situation, I conservatively fall back on the canon of the shorter text in each case.

---

66. "Much more common" being a relative term. "Kingdom of Heaven" is an ascription that occurs three times in the Coptic Thomas (ll. 20, 54, and 114). "Kingdom of God" does not occur in Coptic Thomas and occurs only once in the Greek fragments (l. 27).

67. So DeConick, *Original Gospel of Thomas in Translation*, 52. It does not appear, however, that DeConick considers the possibility that τοῦ οὐρανοῦ could have been replaced by a *nomen sacrum*, thus rendering it too short for the allotted space as well. Each line of the Coptic manuscript has room for between twenty-eight and thirty-three characters. DeConick is correct that if τοῦ οὐρανοῦ were written out fully, it plus the last five characters of βασιλεία would make twenty-nine total characters in the line. If, however, it were not written out fully, the shortened version of τοῦ οὐρανοῦ would make it too short, meaning that length and number of characters should not be the only (or even the most significant) factor in deciding how to fill in the lacuna.

68. Mueller ("Kingdom of Heaven or Kingdom of God?," 271–74) ultimately decides otherwise, but Fitzmyer ("Oxyrhynchus Logoi," 376–77) sticks with τοῦ θεοῦ.

69. Mueller, "Kingdom of Heaven or Kingdom of God?," 268, following Grant and Schoedel (*Secret Sayings of Jesus*, 70) and Otfried Hofius ("Das koptische Thomasevangelium und die Oxyrhynchus Papyri Nr 1, 654, und 655," *EvT* 20 [1960]: 31).

Tim Ricchuiti

P. Oxy. 654—Logion 4

NHC II 2.33.5–10	P. Oxy. 654.21–27
ⲡⲉϫⲉ ⲓ(ⲏⲥⲟⲩ)ⲥ ϥⲛⲁϫⲛⲁⲩ ⲁⲛ ⲛϭⲓ	[λέγει Ἰη(σοῦ)ς]· οὐκ ἀποκνήσει
ⲡⲣⲱⲙⲉ ⲛ̄2ⲗⲗⲟ 2ⲛ̄ ⲛⲉϥ2ⲟⲟⲩ ⲉⲭⲛⲉ	ἄνθ[ρωπος παλαιὸς ἡμε]ρῶν
ⲟⲩⲕⲟⲩⲉⲓ ⲛ̄ϣⲏⲣⲉ ϣⲏⲙ ⲉϥ2ⲛ̄ ⲥⲁϣϥ̄	ἐπερωτῆσαι πα[ιδίον ἑπτὰ ἡμε]ρῶν
ⲛ̄2ⲟⲟⲩ ⲉⲧⲃⲉ ⲡⲧⲟⲡⲟⲥ ⲙ̄ⲡⲱⲛ2 ⲁⲩⲱ	περὶ τοῦ τόπου τῆ[ς ζωῆς, καὶ
ϥⲛⲁⲱⲛ2 ϫⲉ ⲟⲩⲛ̄ 2ⲁ2 ⲛ̄ϣⲟⲣⲡ ⲛⲁⲣ̄	ζή]σετε· ὅτι πολλοὶ ἔσονται π[ρῶτοι
2ⲁⲉ ⲁⲩⲱ ⲛ̄ⲥⲉϣⲱⲡⲉ ⲟⲩⲁ ⲟⲩⲱⲧ[70]	ἔσχατοι καὶ] οἱ ἔσχατοι πρῶτοι, καὶ
	[εἰς γενήσου]σιν.

Jesus said, "The man old in days will not hesitate to ask a child of seven days about the place of life, and he will live. For many who are first will be last, and they will become one.

Jesus said, "The man old in days will not hesitate to ask a child of seven days about the place of life, and he will live. For many who are first will be last, and the last will be first, and they will become one.

Climbing down from the mountain of variants in logion 3, we have only the addition of οἱ ἔσχατοι πρῶτοι to deal with in logion 4. This is yet another variant that could easily go either way: we could argue that it is a predictable addition to the text by the Greek scribe, on the grounds of maintaining parallelism within the text or an attempt to harmonize with the canonical Gospels (cf. Matt 19:30; 20:16; Mark 10:31; Luke 13:30). We could also argue for its originality and attribute its deletion in the Coptic to either an accidental omission or a purposeful attempt to blunt the force of the saying (though it is unclear what kind of understanding or desire would need to be present in the community to generate the deliberate deletion of "the last will be first" while leaving in "the first will be last"). Indeed, it is quite possible to see the accidental deletion of the phrase from the Coptic. The text in the manuscript currently reads like so:

. . . ⲁⲩⲱ
ϥⲛⲁⲱⲛ2ⲭⲉⲟⲩⲛ̄2ⲁ2ⲛ̄ϣⲟⲣⲡⲛⲁⲣ̄2ⲁ
ⲉⲁⲩⲱ̄ⲛ̄ⲥⲉϣⲱⲡⲉⲟⲩⲁⲟⲩⲱⲧ

---

70. See A. F. J. Klijn, "The 'Single One' In the Gospel of Thomas," *JBL* 81 (1962): 271–78, on the equivalence of ⲟⲩⲁ, ⲟⲩⲱⲧ, and εἷς.

The original text, containing the phrase "and the last will be first" (ⲁⲩⲱ ⲛ̅ϩⲁⲉ ⲛⲁⲣ̅ ϣⲟⲣⲡ), could have looked something like this:

. . . ⲁⲩⲱ
ϥⲛⲁⲱⲛϩⲭⲉⲟⲩⲛ̅ϩⲁϩⲛ̅ϣⲟⲣⲡⲛⲁⲣ̅ϩⲁ
ⲉⲁⲩⲱⲛ̅ϩⲁⲉⲛⲁⲣ̅ϣⲟⲣⲡⲁⲩⲱⲛ̅ⲥⲉϣⲱ
ⲡⲉⲟⲩⲁⲟⲩⲱⲧ

As the scribe's eye jumped ahead from the second ⲁⲩⲱ in the passage to the third—

. . . ⲁⲩⲱ
ϥⲛⲁⲱⲛϩⲭⲉⲟⲩⲛ̅ϩⲁϩⲛ̅ϣⲟⲣⲡⲛⲁⲣ̅ϩⲁ
ⲉⲁⲩⲱⲛ̅ϩⲁⲉⲛⲁⲣ̅ϣⲟⲣⲡⲁⲩⲱⲛ̅ⲥⲉϣⲱ
ⲡⲉⲟⲩⲁⲟⲩⲱⲧ

—he would have accidentally deleted the phrase in question, leaving only

. . . ⲁⲩⲱ
ϥⲛⲁⲱⲛϩⲭⲉⲟⲩⲛ̅ϩⲁϩⲛ̅ϣⲟⲣⲡⲛⲁⲣ̅ϩⲁ
ⲉⲁⲩⲱⲛ̅ⲥⲉϣⲱⲡⲉⲟⲩⲁⲟⲩⲱⲧ

This is only one possibility,[71] but it suggests that the Greek contains the original.

P. Oxy. 654—Logion 5

NHC II.2.33.10–14	P. Oxy. 654.27–31
ⲡⲉⲭⲉ ⲓ(ⲏⲥⲟⲩ)ⲥ ⲥⲟⲩⲱⲛ ⲡⲉⲧⲙ̅ⲡⲙ̅ⲧⲟ	λέγει Ἰη(σοῦ)ς· γ[νῶθι τὸ ὂν
ⲙ̅ⲡⲉⲕϩⲟ ⲉⲃⲟⲗ ⲁⲩⲱ ⲡⲉⲑⲏⲡ ⲉⲣⲟⲕ	ἔμπρος]θεν τῆς ὄψεώς σου, καὶ [τὸ
ϥⲛⲁϭⲱⲗⲡ̅ ⲉⲃⲟⲗ ⲛⲁⲕ ⲙⲛ̅ ⲗⲁⲁⲩ ⲅⲁⲣ	κεκαλυμμένον] ἀπό σου
ⲉϥϩⲏⲡ ⲉϥⲛⲁⲟⲩⲱⲛϩ ⲉⲃⲟⲗ ⲁⲛ	ἀποκαλυφήσετ[αί σοι· οὐ γάρ ἐς]τιν

---

71. It is a possibility that works particularly well with Attridge's reconstruction ("Greek Fragments," 115) but not so well with DeConick's (*Original Gospel of Thomas in Translation*, 57). DeConick notes that Attridge's reconstruction would require fifteen characters, while the line appears to have room for only twelve.

Tim Ricchuiti

κρυπτὸν ὃ οὐ φανε[ρὸν γενήσεται],

καὶ θεθαμμένον[72] ὃ ο[ὐκ

ἐγερθήσεται].

Jesus said, "Know what is before

your face, and what is hidden from

you will be revealed to you, for there

is nothing hidden that will not be

manifested."

Jesus said, "Know what is before

your face, and what is hidden from

you will be revealed to you, for there

is nothing hidden that will not be

manifested, nor buried that will not

be raised."

The manuscript of logion 5 reads ἀποκαλυφήσετ[αι, while it should read ἀποκαλυφθήσετ[αι. That is a fairly straightforward misspelling on the part of the Greek scribe (he omitted the θ). The second variant—the addition of the phrase καὶ θεθαμμένον ὃ οὐκ ἐγερθήσεται ("and [nothing] buried that will not be raised")—presents a bit more of a problem. Apparently, this phrase became a rather common burial inscription in Egypt, making it a predictable addition.[73] Once again, it looks as if the canon of the shorter text holds here and as if the Greek is inauthentic. However, we should also note that the burial inscription (fifth or sixth century CE) is known from at least a few hundred years later. It seems odd to not at least recognize the *possibility* that the burial inscription stemmed from recognition that Jesus said something like this (perhaps in original Thomas), rather than the other way around. The possibilities do not end even there, as logion 6 contains a similar Coptic addition (ⲁⲩⲱ ⲙⲛ̄ ⲗⲁⲁⲩ ⲉϥϩⲟⲃⲥ̄ ⲉⲩⲛⲁϭⲱ ⲟⲩⲉϣⲛ̄ ϭⲟⲗⲡϥ, "and nothing that will remain covered without being revealed"), raising the possibility of a transposition similar in kind, though not degree, to the transposition of logion 30+77b.[74] Looking at the dissimilarities between the two sayings, I

---

72. Likely a misspelling of τεθαμμένον.
73. Fitzmyer, "Oxyrhynchus Logoi," 383. See also Grenfell and Hunt, *Oxyrhynchus Papyri*, 4:18; DeConick, *Original Gospel of Thomas in Translation*, 60.
74. Taken up in more detail shortly.

think we can shed light on the original text here. If καὶ θεθαμμένον [*sic*] ὃ οὐκ ἐγερθήσεται is an addition to the Greek of logion 5, it ought to be an addition to the almost identically ending logion 6. But we do not find it there. Instead, we find the altered Coptic addition, which shifts emphasis from a physical resurrection to the more common refrain of *gnosis* and revelation. Indeed, recognizing the theological motivation for such a deletion, it is most likely that P. Oxy. 654 preserves the original text of Thomas 5.

P. Oxy. 654—Logion 6

NHC II 2.33.14–23

ⲁⲩϫⲛⲟⲩϥ ⲛ̄ϭⲓ ⲛⲉϥⲙⲁⲑⲏⲧⲏⲥ ⲡⲉϫⲁⲩ

ⲛ̅ⲁϥ ϫⲉ ⲕⲟⲩⲱϣ ⲉⲧⲣ̅ⲛ̅ⲣ̅ⲛⲏⲥⲧⲉⲩⲉ

ⲁⲩⲱ ⲉϣ ⲧⲉ ⲑⲉ ⲉⲛⲁϣⲗⲏⲗ ⲉⲛⲁϯ

ⲉⲗⲉⲏⲙⲟⲥⲩⲛⲏ ⲁⲩⲱ ⲉⲛⲁⲣ̅ⲡⲁⲣⲁⲧⲏⲣⲉⲓ

ⲉⲟⲩ ⲛ̄ϭⲓ ⲟⲩⲱⲙ ⲡⲉϫⲉ ⲓ(ⲏⲥⲟⲩ)ⲥ ϫⲉ

ⲙ̄ⲡ̅ⲣ̅ ϫⲉ ϭⲟⲗ ⲁⲩⲱ ⲡⲉⲧⲉⲧⲛ̅ⲙⲟⲥⲧⲉ

ⲙ̄ⲙⲟϥ ⲙ̄ⲡ̅ⲣ̅ⲁⲁϥ ϫⲉ ⲥⲉϭⲟⲗⲡ ⲧⲏⲣⲟⲩ

ⲉⲃⲟⲗ ⲙ̄ⲡⲉⲙⲧⲟ ⲉⲃⲟⲗ ⲛ̄ⲧ̅ⲡⲉ ⲙ̄ⲛ̄ ⲗⲁⲁⲩ

ⲅⲁⲣ ⲉϥϩⲏⲡ ⲉϥⲛⲁⲟⲩⲱⲛϩ ⲉⲃⲟⲗ ⲁⲛ

ⲁⲩⲱ ⲙ̄ⲛ̄ ⲗⲁⲁⲩ ⲉϥϩⲟⲃ̅ⲥ̅ ⲉⲩⲛⲁϭⲱ

ⲟⲩⲉϣ̅ⲛ̄ ϭⲟⲗⲡϥ

P. Oxy. 654.32–40

[ἐξ]ετάζουσιν αὐτὸν ο[ἱ μαθηταὶ

αὐτοῦ καὶ λέ]γουσιν· πῶς

νηστεύ[σομεν, καὶ πῶς

προσευξό]μεθα, καὶ πῶς

[ἐλεημοσύνην ποιήσομεν κ]αὶ τί

παρατηρήσ[ομεν περὶ τῶν

βρωμάτω]ν· λέγει Ἰη(σοῦ)ς· [μὴ

ψεύδεσθε καὶ ὅτι μισ]εῖται, μὴ

ποιεῖτ[ε· ὅτι πάντα ἐνώπιον τ]ῆς

ἀληθ[ε]ίας ἀν[αφαίνεται. οὐδὲν γάρ

ἐστίν ἀ[π]οκεκρ[υμμένον ὃ οὐ

φανερὸν ἔσται].

His disciples questioned him and said to him, "Do you want us to fast? And how shall we pray? Shall we give alms? And from what foods shall we abstain?" Jesus said, "Do not tell lies

His disciples questioned him and said, "How should we fast, and how should we pray? And how should we give alms? And what should we observe concerning our food? Jesus

and do not do that which you hate.	*said, "Do not lie, and that which you*
For everything is revealed before	*hate, do not do. For everything is*
heaven. For there is nothing hidden	*revealed before truth. For there is*
that will not be manifested, and	*nothing hidden that will not be made*
nothing that will remain covered	*known."*
without being revealed."	

Each variant of logion 6 is a clear instance of the Coptic's secondary character. The Coptic addition of naq appears to be a scribal alteration toward clarity. Regarding the substitution of πῶς νηστεύσομεν ("How should we fast?") for ϫⲉⲕⲟⲩⲱϣ ⲉⲧⲣⲛ̄ⲣⲛⲏⲥⲧⲉⲩⲉ ("Do you want us to fast?"), DeConick explains particularly well the difference in and significance of these questions beginning the saying: "The questions have a more parallel structure in the Greek than in the Coptic. . . . [T]he Coptic questions appear to have been revised to reflect the practices of later Christians who no longer wished to continue obligatory fasting practices."[75] The substitution of ⲙ̄ⲡⲉⲙⲧⲟ ⲉⲃⲟⲗ ⲛ̄ⲧⲡⲉ ("in the face of heaven/the sky") for ἐνώπιον τῆς ἀληθείας ("in the face of truth") is relatively simple to explain once one realizes that the Coptic for "truth" is ⲙⲉ, only one character off from the Coptic for "sky" (ⲡⲉ).[76] The scribe unintentionally substituted ⲡ for what should have been ⲙ. Finally, the additional statement ⲁⲩⲱ ⲙ̄ⲛ̄ ⲗⲁⲁⲩ ⲉϥϩⲟⲃⲥ̄ ⲉⲩⲛⲁϭⲱ ⲟⲩⲉϣⲛ̄ ϭⲟⲗⲡϥ ("and there is nothing covered that will not be revealed") is almost certainly an expansion and alteration of the original like that previously described for logion 5.[77]

Finally, with logion 7 bringing us to the close of P. Oxy. 654, we have our first example of a text wherein conjecture leaves the arena of external probabilities completely (such probabilities being unlimited by the sparse text available). With only seventeen visible characters remaining in the Greek fragment, it is of little value here to guess about what mistakes the scribe may or may not have made.

Analysis

Overall, there are eighteen variants to deal with between the text of P. Oxy. 654 and logia 1–7 of the Coptic Thomas. There does not

---

75. DeConick, *Original Gospel of Thomas in Translation*, 62.
76. It is also worth noting that the two characters' similar look may have contributed to the confusion.
77. The alteration also shares some verbal familiarity with Matt 10.26 and Luke 12.2.

appear to be any tendency toward a particular type of variant: five are substitutions, seven are additions within the Greek text, and six are additions within the Coptic text. Nor does any particular logion stand out: logion 3 has the highest number of variants, at five; but logia 2 and 6 are just behind, at four variants each. What does stand out is the clearly secondary character of the Coptic text. Of the eighteen variations, I judged the text of P. Oxy. 654 to be original in thirteen cases (72.2%). I judged the Coptic text to be original in just three cases (17%), each of which was an easily detectable spelling variation. Scholars are clearly on solid ground when they assume the primacy of the text of P. Oxy. 654.

Table 5.1. Variation of P. Oxy. 654 by Logion			
	Substitution	Greek Addition	Coptic Addition	Total
Prologue	0	1	1	2
1	0	0	0	0
2	0	2	2	4
3	2	2	1	5
4	0	1	0	1
5	1	1	0	2
6	2	0	2	4
7	0	0	0	0
Total	5	7	6	

The nature of the alterations also stands out. While I remain agnostic on the motivation of the alteration of logion 2, logia 3, 5, and 6 each display theologically motivated alterations. Logion 3 appears unwilling to ascribe the "kingdom" (to which adherents of the text were taught to aspire) to "God" ($\theta\epsilon\acute{o}\varsigma$), who would have been associated with an evil demiurge, rather than the benevolent "Father" seen elsewhere in Thomas. Logia 5 and 6 alter a phrase that would have glorified and endorsed bodily resurrection. To be sure, most variation between the texts can be attributed to natural, neutral, and unintentional alteration; but we must also recognize those places where that is not the case.

Tim Ricchuiti

P. Oxy. 1—Logion 26

NHC II 2.38.12–17	*P. Oxy. 1.1–4*
ⲡⲉϫⲉ ⲓ(ⲏⲥⲟⲩ)ⲥ ϫⲉ ⲡϫⲏ ⲉⲧϩⲙ̄ ⲡⲃⲁⲗ	
ⲙ̄ⲡⲉⲕⲥⲟⲛ ⲕⲛⲁⲩ ⲉⲣⲟϥ ⲡⲥⲟⲉⲓ ⲇⲉ	
ⲉⲧϩⲙ̄ ⲡⲉⲕⲃⲁⲗ ⲕⲛⲁⲩ ⲁⲛ ⲉⲣⲟϥ ϩⲟⲧⲁⲛ	
ⲉⲕϣⲁⲛⲛⲟⲩϫⲉ ⲙ̄ⲡⲥⲟⲉⲓ ⲉⲃⲟⲗ ϩⲙ̄	
ⲡⲉⲕⲃⲁⲗ ⲧⲟⲧⲉ ⲕⲛⲁⲛⲁⲩ ⲉⲃⲟⲗ	καὶ τότε διαβλέψεις ἐκβαλεῖν τὸ
ⲉⲛⲟⲩϫⲉ ⲙ̄ⲡϫⲏ ⲉⲃⲟⲗ ϩⲙ̄ ⲡⲃⲁⲗ	κάρφος τὸ ἐν τῷ ὀφθαλμῷ τοῦ
ⲙ̄ⲡⲉⲕⲥⲟⲛ	ἀδελφοῦ σου.
. . . Then you will see clearly to cast	*And then you will see clearly to cast*
the twig out of *your brother's eye.*	*out the twig* in *your brother's eye.*

The beginning of P. Oxy. 1 agrees almost exactly with the Coptic manuscript, where they overlap.[78] There are two small disagreements: (1) the addition of a καί at the beginning of the verse and (2) the slightly different nuance of the prepositions used in description of the "twig" (ⲉⲃⲟⲗ, "from," vs. ἐν, "in"). The text is parallel to Matthew 7.3–5 and Luke 6.41–42:

Matthew 7.3–5	Luke 6.41–42
τί δὲ βλέπεις τὸ κάρφος τὸ ἐν τῷ	Τί δὲ βλέπεις τὸ κάρφος τὸ ἐν τῷ
ὀφθαλμῷ τοῦ ἀδελφοῦ σου, τὴν δὲ	ὀφθαλμῷ τοῦ ἀδελφοῦ σου, τὴν δὲ
ἐν τῷ σῷ ὀφθαλμῷ δοκὸν οὐ	δοκὸν τὴν ἐν τῷ ἰδίῳ ὀφθαλμῷ οὐ
κατανοεῖς; ἢ πῶς ἐρεῖς τῷ ἀδελφῷ	κατανοεῖς; πῶς δύνασαι λέγειν τῷ
σου· ἄφες ἐκβάλω τὸ κάρφος ἐκ τοῦ	ἀδελφῷ σου· ἀδελφέ, ἄφες ἐκβάλω
ὀφθαλμοῦ σου, καὶ ἰδοὺ ἡ δοκὸς ἐν	τὸ κάρφος τὸ ἐν τῷ ὀφθαλμῷ σου,
τῷ ὀφθαλμῷ σου; ὑποκριτά, ἔκβαλε	αὐτὸς τὴν ἐν τῷ ὀφθαλμῷ σου δοκὸν
πρῶτον ἐκ τοῦ ὀφθαλμοῦ σοῦ τὴν	οὐ βλέπων; ὑποκριτά, ἔκβαλε
δοκόν, καὶ τότε διαβλέψεις ἐκβαλεῖν	πρῶτον τὴν δοκὸν ἐκ τοῦ ὀφθαλμοῦ
τὸ κάρφος ἐκ τοῦ ὀφθαλμοῦ τοῦ	σου, καὶ τότε διαβλέψεις τὸ κάρφος
ἀδελφοῦ σου.	τὸ ἐν τῷ ὀφθαλμῷ τοῦ ἀδελφοῦ σου
	ἐκβαλεῖν.

---

78. The extant papyrus page begins with καὶ τότε διαβλέψεις.

The Luke text is in complete verbal parallel save for the location of ἐκβαλεῖν. The Matthew text is in complete verbal parallel save for the prepositional phrase, which more closely matches the Coptic. The best explanation for these parallels is that the Coptic represents the original text or stems from an earlier tradition that also lies behind the Matthean text.[79] Following this explanation, it appears that the scribe of P. Oxy. 1 attempted to correct his text utilizing the verbal parallel in Luke, which introduced both the καί and the alteration of the original prepositional phrase (which would have looked more like Matt 7.5).[80]

P. Oxy. 1—Logion 27

NHC II 2.38.17–20	P. Oxy. 1.4–11
ⲉⲧⲉⲧⲛⲣⲛⲏⲥⲧⲉⲩⲉ ⲉⲡⲕⲟⲥⲙⲟⲥ	λέγει Ἰ(ησοῦ)ς· ἐὰν μὴ νηστεύσηται
ⲧⲉⲧⲛⲁϩⲉ ⲁⲛ ⲉⲧⲙⲛⲧⲉⲣⲟ	τὸν κόσμον, οὐ μὴ εὕρηται τὴν
ⲉⲧⲉⲧⲛ̄ⲧⲙⲉⲓⲣⲉ ⲙ̄ⲡⲥⲁⲙⲃⲁⲧⲟⲛ	βασιλείαν τοῦ θ(εο)ῦ· καὶ ἐὰν μὴ
ⲛ̄ⲥⲁⲃⲃⲁⲧⲟⲛ ⲛ̄ⲧⲉⲧⲛⲁⲛⲁⲩ ⲁⲛ ⲉⲡⲉⲓⲱⲧ	σαββατίσητε τὸ σάββατον, οὐκ
	ὄψεσθε τὸ(ν) π(ατέ)ρα.
"If you do not fast from the world,	*Jesus said, "If you do not fast from*
you will not find the Kingdom. If you	*the world, you will not find the*
do not keep the Sabbath as Sabbath,	*Kingdom of God. And if you do not*
you will not see the Father."	*keep the Sabbath the Sabbath, you*
	will not see the Father."

---

79. Stephen J. Patterson, *The Gospel of Thomas and Jesus* (Sonoma, CA: Polebridge, 1993), 30–31.

80. DeConick (*Original Gospel of Thomas in Translation*, 128) notes another possibility proposed by John H. Sieber ("A Redactional Analysis of the Synoptic Gospels with Regard to the Question of the Sources of the Gospel according to Thomas" [PhD diss., Claremont Graduate School, 1966], 72–74)—namely, that this type of variant appears to stem from oral tradition, rather than literary development of the gospel.

Tim Ricchuiti

Logion 27 gives us our first identifiable spelling variation in the Coptic Thomas: the Coptic manuscript reads ⲉⲧⲉⲧⲙ̅ⲣⲛⲏⲥⲧⲉⲩⲉ where it should read ⲉⲧⲉⲧⲛ̅ⲧⲙ̅ⲣⲛⲏⲥⲧⲉⲩⲉ. Additionally, P. Oxy. 1 has three additions: (1) the introductory "Jesus said," (2) the genitive modifier τοῦ θεοῦ, and (3) a καί introducing the second half of the logion.[81] Variants 1 and 3 are almost certainly cases where the shorter text (the Coptic text in each case) lines up with the original text. The addition of the introductory formula is a completely predictable adjustment on the part of the scribe.[82] Beyond this, it is not as if logia lacking the introductory formula are unknown (cf. logia 62, 69, 101).[83] The additional καί could be merely a translational issue,[84] but along with the additional καί of logion 26, we can detect the beginnings of a scribal tendency toward additional conjunctions in P. Oxy. 1.

This leaves us only with the addition of τοῦ θεοῦ. This is essentially the same problem seen in logion 3. It is true that "kingdom" is generally found without any modifiers (logia 3, 22, 27, 46, 49, 82, 107, 109, 113),[85] but if anything, that would push us in the direction of affirming the originality of τοῦ θεοῦ.[86] Beyond this, it is easy to detect a motivation to delete τοῦ θεοῦ from the manuscript. A pair of parallel conditional statements form logion 27:

If you do not fast from the world,	you will not find the Kingdom.
If you do not keep the Sabbath as Sabbath,	you will not see the Father.

If τοῦ θεοῦ is original, logion 27 makes an implicit connection between "the Father" and "God." But this would have been unacceptable for adherents to a theology that taught that "God" was to be associated with the demiurge, while the "Father" represented the true Supreme Being. Therefore, the most likely scenario is that τοῦ θεοῦ is original and was deleted due to theological considerations.

---

81. It is a bit of bad form on my part to separate τοῦ θεοῦ καί into two variants when they appear as one addition in the manuscript. However, I believe that I can demonstrate good cause to treat them separately.

82. Interestingly enough, DeConick (*Original Gospel of Thomas in Translation*, 129) views this as the basis for why the Greek is likely authentic here, noting that "this introductory clause is consistent with the manner in which the majority of logia are introduced in the Gospel." However, it is precisely because of that consistency that I find it more likely that the λέγει Ἰησοῦς is secondary.

83. Plisch, *Gospel of Thomas*, 207–8.

84. Indeed, DeConick ignores the καί in her translation (*Original Gospel of Thomas in Translation*, 131).

85. Ibid., 129.

86. It is more likely that a scribe would delete τοῦ θεοῦ to keep the manuscript in line with other logia than that a scribe would add τοῦ θεοῦ and break such parallel.

P. Oxy. 1—Logion 28

NHC II 2.38.20–31

ⲡⲉϫⲉ ⲓ(ⲏⲥⲟⲩ)ⲥ ϫⲉ ⲁⲉⲓⲱϩⲉ ⲉⲣⲁⲧ

ϩⲛ ⲧⲙⲏⲧⲉ ⲙⲡⲕⲟⲥⲙⲟⲥ ⲁⲩⲱ

ⲁⲉⲓⲟⲩⲱⲛϩ ⲉⲃⲟⲗ ⲛⲁⲩ ϩⲛ ⲥⲁⲣⲝ ⲁⲉⲓϩⲉ

ⲉⲣⲟⲟⲩ ⲧⲏⲣⲟⲩ ⲉⲩⲧⲁϩⲉ ⲙⲡⲓϩⲉ

ⲉⲗⲁⲁⲩ ⲛϩⲏⲧⲟⲩ ⲉϥⲟⲃⲉ ⲁⲩⲱ

ⲁⲧⲁⲯⲩⲭⲏ † ⲧⲕⲁⲥ ⲉϫⲛ ⲛϣⲏⲣⲉ

ⲛⲣⲣⲱⲙⲉ ϫⲉ ϩⲛⲃⲗⲗⲉⲉⲩⲉ ⲛⲉ ϩⲙ

ⲡⲟⲩϩⲏⲧ ⲁⲩⲱ ⲥⲉⲛⲁⲩ ⲉⲃⲟⲗ ⲁⲛ ϫⲉ

ⲛⲧⲁⲩⲉⲓ ⲉⲡⲕⲟⲥⲙⲟⲥ ⲉⲩϣⲟⲩⲉⲓⲧ

ⲉⲩϣⲓⲛⲉ ⲟⲛ ⲉⲧⲣⲟⲩⲉⲓ ⲉⲃⲟⲗ ϩⲙ

ⲡⲕⲟⲥⲙⲟⲥ ⲉⲩϣⲟⲩⲉⲓⲧ ⲡⲗⲏⲛ ⲧⲉⲛⲟⲩ

ⲥⲉⲧⲟϩⲉ ϩⲟⲧⲁⲛ ⲉⲩϣⲁⲛⲛⲉϩ ⲡⲟⲩⲏⲣⲡ

ⲧⲟⲧⲉ ⲥⲉⲛⲁⲣⲙⲉⲧⲁⲛⲟⲉⲓ

P. Oxy. 1.11–21

λέγει Ἰ(ησοῦ)ς· ἔ[ς]την ἐν μέσῳ τοῦ

κόσμου καὶ ἐν σαρκεὶ ὤφθην αὐτοῖς

καὶ εὗρον πάντας μεθύοντας καὶ

οὐδένα εὗρον δειψώ(ν)τα ἐν αὐτοῖς

καὶ πονεῖ ἡ ψυχή μου ἐπὶ τοῖς υἱοῖς

τῶν ἀν(θρώπ)ων ὅτι τυφλοί εἰσιν τῇ

καρδίᾳ αὐτῶ[ν] καὶ [οὐ] βλέπ[ουσιν

ὅτι . . .]

Jesus said, "I stood in the midst of the world and I appeared to them in the flesh. I found all of them drunk; I found none of them thirsty. And my soul suffered in pain over the sons of men, for they are blind in their hearts and they do not see . . ."

Jesus said, "I stood in the midst of the world and I appeared to them in the flesh and I found all of them drunk and I found none of them thirsty. And my soul suffered in pain over the sons of men, for they are blind in their hearts and they do not see . . ."

There are no significant differences between the Greek and Coptic in logion 28.[87] However, in keeping with the scribal tendency for P. Oxy. 1, the Greek has two additional instances of καί. One other scribal error has P. Oxy. 1 reading σαρκεί[88] instead of σαρκί.

---

87. To the point that, in keeping with the rest of P. Oxy. 1, most translations leave out each καί entirely.
88. While this could possibly be a spelling variation rather than a scribal error, the fact that the σαρκεί has been corrected within the manuscript itself (σαρκί) pushes us strongly in the direction of error. Of course, it is impossible to know whether a later corrector or the scribe made the correction.

Tim Ricchuiti

P. Oxy. 1—Logion 29

NHC II 2.38.31–39.2   *P. Oxy. 1.22*

ⲡⲉⲭⲉ ⲓ(ⲏⲥⲟⲩ)ⲥ ⲉⲱⲭⲉ ⲛ̄ⲧⲁ ⲧⲥⲁⲣⳅ

ⳤⲱⲡⲉ ⲉⲧⲃⲉ ⲡ̄ⲛ̄ⲁ̄ ⲟⲩⳤⲡⲏⲣⲉ ⲧⲉ

ⲉⳤⲭⲉ ⲡ̄ⲛ̄ⲁ̄ ⲇⲉ ⲉⲧⲃⲉ ⲡⲥⲱⲙⲁ

ⲟⲩⳤⲡⲏⲣⲉ ⲛ̄ⳤⲡⲏⲣⲉ ⲡⲉ ⲁⲗⲗⲁ ⲁⲛⲟⲕ ϯⲣ̄

ⳤⲡⲏⲣⲉ ⲛ̄ⲡⲁⲉⲓ ⲭⲉ ⲡⲱⲥ ⲁⲧⲉⲉⲓⲛⲟϭ

ⲙⲙⲛ̄ⲧⲣⲙ̄ⲙⲁⲟ ⲁⲥⲟⲩⲱⳅ ϩⲛ̄   . . . ἐνοικ]εῖ [ταύτ]η[ν τ]ὴν

ⲧⲉⲉⲓⲙ̄ⲛ̄ⲧϩⲏⲕⲉ   πτωχεία(ν).

. . . *dwelled in this poverty.*   . . . *dwells in this poverty.*

There are no significant differences between the Greek and Coptic in logion 29. [89]

P. Oxy. 1—Logion 30+77b

NHC II 2.39.2–5   *P. Oxy. 1.23–27*

ⲡⲉⲭⲉ ⲓ(ⲏⲥⲟⲩ)ⲥ ⲭⲉ ⲡⲙⲁ ⲉⲩⲛ̄ ⳤⲟⲙⲧ   [λέγ]ει ['Ι(ησοῦ)ς· ὅπ]ου ἐὰν ὦσιν

ⲛ̄ⲛⲟⲩⲧⲉ ⲙⲙⲁⲩ ϩⲛ̄ⲛⲟⲩⲧⲉ ⲛⲉ ⲡⲙⲁ   [τρ]ε[ῖς], ε[ἰς]ὶν θεοί· καὶ [ὅ]που ε[ἷς]

ⲉⲩⲛ̄ ⲥⲛⲁⲩ ⲏ ⲟⲩⲁ ⲁⲛⲟⲕ ϯⳤⲟⲟⲡ   ἐστιν μόνος, [λ]έγω· ἐγώ εἰμι μετ'

ⲛⲙⲙⲁϥ   αὐτ[οῦ] . . .

Jesus said, "Where there are three   *Jesus said, "Where there are three,*

gods, they are gods. Where there are   *they are gods. And where one is*

two or one, I am with him."   *alone, I say, I am with him."*

NHC II 2.46.22–28   *P. Oxy. 1.27–30*

ⲡⲉⲭⲉ ⲓ(ⲏⲥⲟⲩ)ⲥ ⲭⲉ ⲁⲛⲟⲕ ⲡⲉ

ⲡⲟⲩⲟⲉⲓⲛ ⲡⲁⲉⲓ ⲉⲧϩⲓⳤⲱⲟⲩ ⲧⲏⲣⲟⲩ

---

89. As can be seen from the provided translation, there is a possible difference in tense, but the various ways the Greek tense could be interpreted syntactically make this one of those places where we have to assume that semantic difference between Coptic and Greek is a more likely explanation of any difference than is scribal error/textual corruption.

ⲁⲛⲟⲕ ⲡⲉ ⲡⲧⲏⲣϥ ⲛ̅ⲧⲁ ⲡⲧⲏⲣϥ ⲉⲓ ⲉⲃⲟⲗ

ⲛ̅ϩⲏⲧ ⲁⲩⲱ ⲛ̅ⲧⲁ ⲡⲧⲏⲣϥ ⲡⲱϩ ϣⲁⲣⲟⲉⲓ

ⲡⲱϩ ⲛ̅ⲛⲟⲩϣⲉ ⲁⲛⲟⲕ ϯⲙ̅ⲙⲁⲩ ϥⲓ ⲙ̅ⲡⲱⲛⲉ

ⲉϩⲣⲁⲓ ⲁⲩⲱ ⲧⲉⲧⲛⲁϩⲉ ⲉⲣⲟⲉⲓ ⲙ̅ⲙⲁⲩ

. . . Split a piece of wood, I am there.

Lift up the stone and you will find me

there.

. . . ἔγει[ρ]ον τὸν λίθο(ν) κἀκεῖ

εὑρήσεις με· σχίσον τὸ ξύλον κἀγὼ

ἐκεῖ εἰμι.

Lift up the stone and you will find me

there. Split the wood and I am there.

The combination of logia 30 and 77 represents the most difficult, or at the very least the most elaborate, of all Thomasine text-critical problems. To be dealt with are (1) a highly corrupted text in logion 30, in which the original text is in all likelihood no longer maintained in either the Greek or the Coptic; (2) the only occurrence[90] of transposition among any of the variants in any of the manuscripts; and (3) the peculiar problem of the disparate Coptic sayings' combination in the Greek manuscript.

Our first difficulty is in attempting to get behind both the Coptic and Greek of logion 30, as neither appears to preserve the original text. The Coptic contains an additional ⲛ̅ⲛⲟⲩⲧⲉ ("gods") in the initial clause, apparently because of a scribe's attempt to make sense of the following clause ("they are gods"). The Greek contains an additional καί, a pattern that we have seen emerge with respect to P. Oxy. 1 and that is probably inauthentic. It also includes an emphatic λέγω ("I say") in the middle of Jesus' statement, which we will come back to in a moment. Finally, there is a substitution between the Coptic and the Greek. Where the Greek has only "where one is alone," the Coptic has "where there are two or one." The closest biblical parallel is Matthew 18.20 ("For where there are two or three having come together in my name, I am there in their midst").[91] It is possible that the Coptic scribe, remembering that the biblical parallel had two items ("two or three"), simply got the two items wrong (substituting "two or one"). It is also possible that he simply wanted to be more explicit (i.e., answering the question of what happens when there are two gathered).

A final possibility has to do with the extra λέγω. Plisch proposes a scenario wherein the Coptic is closer to the original text.[92] The original Greek *Vorlage* would have therefore read something like ὅπου εἷς ἢ δύο

---

90. Excepting the possible instance of transposition within ll. 5 and 6.

91. NA[27]: οὐ γάρ εἰσιν δύο ἢ τρεῖς συνηγμένοι εἰς τὸ ἐμὸν ὄνομα, ἐκεῖ εἰμι ἐν μέσῳ αὐτῶν.

92. Plisch, *Gospel of Thomas*, 98–99 n. 2.

Tim Ricchuiti

ἐστιν μόνος.[93] The text would have become corrupted at the point of ἢ δύο, and a later scribe would have reconstructed the text according to Matthew 18.19–20 (replacing the four characters with λέγω). This last scenario actually works quite well with an assumption that should be growing more obvious: contrary to the assumptions of most scholars, *the Greek text of P. Oxy. 1 appears to be secondary in nearly every case.* There is no doubt that it was *produced* earlier than the Coptic, but the Coptic was copied (or translated) from a better exemplar than the one that produced P. Oxy. 1.

Moving on to logion 77, there are two variants to deal with. The first is the extra καί (in this case hidden in the crasis κἀγώ). The second is the transposition of the statement "Split the wood, I am there" from the end of the logion in Greek to the beginning of the Coptic state-ment.[94] It is unlikely that the scribe of either manuscript would have made this mistake unintentionally: the Coptic phrase (ⲡⲱϩ ⲛ̄ⲛⲟⲩϣⲉ ⲁⲛⲟⲕ ϯⲙ̄ⲙⲁⲩ) has four words totaling eighteen characters, while the Greek phrase (σχίσον τὸ ξύλον κἀγὼ ἐκεῖ εἰμι) has six words totaling twenty-five characters. The question, then, is what kind of intentional change would bring about the corruption of the text as we have it now, particularly considering the movement of logion 77b.

It appears that this transposition is best explained by the Greek text representing the original more faithfully. This would have come about as a scribe, either in translating from Greek to Coptic or in copying the Coptic text, wished to introduce or reinforce (depending on one's perspective) the Christological assertions of logion 77 ("Jesus said, 'I am the light that is above everything. I am everything. Everything has come from me, and everything has reached [ⲡⲱϩ] up to me.'") To do so, he moved the "stone–wood" phrase from logion 30 to logion 77. Because the verb of logion 77's last statement was a homonym to the verb of the "stone–wood" phrase's last statement ("split [ⲡⲱϩ] a piece of wood, I am there"), the order was reversed on stylistic grounds. What remains unexplained, however, is why that scribe would also delete the "stone–wood" saying from logion 30. The Coptic Thomas is clearly comfortable with repetition (e.g., logia 5/6, 6/14, 11/22, etc.). While this may not be the most elegant solution, it is at least widespread: DeConick and Kuhn come to the same con-clusion, though DeConick explicitly states her assumption of P. Oxy. 1's primacy.[95] Kuhn, while not explicitly endorsing the same, argues

---

93. Marcovich ("Textual Criticism," 67–68) actually proposes ὅπου εἷς ἐστιν μόνος ἢ δύο ἐγώ εἰμι μετ' αὐτῶν as a reconstruction of the corrupted text of P. Oxy. 1, though that reconstruction was criticized by C. H. Roberts ("The Gospel of Thomas: Logion 30a," *JTS* 21 [1970]: 91–92) and Benedict Englezakis ("Thomas, Logion 30," *NTS* 25 [1978]: 262–75).

94. Not the beginning of the logion, but the beginning of this particular statement.

95. DeConick, *Original Gospel of Thomas in Translation*, 138–39.

for the Coptic's secondary nature on the basis of the use of ⲡⲱϩ as a Coptic catchword linking the end of what would have been the original logion 77.[96]

P. Oxy. 1—Logion 31

NHC II 2.39.5–7	*P. Oxy. 30–35*
ⲡⲉⲭⲉ ⲓ(ⲏⲥⲟⲩ)ⲥ ⲙⲛ ⲡⲣⲟⲫⲏⲧⲏⲥ ϣⲏⲡ	λέγει Ἰ(ησοῦ)ς· οὐκ ἔστιν δεκτὸς
ϩⲙ ⲡⲉϥ▮ⲙⲉ▮ ⲙⲁⲣⲉ ⲥⲟⲉⲓⲛ	προφήτης ἐν τῇ ▮π(ατ)ρίδι▮ αὐτ[ο]ῦ,
ⲣ̄ⲑⲉⲣⲁⲡⲉⲩⲉ ⲛ̄ⲛⲉⲧⲥⲟⲟⲩⲛ ⲙ̄ⲙⲟϥ	οὐδὲ ἰατρὸς ποιεῖ θεραπείας εἰς τοὺς
	γεινώσκοντας αὐτό(ν).

Jesus said, "No prophet is accepted in his ▮village▮; no physician heals those who know him."	*Jesus said, "No prophet is accepted in his ▮homeland▮; no physician heals those who know him."*

Logion 31 has only one difference, and while categorizing it as a variant is a bit of a close call, the difference is sufficiently large to merit such a categorization. That sufficiency is not due solely to the semantic range between "village" (ϯⲙⲉ) and "homeland/country" (πατρίδι)—to be sure, a difference large enough to label this as a variant rather than dismiss it as a translational difference. It is also due to the striking manner in which the NT parallels shed light on the discussion. Being that there is certainly a variant here, the problem is in determining if the Greek originally had κώμη ("village") or if the Coptic originally had ⲥⲱϣⲉ ("country"). The NT parallels (Matt 13.57; Mark 6.4; Luke 4.23–24; John 4.44) exclusively contain πατρίδι, in agreement with P. Oxy. 1. The Coptic NT, however, does not match the Coptic Thomas, lining up instead with the Greek NT (ⲥⲏϣ, alternate form of ⲥⲱϣⲉ).[97] I find it much more likely that the Coptic Thomas is preserving the original reading here, as it goes against its own tradition, whereas the Greek appears to be harmonizing within its own tradition.

---

96. K. H. Kuhn, "Some Observations on the Coptic Gospel according to Thomas," *Mus* 73 (1960): 317–19.
97. The Sahidic Coptic NT of Mark 6 also provides evidence that this is *not* a simple semantic issue. Both ⲥⲱϣⲉ and ϯⲙⲉ occur within the space of a few verses, in parallel with their NT counterparts, indicating that these two words are sufficiently separated semantically within Coptic to not merely evidence a translation issue.

P. Oxy. 1—Logion 32

NHC II 2.39.7–10	*P. Oxy. 1.36–41*
ⲡⲉϫⲉ ⲓ(ⲏⲥⲟⲩ)ⲥ ϫⲉ ⲟⲩⲡⲟⲗⲓⲥ	λέγει Ἰ(ησοῦ)ς· πόλις οἰκοδομημένη
ⲉⲩⲕⲱⲧ ⲙ̄ⲙⲟⲥ ϩⲓϫⲛ̄ ⲟⲩⲧⲟⲟⲩ	ἐπ᾽ ἄκρον [ὄ]ρους ὑψηλοῦς καὶ
ⲉϥϫⲟⲥⲉ ⲉⲥⲧⲁϫⲣⲏⲩ ⲙ̄ⲛ̄ ϭⲟⲙ ⲛ̄ⲥ̄ϩⲉ	ἐστηριγμένη οὔτε πε[ς]εῖν δύναται
ⲟⲩⲇⲉ ⲥⲛⲁϣϩⲱⲡ ⲁⲛ	οὔτε κρυ[β]ῆναι.
Jesus said, "A city built on a high mountain and fortified can neither fall nor be hidden."	*Jesus said, "A city that has been built upon the top of a high mountain and that has been fortified can neither fall nor be hidden."*

The Greek scribe inserts a final ς where one should not be (ὑψηλοῦς for ὑψηλοῦ). Other than that, logion 32 has only one addition: an expansion in the Greek text from "on a high mountain" (ϩⲓϫⲛ̄ ⲟⲩⲧⲟⲟⲩ ⲉϥϫⲟⲥⲉ) to "upon *the top* of a high mountain" (ἐπ᾽ ἄκρον [ὄ]ρους ὑψηλοῦ). Lacking any rationale for the longer text, we should prefer the shorter Coptic here.

P. Oxy. 1—Logion 33

NHC II 2.39.10–18	*P. Oxy. 1.41–42*
ⲡⲉϫⲉ ⲓ(ⲏⲥⲟⲩ)ⲥ ⲡⲉⲧⲕ̄ⲛⲁⲥⲱⲧⲙ̄ ⲉⲣⲟϥ	λέγει Ἰ(ησοῦ)ς· ἀκούεις [ε]ἰς τὸ ἓν
ϩⲙ̄ ⲡⲉⲕⲙⲁⲁϫⲉ ϩⲙ̄ ⲡⲕⲉⲙⲁⲁϫⲉ ⲧⲁϣⲉ	ὠτίον σου το[ῦτο κήρυξον . . .]
ⲟⲉⲓϣ ⲙ̄ⲙⲟϥ ϩⲓϫⲛ̄ ⲛⲉⲧⲛ̄ϫⲉⲛⲉⲡⲱⲣ	
ⲙⲁⲣⲉ ⲗⲁⲁⲩ ⲅⲁⲣ ϫⲉⲣⲉ ϩⲏ̄ⲃ̄ⲥ̄ ⲛ̄ϥⲕⲁⲁϥ	
ϩⲁ ⲙⲁⲁϫⲉ ⲟⲩⲇⲉ ⲙⲁϥⲕⲁⲁϥ ϩⲙ̄ ⲙⲁ	
ⲉϥϩⲏⲡ ⲁⲗⲗⲁ ⲉϣⲁⲣⲉϥⲕⲁⲁϥ ϩⲓϫⲛ̄	
ⲧⲗⲩⲭⲛⲓⲁ ϫⲉⲕⲁⲁⲥ ⲟⲩⲟⲛ ⲛⲓⲙ ⲉⲧⲃⲏⲕ	
ⲉϩⲟⲩⲛ ⲁⲩⲱ ⲉⲧⲛ̄ⲛⲏⲩ ⲉⲃⲟⲗ ⲉⲩⲛⲁⲛⲁⲩ	
ⲁⲡⲉϥⲟⲩⲟⲉⲓⲛ	
Jesus said, "What[98] you will hear in your ear. . ."	*Jesus said, "You hear in your one ear. . ."*

This is one of those logia that could easily be interpreted in a number of ways, without any concrete solutions.[99] It is possible that the addition of ἕν ("one") in the Greek could simply be implied in the Coptic phrase ("your ear . . . other ear"). It is also possible that it was deleted from the Coptic or that it is a secondary expansion. In this case, we will remain without a conclusion.

Analysis

Overall, there are nineteen variants to deal with between the text of P. Oxy. 1 and logia 26–33 and 77b of the Coptic Thomas. While there is relatively the same amount of variants within these first two papyri, the similarity between the two ends there. Whereas P. Oxy. 654 did not betray an affinity with any particular type of variant, P. Oxy. 1 has a clear tendency toward additions (ten additions within the Greek compared to just six substitutions, two additions within the Coptic, and one transposition).

Table 5.2. Variation of P. Oxy. 1 by Logion					
	Substitution	Transposition	Greek Addition	Coptic Addition	Total
26	1	0	1	0	2
27	1	0	3	0	4
28	1	0	2	0	3
29	0	0	0	0	0
30+77b	1	1	2	1	5
31	1	0	0	0	1
32	1	0	1	0	2
33	0	0	1	1	2
Total	6	1	10	2	

---

98. Most scholars (Attridge, "Greek Fragments," 121; DeConick, *Original Gospel of Thomas in Translation*, 142–43; Plisch, *Gospel of Thomas*, 101) supply the missing ὅ to the Greek text, as it is certainly an unintentional deletion.

99. Plisch, *Gospel of Thomas*, 102: "The first sentence of *Gos. Thom.* 33 contains a text-critical problem that one can try to solve in different ways without ever attaining absolute certainty."

This weight toward expansion would, by itself, engender questions regarding the Greek's authenticity; as the preceding analysis shows, those questions would be well founded. Of the nineteen variants, the Coptic preserves the more primitive reading fourteen times (74%), while the Greek preserves the original in only four cases (21%). This is a reverse of the case for P. Oxy. 654. This in itself should be surprising, considering the unanimous regard in which the Greek fragments are held as a whole, but it is even more surprising that the main motivation for the Greek text's preservation of the original wording appears to be theological (the deletion of τοῦ θεοῦ from l. 27 and the transposition of l. 77b). Admittedly, this is a small sample (two out of four instances), but it is nevertheless compelling because of the stark contrast between P. Oxy. 1 and the other two papyri.

P. Oxy. 655—Logion 24

NHC II 2.38.3–10 | *P. Oxy. 655 (Fragment d)*

ⲡⲉϫⲉ ⲛⲉϥⲙⲁⲑⲏⲧⲏⲥ ϫⲉ ⲙⲁⲧⲥⲉⲃⲟⲛ

ⲉⲡⲧⲟⲡⲟⲥ ⲉⲧⲕ̄ⲙ̄ⲙⲁⲩ ⲉⲡⲉⲓ ⲧⲁⲛⲁⲅⲕⲏ

ⲉⲣⲟⲛ ⲧⲉ ⲉⲧⲣ̄ⲛ̄ϣⲓⲛⲉ ⲛ̄ⲥⲱϥ ⲡⲉϫⲁϥ

ⲛⲁⲩ ϫⲉ ⲡⲉⲧⲉⲩⲛ̄ ⲙⲁⲁϫⲉ ⲙ̄ⲙⲟϥ

ⲙⲁⲣⲉϥ ⲥⲱⲧⲙ̄ ⲟⲩⲛ̄ ⲟⲩⲟⲉⲓⲛ ϣⲟⲟⲡ

ⲛ̄ⲫⲟⲩⲛ ⲛ̄ⲛⲟⲩⲣ̄ⲙ̄ⲟⲩⲟⲉⲓⲛ ⲁⲩⲱ ϥⲣ̄ | . . . φῶς ἐς]τιν [ἐν ἀνθρώπῳ

ⲟⲩⲟⲉⲓⲛ ⲉⲡⲕⲟⲥⲙⲟⲥ ⲧⲏⲣϥ ⲉϥⲧⲙ̄ⲣ̄ | φ]ωτεινῷ, [ἐν ὅλῳ τῷ κ]όσμῳ

ⲟⲩⲟⲉⲓⲛ ⲟⲩⲕⲁⲕⲉ ⲡⲉ | [φωτίζει· εἰ δὲ μ]ή, [σκοτεινός ἐ]στιν.

. . . there is light within the man of | *. . . there is light in the man full of*

light and he becomes light to the | *light, he gives light to the whole*

whole world. If he does not become | *world. But if not, he is darkness.*

light, he is darkness.

The fragmentary nature of P. Oxy. 655 (eighteen visible characters) prevents any analysis of the differences between the Greek and the Coptic in logion 24.

P. Oxy. 655—Logion 36

NHC II 2.39.24–27	P. Oxy. 655, col. 1.1–17
ΠΕΧΕ Ι(ΗCΟΥ)C ΠΠϤΙ ΡΟΟΥϢ ΧΙΝ	[λέγει Ἰ(ησοῦ)ϲ· μὴ μεριμνᾶτε ἀ]πὸ
2ΤΟΟΥΕ ϢΑ ΡΟΥ2Ε ΑΥϢ ΧΙΝ	πρωὶ ἕ[ως ὀψὲ, μήτ]ε ἀφ᾽ ἑσπ[έρας
2ΙΡΟΥ2Ε ϢΑ 2ΤΟΟΥΕ ΧΕ ΟΥ	ἕως π]ρωί, μήτε [τῇ τροφῇ ὑ]μῶν τὶ
ΠΕΕΤΗΑΤΑΑϤ 2ΙϢΤ ΤΗΥΤΠ	φάγητε, [μήτ]ε τῇ στ[ολῇ ὑμῶν τὶ
	ἐνδύση]σθε. [πολ]λῷ κρεί[σσον]ές
	ἐ[στε] τῶν [κρί]νων, ἅτι[να ο]ὐ
	ξα[ί]νει οὐδὲ ν[ήθ]ει. μ[ηδ]ὲν
	ἔχοντ[ες ἔ]νδ[υ]μα, τὶ ἐν[δύεσθε] καὶ
	ὑμεῖς; τίς ἂν προσθείη ἐπὶ τὴν
	εἰλικίαν ὑμῶν; αὐτὸ[ς δ]ώσει ὑμεῖν
	τὸ ἔνδυμα ὑμῶν.

Jesus said, "Do not be concerned from morning until evening and from evening until morning about what you will wear."

Jesus said, "Do not be concerned from morning until evening, nor from evening until morning, neither with respect to your food, what you should eat, nor with respect to your clothing, what you should wear. You are much greater than the lilies, which do not card or spin. And you, when you have no clothing, what (will) you wear? Who might add to your lifespan? He will give you your clothing.

There are two additions and a substitution to resolve for logion 36. The substitution is a misspelling within the Coptic manuscript: it reads ΠΕΕΤΗΑΤΑΑϤ where it should read ΠΕΤΕΤΗΑΤΑΑϤ. The two additions represent, by far, the biggest chunk present in the Greek but missing in the Coptic. However, this is another instance where the canon on the primacy of the shorter text will be set aside. While the Greek does line up better with the biblical parallels (Matt 6.25–30; Luke 12.22, 27–28), it only just manages to recall the voice of those parallels, to say nothing of the very words. Therefore, it is not a predictable adjustment on the part of a scribe or a purposeful expansion/reconstruction of the text behind the Coptic. Instead, it makes more sense to view the expanded text as original to Thomas and to consider the deletion an act of clarification/correction. The rationale for such a deletion appears to be an attempt by the Coptic scribe to resolve an apparent discrepancy between the recommendation of this logion ("don't worry so much, God will provide your clothing") and the recommendation of the next ("you will not see the Son until you can strip naked, getting rid of your clothing").[100] If the readers of Thomas understood the "garments/clothing" to represent the flesh (as in l. 37), the motivation behind such an alteration becomes clear: we have yet another instance of theological alteration.[101]

P. Oxy. 655—Logion 37

NHC II 2.39.27–40.2	P. Oxy. 655, col. 1.17–col 2.1
ⲡⲉⲭⲉ ⲛⲉϥⲙⲁⲑⲏⲧⲏⲥ ϫⲉ ⲁϣ ⲛ̅ϩⲟⲟⲩ	λέγουσιν αὐτῷ οἱ μαθηταὶ αὐτοῦ·
ⲉⲕⲛⲁⲟⲩⲱⲛϩ ⲉⲃⲟⲗ ⲛⲁⲛ ⲁⲩⲱ ⲁϣ	πότε ἡμεῖν ἐμφανὴς ἔσει, καὶ πότε σε
ⲛ̅ϩⲟⲟⲩ ⲉⲛⲁⲛⲁⲩ ⲉⲣⲟⲕ ⲡⲉⲭⲉ	ὀψόμεθα;
ⲓ̅(ⲏⲥⲟⲩ)ⲥ ϫⲉ ϩⲟⲧⲁⲛ ⲉⲧⲉⲧⲛ̅ϣⲁⲕⲉⲕ	λέγει· ὅταν ἐκδύσησθε καὶ μὴ
ⲧⲏⲩⲧⲛ̅ ⲉϩⲏⲩ ⲙ̅ⲡⲉⲧⲛ̅ϣⲓⲡⲉ ⲁⲩⲱ	αἰσχυνθῆτε ...
ⲛ̅ⲧⲉⲧⲛ̅ϥⲓ ⲛ̅ⲛⲉⲧⲛ̅ϣⲧⲏⲛ ⲛ̅ⲧⲉⲧⲛ̅ⲕⲁⲁⲩ	
ϩⲁ ⲡⲉⲥⲏⲧ ⲛ̅ⲛⲉⲧⲛ̅ⲟⲩⲉⲣⲏⲧⲉ ⲛ̅ⲑⲉ	

---

100. As l. 37 exists in P. Oxy. 655 as well, this same problem would have been present for the Greek scribe. This may offer a glimpse into Thomas in transition: l. 37 had accreted at this point (within DeConick's model, e.g. [*Recovering the Original Gospel of Thomas*]), but the longer text of l. 36 had not yet been adjusted to make the two logia cohere. Perhaps, though, the existence of l. 37 in the Greek fragment is evidence against my view, in which case it would be better to go with Plisch's suggestion that the shorter Coptic text is more in line with other sayings (*Gospel of Thomas*, 105–7).

101. It would go against the theology of Coptic Thomas to have the flesh as "a gift from God that one had to put on" (DeConick, *Original Gospel of Thomas in Translation*, 149).

ⲦⲚⲚⲓⲕⲟⲩⲉⲓ Ⲛϣ̄Ⲏⲣⲉ ϣⲎⲙ Ⲛ̄ⲧⲉⲧⲚⲭⲟⲡⲭ̄ⲡ̄

Ⲙ̄ⲙⲟⲟⲩ ⲧⲟⲧⲉ[ⲧⲉⲧⲚⲁⲛⲁⲩ] ⲉⲡϣⲎⲣⲉ

Ⲙ̄ⲡⲉⲧⲟⲚϩ ⲁⲩⲱ ⲧⲉⲧⲚⲁⲣ̄ ϩ̄ⲟⲧⲉ ⲁⲛ

[οὐδὲ φοβη]θ[ήσεσθε].

His disciples said, "When will you	His disciples said to him, "When will
appear to us? And when will we see	you become visible to us, and when
you?"	will we see you?
Jesus said, "When you strip	He said, "When you disrobe and are
yourselves naked without being	not ashamed...
ashamed. . .	
. . . you will not be afraid."	. . . you will not be afraid."

Much has been written about the theology and meaning of logion 37, particularly as it relates to the view of physicality for the Thomasine community.[102] We will not be interacting with such works here, as the variation between the Greek and Coptic is easily explained on other grounds. Logion 37 contains a Coptic addition and a Greek addition, though neither appears to be authentic. The addition in the Greek of αὐτῷ and the addition in the Coptic of ⲓⲏⲥⲟⲩⲥ each appear to be an expansion toward clarity.

P. Oxy. 655—Logion 38

NHC II 2.40.2–7

ⲡⲉⲭⲉ ⲓ(ⲏⲥⲟⲩ)ⲥ ⲭⲉ ϩⲁϩ Ⲛ̄ⲥⲟⲡ

ⲁⲧⲉⲧⲚ̄ⲣ̄ⲉⲡⲓⲑⳛⲙⲉⲓ ⲉⲥⲱⲧⲙ̄

ⲁⲛⲉⲉⲓϣⲁⲭⲉ ⲛⲁⲉⲓ ⲉϯⲭⲱ Ⲙ̄ⲙⲟⲟⲩ

ⲛⲎⲧⲚ̄ ⲁⲩⲱ Ⲙ̄Ⲛ̄ⲧⲎⲧⲚ̄ ⲕⲉⲟⲩⲁ ⲉⲥⲟⲧⲙⲟⲩ

Ⲛ̄ⲧⲟⲟⲧ[ϥ] ⲟⲩⲚ̄ ϩ̄Ⲛ̄ϩⲟⲟⲩ ⲛⲁϣⲱⲡⲉ

P. Oxy. 655, col. 2.2–11

λέ[γει Ἰ(ησοῦ)ς· πολλάκις] ο[ὖν

ἐπεθυμεῖτε] τ[ούτους τοὺς λό]γ[ους

μου ἀκοῦσαι] κα[ὶ ἔχετε οὐδὲ]ν̣[ὸς

ἄλλου ἀκοῦσαι] κα[ὶ ἐλεύσονται]

ἡμ[έραι ὅτε ζητή]σε[τέ με καὶ οὐ μὴ

102. See, e.g., April D. DeConick and Jarl Fossum, "Stripped before God: A New Interpretation of Logion 37 in the Gospel of Thomas," *VC* 45 (1991): 123–50; Marvin W. Meyer, "Seeing or Coming to the Child of the Living One? More on 'Gospel of Thomas' Saying 37," *HTR* 91 (1998): 413–16; Gregory J. Riley, "A Note on the Text of 'Gospel of Thomas 37," *HTR* 88 (1995): 179–81.

Tim Ricchuiti

ⲛ̅ⲧⲉⲧⲛ̅ϣⲓⲛⲉ ⲛ̅ⲥⲱⲉⲓ ⲧⲉⲧⲛⲁϩⲉ ⲁⲛ
ⲉⲣⲟⲉⲓ

εὑρήσετέ με].

Jesus said, "You desired many times
to listen to these words that I speak
to you, and you do not have another
from whom to hear them. There will
be days when you seek me, (but) you
will not find me."

[Jesus] said . . .

There are no significant differences between the fourteen characters of Greek and the Coptic in logion 38.

P. Oxy. 655—Logion 39

NHC II 2.40.7–13

ⲡⲉⲭⲉ ⲓ(ⲏⲥⲟⲩ)ⲥ ϫⲉ ⲛ̅ⲫⲁⲣⲓⲥⲁⲓⲟⲥ ⲙⲛ̅
ⲛ̅ⲅⲣⲁⲙⲙⲁⲧⲉⲩⲥ ⲁⲩϫⲓ ⲛ̅ϣⲁϣⲧ
ⲛ̅ⲧⲅⲛⲱⲥⲓⲥ ⲁⲩϩⲟⲡⲟⲩ ⲟⲩⲧⲉ ⲙ̅ⲡⲟⲩⲃⲱⲕ
ⲉϩⲟⲩⲛ ⲁⲩⲱ ⲛⲉⲧⲟⲩⲱϣ ⲉⲃⲱⲕ ⲉϩⲟⲩⲛ
ⲙ̅ⲡⲟⲩⲕⲁⲁⲩ ⲛ̅ⲧⲱⲧⲛ̅ ⲇⲉ ϣⲱⲡⲉ
ⲙ̅ⲫⲣⲟⲛⲓⲙⲟⲥ ⲛ̅ⲑⲉ ⲛ̅ⲛ̅ϩⲟϥ ⲁⲩⲱ
ⲛ̅ⲁⲕⲉⲣⲁⲓⲟⲥ ⲛ̅ⲑⲉ ⲛ̅ⲛ̅ϭⲣⲟⲙⲡⲉ

P. Oxy. 655, col. 2.11–23

[λέγει Ἰ(ησοῦ)ς· οἱ Φαρισαῖοι καὶ οἱ
γραμματεῖς] ἔλ[αβον τὰς κλεῖδας]
τῆς [γνώσεως. αὐτοὶ ἔ]κρυψ[αν
αὐτάς. οὔτε] εἰσῆλ[θον, οὔτε τοὺς]
εἰσερ[χομένους ἀφῆ]καν [εἰσελθεῖν.
ὑμεῖς] δὲ γεί[νεσθε φρόνι]μοι ὡ[ς
ὄφεις καὶ ἀ]κέραι[οι ὡς
περιστε]ρα[ί].

Jesus said, "The Pharisees and the
scribes took the keys of knowledge.
They hid them. Neither did they go in,
nor did they permit those who wished
to go in to do so. You, however,
become wise like serpents and
innocent like doves."

Jesus said, "The Pharisees and the
scribes took the keys of knowledge.
They hid them. Neither did they go in,
nor did they permit those who were
going in to go in. But you become
wise like serpents and innocent like
doves."

Although there is some slight variation between the Greek present participle τοὺς εἰσερχομένους and the Coptic phrase ⲛⲉⲧⲟⲩⲱϣ ⲉⲃⲱⲕ ⲉϩⲟⲩⲛ in logion 38, it does not rise to the level of variation. It is much more likely to be due to translational issues than to scribal alterations.

Analysis

With only six variants to analyze, it is a bit precocious to characterize the merit of P. Oxy. 655. While the variants of logion 37 were both secondary, the variants of logion 36 demonstrate the more primary character of P. Oxy. 655 well. Additionally, it is *probably* for theological considerations that such a large amount of material was deleted from logion 36, and so, in this, even the especially small sample of P. Oxy. 655 demonstrates our thesis concerning Thomas's theological corruption.

Table 5.3. Variation of P. Oxy. 655 by Logion				
	Substitution	Greek Addition	Coptic Addition	Total
24	0	0	0	0
36	1	2	0	3
37	0	1	1	2
38	0	0	0	0
39	0	0	0	0
Total	1	3	1	

CONCLUSION

It was my purpose here (1) to conduct a comparison of the Greek fragments of the Gospel of Thomas to the full Coptic manuscript, (2) to assess the merit of the four manuscripts containing Thomas with respect to their originality, and (3) should the assessment yield fruit, to draw a few conclusions on the scholarly consensus regarding both the character of the Greek fragments versus the Coptic text and the amount of theological alteration present, particularly in Thomas, but more generally in noncanonical works as a whole. Considering the preceding analysis of the Gospel of Thomas in both Greek and Coptic, it appears that scholars are on fairly solid ground when it comes to the assumption that the Greek represents an earlier strain of Thomas. The data behind P. Oxy. 654 and 655 certainly bear this out. Of the twenty-three variants, I judged the Coptic to represent the earliest form of the text only three times (13%), while the Greek text preserved the earlier text sixteen times (70%). The Greek text is slightly more expansive, but even that meager tendency disappears when considering the massive addition of logion 36.

Table 5.4. Variation among P. Oxy. 654, 655				
	Substitution	Greek Addition	Coptic Addition	Total
P. Oxy. 654	5	7	6	18
P. Oxy. 655	1	3	1	5
Total	6	10	7	23

However, my initial hypothesis (and some of those scholarly assumptions) must be adjusted in light of P. Oxy. 1's clearly secondary character. As has already been noted, the Coptic text preserves the original reading nearly four times as often as the Greek text (fourteen instances compared to four instances). There is a strong tendency here for the Greek to be more expansive—the text of P. Oxy. 1 expands on the Coptic text ten times, while the reverse happens only twice.

Table 5.5. Variation within P. Oxy. 1				
Substitution	Transposition	Greek Addition	Coptic Addition	Total
6	1	10	2	19

Many of those expansions are due to the tendency of the scribe of P. Oxy. 1[103] to add the connective καί. However, the secondary nature of the Greek fragment is not limited to extra conjunctions: where there is a substitution, the Coptic tends to preserve the original (five out of six times).

As far as conclusions on the fluidity of Thomas goes, it should be noted that the scribes who copied the gospel appear to fall victim to many of the exact same traps that corrupted canonical texts. Beyond the

---

103. Or, of course, some precursor to P. Oxy. 1.

obvious places for overlap, such as haplography, dittography, and so on (errors due to physical limitations), a significant number of the variants were due to harmonization with the relevant biblical parallels or other tradition. At the same time, the Coptic scribe prefers, in at least some cases, secondary readings to theologically difficult readings. That preference accounted for two of the four places in P. Oxy. 1 where the Greek text was judged to be original (ll. 27, 77b). Additionally, it can be argued that the changes demonstrate some theological alterations due to *praxis* (e.g., the alteration of dietary restraints in l. 6) and others due to *pistis* (e.g., the massive deletion in the case of l. 36, the alterations of "Kingdom of God" phrases in ll. 3 and 27, and possibly the alteration of l. 2). Altogether, alterations in the Coptic text evidence theological alteration in at least six places (ll. 3, 5–6, 27, 36, 77b),[104] irrespective of which fragment it occurs in or the fragment's overall character. It does indeed appear that the Coptic scribe altered Thomas in such a way as to make it more amenable to the community that eventually decided to include it in the Nag Hammadi writings.

Ultimately, there were limitations in the present study, with only a little over a thousand words to analyze where the four manuscripts overlap. But there remain hidden avenues and alleyways yet unexplored. In the first place, a more in-depth comparison of the transmission of Thomas in these four manuscripts to the transmission of certain NT passages in comparable manuscripts (e.g., a few early fragments checked against a later, more complete manuscript) could generate substantive conclusions about the relative level of reverence the works were held in by the early Christian communities, notwithstanding the work of some church fathers to discourage their use or ban certain texts outright.[105] The kind of comparison undertaken here of the extant manuscripts of Thomas could be performed on other early Christian literature to determine if Thomas is an outlier in its transmission or if it is in line with what we would expect for noncanonical texts (or, indeed, canonical texts). In any case, the present study ought to demonstrate that textual criticism has a role to play beyond just the New Testament, illuminating issues that might otherwise be missed.

---

104. The process toward "rest" of l. 2 accounting for the "at least."

105. E. J. Epp ("The Oxyrhynchus New Testament Papyri: 'Not without Honor except in Their Hometown'?," *JBL* 123 [2004]: 245–81) proposes something similar to this, though without the same explicit purpose.

6

JESUS AS ΘΕΟΣ

A Textual Examination

Brian J. Wright[1]

From Aland to Zuntz, every major NT scholar has explored the canon of the NT for texts that call Jesus θεός.[2] While this may seem like a painless pursuit with plenty of "proof passages," several stumbling blocks quickly emerge.[3] No author of a Synoptic Gospel explicitly

---

1. I dedicate this work to several people. First, I dedicate it to my mom, Debra L. Wright, whose selfless love and perseverance continues to humble me. Second, I dedicate it to a group of men—Ereke Bruce, Steve Llewellyn, Grant Mayfield, Dustin Walker, et al.—to whom I am eternally grateful for first sharing the gospel with me during my junior year of college and purposefully discipling me with an interdenominational love in/through Christ. Finally, yet importantly, I also dedicate this work to John R. Brown. Although I can point to many books, events, and people that have helped form my cognitive view of Christianity, his life continues to model for me the practicality of the Christian life as Christ commanded in Matt 5.16: "Let your light shine before others, so that they may see your good works and glorify your Father who is in heaven."

    Special thanks are due to J. K. Elliot, Gordon D. Fee, P. J. Williams, Daniel B. Wallace, Tommy Wasserman, Darrell Bock, and Chrys Caragounis for looking at a preliminary draft of this manuscript and making valuable suggestions.

2. For a detailed list of many such views, see Daniel B. Wallace, *Granville Sharp's Canon and Its Kin: Semantics and Significance* (Bern: Peter Lang, 2009), 27–28.

3. Bart Ehrman, in at least three published books and one published lecture series, even suggests that the *Ausgangstext* does not necessarily teach the deity of Christ. He bases these allegations on alleged textual problems that he attributes to manipulative scribal activity, most often pointing to textual problems behind such verses. He almost exclusively leans toward the manipulation of early proto-orthodox scribes in the development of a high Christology in his book *The Orthodox Corruption of Scripture: The Effect of Early Christological Controversies on the Text of the New Testament* (Oxford: Oxford University Press, 1993).

ascribes the title θεός to Jesus.[4] Jesus never uses the term θεός for himself.[5] No sermon in the book of Acts attributes the title θεός to Jesus.[6] No extant Christian confession[7] of Jesus as θεός exists earlier than the late 50s.[8] Prior to the fourth-century Arian controversy, noticeably few Greek MSS attest to such "Jesus-θεός" passages.[9] And possibly the biggest problem for NT Christology regarding this topic

---

4. As Raymond Brown hypothesizes, "The slow development of the usage of the title 'God' for Jesus requires explanation. . . . The most plausible explanation is that in the earliest stage of Christianity the Old Testament heritage dominated the use of 'God'; hence, 'God' was a title too narrow to be applied to Jesus." I am unconvinced that this is the "most" plausible explanation, given the predominately Jewish context that may have dictated the early evangelistic terminology (e.g., Matthew's "kingdom of heaven"). Nevertheless, Brown adds, "[W]e do maintain that in general the *NT* authors were aware that Jesus was being given a title which in the LXX referred to the God of Israel" (Raymond Brown, "Does the New Testament Call Jesus 'God'?" *TS* 26 [1965]: 545–73). At the same time, "To reconstruct the history of titles as if this were the study of christology is like trying to understand the windows of Chartres cathedral by studying the history of coloured glass" (Leander E. Keck, "Toward the Renewal of NT Christology," *NTS* 32 [1986]: 368; whole article on 362–77).

5. In fact, Mark 10.18 records that Jesus differentiates himself from God (= the Father; cf. Matt 19.17; Luke 18.19; Mark 15.34; Matt 27.46; John 20.17). H. W. Montefiore, in his essay "Toward a Christology for Today," notices this as he postulates that Jesus seems to have explicitly denied that he was God (*Soundings* 45 [1962]: 158). In addition, R. H. Fuller believes, similar to Bultmann, that Jesus understood himself as an eschatological prophet (Reginald H. Fuller, *The Foundations of New Testament Christology* [New York: Charles Scribner's Sons, 1965], 130). While none of these texts or interpretations portray a complete NT Christology (Jesus does identify himself with God [e.g., John 10.30; 14.9], he never explicitly rejects that he is God, and he understood himself to be more than an eschatological prophet), it is true that Jesus never uses the term θεός for himself.

6. Acts 20.28 is in a *speech* (and the only one) addressed to a Christian audience. "All the others," John Stott explains, "are either evangelistic sermons, . . . legal defenses, . . . or the five speeches before the Jewish and Roman authorities" (John R. W. Stott, *The Message of Acts: The Son, the Church, and the World* [Downers Grove, IL: InterVarsity, 1990], 323). Cf. Richard I. Pervo, *Acts: A Commentary* (Minneapolis: Fortress, 2009), 515–31.

7. Raymond Brown, however, insightfully notes a danger in judging usage from occurrence, because NT occurrence does not create a usage but testifies to a usage already existing (Raymond E. Brown, *Jesus: God and Man* [Milwaukee: Bruce, 1967]). None of the passages considered in this chapter give any evidence of innovating.

8. With Rom 9.5 probably occurring first, if one could be certain of its punctuation/ grammar (see discussion following).

9. In a recent popular book, *Reinventing Jesus*, the authors note that "there are at least *forty-eight* (and as many as fifty-nine) Greek New Testament manuscripts that predate the fourth-century." In an endnote, the authors go on to explain that these are only Greek New Testament MSS and do not include the early versions or the pre-fourth-century patristic writers. Even so, only four "Jesus-θεός" passages (Rom 9.5; John 1.1, 18; 20.28) are included in these MSS (J. Ed Komoszewski, M. James Sawyer, and Daniel B. Wallace, *Reinventing Jesus: How Contemporary Skeptics Miss the Real Jesus and Mislead Popular Culture* [Grand Rapids: Kregel, 2006], 116).

Brian J. Wright

is that textual variants exist in every potential passage where Jesus is explicitly referred to as θεός.[10]

This plethora of issues may provoke one to repeat, for different reasons, what a Gnostic document once confessed about Jesus, "Whether a god or an angel or what I should call him, I do not know."[11] Yet "it was the Christians' habit on a fixed day to assemble before daylight and recite by turns a form of words to Christ as a god," Pliny the Younger wrote in a letter to Emperor Trajan about Christians.[12] "We must think about Christ as we think about God," the author of 2 Clement opens his homily. "I bid you farewell always in our God Jesus Christ," concludes Ignatius in his letter to Polycarp.[13] "True God from true God," the first ecumenical council ultimately dogmatized concerning Jesus.[14] When, then, did this boldness to call Jesus θεός begin?[15]

---

10. The authors of *Reinventing Jesus* note (114), "If a particular verse does not teach the deity of Christ in some of the manuscripts, does this mean that that doctrine is suspect? It would only be suspect if all the verses that affirm Christ's deity are textually suspect." Unfortunately, regarding the explicit "Jesus-θεός" passages, that may be the case here. At the same time, the authors continue, "And even then the variants would have to be plausible." This further reveals the importance of this study.

11. Infancy Gospel of Thomas 7.4, from the Greek text of Constantin von Tischendorf, *Evangelia Apocrypha* (Hildesheim: George Olms, 1987; original, Leipzig, 1867). For a more recent text-critical work on it, see Tony Chartrand-Burke, "The Greek Manuscript Tradition of the Infancy Gospel of Thomas," *Apocrypha* 14 (2003): 129–51.

12. *Pliny: Letters and Panegyricus*, vol. 2, *Letters Books VIII–X, Panegyricus*, trans. Betty Radice, Loeb Classical Library (Cambridge, MA: Harvard University Press, 1969), 288–89.

13. "Ignatius effortlessly and spontaneously wove within his understanding of the relationship between the Father and the Son the simple and unequivocal proclamation that Jesus Christ is God" (Thomas Weinandy, "The Apostolic Christology of Ignatius of Antioch: The Road to Chalcedon," in *Trajectories through the New Testament and the Apostolic Fathers* [New York: Oxford University Press, 2005], 76). Here are fourteen such occurrences in Ignatius: *Eph.* prol., 1.1, 7.2, 15.3, 18.2, 19.3; *Rom.* prol. (2x), 3.3, 6.3; *Smyrn.* 1.1, 10.1; *Trall.* 7.1; *Pol.* 8.3.

14. θεὸν ἀληθινὸν ἐκ θεοῦ ἀληθινοῦ (Philip Schaff, *The Creeds of Christendom: A History and Critical Notes*, vol. 2 [New York: Harper and Brothers, 1877], 57).

15. I am discussing the origin of the title θεός as applied to Jesus and not the origin of understanding Jesus as divine. That understanding was early and expressed in various ways (see, among others, C. F. D. Moule, *The Origin of Christology* [Cambridge: Cambridge University Press, 1977]; Larry Hurtado, *Lord Jesus Christ: Devotion to Jesus in Earliest Christianity* [Grand Rapids: Eerdmans, 2003]). As for the title θεός, "On the one hand, the dominant Greco-Roman ethos assumed that there were many gods and that human beings could be deified. Many emperors refused to be called gods during their lifetimes, yet were named gods after their deaths. The term 'god' was also used for living rulers, like Agrippa (Acts 12:21–22; Josephus, *Ant.* 19.345) and Nero (Tacitus, *Annals* 14.15). On the other hand, the Jewish tradition centered on faith in one God (Deut 6:4), who was not to be portrayed in human form or to be identified with a human being (Exod 20:4; Deut 5:8; 2 Macc 9:12; cf. John 5:18; 10:33)" (Craig R. Koester, *Hebrews: A New Translation with Introduction and Commentary* [New York: Doubleday, 2001], 202). Further,

CONDENSED EXAMINATION

Although this work will examine the textual certainty of every potential NT ascription of θεός to Jesus,[16] ten of the possible seventeen passages will be dismissed up front for the following reasons:[17]

    1. Punctuation. Romans 9.5 involves a punctuation issue "which our earliest manuscripts do not answer."[18] Moreover, even if the absence of any discernible type of standardized punctuation cannot be *definitively* traced back to the earliest Greek NT MSS, "the presence of punctuation in Greek manuscripts, as well as in versional and patristic sources, cannot be

---

      one should note that the majority of passages in which Jesus is potentially called θεός appear in writings attributed to Jewish settings, whereas only a few might be Pauline (see, e.g., Richard N. Longenecker, *The Christology of Early Jewish Christianity* [Naperville, IL: Allenson, 1970], 139).

16. I will employ a reasoned eclecticism method, the currently reigning view among textual critics. Several limitations exist, however, on the scope of my research. For example, I did not exhaustively examine each critical apparatus to find other variants that potentially affirm Jesus as θεός. I did not work extensively with foreign literature. I relied heavily on the manuscript collations of others. I created no comprehensive comparative analysis of the manuscript relationships for the Pauline corpus or for any individual book(s). I did not determine the scribal habits of every MS or witness cited. I also depended heavily on those whose academic acumen far exceeds mine and whose scholarly contributions are highly regarded.

17. A handful of other verses are sometimes used to implicitly equate Jesus with θεός (Luke 8.39; 9.43; 1 Thess 4.9; 1 Tim 1.1; 5.21; 2 Tim 4.1; Titus 1.3; 3.4; Heb 3.4; James 1.1), yet I did not think enough academic support existed to merit their inclusion in this work.

18. Douglas J. Moo, "The Christology of the Early Pauline Letters," in *Contours of Christology in the New Testament* (Grand Rapids: Eerdmans, 2005), 190. Similarly, Ehrman concludes, "Nor will I take into account variant modes of punctuation that prove christologically significant, as these cannot be traced back to the period of our concern, when most manuscripts were not punctuated" (*Orthodox Corruption of Scripture*, 31). Cf. Robert Jewett, *Romans* (Minneapolis: Fortress, 2007), 555, 566–69; Bruce M. Metzger, *A Textual Commentary on the Greek New Testament*, 2nd ed. (Stuttgart: German Bible Society, 1994), 459-62; Murray J. Harris, *Jesus as God: The New Testament Use of Theos in Reference to Jesus* (Grand Rapids: Baker, 1992), 150–51; and Walter Bauer, *A Greek-English Lexicon of the New Testament and Other Early Christian Literature*, ed. Frederick William Danker, 3rd ed. (Chicago: University of Chicago Press, 2000 [hereinafter BDAG]), s.v. "θεός."
      The earliest MS of Romans to date (𝔓46, ca. 200 [cf. Kurt Aland, *Kurzgefasste Liste der griechischen Handschriften des Neuen Testaments*, 2nd ed. (Berlin: Gruyter, 1994), 31–32]) does not contain any punctuation here. Nevertheless, Lattey shows that a fifth-century codex (C/04) contains a small cross between σάρκα and ὁ ὤν to designate some form of a stop, which the NA27 and UBS4 texts reflect with a comma (Cuthbert Lattey, "The Codex Ephraemi Rescriptus in Romans ix. 5," *ExpTim* 35 [1923–24]: 42–43).

            Brian J. Wright

regarded as more than the reflection of current exegetical understanding of the meaning of the passage."[19]

2. Extenuating circumstances. Although Colossians 2.2 contains "no fewer than fifteen textual options,"[20] the issue is syntax rather than textual pedigree and is outside the scope of this investigation. Other such extenuating circumstances hold true for the following:

Matthew 1.23[21]
John 17.3[22]
Ephesians 5.5[23]
2 Thessalonians 1.12[24]
1 Timothy 3.16[25]

---

19. Metzger, *Textual Commentary*, 167. Cf. H.-C. Kammler, "Die Prädikation Jesu Christi als 'Gott' und die paulinische Christologie: Erwägungen zur Exegese von Röm 9,5b," *ZNW* 94 (2003): 164–80.

20. Douglas J. Moo, *The Letters to the Colossians and to Philemon* (Grand Rapids: Eerdmans, 2008), 168. These options are listed conveniently in Bruce M. Metzger and Bart D. Ehrman, *The Text of the New Testament: Its Transmission, Corruption, and Restoration*, 4th ed. (New York: Oxford University Press, 2005), 334.

21. The text is overwhelmingly certain here, as the author cites Isa 7.14 in relation to the birth of Jesus. Yet, despite its textual certainty, we cannot be sure that the evangelist takes "God with us" literally and attempts to call Jesus θεός (as J. C. Fenton concludes in "Matthew and the Divinity of Jesus: Three Questions concerning Matthew 1:20–23," in *Studia Biblica 1978*, vol 2, *Papers on the Gospels*, ed. E. A. Livingstone [Sheffield: JSOT Press, 1980], 79–82). See, among others, R. T. France, *The Gospel of Matthew* (Grand Rapids: Eerdmans, 2007), esp. 49–50, 56–58.

22. Note the discussion of the grammatical issues relating to this phrase in Harris, *Jesus as God*, 258–59. The text, nonetheless, should be considered certain.

23. The textual evidence is solid here. Ehrman accurately explains, "In the text that is almost certainly original ('the Kingdom of Christ and God'), Christ appears to be given a certain kind of priority over God himself. This problem is resolved by all of the changes, whether attested early or late" (Ehrman, *Orthodox Corruption*, 269). See Harris, *Jesus as God*, 261–63, for grammatical issues.

24. The textual issue in this verse does not pertain to the clause in question, leaving one with two possible Greek genitive translations: (1) "according to the grace of our God and Lord, namely Jesus Christ" or (2) "according to the grace of our God and the Lord Jesus Christ." I favor the latter (which does not attribute the title θεός to Jesus), primarily for the following reason, "Second Thessalonians 1:12 does not have merely 'Lord' in the equation, but 'Lord Jesus Christ.' Only by detaching κυρίου from Ἰησοῦ Χριστοῦ could one apply [Granville] Sharp's rule to this construction" (Wallace, *Sharp's Canon*, 236).

25. The attestation for the variants here is not strong enough to warrant serious consideration (contra Stephen W. Frary, "Who Was Manifested in the Flesh? A Consideration of Internal Evidence in Support of a Variant in 1 Tim 3:16a," *EFN* 16 [2003]: 3–18). Towner notes, "the change to ὅ (D* and Vg plus some Latin Fathers) was a gender adjustment to accord with τὸ μυστήριον; another late solution was the change to θεός (a[2] A[c] C[2] D[2] Ψ 1739 1881 TR vg[mss]), which supplies the antecedent thought to be lacking in ὅς" (Philip Towner, *The Letters to Timothy*

Titus 2.13[26]

1 John 5.20[27]

Jude 4[28]

---

and Titus [Grand Rapids: Eerdmans, 2006], 278). Cf. W. M. Zoba, "When Manuscripts Collide," CT 39, no. 12 (1995): 30-31. Cf. also Robert H. Gundry, "The Form, Meaning, and Background of the Hymn Quoted in 1 Timothy 3:16," in Apostolic History and the Gospel: Biblical and Historical Essays Presented to F. F. Bruce, ed. W. Ward Gasque and Ralph P. Martin (Exeter: Paternoster, 1970), 203–22.

26.   Though I strongly feel that this verse attributes the title θεός to Jesus, a textual examination is unnecessary, since the only viable variant concerns the order of the last two words: Ἰησοῦ Χριστοῦ or Χριστοῦ Ἰησοῦ. The debate, then, will have to continue congregating around syntax. See Gordon Fee, Pauline Christology: An Exegetical-Theological Study (Peabody, MA: Hendrickson, 2007), esp. 442–46. Against Fee's position, see Wallace, Sharp's Canon, 256–64; Robert M. Bowman Jr., "Jesus Christ, God Manifest: Titus 2:13 Revisited," JETS 51 (2008): 733–52; Robert W. Yarbrough, 1–3 John (Grand Rapids: Baker, 2008), 320.

      Several NT scholars put an asterisk by this book because they consider it deutero-Pauline. Yet even if one assumes that Paul did not write Titus, it still would have been written in the first century and, therefore, would be impervious to some of the critiques often given for such texts, such as orthodox corruption(s) due to the third-century Arian controversy. As a matter of fact, although Ehrman did not mention Titus 2.13 specifically in Orthodox Corruption, by his own argument regarding 2 Pet 1.1, Titus 2.13 would explicitly equate Jesus with θεός: "Because the article is not repeated before Ἰησοῦ (in 2 Pet 1:1), it would be natural to understand both 'our God' and 'Savior' in reference to Jesus [our 'God and Savior']" (Orthodox Corruption, 267). In other words, Ehrman recognizes that one article with two nouns joined by καί refers to the same person, making Titus 2.13 an explicit reference to Jesus as θεός.

27.   Of the two notable variants in this verse, neither of them effectually touches our present topic. The crux interpretum is the antecedent of οὗτος, but it is not clear whether it represents a reference to God the Father or Jesus Christ (see Wallace, Sharp's Canon, 273–77 for a discussion of the syntax of 1 John 5.20). Even so, Augustine used this verse to support his argument that Jesus was "not only God, but also true God" (The Trinity: Introduction, Translation, and Notes [New York: New City, 2000], 71). Likewise, Rudolf Schnackenburg argues strongly, from the logic of the context and the flow of the argument, that "This is the true God" refers to Jesus Christ (John E. Rotelle, Die Johannesbriefe, in Herders theologischer Kommentar, 2nd ed. [Freiburg: Herder, 1963], 291). Stephen Smalley notes, "But even if we do not accept the equation (Jesus as God) as explicitly present in this verse, it remains true that there is an association between God and his Son that is articulated here more clearly than anywhere else in 1 John" (Stephen S. Smalley, 1, 2, 3 John [Nashville: Thomas Nelson, 2007], 295). Cf. also Judith M. Lieu, I, II, and III John: A Commentary (Louisville: Westminster John Knox, 2008), 233–34; Peter Rhea Jones, 1, 2 & 3 John (Macon, GA: Smyth and Helwys, 2009), 231–35.

28.   I kept this text in the condensed list primarily because several MSS contain the word θεόν (e.g., K L P S Ψ 049 104 syr^h, ph). Landon persuasively argues that the internal evidence supports δεσπότην θεόν rather than simply δεσπότην and that the expression refers only to God (Charles Landon, The Text of Jude and a Text-Critical Study of the Epistle of Jude, JSNT Supplement 135 [Sheffield: Academic, 1996], 63–67). What makes his argument strong is that if Ehrman is correct about the direction of corruption away from adoptionistic heresies, noting the text of 2 Pet 1.2 in 𝔓^72, this reading alone resists orthodox interference (i.e., shortening by scribes who wish to show God and Jesus as the same entity, thereby stressing Christ's divinity). Yet

Brian J. Wright

This leaves seven texts warranting extended examination.

EXTENDED EXAMINATION

John 1.1[29]

According to Aland's *Kurzgefasste Liste*, the Gospel of John has

---

even with Landon's well thought-out thesis, of which I did not list all his perceptive reasons, I still reject the longer reading for the following reasons: (1) the earliest and best MSS support the shorter reading [e.g., $\mathfrak{P}^{72}$ $\mathfrak{P}^{78}$ ℵ A B C 0251 33 1739 *Lectpt it*ar vg cop$^{sa, bo}$ geo], (2) it is probable that a scribe sought to clarify the shorter reading and/or stay within the NT's normal pattern (i.e., Luke 2.29; Acts 4.24; 2 Tim 2.21; Rev 6.10), and (3) it is the more difficult reading. Therefore, my preference is for the shorter reading: δεσπότην (used of God in Luke 2.29, Acts 4.24, and Rev 6.10 and of Christ in 2 Pet 2.1 and here). For exhaustive MS evidence, see Tommy Wasserman, *The Epistle of Jude: Its Text and Transmission* (Stockholm: Almqvist und Wiksell, 2006), esp. 251–54. Cf. also C. A. Albin, *Judasbrevet: Traditionen, Texten Tolkningen* (Stockholm, 1962), 148, 596.

    In addition, the shorter reading in Jude 4 (where Christ is described as the ruling Master, δεσπότην) would comport well with Jude 5 *if* "Jesus" is indeed the original reading. This would clearly highlight the pre-existence of Christ and thus implicitly argue for his deity. Therefore, both verses taken together make a compelling argument for the pre-existence, as well as the deity, of Jesus Christ (without giving the title θεός to Jesus). For in-depth textual discussion of Jude 5, in which the author argues for Ιησους here, see Philipp F. Bartholomä, "Did Jesus Save the People out of Egypt? A Re-Examination of a Textual Problem in Jude 5," *NovT* 50 (2008): 143–58. For an opposing view on Jude 5, see James R. Royse, *Scribal Habits in Early Greek New Testament Papyri*, New Testament Tools, Studies, and Documents 36 (Boston: Brill, 2008), 610–12.

29. I recognize that the anarthrous θεός denotes the pre-existent λόγος and not explicitly Jesus (yet?). I also acknowledge that some scholars have argued well that John 1.1 is a part of the hymn exalting God's σοφία (the הכמה of Prov 8; cf. Sir 1.1–10) and/or have shown that Philo periodically uses the term θεός without the definite article for λόγος (e.g., *Somn.* 1.230). Nevertheless, without taking the referent for λόγος for granted (even though, e.g., σοφία is never designated the title θεός and though Philo's over 1,300 uses of λόγος are systematically different from John's meaning), I still believe the pre-existent λόγος eventually points to Jesus, the λόγος incarnate (i.e., John 1.14, 17; cf. Rev 19.13), and therefore pertains to this chapter's examination. For similar (recent) conclusions about the pre-existent λόγος eventually pointing to Jesus, see, among others, Martin Hengel, "The Prologue of the Gospel of John as the Gateway to Christological Truth," in *The Gospel of John and Christian Theology*, ed. Richard Bauckham and Carl Mosser (Grand Rapids: Eerdmans, 2008), 271; Uwe-Karsten Plisch, *The Gospel of Thomas: Original Text with Commentary* (Stuttgart: Deutsche Bibelgesellschaft, 2008), 76–77; Moo, *Colossians and the Philemon*, 118; Andreas J. Köstenberger and Scott R. Swain, *Father, Son, and Spirit: The Trinity and John's Gospel*, ed. D. A. Carson (Downers Grove, IL: InterVarsity, 2008), 113; Douglas W. Kennard, *Messiah Jesus: Christology in His Day and Ours* (New York: Peter Lang, 2008), 503; Petr Pokorný, *A Commentary on the Gospel of Thomas: From Interpretations to the Interpreted* (New York: T&T Clark, 2009), 16.

more papyrus fragments than any other book of the NT.[30] Surprisingly, though, neither UBS[4] nor NA[27] list any variants for John 1.1c. Only three major published NT Greek texts—those of Tischendorf[8], Merk, and von Soden—even list textual variants in their apparatus (with 100 percent unanimity as to its *Ausgangstext*: καὶ θεὸς ἦν ὁ λόγος).[31] No textual debates on John 1.1c exist in any standard work on Jesus-θεός passages, and until eighteen years ago,[32] NT textual critics were unanimous in their certainty of John 1:1c. This scholarly agreement continues today even though one textual critic, Bart Ehrman, stated his reluctance to dismiss the testimony of a single eighth-century Alexandrian manuscript, L.[33] To Ehrman, an articular θεός gives him the "distinct impression" that the orthodox party changed it due to the Arian controversies.[34] In other words, Ehrman points out that an articular θεός possibly makes this otherwise implicit identification (Jesus as simply divine) an explicit one (God himself).[35]

Although the most probable understanding of the anarthrous θεός is qualitative (the Word has the same *nature* as God),[36] three points concern us here textually:

---

30. Aland, *Kurzgefasste Liste*, 29–33. This statistic was without the benefit of many more John papyrus fragment discoveries to date (see, e.g., J. K. Elliott, "Five New Papyri of the New Testament," *NovT* 41 [1999]: 209–13; Elliott, "Four New Papyri Containing the Fourth Gospel and Their Relevance for the Apparatus Criticus," *JETS* 59 [2008]: 674–78; Peter Head, "P. Bodmer II (𝔓[66]): Three Fragments Identified; A Correction," *NovT* 50 [2008]: 78–80).

31. This unanimity continues today, e.g., in such specialized (i.e., single book) text-critical works as the IGNTP edition of the Gospel of John (i.e., The American and British Committees of the International Greek New Testament Project, *The New Testament in Greek IV, The Gospel according to St. John*, vol. 1, *The Papyri* [New York: Brill, 1995], 123; vol. 2, *The Majuscules* [Leiden: Brill, 2007], 189).

32. Reference is here made to the publication year (1993) of Bart Ehrman's *Orthodox Corruption*.

33. Ehrman, *Orthodox Corruption*, 179 n. 187.

34. Ibid.

35. Ibid. John could have used θεῖος (e.g., Acts 17.29; 2 Pet 1.3, 4) or some other word meaning "divine," had he wished to convey Jesus as simply divine. Keener helpfully points out, "Regarding Jesus as merely 'divine' but not deity violates the context; identifying him with the Father does the same. For this reason, John might thus have avoided the article even had grammatical convention not suggested it; as a nineteenth-century exegete argued, an articular θεός would have distorted the sense of the passage, 'for then there would be an assertion of the entire identity of the Logos and of God, while the writer is in the very act of bringing to view some distinction between them. . . .' Scholars from across the contemporary theological spectrum recognize that, although Father and Son are distinct in this text, they share deity in the same way" (Craig S. Keener, *The Gospel of John: A Commentary* [Peabody, MA: Hendrickson, 2003], 374).

36. Contra Modalism/Sabellianism (and the Jehovah's Witnesses rendering of John 1.1c in their New World Translation). Philip Harner, after probing the fourth Gospel for passages that use predicate nouns, points out that the qualitative force of the predicate is more prominent than its definiteness or indefiniteness in forty of the fifty-three cases that use anarthrous predicates preceding the verb. He notes

Brian J. Wright

1. Both $\mathfrak{P}^{75}$ and Codex B attest to the absence of the article in John 1.1c. This is significant since "[t]hese MSS seem to represent a 'relatively pure' form of preservation of a 'relatively pure' line of descent from the original text."[37] Kenneth W. Clark concludes, "[I]t is our judgment that $\mathfrak{P}^{75}$ appears to have the best textual character in the third century."[38] Ehrman concurs, "Among all the witnesses, $\mathfrak{P}^{75}$ is generally understood to be the strongest."[39] Thus this evidence significantly strengthens our initial external examination in favor of an anarthrous θεός.

2. Only two MSS (L and W^S) contain the articular θεός in καὶ ὁ θεὸς ἦν ὁ λόγος.[40] In addition, these two MSS are late (eighth century)[41] and have never produced a reading that has found acceptance into the base text of the NA^{27} or UBS^4 without the support of better and earlier MSS. In fact, as Matthew P. Morgan points out regarding Regius (L), the article with θεός in John 1.1c represents the only sensible variant involving a single letter in all (53) of this scribe's singular readings. The best explanation for the addition of the article is the sloppy scribal behavior

---

specifically, "In John 1:1 I think that the qualitative force of the predicate is so prominent that the noun cannot be regarded as definite." He also suggests, "[T]he English language is not as versatile at this point as Greek, and we can avoid misunderstanding the English phrase only if we are aware of the particular force of the Greek expression that it represents" ("Qualitative Anarthrous Predicate Nouns: Mark 15:39 and John 1:1," *JBL* 92 [1973]: 87; whole article on 75–87). Cf. J. G. Griffiths, "A Note on the Anarthrous Predicate in Hellenistic Greek," *ExpTim* 62 (1950–51), 314–16; Robert W. Funk, "The Syntax of the Greek Article: Its Importance for Critical Pauline Problems" (PhD diss., Vanderbilt University, 1953), 148; Robertson, (A. T. Robertson, *A Grammar of the Greek New Testament in the Light of Historical Research*, 4th ed. (New York: Hodder and Stoughton, 1923), 767–68; Daniel B. Wallace, *Greek Grammar beyond the Basics: An Exegetical Syntax of the New Testament* (Grand Rapids: Zondervan, 1996), 266–69.

37. Gordon D. Fee, "$\mathfrak{P}^{75}$, $\mathfrak{P}^{66}$, and Origen: The Myth of Early Textual Recension in Alexandria," in *New Dimensions in New Testament Study*, ed. R. N. Longenecker and M. C. Tenney (Grand Rapids: Eerdmans, 1974], 44). Cf. also Peter M. Head, "Christology and Textual Transmission: Reverential Alterations in the Synoptic Gospels," *NovT* 35 (1993): 105–29, esp. 112–13.

38. Kenneth W. Clark, "The Gospel of John in Third-Century Egypt," *NovT* 5 (1962): 24. Cf. also S. A. Edwards, "$\mathfrak{P}^{75}$ under the Magnifying Glass," *NovT* 18 (1976): 190–212.

39. Ehrman, *Orthodox Corruption*, 112.

40. Only Merk's critical NT text contains Codex Freerianus (W[032-S]). Then again, as Daniel B. Wallace reminded me, Codex W was not discovered until *after* Tischendorf wrote his critical work and *while* von Soden was producing his work (i.e., its publication was shortly before von Soden's final volume).

41. "[T]he first quire of John . . . is a later (probably eighth-century) replacement quire that bears no relation to the rest of the manuscript and made up for the (presumably) lost original portion" (James R. Royse, "The Corrections in the Freer Gospels Codex," in *The Freer Biblical Manuscripts: Fresh Studies of an American Treasure Trove*, ed. Larry W. Hurtado [Atlanta: Society of Biblical Literature, 2006], 186). Cf. Metzger and Ehrman, *Text of the New Testament*, 77–81; Edgar J. Goodspeed, "Notes on the Freer Gospels," *AJT* 13 (1909): 597–603, esp. 599.

evident in every aspect of this manuscript (i.e., the Gospel of John portion of Regius).[42] As for W[S], Morgan points out the following:

1. There is no evidence to establish a *direct relationship* between these two eighth-century manuscripts. As a result, the occurrences of the article with θεός found in John 1.1c in both MSS should be considered isolated readings.

2. Alignment of Codex L and W[S] never merits inclusion in the accepted text of NA[27] *without support* from other key MSS (ℵ, B, C, D, 𝔓[66], 𝔓[75]).

3. There are *no known instances* where a combination of W[S] with a single other witness finds credibility as a potentially "original" reading.

Therefore, the inclusion of W[S] as a subsingular reading in John 1.1c does not negate the egregious nature of the scribal behavior in Codex L, and it further demonstrates that this combination possesses insufficient testimony to consider the reading καὶ ὁ θεὸς ἦν ὁ λόγος to be a plausible original.[43]

This scant evidence, at best, struggles to gain any viability in going back to the *Ausgangstext*. In addition, it is highly improbable that this was a deliberate corruption by the Orthodox Church *five* centuries after the Arian controversy.

Sahidic Coptic MSS,[44] usually considered decent representatives of the Alexandrian form of text,[45] offer an intriguing clue to the textual certainty in John 1.1c. In short, Sahidic has both an indefinite and a

---

42. Matthew P. Morgan, "The Legacy of a Letter: Sabellianism or Scribal Blunder in John 1:1c?", in this volume.

43. Ibid, 116.

44. According to Schüssler, "Today we count about 182 Coptic MSS of the Gospel of John in the Sahidic dialect" (Karlheinz Schüssler, "Some Pecularities of the Coptic (Sahidic) Translations of the Gospel of John," *Journal of Coptic Studies* 10 [2008]: 41–62). That number, Schüssler continues, includes five complete MSS of John's Gospel (i.e., sa 505, 506, 508, 561, 600), 38 lectionaries, and three other liturgical MSS. His recent MS calculation helps explain the "1057 Coptic citations of John's gospel in the 27th edition of the Nestle-Aland *Novum Testamentum Graece*" (Christian Askeland, "Has the Coptic Tradition Been Properly Used in New Testament Textual Criticism?" [paper presented at the annual meeting of the Society of Biblical Literature, Boston, MA, November 22, 2008], 1).

45. Frederik Wisse, "The Coptic Versions of the New Testament," in *The Text of the New Testament in Contemporary Research: Essays on the* Status Quaestionis, ed. Bart D. Ehrman and Michael W. Holmes (Grand Rapids: Eerdmans, 1995), 137. Cf. Metzger, *Textual Commentary*, 15; Metzger, *The Early Versions of the New*

definite article (whereas Koine Greek only has a definite article). What gives this fact significance is that John 1.1c has the *indefinite* article in Sahidic (and Bohairic) MSS[46]: ⲁⲅⲱ ⲛⲉⲩⲛⲟⲩⲧⲉ ⲡⲉ ⲡϣⲁⲝⲉ.[47] It should come as no surprise, then, that the occurrence of the indefinite article (ⲟⲩ, which has contracted) before "God" (ⲛⲟⲩⲧⲉ) in this passage suggests that the Coptic translator was looking at a Greek *Vorlage* with an anarthrous θεός. In other words, the fact that θεός was translated into Sahidic (and Bohairic) as an indefinite noun strongly suggests that the translator was translating a Greek text *without* the article.

To flesh this out a little more, Horner translates John 1.1c into English as follows: "and [a] God was the Word."[48] The apparatus, however, states, "*Square* brackets imply words used by the Coptic and *not* required by the English, while *curved* brackets supply words which *are* necessary to the English idiom."[49] Unlike English, the Sahidic indefinite article is used with abstract nouns (e.g., truth, love, hate) and nouns of substance (e.g., water, bread, meat).[50] An example of this can be seen in Horner's translation of John 19.34b (καὶ ἐξῆλθεν εὐθὺς αἷμα καὶ ὕδωρ), where there are no Greek articles: "and immediately came out [a] blood and [a] water."[51] None of the words in brackets are necessary in English, but they are noted by Horner due to the presence of the indefinite article in the Coptic MSS.

Circling back to the textual assessment, the question we must now answer is, did Coptic translators uniformly translate the nominative

---

Testament: Their Origin, Transmission, and Limitations (Oxford: Clarendon, 1977), esp. 132–37; Metzger and Ehrman, *Text of the New Testament*, 110–15.

46. Bohairic was a different (but new) Coptic translation from Greek. More importantly, though, it is an important witness to the secondary Alexandrian type of text (see, e.g., Metzger, *Textual Commentary*, 15).

47. George W. Horner, ed., *The Coptic Version of the New Testament in the Southern Dialect, Otherwise Called Sahidic and Thebaic, with Critical Apparatus, Literal English Translation, Register of Fragments, and Estimate of the Version*, 7 vols. (Oxford: Clarendon, 1911–24), 3:2. Cf. Hans Quecke, *Das Johannesevangelium saïdisch: Text der Handschrift PPalau Rib. Inv.-Nr. 183 mit den Varianten der Handschriften 813 und 814 der Chester Beatty Library und der Handscrift M569* (Barcelona: Papyrologica Castroctaviana, 1984), 73. For Bohairic, see George W. Horner, ed., *The Coptic Version of the New Testament in the Northern Dialect, Otherwise Called Memphitic and Bohairic, with Introduction, Critical Apparatus, and Literal English Translation*, 4 vols. (Oxford: Clarendon, 1898–1905), 3:2.

48. Horner, *Coptic Version of the New Testament in the Southern Dialect*, 3:3.

49. Ibid., 3:376 (italics added).

50. Thomas Lambdin, *Introduction to Sahidic Coptic* (Macon, GA: Mercer, 1983), 5. Cf. also Bentley Layton, *A Coptic Grammar: Sahidic Dialect* (Wiesbaden: Harrassowitz, 2000).

51. Horner, *Coptic Version of the New Testament in the Southern Dialect*, 3:307. A few other examples from the Gospel of John include 1.16, 26, 33; 3.5, 6; 5.39; 6.10; 16.33.

singular θεός?[52] To answer this, I examined every occurrence of the nominative singular θεός in every potential Johannine writing (i.e., John, 1 John, 2 John, 3 John, Revelation).[53] This examination revealed that John 1.1c was the *only* time the nominative singular θεός (articular or anarthrous) was translated with a Coptic *indefinite* article. Putting this in further perspective, of the five NT books examined, there were only four other anarthrous uses of θεός (if one includes the textual variant in Rev 21.3).[54] Still, despite whatever one understands the Coptic translator to have done with the other four potential instances (assuming their *Vorlage* contained them), John 1.1c is the only text for which we can be certain that the Coptic translator was in fact looking at a *Vorlage* that contained an anarthrous θεός (i.e., no evidence to the contrary exists to date). As stated already, only two, late eighth-century MSS contain the articular θεός, and both the Sahidic and Bohairic versions were composed prior to then. In other words, until (or unless) new evidence is discovered to the contrary, it is highly probable that the Coptic translator(s) were looking at a Greek *Vorlage* with an anarthrous θεός, as reflected by the only Coptic indefinite article with a nominative singular θεός in the five NT books previously mentioned.

In sum, it is highly improbable that the Coptic translator was translating a Greek *Vorlage* containing an articular θεός. Internally (and syntactically), the absence of the article does not necessarily deny the full deity of Jesus. "Neither in LXX Greek nor in secular Greek," Harris explains, "is a firm or a fine distinction drawn between the articular and the anarthrous θεός. This judgment is confirmed, as far as Hellenistic Greek writings contemporaneous with the NT are concerned, by Meecham, who cites specific examples from the Epistle to Diognetus."[55]

---

52. For a more in-depth work dealing specifically with this question, see Timothy Ricchuiti and Brian J. Wright, "From 'God' (θεός) to 'God' (ⲛⲟⲩⲧⲉ): A New Discussion and Proposal regarding John 1:1c and the Sahidic Coptic Version of the New Testament," *JTS* 62.2 (2011): 494–512.

53. The following statistics were produced via the base text of the NA[27] and UBS[4] in Bibleworks 8.0. For the Sahidic Coptic version, I examined Horner, *Coptic Version of the New Testament in the Southern Dialect*; Quecke, *Das Johannesevangelium saidisch*; and Herbert Thomas, ed., *The Coptic Version of the Acts of the Apostles and the Pauline Epistles in the Sahidic Dialect* (Cambridge: Cambridge University Press, 1932) (Chester Beatty MSS). Admittedly, a slight distortion of the database might occur due to text-critical issues (e.g., John 8.54). I did not exhaustively examine each critical apparatus, MS, or witness, to find other viable variants that attest to a nominative singular θεός/ⲛⲟⲩⲧⲉ. My purpose here was merely to obtain a highly probable snapshot of occurrences and patterns via several modern Greek NT editions.

54. θεός occurs twice in this verse (with the second occurrence placed in brackets in both the NA[27] and UBS[4]), but only the second (anarthrous) one is reflected in the Coptic. The other three are John 1.18, John 8.54, and Rev 21.7.

55. Harris, *Jesus as God*, 29.

Brian J. Wright

Another critic puts it more specifically: "The term θεός appears in some form 83 times. Of these 63 are articular and 20 anarthrous. Still, it is highly improbable that the Fourth Evangelist intends any consistent distinction to be drawn between θεός and ὁ θεός."[56] At any rate, the scholarly consensus is correct that the text is certain and that every viable MS ascribes the title θεός to Jesus.

John 1.18

At least thirteen variant readings[57] exist for John 1.18, of which three are viable.[58] All three viable variants divide into two distinct groups, reading with either υἱός or θεός.[59] If the latter group is chosen, the final categorization ultimately depends on the presence or absence of the article:

1. **μονογενὴς θεός**—𝔓[66] ℵ* B C* L S* 423 Diatessaron[Arabic] syr[p, h(mg)] geo[2] Apostolic Constitutions Arius[acc. to Epiphanius] Basil Clement[grlat] Cyril[1/4] Didymus Epiphanius Gregory-Nyssa Heracleon Hilary Irenaeus[lat] [1/3] Jerome Origen[gr 2/4] Pseudo-Ignatius Ptolemy Synesius[acc. to Epiphanius] Theodotus[acc. to Clement] Valentinians[acc. to Irenaeus and Clement]

2. **ὁ μονογενὴς θεός**—𝔓[75] ℵ[1] 33 cop[sa, bo] Basil[1/2] Clement[2/3] Clement[from Theodotus 1/2] Cyril[2/4] Epiphanius Eusebius[3/7] Gregory-Nyssa Origen[gr 2/4] Serapion[1/2]

3. **ὁ μονογενὴς υἱός**—A C[3] G Θ K T X Ψ W[supp] Δ Π 063 0141 0211 1 13 22 24 63 68 69 79 106 114 118 124 131 138 152 154 157 158 160 165 168 173 178 180 185 191 205 209 213 220 222 228 245 265 268 270 280 295 333 345 346 348 352[c] 357 370 377 382 389 391 397 401 423 430 472 482 489 508 513 515 537 543 544 555 557 565 579 589 597 649 679 683 700 709 713 716 720 726 731 732 733 736 740 744 747 775 787 788 792 799 807 809 821 826 827 828 829 833 841 851 863 865 873 874 878 883 884 888 889 891 892 899 904 931 968 969 979 982 983 989 992 994 1006 1009 1010 1014 1021 1026 1029 1038 1043 1071 1079 1085 1087 1093 1113 1118 1128 1187

---

56. Daniel Rathnakara Sadananda, *The Johannine Exegesis of God: An Exploration into the Johannine Understanding of God* (New York: Gruyter, 2004), 177.

57. Kurt Aland, Barbara Aland, and Klaus Wachtel, *Text und Textwert der griechischen Handschriften des Neuen Testaments: Johannesevangelium* (New York: Gruyter, 2005), 3–5.

58. Several exegetical and historical details exist that will not be canvassed here.

59. John 1.18 is actually the only verse listed under textual issues in both major works on this topic: the standard work by Murray Harris, *Jesus as God*, lists only three problems as "textual" (Heb 1.8; 2 Pet 1.1; John 1.18), and Raymond Brown's *An Introduction to New Testament Christology* lists three under "textual": Gal 2.20; Acts 20.28; John 1.18.

1188 1195 1200 1216 1230 1241 1242 1243 1253 1292 1342 1344 1365 1424 1505 1546 1646 2148 *Byz* [E F G H] *Lect* it[a, aur, b, c, e, f, ff(2), l] vg syr[c, h, pal] arm eth geo[l] slav Alexander Ambrose[10/11] Ambrosiaster Athanasius Augustine Basil[1/2] Caesarius Irenaeus[lat 1/3] Irenaeus[lat 2/3] Clement[from Theodotus 1/2] Clement[1/3] Cyril[1/4] Chrysostom Hippolytus Origen[lat 1/2] Letter of Hymenaeus Eustathius Eusebius[4/7] Serapion[1/2] Gregory-Nazianzus Proclus Theodoret John-Damascus Tertullian Hegemonius Victorinus-Rome Hilary[5/7] Pseudo-Priscillian Faustinus Fulgentius Gregory-Elvira Phoebadius Jerome Varimadum Letter of Hymenaeus Nonnus Synesius Titus of Bostra Victorinus of Rome

External Evidence[60]

Θεός is attested in the best Alexandrian majuscule (B) and in the earliest available MSS ($\mathfrak{P}^{66}$ $\mathfrak{P}^{75}$).[61] The significance of this is that if the Alexandrian witnesses for υἱός (e.g., T Δ Ψ 892 1241) cannot reasonably go back to the Alexandrian archetype, its attestation therein is almost a moot point.[62] Ehrman rightly concludes that the semirecent discovery of $\mathfrak{P}^{66}$ and $\mathfrak{P}^{75}$ did "very little (in this instance) to change the character of the documentary alignment" and has "done nothing to change the picture."[63] Granted, no scholar, to my knowledge, argues against this fact. Nevertheless, these two MSS continue to persuade certain scholars (particularly in evangelical circles) that θεός is now the superior reading. For example, Köstenberger and Swain recently concluded, "With the acquisition of $\mathfrak{P}^{66}$ and $\mathfrak{P}^{75}$, both of which read *monogenēs theos*, the preponderance of the evidence now leans in the direction of the latter reading [*monogenēs theos*]."[64] This evidence, albeit strong, has not really changed the picture. That is why scholars who opt for υἱός consistently point out the apparent isolation of θεός in the Alexandrian form of text. In fact, Ehrman argues that because "virtually *every* other representa-

---

60. Several major published Greek NT texts are evenly divided here as to the *Ausgangstext* (e.g., von Soden, Bover, and Tischendorf[8] choose ὁ μονογενὴς υἱός [though it should be noted that the discoveries of $\mathfrak{P}^{66}$ and $\mathfrak{P}^{75}$ occurred after two of these texts were published], while UBS[4], NA[27], and Merk favored μονογενὴς θεός).

61. For the chief characteristics regarding the copying activity of the scribes of both $\mathfrak{P}^{66}$ and $\mathfrak{P}^{75}$, consult Royse, *Scribal Habits*, esp. 544, 704.

62. Nevertheless, as Clark admonishes, "We are mindful that these papyri cannot claim unquestioned priority on the ground alone of their greater antiquity . . . [nor can we] blindly follow their textual testimony even when the two are in agreement with one another" ("Gospel of John in Third-Century Egypt," 23). Cf. also Eldon J. Epp, "A Dynamic View of Textual Transmission," in *Studies in the Theory and Method of New Testament Textual Criticism*, ed. Eldon J. Epp and Gordon D. Fee (Grand Rapids: Eerdmans, 1993), 274.

63. Ehrman, *Orthodox Corruption*, 112.

64. Köstenberger and Swain, *Father, Son, and Spirit*, 78. Cf. also Andreas J. Köstenberger, *John* (Grand Rapids: Baker, 2004), 50.

Brian J. Wright

tive of *every* other textual grouping—Western, Caesarean, Byzantine—attests to υἱός," θεός does not "fare well at all."[65] Let us assess, then, the remaining textual groupings Ehrman mentioned, since no one, to my knowledge, is arguing against θεός going back to the Alexandrian archetype.

Three main issues require comment concerning the Western tradition:

1. The quality of the Western MS supporting θεός (ℵ)[66] is comparatively greater than all Alexandrian MSS supporting υἱός. Therefore, unlike the overwhelming improbability of υἱός going back to the Alexandrian archetype, θεός does have a viable possibility of doing so in the Western tradition.

2. ℵ is the earliest Western MS containing this passage (thus strengthening its possible connection with the Western archetype). In the least, this demonstrates that θεός is *not* isolated in the Alexandrian form of text, with weak attestation elsewhere.

3. Although υἱός has relatively stronger support in the Western form of text (e.g., W^S it vg syr^c Irenaeus), one could still argue that "in the early period [pre-180] there was no textual tradition in the West that was not shared with the East."[67] In other words, "the origin of the 'Western' text lies anywhere but in the direction its name would suggest."[68] Ehrman concludes, "Above all, it is significant in saying something about the transmission of the so-called 'Western' text of the Fourth Gospel. To be sure, we have not uncovered any evidence of a consolidated form of this text that could match the carefully

---

65. Ehrman, *Orthodox Corruption*, 79 (italics added). Later, we shall see that he reverses the same external appraisal he employs here (see the discussion of Heb 1.8 in this chapter).

66. Sinaiticus (ℵ) aligns with the "West" in John 1.1–8.38. See Gordon Fee, "Codex Sinaiticus in the Gospel of John: A Contribution to Methodology in Establishing Textual Relationships," in Epp and Fee, *Studies in the Theory and Method of New Testament Textual Criticism*, 221-43.

67. Kurt Aland and Barbara Aland, *The Text of the New Testament: An Introduction to the Critical Editions and to the Theory and Practice of Modern Textual Criticism*, 2nd ed. (Grand Rapids: Eerdmans, 1989), 54. Aland and Aland argue, "Hardly anyone today refers to this putative Western text without placing the term in quotation marks, i.e., as the 'Western text'" (ibid.). Likewise, Scrivener concludes that "the text of Codex Bezae, as it stands at present, is *in the main* identical with one that was current both in the East and West" (Frederick H. Scrivener, *Bezae Codex Cantabrigiensis* [London: Bell and Daldy, 1864], xlv).

68. Aland and Aland, *Text of the New Testament*, 67. Cf. Roger L. Omanson, *A Textual Guide to the Greek New Testament: An Adaptation of Bruce M. Metzger's "Textual Commentary" for the Needs of Translators* (Peabody, MA: Hendrickson, 2006), 22.

---

controlled tradition of Alexandria."[69] The possible implication of this, then, is that even the attestation of υἱός in the majority of MSS in the Western form of text does not necessarily add a lot of textual weight to its authenticity (especially without ℵ or stronger Western support).

Does the Caesarean textual grouping strengthen the argument in support for υἱός? Again, the overwhelming majority read υἱός (Θ 565 579 700 f^1 f^{13} geo^1). This, however, is problematic for at least two reasons:

1. More recent nomenclature moves away from the label "Caesarean," since strong argumentation exists against it being a fourth form of text.[70] Admittedly, some merit might exist in using the label with the result that further geographical distribution might be exposed.

2. Assuming the Caesarean group does reveal further geographical distribution, θεός is attested in it, albeit scarcely (geo^2): "Like the Armenian version, it [Georgian] is an important witness to the Caesarean type of text. Among the oldest known Gospel manuscripts are the Adysh manuscript of A.D. 897, the Opiza manuscript of 913, and the Tbet' manuscript of 995. In most *apparatus critici*, the Adysh manuscript is cited as Geo^1 and the testimony of the other two, as Geo^2."[71] Again, the evidence here shows that θεός is present outside an exclusively Alexandrian tradition, with a viable witness to an archetype (increasing its geographical distribution).

Regarding the Latin and Syriac traditions (aligning with the "Western" type of text), υἱός occurs most frequently, with θεός still present in some Syriac MSS (syr$^{h(mg)}$ syr^p).[72] At first glance, this scant evidence seems irrelevant. Impressive here, though, is that θεός is attested again outside the Alexandrian tradition (e.g., the Peshitta [syr^p] was "transmitted with remarkable fidelity," and syr$^{h(mg)}$ is close to the

---

69. Bart Ehrman, "Heracleon and the 'Western' Textual Tradition," *NTS* 40 (1994): 178–79.

70. See Bruce Metzger, "The Caesarean Text of the Gospels," in *Chapters in the History of New Testament Textual Criticism* (Grand Rapids: Eerdmans, 1963), 42–72; Larry Hurtado, *Text-Critical Methodology and the Pre-Caesarean Text: Codex W in the Gospel of Mark* (Grand Rapids: Eerdmans, 1981), 24–45; Eldon Epp, "Issues in New Testament Criticism," in *Rethinking New Testament Textual Criticism*, ed. David A. Black (Grand Rapids: Baker, 2002), 39.

71. Metzger and Ehrman, *Text of the New Testament*, 118–19. Cf. Robert Blake and Maurice Brière, "The Old Georgian Version of the Gospel of John," Patrologia Orientalis 26, no. 4 (Paris: Firmin-Didot, 1950).

72. For certain cautions when using Syriac, see P. J. Williams, *Early Syriac Translation Technique and the Textual Criticism of the Greek Gospels* (Piscataway, NJ: Gorgias, 2004).

Brian J. Wright

"Western" type of text).[73] At the same time, θεός is the exclusive reading in both the Arabic and Coptic traditions.[74] θεός, then, is attested in one of the earliest versions of the NT where υἱός is completely absent (the Coptic versions).

Turning now to the church fathers, Ehrman emphasizes the early date of υἱός by listing three specific fathers "who were writing before our earliest surviving manuscripts were produced" (Irenaeus, Clement, and Tertullian).[75] Regrettably, he does this without acknowledging any fathers (let alone 𝔓[66]) supporting θεός around the same period. We can, however, list three: Irenaeus, Clement, and Eusebius. One may notice that two of the names appear on both sides of the debate. This redundancy reveals the fact that many fathers (both Greek and Latin) use υἱός as well as θεός in their writings on John 1.18. The point is that there are many names that could be used to support either reading. In fact, here are three more: Basil, Cyril, and Origen. At the risk of sounding repetitive, θεός here shows up again outside the Alexandrian tradition (e.g., early Latin fathers in the Gospels are Western witnesses),[76] with relatively strong textual weight (per Ehrman's argument).

At least two more issues, though, are critical regarding the church fathers. First, McReynolds warns us that any reference to ὁ μονογενὴς υἱός by a father is unsubstantiated unless it specifically denotes John 1.18. The citation or allusion alone could equally apply to any of the other passages in John (1.14; 3.16) or in the NT (Luke 7.12; Heb 11.17; 1 John 4.9) where μονογενής refers to the "Son." The same problem does *not* apply to μονογενὴς θεός, since it occurs nowhere else. Thus one can be sure that John 1.18 is in view if μονογενὴς θεός, with or without the article, is read (e.g., Arius, Basil, Clement, Cyril, Didymus, Epiphanius, Eusebius, Gregory of Nyssa, Heracleon, Hilary, Irenaeus, Jerome, Origen, Pseudo-Ignatius, Ptolemy, Serapion, Synesius, Tatian, Theodotus, Valentinius). McReynolds concludes "that patristic evidence for various readings needs to be used much more carefully, and with a full view of the context of the Father being quoted."[77]

---

73. Metzger and Ehrman, *Text of the New Testament*, 98. For a recent discussion on the genetic relationship between the Old Syriac and the Peshitta, see Andreas Juckel, "Research on the Old Syriac Heritage of the Peshitta Gospels," in *Journal of Syriac Studies* 12, no. 1 (2009): 41–115.

74. See, e.g., Quecke, *Das Johannesevangelium saïdisch*, 75.

75. Ehrman, *Orthodox Corruption*, 79.

76. Contra Sadananda, *Johannine Exegesis of God*, 210. Cf. Metzger, *Textual Commentary*, 15.

77. Paul McReynolds, "John 1:18 in Textual Variation and Translation," in *New Testament Textual Criticism* (Oxford: Clarendon, 1981), 118. Cf. Carroll Osburn, "Methodology in Identifying Patristic Citations in NT Textual Criticism," in *NovT* 47 (2005): 313–43.

Second, the reading μονογενὴς θεός is *not* an anti-Arian polemic. Arians did not balk at giving the title θεός to Jesus.[78] In fact, Arius supports the reading θεός here (according to Epiphanius)[79] and even called Jesus "God" in a letter he wrote to Eusebius bishop of Nicomedia:

> But what do we say and think? What have we taught and what do we teach? That the Son is not unbegotten or a portion of the unbegotten in any manner or from any substratum, but that by the will and counsel of the Father he subsisted before times and ages, full of grace and truth, God, only-begotten, unchangeable.[80]

If this is true, it throws into doubt that an orthodox scribe would change the text away from Arius if θεός bolsters the complete deity of Christ. Even if the reverse is true (if Epiphanius's testimony is wrong and/or if Arius never wrote that letter), one would have to assume that each scribe that changed υἱός to θεός knew about the Arian controversy. But it did not change the text to the higher Christology (examples of which would be many, given the MS evidence previously listed). Even then, the evidence shows inconsistency in their alleged corruption(s) given John 1.1 and 20.28. On top of all that, it would also have to be shown that all the textual evidence originated during or subsequent to this Arian controversy (which it does not). One might still argue, though, that there only needed to be one extremely early scribe who generated θεός. The real question would then become how early this occurred. To answer this objection, the evidence reveals that earlier MSS (in fact, the earliest, well before the Arian controversy) attest to θεός. This indicates that the objection would remain highly speculative and against the clearer testimony of earlier and better MSS. In other words, the *earliest* and *best* MSS (as well as the fact that both sides of this Christological

---

78. "'Ἦν ποτε ὅτε οὐκ ἦν'—'At one time he did not exist'—became the slogan that best expresses the core of Arius's theology, which he shaped in the *Thalia* (θάλεια = 'banquet'), his main work, which is cited in almost all of the sources dealing with Arius" (Hubertus R. Drobner, *The Fathers of the Church: A Comprehensive Introduction* [Peabody, MA: Hendrickson, 2007], 236). Cf. also Raymond E. Brown, *The Gospel according to John (i–xii): Introduction, Translation, and Notes* (Garden City, NY: Doubleday, 1966), 17.

79. Valentinus (another theologian deemed heretical) also accepted the same reading: Valentinians[acc. to Irenaeus and Clement]. Furthermore, no church father accuses him of changing the text. Hort argued here that μονογενὴς θεός was original because the Gnostics (such as Valentinus) did not invent this phrase; instead, they quoted it (F. J. A. Hort, *Two Dissertations* [Cambridge: Macmillan, 1876]).

80. William Rusch, *The Trinitarian Controversy* (Philadelphia: Fortress, 1983), 29–30. For Greek text, see *Urkunden zur Geschichte des arianischen Streites*, ed. H. G. Opitz (Berlin: Gruyter, 1934). Cf. R. P. C. Hanson, *The Search for the Christian Doctrine of God: The Arian Controversy, 318–381* (Grand Rapids: Baker, 2005), 6; Lewis Ayres, *Nicaea and Its Legacy: An Approach to Fourth-Century Trinitarian Theology* (New York: Oxford University Press, 2004), 105–26.

controversy use/quote θεός) heighten the argument away from the allegation that this is an orthodox corruption.[81]

Two other plausible reasons might explain the mainstream survival of υἱός. One, "Son" may have prevailed as the easier (more predictable) reading before the composition of most extant versions. In support of this, "Son" has *universal* agreement in *later* copies, with *no* observable evidence of scribes to alter it. Two, given the preceding external arguments, even though θεός has wide geographical distribution, it remains weak compared to the distribution of υἱός in other non-Alexandrian forms of text. A probable explanation is that θεός is by far the more difficult reading theologically, statistically, and stylistically, which generally produces various textual variants (see the following discussion of the internal evidence).

In sum, externally, *both* readings enjoy wide geographical distribution, even though υἱός is relatively stronger in non-Alexandrian forms of text. Both readings coexisted in the second century, although weightier MSS support θεός.[82] As a whole, then, θεός is more probable due to the quality, antiquity, and transmissional history of the witnesses previously listed. Nevertheless, this external evidence alone does not make θεός the exclusive heir to the throne.

Internal Evidence

Several internal observations initially seem convincing in support of υἱός. For starters, statistically, μονογενής refers to the "Son" elsewhere in John (1.14; 3.16) and in the NT (Luke 7.12; Heb 11.17; 1 John 4.9). "The only occasion in the NT where μονογενής is not used of an 'only son,'" Harris observes, "is Luke 8:42, where it qualifies θυγάτηρ."[83] Stylistically, the reading "Son" is more natural with the mention of "God" earlier in the verse as well as the mention of "Father" later in the verse. Otherwise, why would "God" be repeated twice, and how could God reside in the bosom of another God ("the Father")? Theologically, the NT rarely calls Jesus θεός, making the reading almost too difficult. All of these observations seem to point one in the direction of an original reading of ὁ μονογενὴς υἱός.[84]

---

81. See also Royse, *Scribal Habits*, esp. 19–27.

82. Given my methodology previously stated, merely *counting* MSS is inadequate; one must also *weigh* them.

83. Harris, *Jesus as God*, 92.

84. For a more extensive grammatical examination, especially whether the adjective μονογενής can be used substantivally when it immediately precedes a noun of the same inflection, see Stratton L. Ladewig, "An Examination of the Orthodoxy of the Variants in Light of Bart Ehrman's *The Orthodox Corruption of Scripture*" (ThM thesis, Dallas Theological Seminary, 2000), 51–62; Daniel B. Wallace, "The Gospel according to Bart: A Review Article of *Misquoting Jesus* by Bart Ehrman," *JETS* 49 (2006): 344–46.

In response, the offense of using θεός probably drove a scribe to the less offensive Christology of υἱός, which comports well with the scribal tendency to simplify the text (substituting "God" for "Son" is highly improbable, perhaps best explaining the absence of θεός in later Greek MSS). Even more, μονογενὴς θεός is *never* used elsewhere.[85] One must ask, then, why here and only here do we have the textual variant μονογενὴς θεός (with or without the article)? The answer, given this scenario alone, seems to be that θεός best explains the rise of the other variants.

Stylistically, θεός closes the inclusio begun in 1.1c, also possibly providing a parallel with 20.28 (the gospel as a whole). Perhaps the intention was to shock the reader. If this phrase occurred frequently, the author may have failed in achieving his desired result. The reference "who is in the bosom of the Father" is an anthropomorphic metaphor for intimacy and fellowship.[86] In other words, it is an idiom for closeness and does not truly affect either reading. Lastly, the author of John's Gospel has a penchant for varying Christological designations (cf., e.g., 1.49; 4.42; 6.69; 9.38; 11.27; 20.16).

Another internal argument sometimes given is that a scribe could have easily erred, since only one Greek majuscule letter differentiates "Son" from "God": $\overline{ΥC}$ or $\overline{ΘC}$. One problem with this option, however, is that υἱός was not one of the original (or earliest) *nomina sacra*.[87] At the same time, though, θεός ($\overline{ΘC}$) was one of the four earliest (i.e., Ἰησοῦς, Χριστός, κύριος, and θεός) and most consistently rendered *nomina sacra* from the second century onward.[88] To state this differently, although this option is not impossible, it is highly improbable given the transmissional evidence we have.

What variant, then, best explains the rise of the others? The subtle meaning of the two words in their original apposition, μονογενὴς θεός, may have caused an early misconception. Thus an article was assigned to the original reading, now ὁ μονογενὴς θεός, as early as 𝔓75, ℵ, and cop[bo, sa]. Ironically, this change wound up alleviating nothing and was inconsistent with other Johannine and NT usage. Accordingly, the next stage of evolution changed "God" to "Son": ὁ μονογενὴς υἱός. Finally, although a few other variants arose that either combined the two readings (ὁ μονογενὴς υἱὸς θεός)[89] or simply omitted both (ὁ

---

85. Certain texts (John 5.44; 17.3; Rom 16.27; 1 Tim 1.17; Jude 25) do not legitimately belong here since they all use μόνος and not μονογενής.

86. See BDAG, 556–57; L&N, 34.18 (*The Greek/English Lexicon of the NT Based on Semantic Domains.* Edited by Johannes P. Nouw and Eugene A. Nida [New York, United Bible Societies, 1989]),

87. See, e.g., Larry W. Hurtado, "The Origin of the *Nomina Sacra*: A Proposal," *JBL* 117, no. 4 (1998): 655–73; Dirk Jongkind, *Scribal Habits of Codex Sinaiticus*, Text and Studies: Contributions to Biblical and Patristic Literature, 3rd ser., vol. 5 (Piscataway, NJ: Gorgias, 2007), 62–84.

88. Hurtado, "Origin of the *Nomina Sacra*," 655, 657.

89. E.g., it[q] Ambrose[1/11] Irenaeus lat [1/3] Origen[pt].

μονογενής),[90] ὁ μονογενὴς υἱός became the majority reading, with *no* viable evidence of change in later Greek MSS.[91]

In retrospect, μονογενὴς θεός is the best reading given all the evidence we have internally and externally. As a result, it is highly probable that the text of John 1.18 calls Jesus θεός.

John 20.28

Far beyond the confession of Nathanael in John 1.49 ("Rabbi, you are the Son of God; you are the king of Israel!"),[92] the Gospel of John ends with the fullest Christological confession of faith in the entire Gospel of John:[93] ἀπεκρίθη Θωμᾶς καὶ εἶπεν αὐτῷ· ὁ κύριός μου καὶ ὁ θεός μου ("Thomas answered and said to him, 'My Lord and my God'"). While this chapter does not seek to demonstrate or articulate the sense in which Jesus was understood to be θεός,[94] the aim here, again, is to find out whether a textual analysis will reveal a particular degree of textual certainty that this title was even ascribed to him.

Externally, a single fifth-century Western manuscript, D (05), omits the second article in this verse, thus rendering θεός μου instead of ὁ θεός μου.[95] While this changes nothing contextually,[96] D is arguably one of the most important Western MSS textually. As Aland and Aland note, "When D supports the early tradition the manuscript has a genuine significance, but it (as well as its precursors and followers) should be examined most carefully when it opposes the early tradition."[97] In

---

90. I consider ὁ μονογενής so poorly attested externally (vg^ms Ambrose Aphrahat Cyril of Jerusalem Diatessaron Ephraem Jacob of Nisibis Nestorius Ps-Athanasius Ps-Ignatius Ps-Vigilius[1/2] Victorinus-Rome) and too easily explainable transmissionally to necessitate the reverse hypothesis of starting with it.

91. For similar conclusions, see Jack Finegan, *Encountering New Testament Manuscripts: A Working Introduction to Textual Criticism* (Grand Rapids: Eerdmans, 1974), esp. 174–77; Lieu, *I, II, and III John*, 182 n. 113, 233 n. 163.

92. ἀπεκρίθη αὐτῷ Ναθαναήλ· ῥαββί, σὺ εἶ ὁ υἱὸς τοῦ θεοῦ, σὺ βασιλεὺς εἶ τοῦ Ἰσραήλ.

93. N. T. Wright, *The Resurrection of the Son of God* (Minneapolis: Fortress, 2003), 664.

94. For example, some have felt that Jesus allowed this statement in order not to "ruin the moment." Yet Jesus quotes Deut 6:13, "You are to worship the Lord your God and serve only him," in Matt 4:10 and Luke 4:8. Therefore, his teachings and convictions seem to strongly negate this option. Likewise, it is important to note that Jesus is the sole object of Thomas's interjection (αὐτῷ), while, at the same time, the two exclamations are impossible to unlink due to the conjunction καί. Nevertheless, for the most plausible interpretive options of Thomas's confession, see Sadananda, *Johannine Exegesis of God*, 11–44. Cf. also Bruce M. Metzger, "Jehovah's Witnesses and Jesus Christ," *ThTo* 10 (1953): 65–85, esp. 71.

95. Cf. Frederick H. A. Scrivener, *Bezae Codex Cantabrigiensis* (London: Bell and Daldy, 1864), 156; IGNTP, *Gospel according to St. John*, 2:541.

96. Harris lists four solid reasons in *Jesus as God* (109), though I believe his third reason can be stated much stronger, since ὁ κύριος is never used of God the Father in John's Gospel except in two OT quotations (12.13, 38).

97. Aland and Aland, *Text of the New Testament*, 110.

this case, the latter is true. Furthermore, D is an eccentric MS and regularly drops the article.[98] Yet even if D is original and the second article is absent, this verse (ὁ κύριός μου καὶ θεός μου) grammatically falls under the criteria of Granville Sharp's rule:

> In native Greek constructions (i.e., not translation Greek), when a single article modifies *two* substantives connected by καί (thus, article-substantive-καί-substantive), when both substantives are (1) singular (both grammatically and semantically), (2) personal, (3) and common nouns (not proper names or ordinals), they have the same referent."[99]

In other words, if D is correct and there is no article before θεός, both "Lord" and "God" in this verse explicitly refer to Jesus because of this grammatical construction (cf. also 2 Pet 1.1, discussed later in this chapter). Thus Granville Sharp's rule makes the phrase even more explicit and leaves "no wiggle room for doubt."[100] John 20.28, no matter which variant or MS one chooses, is categorically secure for referring to Jesus as θεός.[101]

---

98. "By actual count, there is a parsimonious use of the article in D; in fact, this situation obtains in each book except Luke" (James D. Yoder, "The Language of the Greek Variants of Codex Bezae," *NovT* 3 [1959]: 245).

99. Wallace, *Sharp's Canon*, 132. For brief discussion of personal pronouns within these constructions (e.g., μου following θεός), see n. 144 in the present chapter. In addition, regarding "my God," Schnabel points out, "[A]ccording to Aristotle, 'It would be an absurdity to profess a friend's affection for Zeus' (φιλεῖν τὸν Δία [*Mag. mor.* 1208 b 30]). The exclamation of Euripides' choir upon seeing the sculptures at the temple in Delphi, 'I see Pallas, my own goddess' (Euripides, *Ion* 211), is one of the very few references in Greek literature that uses the phrase 'my God.' Burkert ["'Mein Gott?' Persönliche Frömmigkeit und unverfügbare Götter," in *Geschichte—Tradition—Reflexion: Festschrift für Martin Hengel zum 70* (Tübingen: Mohr Siebeck, 1996), 3–14] points out, however, that this exclamation must be understood as the 'aesthetic wow-experience' of a collective. There is very little archaeological evidence for Greek cults of a 'personal' god who was interested in or connected with the individual person. In the context of the Anatolian cult of Men, dedications refer to, for example, 'the Men of Artemidoros' (*CMRDM* III 67-70), but such formulations do not imply a particular 'pact' with the god. In a Greek polis the gods of the city were important, not the god worshiped by the individual. In everyday life people established contacts with gods only when needed. Burkert concludes that 'insofar a person fulfills his religious obligations, there remained normally a realm of freedom, of the ὅσιον ['profane'], in which religious concerns vanished. This would be contradicted by a unique or comprehensive obligation or affiliation. Resort to the gods becomes important in a time of need, however. . . . The pious person was prepared for being saved, but he does not have a revelation on a document and no treaty with 'his' god. Gods are not at his disposal" (Eckhard J. Schnabel, *Early Christian Mission: Jesus and the Twelve*, vol. 1 [Downers Grove, IL: InterVarsity, 2004], 615).

100. Wallace, *Sharp's Canon*, 132.

101. Moreover, these two OT expressions are frequently juxtaposed when referring to Israel's one God. Waltke further defines, "The distinct meaning of these two

Acts 20.28

Acts 20.28 involves two distinct textual problems, of which at least nine variants (seven and two, respectively) exist. The viable options are as follows:

Textual Problem 1

τὴν ἐκκλησίαν τοῦ θεοῦ—ℵ B H M S V W Θ 056 0142 4 104 218 257 312 314 322 383 424 454 459 614 621 629 917 1175 1409 1495 1505 1522 1611 1758 1831 2138 2147 2298 2412 2495 *l*60 *l*592 *l*598 *l*603 *l*1021 *l*1439 cop[bo] vg it[ar, c, dem, ph, ro, w] syr[h, p] geo Ambrose Athanasius Basil Chrysostom Cyril-Alexandria Epiphanius

τὴν ἐκκλησίαν τοῦ κυρίου—𝔓[74] A C* D E S T Ψ 13 33 36 40 81 94 104 181 206 209 307 337 429 431 436 453 522 610 630 623 945 1678 1739 1829 1891 2344 2464 *l*164 *l*599 arm cop[sa] it[d, e, gig, p] syr[hmg] Ambrosiaster Didymus[dub, lat] Irenaeus[lat] Jerome Lucifer Pelagius Theodoret[1/2]

Textual Problem 2

τοῦ αἵματος τοῦ ἰδίου—𝔓[41] 𝔓[74] ℵ* A B C* D E Ψ 33 36 69 181 307 326 453 610 945 1175 1611 1678 1739 1837 1891 2464 *l*60 arm geo syr[hgr] Cyril Theodoret

τοῦ ἰδίου αἵματος—H L P 049 056 0142 1 88 104 226 323 330 440 547 614 618 927 1241 1243 1245 1270 1409 1505 1646 1828 1854 2147 2344 2412 2492 2495 *Byz Lect* slav Athanasius Chrysostom Didymus[dub vid]

With the external evidence geographically and genealogically pro-portionate on the first textual problem (the other five readings lack

---

names [the appellative Elohim and Yahweh] is widely recognized: whereas the title Elohim contrasts God with man in their natures, the name Yahweh presents God as entering into a personal relationship with man and revealing Himself to him" (Bruce K. Waltke, "The Book of Proverbs and Old Testament Theology" *BibSac* 136 [1979]: 305). Barrett also notes that John's "My Lord and My God" directed to Jesus reflects the LXX, where it represents יהוה אלהים and similar expressions, but also makes contact with an expression fairly common in pagan religious literature (C. K. Barrett, *The Gospel according to John: An Introduction with Commentary and Notes on the Greek Text* [Philadelphia: Westminster, 1978], 572). Cf. B. A. Mastin, "*Theos* in the Christology of John: A Neglected Feature of the Christology of the Fourth Gospel," *NTS* 22 [1975–76]: 32–51, esp. 37–41; G. Deissmann, *Light from the Ancient East* (New York: George H. Doran, 1927), 366–67; H. D. Betz, *Lukian von Samosata und das Neue Testament* (Leiden: Brill, 1961), 102.

sufficient external support, are obvious conflations, or both),[102] the only thing a textual critic can do is appeal to the internal evidence. Yet this, too, is equally balanced.[103] Of course, it must be noted that "church of the Lord" is absent from the NT and apostolic fathers, while "church of God" occurs eleven other times in the NT (1 Cor 1.2; 10.32; 11.16, 22; 15.9; 2 Cor 1.1; Gal 1.3; 1 Thess 2.14; 2 Thess 1.4; 1 Tim 3.5, 15) and twelve times in the apostolic fathers (*1 Clem.* 1.1; Ign., *Eph.* 17.1; Ign., *Trall.* 2.3; 12.1; Ign., *Phld.* 1.1; 10:1; Ign., *Smyrn.* 1.1; Pol., *Phil.* 1.1; *Mart. Pol.* 1.1; *Herm. Sim.* 18.2, 3, 4).[104]

Most scholars accept θεοῦ as original not merely because of its difficulty but also because of their confidence that, in the second textual problem, the authentic reading is τοῦ αἵματος τοῦ ἰδίου ("the blood of his own [Son]" or "his own blood"). Transmissionally, Lars Aejmelaeus proposes an actual literary dependence of Acts 20.28 on 1 Thessalonians 5.9–10 and Ephesians 1.7. This is in keeping with his overall thesis that Pauline allusions in Acts are invariably due to Luke's knowledge of the Pauline letters.[105] In addition, τοῦ αἵματος τοῦ ἰδίου is undeniably superior externally (𝔓⁴¹ 𝔓⁷⁴ ℵ* A B C* D E Ψ 33 1739 geo syr). Its strength also rests on the logic that it is the harder reading and best explains the rise of the others. "That God suffered was acceptable language," Harnack notes, "before criticism required some refinement of the conviction that God (or God's Son) had become man and died on the cross."[106] In addition, τοῦ αἵματος τοῦ ἰδίου received an "A" rating by the UBS⁴ editorial committee,[107] and most major published NT Greek texts agree (e.g., NA²⁷, Tischendorf⁸, Bover, Merk, von Soden, Westcott and Hort, Vogels, and Weiss).

The text most likely originally read τὴν ἐκκλησίαν τοῦ θεοῦ, ἣν

---

102. For a better understanding of the individual witnesses for the book of Acts, see Joseph A. Fitzmyer, *The Acts of the Apostles: A New Translation with Introduction and Commentary* (New York: Doubleday, 1998), 66–79; C. K. Barrett, *A Critical and Exegetical Commentary on the Acts of the Apostles,* vol. 1 (New York: T&T Clark, 2004), 2–29; Darrell L. Bock, *Acts* (Grand Rapids: Baker, 2007), 28–29.

103. Metzger, *Textual Commentary,* 425–27. Cf. Pervo, *Acts,* 523.

104. The phrase "assembly of the Lord," (ἐκκλησία κυρίου), however, does occur in the LXX (e.g., Deut 23.2, 3, 4*bis,* 9; 1 Chron 28.8; Mic 2.5), but never as an articular construction (i.e., ἡ ἐκκλησία τοῦ κυρίου) or with ἐκκλησία having the semitechnical sense that it does in the NT.

105. Lars Aejmelaeus, *Die Rezeption der Paulusbriefe in der Miletrede: Apg 20:18–35* (Helsinki: Suomalainen Tiedeakatemia, 1987), 132–42. Cf. Pervo, *Acts,* 524.

106. Adolf Harnack, *History of Dogma* (London: Constable, [ca. 1900]; repr., New York: Dover, 1961), 1:187 n. 1. For further discussion on the imagery of "the blood" in the history of the church, as related to the work and person of Christ as God, see Jaroslav Pelikan, *Acts* (Grand Rapids: Brazos, 2005), 221–22. Cf. also Charles F. Devine, "The 'Blood of God' in Acts 20:28," *CBQ* 9 (1947): 381–408.

107. Metzger, *Textual Commentary,* 427.

περιεποιήσατο διὰ τοῦ αἵματος τοῦ ἰδίου.[108] The reading θεοῦ soon changed to κυρίου because of the difficulty in reconciling it with αἵματος τοῦ ἰδίου.[109] This conclusion seems verifiable and reinforced by the combination of variants in the witnesses. Here are a few examples of such combinations (in order of the proposed transmissional history):

1. Witnesses that read both originals (θεοῦ and αἵματος τοῦ ἰδίου): ℵ* B 1175 *l*60

2. Witnesses that changed θεοῦ to κυρίου because of the second original (αἵματος τοῦ ἰδίου): 𝔓74 A C* D E Ψ 33 453 945 1739 1891 36 181 307 610 1678 arm Theodoret

3. Witnesses that kept θεοῦ because of the second nonoriginal (ἰδίου αἵματος): H 056 104 614 1409 1505 2412 2495 Athanasius Chrysostom

4. Witnesses that support both nonoriginals (κυρίου and ἰδίου αἵματος): 2344 Didymus

To summarize, the variants that best explain the rise of the others are θεοῦ and αἵματος τοῦ ἰδίου. Acts 20.28, therefore, does not necessarily equate Jesus with θεός (especially with solid evidence for both of these readings). The decision ultimately comes down to one's understanding and interpretation of the phrase διὰ τοῦ αἵματος τοῦ ἰδίου: "with the blood of his own [Son]" or "with his own blood.[110]

---

108. Also, "ἐκκλησία του θεου occurs eleven times in Paul; ἐκκλησια κυριου occurs seven times in the LXX but never without *v.l.* θεου in the New Testament" (J. Keith Elliott, "An Eclectic Textual Study of the Book of Acts," in *The Book of Acts as Church History: Text, Textual Traditions, and Ancient Interpretations*, ed. Tobias Nicklas and Michael Tilly [New York: Gruyter, 2003], 29).

109. "The text [Acts 20.28] caused such puzzlement (God's own blood?) that some of the scribes responsible for making copies of Luke's book evidently attempted to improve or clarify it—particularly by reading 'the church of *the Lord*, which he obtained through his own blood' (cf. Heb. 9.12)" (James D. G. Dunn, *The Acts of the Apostles* [London: Epworth, 1996], 272).

110. Barrett suggests, "It is very unlikely that a trained theologian would write 'his own blood'; but Luke was not such a theologian, and the natural way of reading the Greek should probably be adopted ["with his own blood"]. It was enough for Luke that when Jesus Christ shed his blood on the cross he was acting as the representative of God; he was God's way of giving life, blood, for the world" (C. K. Barrett, *A Critical and Exegetical Commentary on the Acts of the Apostles*, vol. 2, *Introduction and Commentary on Acts XV–XXVIII* [New York: T&T Clark, 1998], 977). Cf. also Harris, *Jesus as God*, 131–41; "blood of God" as used in the apostolic fathers: Ign., *Eph.* 1.1; Ign., *Rom.* 6.3 (cf. Tertullian, *Ad uxor.* 2.3.1 [*sanguine dei*]).

Galatians 2.20[111]

The original text of Galatians 2.20, according to Metzger, Ehrman, and others, must have read, τοῦ υἱοῦ τοῦ θεοῦ ("the Son of God"). In fact, all major published NT Greek texts have this reading with the exception of Bover (who reads θεοῦ καὶ Χριστοῦ). The UBS⁴ committee continues their support and certainty of it. In fact, the committee agreed to increase their rating from a "B" (found in the third edition) to an "A" (found in the fourth edition). Additionally, the authors of the text-critical notes in the *New English Translation*, using different arguments (e.g., progressive revelation),[112] came to the same textual conclusion.[113] Yet after considering the internal and external evidence (as well as the arguments from many secondary sources), I still think that several stones have been left unturned and that discourse has been left unsaid regarding the reading θεοῦ καὶ Χριστοῦ. Therefore, although I ultimately accept the reading υἱοῦ τοῦ θεοῦ, I will give several reasons why I am reluctant to give it an "A" rating or exclude it among the list of passages potentially proclaiming Jesus as θεός.

The four noted variants for this passage, in no particular order, are

1. **τοῦ θεοῦ**—1985

2. **τοῦ θεοῦ τοῦ υἱοῦ**—330

3. **τοῦ υἱοῦ τοῦ θεοῦ**—ℵ A C D² H K L P S T V Ψ 056 075 0151 0278 6 33 69 81 88 104 131 205 209 226 256 263 323 326 365 424 436 440 459 460 489 517 547 614 618 796 910 927 945 999 1175 1241 1242 1243 1245 1270 1315 1319 1352 1424 1448 1505 1573 1611 1646 1734 1735 1738 1739 1827 1836 1837 1852 1854 1874 1881 1891 1912 1962 1982 2125 2127 2147 2200 2400 2412 2464 2495 2815 it^ar, f, r cop^sa, bo syr^h, p *Lect* vg arm eth geo slav Ambrosiaster Augustine Chrysostom Clement Cyril Didymus^dub Jerome Marcion^acc to Adamantius Pelagius Severian Theodoret Varimadum

---

111. Two primary reasons encouraged me to include Gal 2.20 in this study: (1) most standard works on this topic include this passage (e.g., Brown, "Does the New Testament Call Jesus God?"; Harris, *Jesus as God*, 259–61; A. W. Wainwright, "The Confession 'Jesus as God' in the New Testament," *SJT* 10 [1957]: 274–99), and (2) it is possible (though I do not think highly probable) to translate two of the textual variants as either "God even Christ" (θεοῦ καὶ Χριστοῦ) or "God the Son" (τοῦ θεοῦ τοῦ υἱοῦ) (see, e.g., Ehrman, *Orthodox Corruption*, 86).

112. "Although Paul certainly has an elevated Christology, explicit 'God-talk' with reference to Jesus does not normally appear until the later books" (*New Testament: New English Translation, Novum Testamentum Graece*, ed. Michael H. Burer, W. Hall Harris, Daniel B. Wallace [Stuttgart: Deutsche Bibelgesellschaft; Dallas: NET Bible, 2004], 860).

113. Ibid.

Brian J. Wright

4. θεοῦ καὶ Χριστοῦ—𝔓⁴⁶ B D* G it⁽ᵇ⁾, ᵈ, ᵍ Marius Victorinus-Rome Pelagius

Externally, although the majority of witnesses favor τοῦ υἱοῦ τοῦ θεοῦ, the two oldest MSS support θεοῦ καὶ Χριστοῦ (𝔓⁴⁶ B) along with several other important witnesses (D* G it⁽ᵇ⁾, ᵈ, ᵍ Marius Victorinus-Rome Pelagius) . Furthermore, along with its early "proto-Alexandrian" support (𝔓⁴⁶ B),[114] a strong group of Western witnesses concur (D* F G it⁽ᵇ⁾, ᵈ, ᵍ Victorinus-Rome). This variant, then, is relatively early and possesses agreement between good Western and Alexandrian witnesses (though it is not attested in the Byzantine, Caesarean, or secondary Alexandrian form of text).

Next, two main internal arguments against this reading exist: (1) Paul nowhere else expressly speaks of God as the object of a Christian's faith; and (2) during the copying process, a scribe's eye probably passed over the first article to the second, so that only τοῦ θεοῦ was written (as in MS 330).[115] In response to the former, God is the object of a believer's faith in Romans 4.24. Moo writes, "It is typical for Paul to designate God as the one who raised Jesus from the dead (cf. [Rom] 8.11; 10.9; 1 Cor 6.14; 15.15; 2 Cor 4.14), but it is somewhat unusual for him to designate God himself as the object of Christian faith. Undoubtedly he does so here [Rom 4.24] to bring Christian faith into the closest possible relationship to Abraham's faith."[116] As to the latter, that theory best explains only one of the four previously noted variants, τοῦ θεοῦ, not all of them.

Furthermore, θεοῦ καὶ Χριστοῦ does find some syntactical parallel in the *corpus Paulinum*: 1 Timothy 5.21 and 2 Timothy 4.1 (cf. also 1 Tim 6.13).[117] Beyond this, "Son of God" is the easier reading and pos-

---

114. Cf. Philip W. Comfort and David P. Barrett, *The Text of the Earliest New Testament Greek Manuscripts: New and Complete Transcriptions with Photographs* (Wheaton, IL: Tyndale House, 2001), esp. 27–29; E. C. Colwell, "Method in Establishing the Nature of Text-Types of New Testament Manuscripts," in *Studies in Methodology in Textual Criticism of the New Testament*, New Testament Tools and Studies 9 (Leiden: Brill, 1969), 45–55, esp. 48.

115. Metzger, *Textual Commentary*, 524. For other scribal possibilities, see Colwell, *Studies in Methodology in Textual Criticism of the New Testament*, 106–24. Cf. J. R. Royse, "Scribal Tendencies in the Transmission of the Text of the New Testament," in Ehrman and Holmes, *The Text of the New Testament in Contemporary Research*, 239–52; J. R. Royse, "The Treatment of Scribal Leaps in Metzger's *Textual Commentary*," *NTS* 29 (1983): 539-51; Metzger and Ehrman, *Text of the New Testament*, 250–71.

116. Douglas Moo, *The Epistle to the Romans* (Grand Rapids: Eerdmans, 1996), 287. Cf. Moo, *Colossians and the Philemon*, 84 n. 13. The question remains, however, whether Paul, anywhere in his writings, speaks of both God and Christ Jesus together as the object of faith, which is the case in Gal 2.20 if the authentic reading is θεοῦ καὶ Χριστοῦ.

117. Contra Ehrman, "neither of the other expressions ("God even Christ," "God the Son") occurs in this way in Paul" (*Orthodox Corruption*, 86). The position of the pronoun does not affect the sense. 1 Tim 5.21 is surely not ascribing the title θεός

sibly explains why a scribe preferred it. It is also possible that there is a contextual harmonization of verses 19 ("live to God") and 20 ("Christ lives in me"), keeping with the Western tradition and Pauline theology.[118] Of course, textually speaking, harmonization seems to be more literal than conceptual.

Externally and internally, several issues still need more clarification and resolution; nevertheless, the traditional reading υἱοῦ τοῦ θεοῦ is the best of all probable scenarios. At the same time, this reading may not merit an "A" rating (despite the assessment of the UBS[4] committee) and needs further study.

Hebrews 1.8[119]

Two main interconnected textual issues exist in Hebrews 1.8 that possibly resolve the broader grammatical dilemma of how to interpret and translate ὁ θεός in verses 8 and 9:[120]

πρὸς δὲ τὸν υἱόν,
Ὁ θρόνος σου ὁ θεὸς εἰς τὸν αἰῶνα τοῦ αἰῶνος,
καὶ ἡ ῥάβδος τῆς εὐθύτητος ῥάβδος τῆς βασιλείας σου (v 8)

ἠγάπησας δικαιοσύνην καὶ ἐμίσησας ἀνομίαν·
διὰ τοῦτο ἔχρισέν σε ὁ θεὸς ὁ θεός σου
ἔλαιον ἀγαλλιάσεως παρὰ τοὺς μετόχους σου (v 9).

1. The first textual variant involves the presence or absence of τοῦ αἰῶνος after εἰς τὸν αἰῶνα:

ὁ θρόνος σου ὁ θεὸς εἰς τὸν αἰῶνα τοῦ αἰῶνος

ὁ θρόνος σου ὁ θεὸς εἰς τὸν αἰῶνα_____

---

to the chosen angels as well by adding καὶ τῶν ἐκλεκτῶν ἀγγέλων after θεοῦ καὶ Χριστοῦ Ἰησοῦ.

118. Paul seems to adhere to a bidirectional life for the believer, with the two foci being God and Christ.

119. Although Hebrews' author is anonymous, the author was at least a male (11.32) contemporary of the apostle Paul's protégé Timothy (Heb 13:23), placing Hebrews in the first century.

120. There are two other variants in this verse that do not need further discussion here: the omission of the conjunction καί and the word order of ἡ ῥάβδος τῆς εὐθύτητος. The second one in no way affects our question of whether Jesus is explicitly called θεός, and the first one, according to Metzger and others, would only slightly reduce the difficulty of the last variant if it were to read αὐτοῦ. Still, for clarity's sake, I feel confident that these two variants together should read καὶ ἡ ῥάβδος τῆς εὐθύτητος (maintaining the καί and subsequent word order).

Externally, the absence of τοῦ αἰῶνος is significantly inferior, with only a small handful of concentrated MSS omitting it (B 33 t vg^ms). Although it is true that scribes often expanded readings, that is not the situation here, for several reasons. First, τοῦ αἰῶνος is a direct quotation from the LXX (Ps 44.7; MT Ps 45.7). Second, this reading is supported by some of the best and earliest MSS (only a few omit it: B 33 t vg^ms). Third, almost every place עד עולם occurs in the Psalms according to the MT, the LXX translates it with τοῦ αἰῶνος (e.g., Ps 10.16; 45.7; 48.15; 52.10; 104.5). Even when this is not the case (e.g., Ps 20.5), it maintains a resemblance (εἰς αἰῶνα αἰῶνος).

Putting it another way, if one accepts the shorter Greek rendering of the OT quotation in Hebrews 1.8 (simply by εἰς τὸν αἰῶνα) and does not include τοῦ αἰῶνος, it goes against all the ancient versions of the OT. This variant's potential implication for our study, though not directly determinative on the Jesus-θεός issue, is to establish all possible links to a *Vorlage*, best understand the grammatical structure, and assess every possible textual alignment (i.e., character count) in various MSS. In this case, its OT reference (or even *Vorlage*) was probably the LXX.

2. The second main textual issue in verse 8 is whether the last word in the verse should read αὐτοῦ or σου (i.e., πρὸς δὲ τὸν υἱόν ὁ θρόνος σου ὁ θεὸς εἰς τὸν αἰῶνα τοῦ αἰῶνος, καὶ ἡ ῥάβδος τῆς εὐθύτητος ῥάβδος τῆς βασιλείας [σου/αὐτοῦ?]). The outcome, simply put, will help determine whether ὁ θεός is a case of the nominative used for the vocative (if σου) or a subject-predicate nominative (S-PN) construction (if αὐτοῦ):

Nominative for vocative = "Your throne, O God, is forever and ever, and a righteous scepter is the scepter of your kingdom."

S-PN = "God is your throne [or, more likely, Your throne is God] forever and ever, and a righteous scepter is the scepter of his [i.e., God's] kingdom."[121]

---

121. Harris writes, "Grammatically, no valid objection may be raised against these renderings, but conceptually they are harsh"; "To render ὁ θρόνος σου ὁ θεός by 'Your throne is God' is implausible in light of the articular θεός. . . . No more probable is the translation 'God is your throne'" (Murray Harris, "The Translation of *Elohim* in Psalm 45," *TynBul* 35 [1984]: 72, 89; whole article on 65–89). Even more, though, nowhere else is the phrase "God is your throne" ever used. The expression, according to T. K. Cheyne, is not "consistent with the religion of the psalmists" (*The Book of Psalms: A New Translation with Commentary* [London: Kegan, Paul, Trench, Trubner, 1888], 127). Cf. Peter Craigie, *Psalms 1–50* (Waco, TX: Word, 1983), 33–37. For an opposing view, see K. J. Thomas, "The Old Testament Citations in the Epistle to the Hebrews," *NTS* 11 (1965): 303–25, esp. 305; A. Nairne, *The Epistle to the Hebrews* (Cambridge: Cambridge University Press, 1917), 31–34.

Internally, whereas they are both grammatically possible,[122] only the first construction resonates with the central theme of the section and book (i.e., the exalted Christ). Ehrman believes, however, that the orthodox party corrupted this text, because of their "need to differentiate Christ from God."[123] He concludes by saying, "[W]e are now dealing not with a corruption of the original text but with a corruption of a corruption."[124] What Ehrman may be missing is that the author of Hebrews stands in the exegetical tradition of the quoted Psalm. "That Jewish exegetes regularly understood the text as an address is clear," Attridge points out, "both from the Targum and from the revision of the LXX by Aquila."[125] Little doubt remains, then, that the LXX translator construed it so, suggesting that ὁ θεός in Hebrews 1.8 points to Jesus' essential unity with God while preserving his functional subordination (see ὁ θεός σου in v 9).[126] "It is not impossible that the uniform testimony of the ancient versions in support of the vocative may reflect a messianic re-reading which stresses the transcendence of the King—Messiah," Harris writes, "but it is at least equally possible that all these versions testify to the most natural way of construing אֱלֹהִים, whether they understood the word in reference to the Messiah, or, as Mulder believes (*Psalm 45* 48), to God."[127]

Caragounis summarizes several other salient points regarding the use of the nominative for vocative: (1) it occurred very early in classical Greek, (2) it originally applied to deities, (3) it was more frequent in poetry than prose, (4) it gave greater emphasis, and (5) its usage increased substantially in the NT from classical Greek.[128] In addition, after probing the centuries (from ancient to modern times) for the use of the nominative ὁ θεός in lieu of the vocative, he concludes, "[T]he articular nominative ὁ θεός when used as vocative has a more exalted,

---

122. E.g., Mitchell claims, "The predicate nominative is preferred here to the nominative as a vocative, so that God is not directly addressing the son as 'God'" (Alan C. Mitchell, *Hebrews*, ed. Daniel J. Harrington [Collegeville, MN: Liturgical, 2007], 49). Harris (*Jesus as God*, 212) lists two other commentators, Hort and Nairne, who hold to this view. Wallace points out, though, "As to which of these two options is better [subject or predicate nominative], we have already argued that with two articular nouns, the first in order is the subject.... Hence, ὁ θρόνος σου would be the subject rather than ὁ θεός (*contra* most NT scholars who opt for either of these views)" (*Exegetical Syntax*, 59).

123. Ehrman, *Orthodox Corruption*, 265.

124. Ibid.

125. Harold W. Attridge and Helmut Koester, ed., *The Epistle to the Hebrews* (Philadelphia: Fortress, 1989), 58. Cf. Cheyne, *Psalms*, 127.

126. See, e.g., Murray Harris, "The Translation and Significance of Ὁ ΘΕΟΣ in Hebrews 1:8–9," *TynBul* 36 (1985): 129–62.

127. Harris, "*Elohim* in Psalm 45," 77–78. Cf. Gert J. Steyn, "The *Vorlage* of Psalm 45:6-7 (44:7–8) in Hebrews 1:8–9," *HTS* 60, no. 3 (2004): 1088.

128. Chrys C. Caragounis, *The Development of Greek and the New Testament: Morphology, Syntax, Phonology, and Textual Transmission* (Grand Rapids: Baker, 2006), 141–43.

a more distanced, tone belonging to a more formal, solemn and elevated diction . . . [and h]ardly a more solemn or dignified context could be imagined than the one in which this address is placed [Heb 1.8]."[129] In other words, all of these observations together strengthen the internal probability of understanding ὁ θεός as a nominative for vocative and thus supporting the more natural reading, σου.

With all that in mind, there is also a μέν . . . δέ construction in verses 7–8. Wallace feels that the syntax of nominative for vocative adequately handles this construction; the predicate nominative does not: "Specifically, if we read v 8 as 'your throne is God' the δέ loses its adversative force, for such a statement could also be made of the angels, viz., that God reigns over them."[130] To sum this up another way, if one holds to the predicate nominative view, there is no clear distinction here between the angels (subordinate; ephemeral; servants) and Christ (superior; eternal; deity).

Lastly, various translators handle the preposition πρός differently throughout this pericope (namely, 1.7, 8, 13). Several translations render it "of" (e.g., ESV, NASB, NET, RSV), some "to" (e.g., KJV, NJB, NLT), and still others "about" (e.g. CSB, NIV); with varying combinations of all three instances. However, the translations with "of" or "about" reflect a "misconstrual of the citation as a word about [of] the Son, not to him."[131] In other words, πρός in verses 8 and 13 "must be translated 'to.'"[132] This pertains to the present internal investigation because it strengthens the preceding μέν . . . δέ discussion toward translating the nominative as for vocative. I agree with Attridge, then, that "the variant 'his' was probably occasioned by the ambiguity of the preposition used to introduce the citations and the failure to construe the whole citation as an address."[133]

Externally, though both are well attested in the Alexandrian tradition, the pronoun σου has more impressive weight and variety than αὐτοῦ.[134] Here is a snapshot of the witnesses supporting each:

---

129. Chrys C. Caragounis, "The Use of the Nominative ὁ Θεός as Vocative in the Septuagint and the New Testament," in *Holy Scripture and the Ancient Word: Festschrift for Professor Ioannis Galanis* (Thessalonica: P.Pournaras, 2011).

130. Wallace, *Exegetical Syntax*, 59. Similarly, F. F. Bruce says, "Whatever be said of the force of δέ in v. 6, there is no doubt about its strongly adversative force here, where it harks back to μέν in v. 7 (καὶ πρὸς μὲν τοὺς ἀγγέλους . . . πρὸς δὲ τὸν υἱόν)" (*The Epistle to the Hebrews*, rev. ed. [Grand Rapids: Eerdmans, 1990], 59).

131. Attridge, *Hebrews*, 57.

132. Ibid. Cf. George H. Guthrie, "Hebrews," in *Commentary on the New Testament Use of the Old Testament*, ed. G. K. Beale and D. A. Carson (Grand Rapids: Baker, 2007), 936; L. Timothy Swinson, "'Wind' and 'Fire' in Hebrews 1:7 A Reflection upon the Use of Psalm 104 (103)," *TJ* 28 (2007): 218 n. 17; Wallace, *Exegetical Syntax*, 59.

133. Ibid., 59.

134. This assessment was kept even after recognizing that the combination of 𝔓⁴⁶ ℵ B "has the original reading in eleven other cases of minority readings in Hebrews"

1. αὐτοῦ—𝔓⁴⁶ ℵ B H S

2. σου—A D F K L P Ψ 075 0121 0150 0243 0278 6 33 81 104 256 263 326 365 424 436 459 1175 1241 1319 1739 1852 1881 1912 1962 2127 2200 2464 arm *Byz* cop^sa, bo, fay geo *Lect* it^ar, b, comp, d, t, v slav syr^h, p, pal(ms) vg Chrysostom Cyril Gregory-Nyssa Jerome Theodoret

Outside the Alexandrian tradition (primary, 𝔓⁴⁶ ℵ B; secondary, H), αὐτοῦ is almost nonexistent to date (one majuscule, S). And of these six MSS, they are only present in one class of NT witnesses (Greek MSS), two categories of Greek MSS (papyri and majuscules), and four centuries (i.e., 𝔓⁴⁶ [III] ℵ [IV] B [IV] H [VI] S [949]). In comparison, σου is ubiquitous. *Every* possible geographic area—Alexandrian (e.g., primary, 1739; secondary, 0243), Western (e.g., D), Byzantine (e.g., K), and other important MSS (e.g., Ψ)—and *every* century from the third to the fourteenth century (e.g., cop^sa [III] Gregory-Nyssa [IV] A [V] D [VI] syr^h [616] Ψ [VIII] 33 [IX] 1739 [X] 424 [XI] 365 [XII] 263 [XIII] 2200 [XIV]) contains *at least* one witness to σου. What is more, σου is present in *every* class of NT witnesses (Greek MSS, ancient translations into other languages, and quotations by early ecclesiastical writers) and virtually every category of Greek MSS (papyri, majuscules, and minuscules).

One more external issue requires a response. Ehrman remarks, "It is interesting to observe that the same MSS that evidence corruption in Hebrews 1:8 do so in John 1:18 as well, one of the other passages."[135] While this brief statement is basically correct, he leaves the reader with a distorted view of scribal activity and transmissional history. Indeed, many examples of the reverse exist. Here are five examples from the MSS he used numerous times regarding our present topic:

1. 𝔓⁴⁶
   a. Corrupted text according to Ehrman (i.e., calls Jesus θεός): Gal 2.20.
   b. Texts that supports the reading that Ehrman's entertains (i.e., does not call Jesus θεός): Heb 1.8.

2. ℵ (01)
   a. Corrupted texts according to Ehrman (i.e., calls Jesus θεός): John 1.18; 20.28.
   b. Texts that support Ehrman's reading (i.e., does not call Jesus θεός): Acts 20.28; Gal 2.20; Heb 1.8; 2 Pet 1.1.

(Harris, *Jesus as God*, 210). For detailed understanding of the MSS for Hebrews, see Attridge, *Hebrews*, 31–32. Cf. Frank W. Beare, "The Text of the Epistle to the Hebrews in 𝔓⁴⁶," *JBL* 63 (1944): 379–96; Ceslas Spicq, *L'Épître aux Hébreux*, 3rd ed. (Paris: Gabalda, 1952), 1:412–32.

135. Ehrman, *Orthodox Corruption*, 265.

3. **L (019)**
   a. Corrupted texts according to Ehrman (i.e., calls Jesus θεός): John 1.18; 20.28.
   b. Text that supports the reading that Ehrman entertains (i.e., does not call Jesus θεός): John 1.1.

4. **L (020)**
   a. Corrupted texts according to Ehrman (i.e., calls Jesus θεός): Heb 1.8; Jude 4 (Ehrman does not mention this text directly, but see n. 28 above).
   b. Text that supports Ehrman's reading (i.e., does not call Jesus θεός): Gal 2.20.

5. **W (032)**
   a. Corrupted texts according to Ehrman (i.e., calls Jesus θεός): John 1.1; John 20.28.
   b. Text that supports Ehrman's reading (i.e., does not call Jesus θεός): John 1.18.

In light of these five examples, which are only a small sampling, much more work needs to be done in the realm of transmissional history. More important, though, just given the preceding examples, no one would have received a purely truncated view of the deity of Christ if they only received their manuscript. This means that each manuscript in the preceding list has at least one "Jesus-θεός" verse that affirms the deity of Christ. It is inconsequential, then, that *every* potential "Jesus-θεός" passage in *every* manuscript affirm the same. This evidential conclusion causes another major problem in Ehrman's overall orthodox corruption thesis.[136]

In the end, the preponderance of evidence (geographically, genealogically, and internally) points to the true textual reading "but to the Son [he declares], 'Your throne, O God, is forever and ever, and a righteous scepter is the scepter of your kingdom.'" The probability, then, is high that Hebrews 1.8 explicitly calls Jesus θεός.

2 Peter 1.1

Second Peter 1.1 is another NT verse potentially calling Jesus θεός. Some MSS (א Ψ 398 442 621 *l*596 syr^ph vg^mss cop^sa)[137] read κυρίου instead of θεοῦ in verse 1:

---

136. "It is rare to find a single manuscript consistently supporting a particular type of reading in Ehrman's categories," concludes Parker (David C. Parker, *An Introduction to the New Testament Manuscripts and Their Texts* [New York: Cambridge University Press, 2008], 302).

137. NA^27 and Tischendorf^8 differ on 2 Pet 1.1 regarding א. Nevertheless, after personally checking a high-resolution digital photograph posted online by the Center for

ἐν δικαιοσύνῃ τοῦ θεοῦ ἡμῶν καὶ σωτῆρος ᾽Ιησοῦ Χριστοῦ
ἐν δικαιοσύνῃ τοῦ κυρίου ἡμῶν καὶ σωτῆρος ᾽Ιησοῦ Χριστοῦ

The external support, however, overwhelmingly favors θεοῦ. In fact, the NA[27] and the Editio Critica Maior together only list nine witnesses for κυρίου (mentioned previously, with only the NA[27] listing vg[mss]). This means that virtually all other witnesses support θεοῦ.

Nevertheless, there are several factors that appear to support κυρίου:

1. θεοῦ could have arisen due to a scribal oversight of the *nomen sacrum*: K̄Ῡ vs. ΘῩ.[138]

2. The phrase "Lord and Savior" is statistically superior when referring to Christ in 2 Peter. It reads "Lord and Savior" four times (1.11; 2.20; 3.2, 18), while it reads "God and Savior" only once (if one accepts it in 1.1).

3. A shift to θεοῦ could have been a motivated orthodox corruption to make the text speak unambiguously of Jesus as θεός due to the Christological controversies during the early centuries.

4. Κυρίου maintains the alleged parallelism between 1.1 and 1.2, distinguishing θεός and Jesus.

5. θεός is rarely used of Jesus in the NT.

As for θεοῦ, most of the preceding critiques can be justifiably reversed, while adding a few more arguments.

1. Although κύριος and θεός are among the earliest *nomina sacra*,[139] no other viable variants for κύριος or θεός exist in 2 Peter (1.14; 2.4, 9; 3.9).

2. "Lord and Savior" is to the NT (and 2 Peter) norm, and a scribe could have easily harmonized to it.

---

the Study of New Testament Manuscripts (http://images.csntm.org/Manuscripts/GA_01/GA01_122a.jpg [accessed July 27, 2011]), I determined that the NA[27] is correct. In other words, א attests to κυρίου. Cf. also *Novum Testamentum Graecum: Editio Critica Maior*, vol. 4, *Catholic Letters*, installment 2, *The Letters of Peter*, ed. Barbara Aland, Kurt Aland, Gerd Mink, and Klaus Wachtel (Stuttgart: Deutsche Bibelgesellschaft, 2000), part 1 (Text), 204.

138. These forms are reflecting their textual inflection in the verse, since that is the way they would have been written (i.e., the last letter changes to reflect the form).

139. Hurtado, "Origin of the *Nomina Sacra*," 655, 657.

3. Κυρίου might have been sought to maintain the alleged parallelism between 1.1 and 1.2 (even though the alleged parallelism would be extremely rare in the NT).

4. θεοῦ is the harder reading, as the opposing critiques reveal.

5. The construction is different when an author desires to distinguish two persons (e.g., 2 Pet 1.2: τοῦ θεοῦ καὶ Ἰησοῦ τοῦ κυρίου ἡμῶν).[140]

6. The doxology in 2 Peter 3.18 and the phrase in 1.1 are attesting to Jesus' exalted status and are both consistent Christologically with the rest of the NT.[141] It should not be argued that the differing words ("God" in 1.1 and "Lord" in 3.18) refute this concept, since similar parallels can be shown elsewhere with differing words (e.g., Matt 1.23 and 28.20; Mark 1.1 and 15.39; John 1.1 and 20.28).

7. This phrase might be in sync with Hellenistic religious language in order to communicate the gospel meaningfully to Gentile converts.[142]

8. The external evidence is far better and earlier (not to mention the existing unanimity among all major published NT Greek texts, e.g., NA[27], Tischendorf[8], UBS[4], Bover, Merk, von Soden, Westcott and Hort, Vogels, and Weiss).

9. The identification of Jesus as θεός here is entirely realistic in light of progressive revelation (2 Peter being one of the last NT books written).[143]

10. The Granville Sharp rule undoubtedly applies to this construction, thereby referring both titles ("God" and "Savior") to Jesus Christ.[144]

---

140. The Granville Sharp rule does not include proper names, and thus 2 Pet 1.2 does not fit the rule ("Jesus" and "Lord Jesus Christ" are both proper names). Cf. Wallace, *Sharp's Canon*, 159–62. On the use of the article with the name of God, see B. Weiss, "Der Gebrauch des Artikels bei den Gottesnamen," *TSK* 84 (1911): 319–92, 503–38.

141. See, e.g., Thomas R. Schreiner, *1, 2 Peter, Jude* (Nashville: Broadman and Holman, 2003), 287.

142. See Tord Fornberg, "An Early Church in a Pluralistic Society: A Study of 2 Peter" (PhD diss., Uppsala University, 1977), 143. Cf. Michael Amaladoss, *Making All Things New* (Maryknoll: Orbis, 1990).

143. In addition, although 1.1 is the only explicit place Jesus is called θεός in 2 Peter, "other things 2 Peter says about Jesus more or less imply this same understanding. One of the clearest instances is 1.3 where the author of 2 Peter speaks of τῆς θείας δυνάμεως αὐτοῦ, and the antecedent of αὐτοῦ is probably Jesus, the last named substantive (in v. 2)" (Terrance Callan, "The Christology of the Second Letter of Peter," *Bib* 82 [2001]: 253; whole article on 253–63).

144. Furthermore, "The construction occurs elsewhere in 2 Peter [cf. 1.11 and 2.20], strongly suggesting that the author's idiom was the same as the rest of the NT

Michael Green argues, "It is hardly open for anyone to translate 1 Pet 1:3 'the God and Father' and yet here decline to translate 'the God and Saviour.'"[145] Likewise, Hiebert concludes, "Elsewhere, this epistle never uses the word Savior alone but always coupled with another name under the same article (cf. 1:11; 2:20; 3:2, 18)."[146]

At the end of the day, θεοῦ best accounts for all the evidence. If this verdict is correct, it is highly probable that Jesus is explicitly called θεός in 2 Peter 1.1.

CONCLUSION

No one contests that the NT usually reserves the title θεός for God the Father. Yet this usage, though dominant, is not exclusive.[147] The textual proof of the designation θεός as applied to Jesus in the NT merely confirms what other grounds have already established. In fact, the title θεός only makes explicit what is implied by other Christological titles, such as κύριος and υἱὸς θεοῦ. Harris adds,

Even if the early Church had never applied the title θεός to Jesus, his deity would still be apparent in his being the object of human and angelic worship and of saving faith; the exerciser of exclusively divine functions such as creatorial agency, the forgiveness of sins, and the final judgment; the addressee in petitionary prayer; the possessor of all divine attributes; the bearer of numerous titles used of Yahweh in the OT; and the co-author of divine blessing. Faith in the deity of Christ

---

authors'" (*New Testament: New English Translation, Novum Testamentum Graece*, 608 n. 10). Of course, as some scholars note, one can hardly overlook the significance of the personal pronoun ἡμῶν added to θεός in 2 Pet 1.1 (arguably disrupting the Granville Sharp construction). Yet, after exhaustively examining 2 Peter, the NT, and hundreds of nonbiblical papyri, Wallace states, "In all such instances the possessive pronoun had no effect on breaking the construction. The fact, then, that a possessive pronoun attached only to the first substantive never nullifies Sharp's principle—either in 2 Peter or in the NT or in the papyri that I have examined—is strong confirmation of the validity of the rule in 2 Pet 1:1. In this case, as always, presumption must give way to evidence" (Wallace, *Sharp's Canon*, 266). Cf. also Gene L. Green, *Jude and 2 Peter* (Grand Rapids: Baker, 2008), 175.

145. Michael Green, *2 Peter and Jude* (Grand Rapids: Eerdmans, 1993), 69.
146. D. Edmond Hiebert, *Second Peter and Jude: An Expositional Commentary* (Greenville, SC: Unusual Publications, 1989), 37.
147. An argument based on the NT's usage or nonusage of the title θεός for Jesus is different from the claim that the NT authors were so entrenched in Jewish monotheism that they could not have thought of Jesus as θεός. Such a claim assumes that they could not reconcile two truths or break away from their prior presuppositions. Even though they may use "contradictory" terminology, they appear to believe in the divinity of Jesus, sometimes even using preexistent categories (cf., e.g., 1 Cor 8.6; Col 1.15–17; Phil 2.6–11).

does not rest on the evidence or validity of a series of "proof-texts" in which Jesus may receive the title θεός but on the general testimony of the NT corroborated at the bar of personal experience.[148]

The question now before us is not whether the NT explicitly ascribes the title θεός to Jesus but how many times he is thus identified and by whom.[149] Therefore, with *at least* one text that undoubtedly calls Jesus θεός in every respect (John 20.28) and with several others that we can assume as much of with a similar degree of certainty (John 1.1, 18; Rom 9.5; Titus 2.13; Heb 1.8; 2 Pet 1.1; 1 John 5.20), we come back to our initial question: when did this boldness to call Jesus θεός begin? It began in the first century. It was not a creation of Constantine in the fourth century. It was not a doctrinal innovation to combat Arianism in the third century. Nor was it a subapostolic distortion of the apostolic kerygma in the second century. Rather, the church's confession of Christ as θεός began in the first century, with the apostles themselves and/or their closest followers. Such an affirmation therefore reaches back, in some sense, to Jesus himself.

---

148. Murray Harris, "Titus 2:13 and the Deity of Christ," in *Pauline Studies: Essays Presented to F. F. Bruce*, ed. Donald A. Hagner and Murray J. Harris (Grand Rapids: Eerdmans, 1980), 271.

149. A conceptual fallacy exists for any scholar to reject every possible text to show that the original author(s) did not support this concept. Nevertheless, the answer to this question will inevitably boil down to the presuppositions of each scholar (cf. Robert H. Stein, *Jesus the Messiah: A Survey of the Life of Christ* [Downers Grove, IL: InterVarsity, 1996], 17).

Table 6.1—Degree of Certainty for Jesus as Θεός				
Passage	No Reason to Doubt	A High Degree of Probability*	A Lower Degree of Probability	Too Uncertain to Allow Any Reliance
Matt 1.23			X	
John 1.1	X			
John 1.18		X		
John 17.3			X	
John 20.28	X			
Acts 20.28			X	
Rom 9.5		X		
Gal 2.20			X	
Eph 5.5			X	
Col 2.2			X	
2 Thess 1.12			X	
1 Tim 3.16				X
Titus 2.13	X			
Heb 1.8		X		
2 Pet 1.1	X			
1 John 5.20		X		
Jude 4			X	

*While it is still *possible* to interpret the text another way, it is not highly *probable*.

Brian J. Wright

Scripture Index

Ancient Sources Index

Person and Subject Index